Global Philadelphia

IN THE SERIES *Philadelphia Voices, Philadelphia Visions,*
EDITED BY DAVID W. BARTELT

ALSO IN THE SERIES:

Carolyn Adams, David Bartelt, David Elesh, and Ira Goldstein, *Restructuring the Philadelphia Region: Metropolitan Divisions and Inequality*

Richardson Dilworth, ed., *Social Capital in the City: Community and Civic Life in Philadelphia*

Global Philadelphia

Immigrant Communities Old and New

Edited by

AYUMI TAKENAKA AND MARY JOHNSON OSIRIM

TEMPLE UNIVERSITY PRESS
Philadelphia

TEMPLE UNIVERSITY PRESS
Philadelphia, Pennsylvania 19122
www.temple.edu/tempress

Library of Congress Cataloging-in-Publication Data

Global Philadelphia : immigrant communities old and new / edited by Ayumi Takenaka and Mary Johnson Osirim.
    p. cm. — (Philadelphia voices, Philadelphia visions)
    Includes bibliographical references and index.
    ISBN 978-1-4399-0012-3 (cloth : alk. paper)
    ISBN 978-1-4399-0013-0 (paper : alk. paper)
    ISBN 978-1-4399-0014-7 (electronic)
    1. Philadelphia (Pa.)—Ethnic relations.   2. Philadelphia (Pa.)—Emigration and immigration.   3. Immigrants—Pennsylvania—Philadelphia—History.   4. Minorities—Pennsylvania—Philadelphia—History.   5. Immigrants—Pennsylvania—Philadelphia—Social conditions.   6. Minorities—Pennsylvania—Philadelphia—Social conditions.   7. Community life—Pennsylvania—Philadelphia.   8. Ethnicity—Pennsylvania—Philadelphia.   9. Transnationalism.   10. Philadelphia (Pa.)—Social conditions.
I. Takenaka, Ayumi.   II. Osirim, Mary Johnson.

    F158.9.A1G55 2010
    305.8009748'11—dc22
                                                 2009052960

Printed in the United States of America

042910-P

To our families and to Philadelphia's immigrant communities

Contents

Acknowledgments

This volume is truly a collaborative project—one that has brought together scholars from anthropology, economics, education, history, linguistics, psychology, public health, and sociology in the Greater Philadelphia area and beyond—to examine the development of immigrant communities in the city, both past and present. It is a product of two conferences in addition to numerous classroom discussions and informal gatherings at local cafes in Philadelphia. We are grateful to our colleagues and students at Bryn Mawr College, as well as to other scholars, policy makers, and leaders and members of immigrant communities who participated. We also thank Bryn Mawr's former Center for Ethnicities, Communities, and Social Policy, the Office of Intercultural Affairs, especially the director and assistant director of that office, Christopher MacDonald-Dennis and Vanessa Christman, respectively, and the Bryn Mawr–Haverford–Swarthmore (Tri-College) Mellon Program for providing us with funding to organize the two conferences. The conferences, held at Bryn Mawr in 2005 and 2006, brought together most of the contributors for this volume and other scholars from the region and served as a basis for the book. Our special thanks are extended to The Social Science Center of Bryn Mawr College and particularly to the co-directors, Rick Davis and Marc Ross, for providing us with additional funds toward our publication expenses. We are especially grateful to the provost of Bryn Mawr College, Kim Cassidy, and her office for their generosity in meeting our final production costs.

Our thanks also go to Mick Gusinde-Duffy of Temple University Press, David Bartelt, editor of the Philadelphia Voices, Philadelphia Visions series of the Press, and to the anonymous reviewers who provided detailed and helpful comments on various versions of the manuscript. We are very grateful to Chel Avery, Linda Hallinger, Lynne Frost, and Charles Ault for the final editing, indexing, and production of our book. Finally, our most heartfelt thanks are extended to Karen Sulpizio, who helped us with every step in preparing the publication of the book. Her careful and efficient administrative work and overall tireless efforts were indispensable in bringing this project to fruition. We are eternally grateful to her.

Back in 2005, we began to work on this project, hoping to provide a growing number of undergraduates interested in immigration with rich local material. In the process we learned much about the city and region we inhabit, as well as discovering a community of immigration scholars, which we hope will continue to thrive. It is our intention that the book will serve as a guide for students as well as a means to promote further dialogue and action among scholars, policy makers, community leaders, immigrants, and other residents of Philadelphia and beyond.

1

Philadelphia's Immigrant Communities in Historical Perspective

Ayumi Takenaka and Mary Johnson Osirim

P hiladelphia has remained an understudied site of immigration to the United States, yet, immigration has, in fact, played a significant role in shaping the life of the city. Once a center of industrialization and a haven of religious freedom, Philadelphia served as a major port of entry and destination for immigrants throughout the eighteenth and nineteenth centuries. In the 1850s, three out of ten Philadelphians were foreign-born (Miller 2006), and during the peak period of immigration from Southern and Eastern Europe between 1910 and 1914, the city was the third most important immigrant port in the country (Welcoming Center for New Pennsylvanians 2004a).

Recently, however, Philadelphia has lagged behind other major cities in attracting immigrants. Across the country, the volume of immigration dwindled between the two World Wars and picked up again thereafter, especially after the 1965 Hart-Cellar Immigration Act. Mostly from Latin America and Asia, post-1965 immigrants have brought about major changes to the racial and ethnic dynamics of many urban centers. The foreign-born in Philadelphia, by contrast, remained relatively small during the 1970s and 1980s. Unlike other major cities in the country, Philadelphia largely remained Black and White.

The 1990s began to see changes. During the decade, Philadelphia's foreign-born population grew by 30 percent, from 104,816 to 136,000, while the city's overall population decreased by 4 percent (Patusky and Ceffalio 2004).

According to the 2000 U.S. Census (U.S. Census Bureau 2000), foreign-born residents constituted 9 percent of the city's population (one out of every eleven Philadelphia residents). In 2005, the figure increased further to 11 percent (U.S. Census Bureau 2005). The rate at which the immigrant population grew is, indeed, one of the fastest among major metropolitan areas, according to Singer et al. (2008).[1]

Still relatively few in number, however, immigrants are becoming increasingly visible in the life of the city. The racial and ethnic composition of the city has become more diverse, as has the city's urban and cultural landscape. Between 1990 and 2000, the White population shrank by 180,000, while Hispanic, Black, and Asian residents increased, many of whom were new immigrants from abroad (Brookings Institution 2005). Immigrants have also helped revitalize neighborhoods by investing in homes and businesses and by introducing different cultures and foods (Gupta 2000; Welcoming Center for New Pennsylvanians 2004b).

Today, immigration is occurring in the context of significant demographic changes and economic challenges. Demographically, Philadelphia lost 22 percent of its population between 1970 and 2000, well above the rate of other cities, such as New York, Boston, and Chicago (Patusky and Ceffalio 2004), and the population continues to decrease. Failing to add as many newcomers as some other major urban areas, the population is also ageing more rapidly than in many other cities of the country. Economically, the urban core continued to lose its strength in the 1990s. More jobs shifted outward in the metropolitan area, and in 2000, fewer than 30 percent of the region's workers were employed in the central city (Brookings Institution 2000). As a result, the city's median household income dropped (in real terms) and poverty rose, while the size of the middle class shrank (Brookings Institution 2000). The shift to postindustrialism, moreover, has exacerbated the already noticeable divisions among classes, races, and neighborhoods (Adams et al. 1991). In short, Philadelphia, to this day, has continued to struggle as an old industrial city made up of "populations still being educated as industrial immigrants" and "communities still organized around traditional ethnic and racial lines, and still excluded, in the main, from the benefits of the new economic order" (Adams et al. 1991: 26).

Faced with these demographic and economic problems, policy makers have turned to immigration as a means to revitalize the city (e.g., Gupta 2000; Pennsylvania Economy League 2000; Welcoming Center for New Pennsylvanians 2004a). In 2001, City Councilman James F. Kenney led an initiative to attract more immigrants by proposing a plan of action, including the creation of a city-funded Office of New Philadelphians (Kenney 2001). Although this proposal did not materialize, a nonprofit organization, the Welcoming Center for New Pennsylvanians, was established in 2003 by a group of immigrant advocates (*Philadelphia Inquirer,* June 11, 2003). Within the city government, the

Managing Director's Office launched the "Global Philadelphia" project to provide more city information and services in multiple languages, and the Mayor's Commission on African and Caribbean Immigrant Affairs was launched within the city government in order to "improve cultural, social, political, health and other conditions for immigrants" (*Philadelphia Inquirer,* July 1, 2005). Immigration, thus, is increasingly recognized as an important component of Philadelphia's economic growth and revitalization (Welcoming Center for New Pennsylvanians 2004b). To the extent that immigration will likely play a vital role in shaping the future of the area, it is critical to understand the characteristics of growing foreign-born populations today (Welcoming Center for New Pennsylvanians 2004a).

In this context, this volume aims to examine the role of immigration[2] in Philadelphia's social and economic dynamics. With each chapter focusing on a specific group and a time period, the volume, as a whole, provides a comprehensive analysis of the processes and consequences of immigration to Philadelphia over time. Today's newcomers are coming to a city that has lost jobs and people and to a city that is largely characterized as Black and White. How have foreign newcomers adapted and fared in the city? Who has come to Philadelphia, and why? And how have they affected the city's economic landscape as well as its racial and ethnic boundaries? Our main questions in the volume are twofold: how has Philadelphia affected immigrants' lives, and how have they, in turn, shaped Philadelphia? We address these questions by comparing the experiences of different immigrant communities over the past few centuries. The similarities and differences we can draw from this historical, comparative approach, we hope, will provide a better understanding of the processes and implications of contemporary immigration to the area.

While a burgeoning volume of works has emerged on immigrant populations in New York City (e.g., Foner 2001; New York City Department of City Planning Population Division 2004), Miami (e.g., Stepick et al. 2003), and Los Angeles (e.g., Waldinger and Bozorgmehr 1996; Lopez-Garza and Diaz 2002), there is a dearth of literature on immigration to Philadelphia, particularly for the contemporary period. To date, most of the existing studies on immigration to Philadelphia are historical (e.g., Luconi 2001; Peltz 1997). The few that examine contemporary immigration tend to focus on specific groups or topics (e.g., Lee 1998; Kibria 1995), and the most comprehensive volume to date, by Goode and Schneider (1994), was published more than a decade ago. Since then, Philadelphia has undergone major transformations, and the city's foreign-born population has grown rapidly. As the settlement patterns of immigrants to the United States have become more diverse, a growing literature has focused on new destinations of immigrants (e.g., Zuniga and Hernandez-Leon 2005; Massey 2008). Philadelphia is an important, though neglected, destination of immigrants, we argue, and understanding the process of their adaptation will elucidate

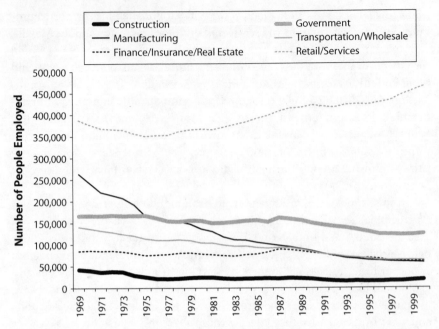

FIGURE 1.1 Change in the industrial structure in Philadelphia. (*Source:* Delaware Valley Regional Planning Commission, Employment Data.)

the patterns of immigrant settlement and mobility in general as well as how cities, their people, and economies cope with foreign-born newcomers.

Context of Immigration

Today's newcomers are coming to the city in the context of demographic shifts, economic shifts, and increased social inequality and racial segregation. Before looking at the profile of new migrants, we shall examine the context in which they are coming today. Formerly a railroad, shipping, and manufacturing center, Philadelphia once prospered as the industrial center of the region (Adams et al. 1991; Warner 1968). The Great Depression, however, brought an end to the city's industrial expansion, and what happened after World War II has been well documented: deindustrialization, job loss, and suburbanization (Adams et al. 1991; Goode 1994; Summers and Luce 1987).

Like many other old industrial cities, Philadelphia underwent a major transition from manufacturing to services (see Figure 1.1). And like other cities, Philadelphia also lost jobs in the context of growing global economic integration. Faced with intense economic competition, some locally based firms were bought by large multinational corporations. Some moved out in search of cheaper land and labor, while others simply closed down (Goode and Schneider 1994).

Unlike other cities, however, Philadelphia's industry was hit particularly hard. Its manufacturing base declined more rapidly than the nation's as a whole, and the city lost 75 percent of its manufacturing jobs between 1955 and 1970 (Adams et al. 1991: 37, fig. 2.1). In 2000, manufacturing constituted only 9 percent, in comparison to 14 percent of jobs nationwide.

Philadelphia suffered severe industrial decline due to a number of factors. One was its high dependence on the production of nondurable goods (e.g., apparel and textiles which had long dominated the city's economy) instead of durable goods (e.g., machinery) (Adams et al. 1991). Smaller in scale and less capital-intensive, the production of nondurable goods was more easily removed and replaced at the time of economic contraction. It was also more vulnerable to shifting economic environments. In 1947, about 30 percent of Philadelphia's privately employed labor force was in nondurable manufactures in contrast to the national average of 19 percent (Adams et al. 1991).

Another factor was Philadelphia's disadvantaged geography. Located between Washington and New York, Philadelphia failed to establish itself as a regional economic center, and unlike Pittsburgh, it did not have a clearly defined region to serve (Goode and Schneider 1994). International trade also favored Washington and New York, often bypassing Philadelphia.

Furthermore, Philadelphia particularly suffered from suburbanization due to relatively greater discrepancies between the city and its suburbs. Between 1970 and 1980, Goode and Schneider (1994) found that Philadelphia lost more jobs to its suburbs than other major cities across the nation. According to the Delaware Valley Regional Planning Commission (2006), the rates of employment have increased in all the suburbs of Philadelphia (especially in Chester, Gloucester, Bucks, and Montgomery counties) during the last decades, in sharp contrast to the city's "sluggish" performance. The disparity in income between the city and its suburbs is quite significant, and indeed is greater than most other cities in the nation, according to Logan (2002: 6, table 2). The gap in employment generation between the city and its suburbs is even more evident today as noted in a recent article in *The Philadelphia Inquirer* (April 6, 2009). Between 1996 and 2006, downtown Philadelphia experienced a decrease in employment, as more jobs relocated to the suburbs. In fact, the Philadelphia-Camden-Wilmington metropolitan area "ranked fifth worst of the 98 regions studied, with 63.7 percent of its jobs more than 10 miles from the city centers," as noted by the Brookings Institution (Mastrull 2009).

In addition, some have blamed the city government for failing to cope with the changing economy. The city's relatively high taxes, poor roads, poor security, large bureaucracy, and bureaucratic regulation have all encouraged the private sector to flee the city. Instead of investing resources to create a competitive labor force, according to them, the government has been a barrier, rather than a stimulant, to economic change.[3]

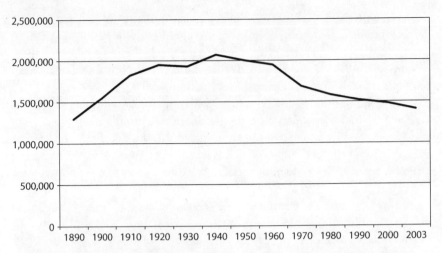

FIGURE 1.2 Population change in Philadelphia. (*Source:* U.S. Census and American Community Survey. Available at http://www.census.gov.)

In tandem with job loss, Philadelphia also began to lose its population. Up until the 1950s, the population kept growing with a significant volume of immigration from Eastern and Southern Europe as well as inflows of African Americans who migrated in search of industrial jobs from the depressed economy of the rural South. In this volume, Birte Pfleger also notes that German immigration to Philadelphia declined during the postwar period and continued on a downward spiral with increased deindustrialization in the city. After reaching a peak of over two million in the 1950s, the population has since continued to decline to the level of 1.4 million in 2005 (Figure 1.2). Particularly noticeable in the most recent decade is a loss of young workers; the state of Pennsylvania lost more young workers than any other state in the years 1990–2000 (Brookings Institution 2005).

The 1980s saw economic growth in the city, yet prosperity was uneven; skewed by the legacy of past patterns of employment, ownership, education, and residence, the economic restructuring exacerbated racial and class divides in the city (Adams et al. 1991). This pattern was also observed in the earlier decades (Warner 1968). Jobs increased in both the low-wage and high-wage sectors, but not in the moderate-wage range, and full-time, stable manufacturing jobs were increasingly replaced by part-time temporary service jobs (Adams et al. 1991).

This trend largely continues until this day. The share of part-time employment has steadily increased (from 6.5 percent in 1970 to 11 percent in 1988). The unemployment rate has increased (from 5.6 percent in 1990 to 6.3 percent in 2006) and has been higher than the national average (4 percent in 1990 and 4.4 percent in 2006). And so has the rate of poverty (20.3 percent in 1990 to 24.5

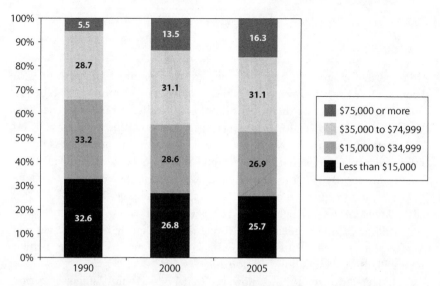

FIGURE 1.3 Household income distribution in Philadelphia. (*Source:* U.S. Census and American Community Survey. Available at http://www.census.gov.)

percent in 2005, compared to the national figures of 13.1 percent in 1990 and 13.3 percent in 2005). The overall rate of employment has also dropped significantly and more significantly than elsewhere (Fair Data 2006). In addition, there are growing disparities in unemployment rates among communities within Philadelphia; some neighborhoods are essentially at full employment (3.8 percent unemployment rate) while others have unemployment rates as high as 30 percent.[4] Moreover, household incomes dropped in real terms (Brookings Institution 2005: fig. 9), and the growth in household income has not kept up with that of the nation as a whole. (In 2005, the median household income in Philadelphia was just over 70 percent of the national average, according to the U.S. Census Bureau [2005].) At the same time, relatively high-income jobs (e.g., management and education) have grown in number (Pennsylvania Department of Labor and Industry 2006; Fair Data 2006). As a consequence, what we see today are growing disparities in earnings (see Figure 1.3). As the figures indicate, income inequality has increased in that relative to the growth in income among the bottom 20 percent of earners, the income of the richest families increased much more. The *Philadelphia Business Journal* (January 17, 2006) reports that between the early 1980s and the early 2000s, the income of the poorest fifth of Pennsylvania families increased about $160 a year, while it went up $540 a year for the middle fifth and $2,650 a year for the top fifth.

Today's immigrants, therefore, are coming to the city in the context of population decline, economic deterioration, and growing income disparities. Who has come to the city and why?

Profile of the Newest Philadelphians

Overall Trend

Although its foreign-born residents have grown in number and percentage in the most recent decades, overall, as Table 1.1 shows, Philadelphia still lags behind other cities in attracting them (e.g., Brookings Institution 2000; Gupta 2000; Patusky and Ceffalio 2004; Welcoming Center for New Pennsylvanians 2004a). The fourth largest city in overall population, Philadelphia nonetheless ranked only sixteenth as a destination for immigrants in 1997–2001, and this trend remains until today (Patusky and Ceffalio 2004; also see Singer et al. 2008: table 2). While the foreign-born made up 36 percent of the population in New York City, 30 percent in Los Angeles, and 12.5 percent in Boston in 2000, just 9 percent of Philadelphia residents were foreign-born, slightly below the national average of 11 percent (Patusky and Ceffalio 2004; New York City Department of City Planning Population Division 2004).

A longer-term trend shows, however, that Philadelphia's "sluggish" performance in attracting immigrants is a recent phenomenon. Prior to 1980, Philadelphia, compared to the nation as a whole, was consistently successful in attracting immigrants (Figure 1.4). Moreover, although Philadelphia experienced a net loss of the foreign-born, as well as of the native-born, until the 1980s, the number of the foreign-born has recently increased, despite a continuous decline in total population.

The Characteristics of Philadelphia's Foreign-Born Population Today

In comparison to other cities, Philadelphia's foreign-born residents stand out in a number of ways. While motives of migration are more or less comparable,

TABLE 1.1   MAJOR IMMIGRANT DESTINATIONS (1997–2001)

Rank	Major MSA	No. of new arrivals
1	New York	490,135
2	LA/Long Beach	360,660
3	Miami	268,074
4	Chicago	190,827
5	Washington, DC	157,548
9	San Francisco	82,669
10	Boston	81,159
11	San Diego	76,541
16	Philadelphia	61,468

[a]Metropolitan Statistical Area.

Source: Patusky and Ceffalio (2004).

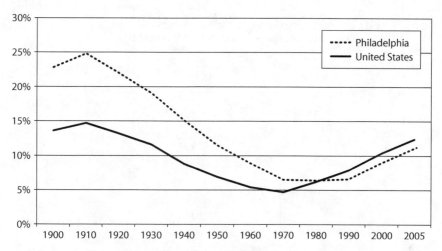

FIGURE 1.4 Percent change in foreign-born population: Philadelphia and the United States. (*Source:* U.S. Census and American Community Survey. Available at http://www.census.gov.)

newcomers to Philadelphia, as pointed out by various chapters in the volume, are likely to cite the city's affordable housing and living conditions, its large number and variety of institutions of higher learning, and its geographical proximity to other metropolises, most notably New York, as major reasons for moving here. Important also are family connections and the existence of ethnic communities, both resulting from past immigration streams. The role of religious and secular aid organizations is also frequently cited as a reason for coming to the city, reflecting the city's strong Quaker and Jewish traditions that have long led in initiating civil rights organizations and assisting refugees (Morawska 2004; Goode and Schneider 1994).

Consequently, a higher proportion of Philadelphia's foreign-born population are refugees. Among the major sending countries of immigrants to Philadelphia are Vietnam, Ukraine, Russia, and Cambodia, which are main source countries of refugees elsewhere to the United States; yet these countries typically do not top the list of sending countries of immigrants in other major cities throughout the country. Philadelphia is home to a major Vietnamese community and the second largest Cambodian community (after Los Angeles) in the country. Perhaps because of the relatively high proportion of refugees, the foreign-born in Philadelphia are more likely to be naturalized citizens (47 percent) than the national average (40 percent).

Reflecting the national trend, foreign newcomers to Philadelphia largely come from Latin America and Asia. In 2000, migrants from Vietnam, China, Ukraine, India, and Jamaica made up a third of the city's foreign-born population. More recent years saw rapid increases in the number of people from India, Mexico, Brazil, and Liberia (U.S. Census Bureau 2005) (see Table 1.2),

TABLE 1.2   MAJOR IMMIGRANT GROUPS IN 2000 AND 2005:
THE NUMBER OF THE FOREIGN-BORN IN PHILADELPHIA

Country of birth	2000	2005
Vietnam	11,533	12,187
China	10,354	10,754
Ukraine	8,326	10,242
India	7,610	12,841
Jamaica	6,994	8,223
Italy	6,097	3,014
Russia	5,275	3,283
Korea	5,209	3,014
Cambodia	4,536	2,254
Dominican Republic	4,281	4,614
Poland	3,765	4,446
Haiti	3,335	4,014
Germany	3,078	3,366
Philippines	3,068	2,424
Mexico	2,679	6,385
Brazil		6,385
Liberia		4,014

Source: U.S. Census and American Community Survey. Available at http://www.census.gov.

and particularly noteworthy is the growth of the Indian population. This population, as described by Rasika Chakravarthy and Ajay Nair in Chapter 11 of this volume, has a distinct characteristic; while a majority of recent migrants from India to the United States are high-skilled male workers, a good portion of Indians in Philadelphia, they find, are female nurses from Kerala, recruited initially in the context of a growing shortage of nurses in the area.

In contrast to other major cities, Philadelphia's foreign-born population is more likely to be re-migrants who, after having settled elsewhere in the country, migrated again to Philadelphia. For instance, a large number of Haitians, as Garvey Lundy shows in Chapter 9 of this volume, arrived in Philadelphia from New York City. Like Haitians, many immigrants come to Philadelphia from another city because they often find it more affordable to purchase homes and begin businesses (Welcoming Center for New Pennsylvanians 2004b). The fact that re-migrants make up a relatively large proportion of the foreign-born determines, in part, the nature of that population in Philadelphia. That is because these migrants, by virtue of migrating more than once, would likely have more skills, as well as motivation or entrepreneurial drive, than their peers who stayed in the original gateway.[5] Indeed, immigrants in Philadelphia today, as shown in the next section, are more educated, on average, than their counterparts in other major cities, such as New York.

Another characteristic of Philadelphia's foreign-born population is the relatively low proportion of the foreign-born among Hispanics/Latinos. This is due to the large presence of Puerto Ricans (who are native-born) in the area. While 40 percent of Hispanics/Latinos nationwide were foreign-born in 2005, only 17 percent of them in Philadelphia were born abroad. About a quarter (24.7 percent) of Hispanics/Latinos in the area were natives who were born outside the continental United States (mostly Puerto Rico) (U.S. Census Bureau 2005). As Victor Vazquez-Hernandez (Chapter 4) points out, the Latino community in Philadelphia has a long history dating back at least to the 1890s. While the community is being transformed amid the current inflows of migration from elsewhere in Latin America, most notably Mexico (see Chapter 8), the community, still predominantly Puerto Rican today, cannot be adequately understood without assessing its historical development over time.

Socioeconomic Characteristics

Foreign-born residents in Philadelphia are heterogeneous, even more so than the native-born, in terms of their socioeconomic backgrounds. A greater proportion of the foreign-born (25 percent), compared to the native-born (21 percent), had less than a high school education in 2005, but they were also more likely to possess graduate or professional degrees (14 percent compared to 9 percent of natives) (U.S. Census Bureau 2005). Overall, foreign-born residents[6] were relatively well educated in comparison to the native-born in the city; while 28 percent of the former had obtained at least a college diploma, the rate was only 20.7 percent for the latter. Compared to the national average, Philadelphia's foreign-born were better educated, in general, while native-born residents lagged behind their counterparts elsewhere. (In a ranking of major cities nationwide, Philadelphia, overall, ranked ninety-second out of one hundred cities in the percentage of its residents who hold bachelor's degrees.) Gupta (2000) also found that Philadelphia drew a more educated immigrant pool than other metropolitan areas in 1997 and 1998. According to the Pennsylvania Economy League (2000), professional workers with H1-B visas (allocated to high-skilled workers) represented a larger share among the foreign-born in the state of Pennsylvania (22.6 percent) than in other states, including New York (17.7 percent) and California (12 percent). Reflecting their higher educational attainment, foreign-born residents in Philadelphia also earned higher annual incomes (personal income), on average, than the native-born: $19,542 versus $17,291 (U.S. Census Bureau 2005).

The socioeconomic backgrounds of foreign-born residents, however, varied significantly by region and country of origin. While 56 percent of South Asians and 49.6 percent of Middle Easterners had at least a college diploma, only 17.6 percent of those from Central American and Caribbean countries did in 2000. Similarly, the median household income of South Asians, $60,000, was double that of those from Central America and the Caribbean ($30,000) in 2000. The difference is reflected in the various patterns of adaptation and community organizing as discussed in the chapters in the volume (for examples, see Chapter 8 on Mexicans, Chapter 11 on Indians, and Chapter 12 on Cambodians).

Settlement Patterns

Settlement patterns of the foreign-born are equally diverse. While they have tended to concentrate in neighborhoods that traditionally attracted immigrants—South Philadelphia, Elmwood, the Far Northeast, and Olney—a growing number of them have also settled in higher-income neighborhoods in Center City. Together, these areas were home to 31 percent of Philadelphia's foreign-born population in 2000, after seeing 83 percent growth in foreign-born population during the 1990s (Patusky and Ceffalio 2004).

Foreign-born newcomers also tended to congregate by nationality. As illustrated by the chapters in this volume, the Vietnamese and Cambodians have largely settled in South Philadelphia and Elmwood, Russians and Ukrainians in the Far Northeast, and Africans in Elmwood and West Philadelphia. Olney has long attracted a diverse group of immigrants, including Indians, Filipinos, Chinese, and those from the Caribbean and Latin America, and Center City has drawn a large number of professionals from diverse countries, including China, India, and the United Kingdom. Amid current inflows of migration to the city, some neighborhoods have undergone significant transformation. Rakhmiel Peltz illustrates in Chapter 2 that South Philadelphia, which traditionally attracted large numbers of Italian and Jewish immigrants to the city, has recently received newcomers from Vietnam, Cambodia, and elsewhere. Consequently, Peltz states, a series of ethnic successions have taken place in South Philadelphia, while Jewish communities have expanded and diversified into the northern areas of the city.

The patterns of residential concentration, however, have varied by country of origin. Generally, newcomers have been most likely to congregate among themselves when there is already a well-established ethnic community. Consequently, the Vietnamese, Cambodians, and Russians (Jews) are more concentrated than others, while the least concentrated are Britons and Germans (Patusky and Ceffalio 2004).

Impact of Immigration

A growing volume of immigration of diverse backgrounds has had, and is likely to have, an impact on Philadelphia. In a report called "A Call to Action," Gupta (2000) discusses various benefits of immigration, including the demographic, economic, and cultural contributions that immigrants make to the city. Immi-

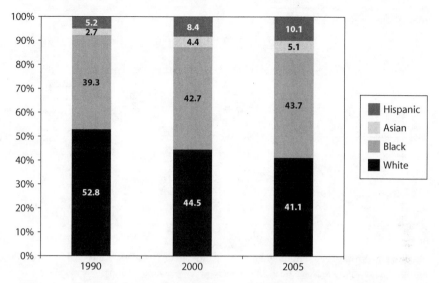

FIGURE 1.5 Change in the racial/ethnic composition of the population in Philadelphia.
(*Source:* U.S. Census and American Community Survey. Available at http://www.census.gov.)

grants have helped replenish the population exodus in many other old industrial cities in the nation, and so, he argues, they could also offset Philadelphia's continuous population decline. While Philadelphia's total population declined by 4.3 percent during the 1990s, the neighborhoods that received the most immigrants, as mentioned above, actually saw an increase of 4 percent in population (Patusky and Ceffalio 2004). Yet others (e.g., Goode and Schneider 1994) argue that the demographic impact of immigrants has been small due to their relatively small presence.

Immigrant advocates have also argued that immigration has contributed to the city's economic revitalization (e.g., Gupta 2000; Welcoming Center for New Pennsylvanians 2004b). In Chapter 10, Mary Johnson Osirim discusses how African immigrants of various nationalities and religious backgrounds have contributed to the economic revitalization of West Philadelphia by establishing businesses, engaging in transnational activities with their native countries in Africa, and by building coalitions with African Americans and Afro-Caribbeans in their neighborhoods.

More direct impact may yet be found on the racial and ethnic composition of the city's population. Today's newcomers, as seen in Figure 1.5, are mostly (66 percent) from Latin America and Asia. The number of Latin Americans and Asians has steadily increased, making up 15.6 percent of the city's population in 2005. Immigrants from Africa, though still relatively small in number, also grew rapidly, by 75 percent (from 9,175 to 16,085) between 2000 and 2005.

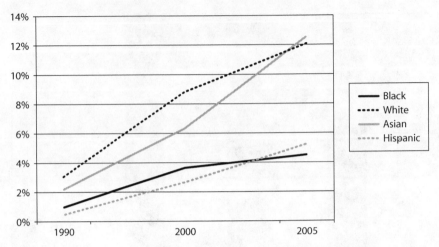

FIGURE 1.6 Proportion of households making more than $100,000 within each racial/ethnic group. (*Source:* U.S. Census and American Community Survey. Available at http://www.census.gov.)

Meanwhile, Whites have continued to decline in number and percentage, and Blacks have surpassed Whites to become the city's largest racial group. In short, Philadelphia's population has become more diverse, and this is largely attributable to growing immigration in recent decades.

At the same time, immigration may also have contributed to the growing income disparity in the city. That is because foreign-born migrants today, as discussed earlier, are more heterogeneous than their native counterparts in their socioeconomic backgrounds. Citing previous research, Clark (2003) argues that immigration does contribute to increasing income inequality in the United States. While the precise impact of immigration on wages continues to be debated, immigrants seem to both reduce the wages of natives with low levels of education and push others upward in the occupational stratification system (Clark 2003).

In Philadelphia, as in the rest of the country, income disparities have grown in recent decades. Within each racial or ethnic group, the income distribution has become more skewed with a noticeable increase in high-income earners. The trend is most noticeable among Blacks where the earnings of the richest 20 percent increased over time (as in other groups) at the same time that the bottom 20 percent remained very poor, earning less than $10,000 per household. Indeed, while the proportion of Black households making more than $100,000 annually increased over time, the comparable figure for Black households making less than $15,000 has also increased, albeit slowly (Figures 1.6 and 1.7). Given that, on average, foreign-born Blacks make more than native-born Blacks—the average household income of African-born immigrants, for

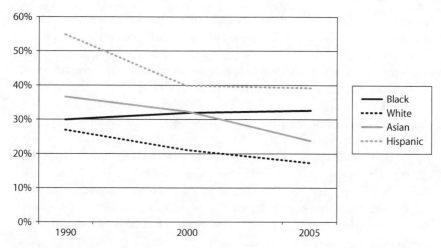

FIGURE 1.7 Proportion of households making less than $15,000 within each racial/ethnic group. (*Source:* U.S. Census and American Community Survey. Available at http://www.census.gov.)

instance, was $37,000, compared with $27,000 among native Blacks—immigration may contribute to diversifying the socioeconomic profile of the Black population in the city.

The growing income disparity, along with increasing racial diversity, may also have contributed to the decreased level of segregation along racial/ethnic lines in the city. Although segregation, particularly between Blacks and Whites, has been consistently high during the past several decades, it has decreased in recent decades (Frey and Myers 2005; Massey and Denton 1993; Logan 2002).[7] In 1990, 78 percent of Blacks had to move in order to reach an even residential pattern between Blacks and Whites, but the rate decreased to 72 percent in 2000. Likewise, the average Black in the Philadelphia metropolitan area lived in a census tract that was 62 percent Black in 2000, a decrease by seven points from 1980. Racial segregation decreased in many other metropolitan areas, but Frey and Myers (2005) show that the rate of decline was greater in Philadelphia than in other major cities in the Northeast. This may, in part, be attributable to immigration as today's immigrants tend to settle in boundary areas between demarcated Black and White communities, and refugees, moreover, often settle in the heart of Black or White neighborhoods (Somekawa 1995). The growth in high-income earners among Blacks may also have contributed to racial desegregation, and Black high-income earners, as we have seen, are increasingly coming from abroad.

Much of the Philadelphia story described here echoes what is happening around the country. Immigrants are increasingly entering a divided society, and immigrants, in turn, shape these divisions. This reflects the fact that today's immigrants are not only coming in the context of growing economic competition; they are also more diverse in their geographical and socioeconomic backgrounds compared to the turn-of-the-century immigrants who were largely European and uneducated. Manufacturing is no longer available as a major source of stable income, and the gap between rich and poor is growing.

Immigrants themselves cope with these challenges in various ways. As the chapters in this volume show, institution building and community support have always been an important strategy of adaptation. And today, immigrants increasingly resort to transnational connections. As described by several chapters in this volume, newcomers to Philadelphia actively maintain ties with their countries of origin and draw on these ties to establish businesses (see Chapter 10), negotiate their identities (see Chapter 9), and organize themselves (see Chapter 5) as a strategy to adapt in the new environment. The stories of immigrant lives presented in each chapter, we hope, will provide both a historical and comparative framework to understand how immigrant communities have shaped, and have been shaped by, the city over time and across groups.

Presenting the Stories of Immigrant Philadelphia

The chapters in this volume cover immigrant populations that have had a major presence in Philadelphia over the past century. Among contemporary immigrant populations, we have strived to include those that are both rapidly growing (such as Mexicans, Indians, and Chinese) and representative of different regions and experiences (Cambodians, Haitians, Africans). While its coverage is in no way comprehensive (for instance, Koreans and Brazilians are not included), we nevertheless hope that the book provides a representative overview of immigrants' experiences over time in Philadelphia. Our contributors also represent diverse disciplines—anthropology, economics, education, history, linguistics, public health, psychology and sociology—making the book a truly interdisciplinary endeavor.

The chapters in this volume reveal the rich diversity and dynamics of the city's immigrant populations and communities. Not only was Philadelphia home to European immigrants who migrated from the old world to the new from the colonial period through the twentieth century, but it also witnessed the establishment of early twentieth century enclave communities among populations that are often most associated with post-1965 migration to the northeastern United States, such as Latinos. Despite the diversity of experiences that African, Asian, Caribbean, European, and Latino populations encountered in the Philadelphia region, there are some themes that unite these experiences across time and space, namely institutions and community development, identities, transnational ties, intra-group differences and inter-group interactions, and socioeconomic mobility. The book is organized around these themes.

The next section of this volume focuses on community formation and intra-(and inter-) ethnic relations, drawing on the experiences of Jewish, Italian, Puerto Rican (and other Latin American), and Chinese immigrants. These chapters explore the patterns of migration and community formation over a span of a century, highlighting the importance of historical continuity and change in understanding these processes. In Chapter 2, Rahkmiel Peltz examines the development of community and intra-group differences in the Jewish community from the late nineteenth century to the present. He focuses, in particular, on generational changes and transitions in major fraternal, ethnic, and social service institutions among successive waves of Jewish immigrants to the area—from early migrants in the 1880s, to Holocaust survivors in the 1940s and 1950s, to the Soviet Jews of the 1970s and 1980s, and the Israelis since the establishment of Israel.

Joan Saverino, in Chapter 3, discusses how Italian artisans in Chestnut Hill, a secondary area of settlement for this group, contributed to the built environment and material culture in Philadelphia. In her analysis, she explores the shifting boundaries of inter- and intra-ethnic social relations and the class and power dynamics embodied in relationships with co-ethnics and the elite Anglo population of Chestnut Hill.

Exploring the diversity of the early Latino community, Victor Vazquez-Hernandez, in Chapter 4, discusses the focal role played by religious and social service organizations in the Latino enclaves of Spring Garden, Southwark, and Northern Liberties. Organizations such as La Milagrosa, the Hispanic American Fraternal Association, the First Spanish Baptist Church, and the International Institute, through providing social services and sponsoring social events, helped consolidate the Puerto Ricans, Cubans, Mexicans, and other Latin Americans into a Pan-Latino community. Not only were immigrant organizations vital in the establishment of many ethnic communities, but they also contributed to the expansion of educational opportunities and early industrial development in the city.

In Chapter 5, Lena Sze indicates that despite the greater diversity within the Chinese population of Philadelphia—from the earlier Cantonese- or Toisan-speaking Chinese to the Fujianese of today—major religious and social service groups have united these populations and come together in the "Save Chinatown" movement. This movement, under the leadership of such institutions as the Holy Redeemer Chinese Catholic Church and School and the Chinese Christian Church Center, have preserved Chinatown from the potential "wrecking balls" of developers who planned to expand a highway and create a stadium in their community. In the process, these religious organizations and others have forged a larger ethnic identity for the Chinese.

Chapters in Part II highlight the critical roles of institutions in the process of immigrant adaptation over time. Birte Pfleger, in Chapter 6, demonstrates how the German Society of Pennsylvania, the oldest German immigrant aid organization in the nation, quickly became an advocate for German-speakers beginning in 1764. Like the Irish social clubs and the Catholic Church discussed by Noel Farley and Philip Kilbride (Chapter 7), the German Society assisted recent German immigrants in obtaining employment, health care, and legal advice, and provided financial assistance for food, housing, and transportation.

Farley and Kilbride, in Chapter 7, illustrate how Irish social clubs provided recent immigrants with assistance in finding jobs, while the Catholic Church provided education, health care, and family counseling. They further explore the establishment of the parochial school system and many noted Catholic colleges and universities by the Irish, whose significant contributions to urban education remain evident today.

Chapter 8, focuses on Mexicans, a group that has rapidly grown in number in the last decade and a half. In this chapter, Jennifer Atlas carefully documents this migration, focusing on critical issues facing many of these migrants today: health conditions and health care. Drawing on interviews with health professionals and some migrants, she examines the inadequate healthcare services that exist in Philadelphia's Mexican community as well as how national legislation affects access to health care for this population.

Part III of this collection explores identities and transnational ties, focusing on the migration of largely post-1965 immigrants from Africa, Asia, and the Caribbean. In Chapter 9, Garvey Lundy examines transnationalism among Haitian immigrants. Through interviewing and participant-observation among seventy Haitians in Philadelphia, he investigates the challenges to unity for this population given the problems of political development in Haiti and Haitians' ties to their home and host societies.

Transnationalism and the emergence of transnational identities are also critical issues in understanding contemporary immigrant groups. In Chapter 10, Mary Johnson Osirim explores the development of transnational and pan-African identities based on in-depth interviews with African entrepreneurs and leaders of community organizations. This population has succeeded in making important contributions to the revitalization of West Philadelphia due in part to the significant presence of African Americans in the city.

In Chapter 11, Rasika Chakravarthy and Ajay Nair argue that with migration to the Philadelphia area, Keralite Hindu nurses experience an increase in socioeconomic status relative to the declining occupational status of their husbands. At the same time, leadership of Nair community organizations serves as a vehicle through which men can regain some of the status they lost in the household and professional realms.

Finally, Ellen Skilton-Sylvester and Keo Chea-Young focus on the experiences of Cambodian migrants in Philadelphia. In contrast to relatively well educated Indian and African immigrants in the city, Cambodians are largely a disadvantaged and "invisible" group, Skilton-Sylvester and Chea-Young argue, and they examine why it is the case and how their "invisibility" shapes their adaptation patterns in the city.

Several chapters in this section also highlight the major role of institutions in the establishment of immigrant communities. Religious and social service organizations played a significant role in the development of many contemporary communities in this volume. Chakravarthy and Nair indicate that the Nair Society of the Delaware Valley, the Kerala Art and Literary Association of Philadelphia, and the Keralite Syrian Christians, among other groups, contributed to unity and community development among the Keralites; Mary Johnson Osirim discusses the major roles that the Coalition of African Communities—Philadelphia (AFRICOM) and the Mayor's Commission on African and Caribbean Immigrant Affairs played in the revitalization of West Philadelphia, and Skilton-Sylvester and Chea-Young illustrate that English as a second language (ESL) programs were central elements in the establishment of the Cambodian community. These, as well as many other institutions, not only strengthened ethnic communities, but they contributed to urban renewal and the transformation of Philadelphia from a largely Black-White venue to a more multicultural city.

Altogether, these stories show how immigrants have shaped Philadelphia and how they have adapted and fared in the city in which they have settled. Although immigrants' experiences are diverse, depending on the kinds of skills they bring with them, the nature of existing communities, and the reception of the host society (Portes and Rumbaut 2005), there are commonalities they have shared throughout the centuries: the importance of community, institutions, and transnational ties, real or imagined. The chapters in this volume also show how central immigration has been to the city of Philadelphia—and that its significance will only increase in the future. Given the extremely heterogeneous nature of immigration today, immigrants will most likely affect, in some fundamental way, the city's ethnic and cultural diversity, as well as racial segregation and economic disparity. Moreover, in the context of a globalized economy and a shrinking and ageing population, immigration is a key to the city's survival and competitiveness. In figuring out how to attract immigrants—and particularly the kinds of immigrants the economy demands—it is critical to understand immigrants' experiences in the city. We hope this volume will contribute to such understanding.

Notes

1. They report that between 2000 and 2006, metropolitan Philadelphia's immigrant population increased by 29 percent.

2. *Immigrants* (in the U.S.) legally refers to those who are admitted to the U.S. for lawful permanent residence under the provisions of the Immigration and Nationality Act. Although all immigrants, by definition, are foreign-born, not all the foreign-born are

immigrants. The foreign-born population includes nonimmigrants, such as students, business personnel, and diplomats, who have been admitted to the U.S. for a temporary duration. Neither are all the foreign-born recent entrants. Some have spent many years in the U.S. and are naturalized U.S. citizens. In this chapter, however, we are using the terms *immigrant* and *foreign-born* interchangeably, as immigrants comprise most of the foreign-born population (New York City Department of City Planning Population Division 2004).

3. Comments provided by Noel Farley on an earlier version of this chapter.

4. Discussion of Philadelphia's mayoral race on Marty Moss-Coane's *Radio Times,* WHYY-FM, April 20, 2007.

5. We are grateful to an anonymous reviewer who suggested this and other points.

6. See Chapter 10 for an example of these proportions among African immigrants in Philadelphia.

7. This is reflected in two commonly used measures of racial segregation—the index of segregation (or the percentage of one group that would have to move to achieve an even residential pattern) and the index of isolation (which measures the percentage of the minority in a neighborhood where the average member of the minority group lives).

References

Adams, Carolyn, David Bartelt, David Elesh, Ira Goldstein, Nancy Kleniewski, and William Yancey. 1991. *Philadelphia: Neighborhoods, Divisions and Conflict in a Postindustrial City.* Philadelphia: Temple University Press.

Brookings Institution. 2000. "Philadelphia in Focus: A Profile from Census 2000." Center on Urban and Metropolitan Policy. Available at http://www.brookings.edu/es/urban/livingcities/Philadelphia.htm.

———. 2005. "Executive Summary." Available at http://www.brookings.edu/metro/pubs/20050404_PriceIsWrongES.pdf.

Clark, William A. V. 2003. *Immigrants and the American Dream.* New York: Guilford Press.

Delaware Valley Regional Planning Commission. 2006. Available at http://www.dvrpc.org (accessed November 1, 2006).

Fair Data. 2006. Available at http://www.fairdata2000.com (accessed November 1, 2006).

Foner, Nancy, ed. 2001. *New Immigrants in New York.* New York: Columbia University Press.

Frey, William, and Dowell Myers. 2005. "Racial Segregation in U.S. Metropolitan Areas and Cities, 1990–2000: Patterns, Trends, and Explanations." Research Report 05-573. Population Studies Center, University of Michigan.

Goode, Judith. 1994. "Polishing the Rustbelt: Immigrants Enter a Restructuring Philadelphia." In *Newcomers in the Workplace: Immigrants in the Restructuring of the U.S. Economy,* ed. Louise Lamphere, Alex Stepick, and Guillermo J. Grenier, 199–230. Philadelphia: Temple University Press.

Goode, Judith, and Jo Anne Schneider. 1994. *Reshaping Ethnic and Racial Relations in Philadelphia: Immigrants in a Divided City.* Philadelphia: Temple University Press.

Gupta, Anuj. 2000. "Immigration in Philadelphia: A Call to Action." Available at http://www.peleast.org/images/wintere.pdf (accessed November 1, 2006).

Kenney, James F. 2001. "A Plan to Attract New Philadelphians." Available at http://www.jameskenney.com/issues.htm (accessed in 2006).

Kibria, Nazli. 1995. *Family Tightrope.* Princeton, NJ: Princeton University Press.

Lee, Jae-Hyup. 1998. *Dynamics of Ethnic Identity: Three Asian American Communities in Philadelphia*. New York: Routledge.

Logan, John R. 2002. "The Suburban Advantage." Available at http://mumford.albany.edu/census/CityProfiles/SuburbanReport/page1.html.

Lopez-Garza, Marta, and David R. Diaz, eds. 2002. *Asian and Latino Immigrants in a Restructuring Economy: The Metamorphosis of Southern California*. Palo Alto, CA: Stanford University Press.

Luconi, Stefano. 2001. *From Paesani to White Ethnics: The Italian Experience in Philadelphia*. Albany: State University of New York Press.

Massey, Douglas S., ed. 2008. *New Faces in New Places: The Changing Geography of American Immigration*. New York: Russell Sage Foundation.

Massey, Douglas S., and Nancy Denton. 1993. *American Apartheid: Segregation and the Making of the Underclass*. Cambridge, MA: Harvard University Press.

Mastrull, Diane. 2009. "Job Sprawl Threatens Urban Poor, Study Says." *Philadelphia Inquirer*, April 6, 2009.

Miller, Fredric M. 2006. "Philadelphia: Immigrant City." Available at http://www.balch institute.org/resources/phila_ellis_island.html (accessed November 1, 2006).

Morawska, Ewa. 2004. "Exploring Diversity in Immigrant Assimilation: Poles and Russian Jews in Philadelphia." *International Migration Review* 38 (4): 1372–1412.

New York City Department of City Planning Population Division. 2004. *The Newest New Yorkers 2000*. New York: New York City Department of City Planning Population Division.

Patusky, Christopher, and Johnny Ceffalio. 2004. "Recent Trends in Immigration to Philadelphia, Pennsylvania: Who Came and Where Do They Live?" Philadelphia: Fels Institute of Government, University of Pennsylvania. Available at https://www.fels.upenn.edu/sites/www.fels.upenn.edu/files/Philadelphia_Immigration_Trends_0.pdf (accessed October 7, 2005).

Peltz, Rakhmiel. 1997. *From Immigrant to Ethnic Culture: American Yiddish in South Philadelphia*. Palo Alto, CA: Stanford University Press.

Pennsylvania Department of Labor and Industry. 2006. Available at http://www.dli.state.pa.us (accessed November 1, 2006).

Pennsylvania Economy League. 2000. "Immigration in Pennsylvania: A Call to Action." Available at http://economyleague.org/files/File/reports/Immigration%20report.pdf.

Portes, Alejandro, and Ruben Rumbaut. 2005. *Immigrant America: A Portrait*. Berkeley: University of California Press.

Singer, Audrey, Domenic Vitiello, Michael Katz, and David Park. 2008. *Recent Immigration to Philadelphia: Regional Change in a Re-Emerging Gateway*. Washington, DC: Brookings Institution.

Somekawa, Ellen. 1995. "On the Edge: Southeast Asians in Philadelphia and the Struggle for Space." In *Reviewing Asian America: Locating Diversity,* ed. Soo-Young Chin, James S. Moy, Wendy L. Ng, and Gary Y. Okihiro, 33–47. Pullman: Washington State University Press.

Stepick, Alex, Guillermo Grenier, Max Castro, and Marvin Dunn. 2003. *This Land Is Our Land: Immigrants and Power in Miami*. Berkeley: University of California Press.

Summers, Anita, and Thomas Luce. 1987. *Economic Development within the Philadelphia Metropolitan Area*. Philadelphia: University of Pennsylvania Press.

U.S. Census Bureau. 2000. United States Census 2000. Available at http://www.census.gov/main/www/cen2000.html.

————. 2005. American Community Survey. Available at http://www.census.gov/acs/www/.

Waldinger, Roger, and Mehdi Bozorgmehr, eds. 1996. *Ethnic Los Angeles.* New York: Russell Sage Foundation.

Warner, Sam B. 1968. *The Private City: Philadelphia in Three Periods of Its Growth.* Philadelphia: University of Pennsylvania Press.

Welcoming Center for New Pennsylvanians. 2004a. *Immigrant Philadelphia: From Cobblestone Streets to Korean Soap-Operas.* Philadelphia: Welcoming Center for New Pennsylvanians.

————. 2004b. "Immigration and Urban Revitalization in Philadelphia: Immigrant Entrepreneurship and Improving Opportunity in the Local Economy." Available at http://www.welcomingcenter.org/pdfs/ImmigrantEntrepreneurship.pdf.

Zuniga, Victor, and Ruben Hernandez-Leon, eds. 2005. *New Destinations: Mexican Immigration in the United States.* New York: Russell Sage Foundation.

PART I

Community Formation and Intra- (and Inter-) Ethnic Relations

The chapters in this section offer a number of important lessons for understanding immigration. The first lesson is the importance of historical continuity; we cannot understand contemporary immigration to Philadelphia without looking at its history. Vazquez-Hernandez (Chapter 4) reminds us that the "Latino" community in Philadelphia dates back at least to the 1890s. Sze (Chapter 5) also argues that today's influx of immigrants in Philadelphia "has roots in prior periods of Philadelphia's history and earlier global economic and political shifts" (p. 97). These chapters together address the importance of personal networks that have shaped immigration throughout the centuries. Saverino (Chapter 3) discusses how Italian immigrants from the Friuli region ended up in Chestnut Hill by way of chain migration, while Sze (Chapter 5) discusses the role of Chinatown as a magnet for further migration from China and elsewhere to Philadelphia. The chapters also address how inter-ethnic relations have shaped immigration and immigrant communities. According to Vazquez-Hernandez (Chapter 4), Puerto Ricans began to migrate to Philadelphia in large numbers in the 1920s as a result of labor recruitment that targeted them after the immigration of Spaniards was cut off by U.S. immigration policy. Saverino (Chapter 3) also discusses how Italians migrated and settled by joining the Irish in domestic service for wealthy Anglos in the city.

Second, the chapters tell us that immigrant "communities" are far from monolithic. Intra-ethnic relations (and tensions) have, indeed, been a crucial component of immigrant experiences, and it is important to pay attention to them. Saverino (Chapter 3) discusses the hierarchy created among Italian migrants—how Northern Italians, such as the Friulani, looked down on Southern Italians, who tended to be darker skinned and less educated than Northerners. The Jewish, Chinese, and Latino communities discussed in this section also show how continuous immigration has expanded, diversified, and transformed these communities over time. Peltz (Chapter 2) and Vazquez-Hernandez (Chapter 4) discuss the diversity within Jewish and Latino communities, respectively, especially in terms of immigrants' regions and countries of origin. Similarly, Sze (Chapter 5) talks about the diverse character of Chinese immigrants today with respect to their political orientation and linguistic and socioeconomic backgrounds.

Third, however complex this concept may be, "community"—or more precisely, a sense thereof—has always been key to immigrants' adaptation. Their "community," typically composed of families, relatives, friends, or others who may share a common language, customs, or migration experience, has always provided immigrants with the critical support they needed, including psychological comfort and financial assistance. Saverino (Chapter 3) talks about the critical role "*paesani* relationship" (p. 52) played in providing new immigrants from Italy with employment opportunities in the 20th century, the kind of system that is prominent in other immigrant communities today. Moreover, this sense of community has typically been rooted in a specific place or neighborhood. In other words, there has been an intricate relationship between place and identity, as Saverino (Chapter 3) put it, or "the neighborhood environment is fundamental to the development of the life of the individual and the family" (Peltz, Chapter 2, p. 27). Even though the traditional Jewish neighborhood of South Philadelphia has transformed itself, this place has continued to have special significance to many Jewish immigrants today (Peltz, Chapter 2). For the Friulani immigrants and their descendants, their sense of community is deeply tied with Chestnut Hill where they have left many legacies through architecture, stones, and other landmarks. For Chinese immigrants in Philadelphia, who have grown increasingly diverse and geographically dispersed in recent decades, Chinatown has continued to serve as an important cultural symbol for many (Sze, Chapter 5).

The significance of neighborhood (thus the nature of community) may be changing in recent years when immigrants have become more dispersed and geographically mobile with extensive transnational ties (see Part III of this volume). However, the salience of community itself has remained unchanged. Community has continued to serve as an important means for immigrants to adapt in the United States—and also in Philadelphia. And to understand the role of immigrant communities and the processes of community formation, these chapters show us, once again, the importance of looking at history—how immigrants settled, how they interacted with others, and how immigration has changed over time.

2

125 Years of Building Jewish Immigrant Communities in Philadelphia

RAKHMIEL PELTZ

Life in the Primary Neighborhood of Immigration: An Introduction

It is an afternoon in July 1997, and I am sitting and recording a conversation in Tsine's South Philadelphia home of fifty years, down the street from her family's house of almost seventy years, the building in which she grew up, where her parents lived when they were alive and which her younger sister still occupies. Tsine was born in South Philadelphia in 1924 and never left the neighborhood. At several junctions, her husband wanted to leave the neighborhood, but Tsine felt too close to her mother to be able to leave. "I don't think that I could stay away—my mother and I were girlfriends. I loved her as a mother—but I—she was my confidante." Tsine's parents hailed from a shtetl near Vinitse, Ukraine. Her father came before World War I and the mother and their first child were separated from him for ten years. They arrived in Philadelphia in 1923 and Tsine was the first of four American-born daughters. Neither parent had parents or siblings in the United States and Tsine understands this to be the reason for the closeness of the immediate family. "I think that maybe because we had nobody else, we cleave—we were closer to one another, at that time . . . and there were a lot of good, good times." The closeness of those first years is recalled by Tsine only in positive terms, although the family was poor.

But Tsine's story is not an aberration. The next day I interview Malke and Froym in their kitchen, about four streets over from Tsine's house, and I learn that we are sitting in a house that had belonged to Malke's grandfather. But even when I walk over two blocks to talk with Freyde, a Holocaust survivor, part of a different immigration wave that came after World War II, I learn that Freyde has been living in her house for fifty years. Her husband died two years ago and her children do not live in the neighborhood. Nevertheless, Freyde would not think of moving. All these cases point to the fact that neighborhoods of primary immigration like South Philadelphia hold special meaning for their residents, be they immigrant or second generation.

Research on factors that promote attachment to place shows that "residing in a neighborhood a long time is not, by itself, enough to create affective attachment." Such feelings are promoted rather by voluntary ties and local friends (Gerson, Stueve, and Fischer 1977: 156). Immigrant neighborhoods during the late nineteenth and early twentieth centuries developed an array of locally based secondary, voluntary associations, including synagogues, political clubs, sports teams, and fraternal groups, as well as ethnic schools, recreational clubs, and restaurants. If the prevalence of such organizations was indeed diminished as the children of immigrants aged, the personal recognition and friendship opportunities persisted. Representatives of the second generation at the end of the twentieth and beginning of the twenty-first centuries are quick to underscore that this is what makes their neighborhood special when it is compared with other areas, despite the fact that the proportion of the original ethnic group residing in the neighborhood is smaller. This characteristic persists in South Philadelphia, Philadelphia's premier immigrant neighborhood of the mass immigration from Europe (cf. Dubin 1996 and Peltz 1998). Today, one hundred twenty-five years after the beginning of Russian Jewish immigration, although most families left the neighborhood, one can still find hundreds of descendants of the immigrants there.

The elderly children of immigrants, who were born in South Philadelphia and spent their entire lives there, sum up their warm feelings toward the neighborhood by pointing to the preponderance of caring neighbors. "*Ven di voynst in South Philadelphia, iz yeyder eyner bakentlekh mit dir,*" said Rosa (When you live in South Philadelphia, you are familiar with everyone). "*Du iz geven mentshn, in ergets ondersh hot men gehot fley in de nuz. . . . Farshteyt ir? Du iz gevin di beste yidn fin gonts Filadelfye,*" commented Feygl-Asye (Here were real people, elsewhere people were snobs. . . . Do you understand? Here were the best Jews in all of Philadelphia). After World War II much of the exodus of Jews from South Philadelphia was directed toward Northeast Philadelphia and the Cherry Hill area of South Jersey. Basye emphasized the contrast with the insular life in the new neighborhood: "When they moved away to the Northeast, they went into their own little houses, they closed the door, turned on the air conditioner and forgot the rest of the world." The main advantage of the neighborhood of primary immigration to the immigrants and their children, according to the residents, was that people knew you and cared about you.

125 Years of Building Jewish Immigrant Communities in Philadelphia

Although South Philadelphia, as an example of a neighborhood of initial immigrant settlement, may at first glance seem simple in structure, since everyone claims to be familiar with everyone else, closer perusal reveals a great complexity of mutually exclusive social networks, even in recent years when the neighborhood's Jewish population has dwindled (Peltz 1998: 94–97, 100). For example, in the mid-1980s, I found that residents who attended one synagogue would also belong to the Jewish Masonic lodge, but not to the local Jewish senior day center; whereas those who attended a second synagogue belonged to the Jewish War Veterans Post as well as the senior center. Nevertheless, the long neighborhood history demonstrated institutions that served a large and diverse Jewish membership, as well as those that attracted a specific Jewish subgroup. I plan to delve into the history and functioning of two kinds of institutions that provided immigrants and their children with various services, the settlement house and the fraternal hometown association.

By way of contrast with an examination of the neighborhood that housed the first large groups of Jews that came to Philadelphia largely from the former Polish lands of the Russian and Austro-Hungarian empires at the turn of the twentieth century as well as the institutions that served them, I will present information on the acculturation of new Jewish immigrants to Philadelphia after World War II. Three waves of Jewish immigrants came to these shores under very different circumstances in regard to their relationship to their societies of origin and to conditions within the American society and the Jewish community they found after immigration. First, I will examine the immigration of European Jews who were Holocaust survivors and arrived here at the end of the 1940s and the beginning of the 1950s. Next I will analyze the adjustments made by Jews from the Soviet Union and the former Soviet Union who came to Philadelphia from about 1970 through the 1990s. Last, I will present some limited evidence that relates to former Israelis, a group of diverse Jewish subethnic origins that came to the city from the late 1950s until the current day. All the while I will be keeping in mind the relative wealth of information we possess on the social and cultural effects of the earlier mass immigration of east European Jews. The first boatload reached the Catherine Street docks in February 1882 and by 1924 restrictive federal legislation had all but stopped immigration from eastern Europe.

My focus will remain on the mass of eastern European Jews who arrived at the end of the nineteenth century, thereby neglecting the small numbers of Jews that arrived in Philadelphia earlier. However, I should mention that the German Jews who arrived in Philadelphia from central Europe in the mid-nineteenth century had achieved much socially and economically by the time the eastern Europeans arrived at the end of the century. These German Jews were far less traditional upon arrival than the eastern Europeans and assimilated into American society rapidly. When the eastern Europeans arrived, the German Jews, ashamed of their kinsmen, attempted to help Americanize them through the settlement house.

During the first wave of eastern European immigration, institutions were developed by the immigrants themselves, such as *landsmanshaftn* ("hometown associations," called *farein*—"union"—in Philadelphia) and neighborhood synagogues that provided a warm, familiar environment in which to learn about American society but also maintain Jewish customs that were particular to the specific locale of origin in the old country. At the same time, the welcoming general and Jewish communities organized institutions, such as settlement houses and immigrant aid societies, to educate new immigrants about the new world and provide needed health and social services for successful immigration and acculturation. Two of the oldest of such institutions to serve Philadelphia Jews were the Neighborhood Centre and the Hebrew Immigrant Aid Society and Council Migration Service of Philadelphia (HIAS). Immigrants were able to take advantage of many of these facilities within their neighborhood, initially South Philadelphia. In addition to close family relationships that lent support for the immigrant experience, these institutions, often down the street from the houses in which they lived, provided the members of immigrant families with "intimate secondary relationships" (Wireman 1984).

The subsequent Jewish immigrant waves that arrived in Philadelphia in the second half of the twentieth century, although in many ways experiencing an easier process of adjustment, were not supported by the extensive, embedded institutional matrix on the local level. The groups they joined were in no way as intimate to their specific lives, neither in relation to their connection to and memory of their hometowns, nor through location in the immigrant neighborhood. This observation is obviously in part a reflection of changes in American society during these years in the late twentieth century in which people became less involved in voluntary associations and in intimate, neighborhood-based, secondary institutions, while they populated areas of the suburbs that covered larger geographic expanses and provided little opportunity for getting together in the neighborhood. Although some Holocaust survivors settled initially in South Philadelphia, they moved on to newer neighborhoods, especially Northeast Philadelphia. Even though there were still Jewish residents and synagogues in South Philadelphia when the Soviet Jews first arrived, the Jewish organizations responsible for their resettlement arranged for housing largely in the Far

Northeast. Over the years, few, if any, Israelis made South Philadelphia home. The allure of higher socioeconomic status areas was far greater.

At the same time, the experience of the later immigrants reflects changes in Jewish life, wherein the old country of most of world Jewry in the early twentieth century, the communities of eastern Europe, were wiped off the face of the earth during the Holocaust. In addition, the history of repression of Jews in the Soviet Union left the survivors from those communities with little positive feeling for that homeland. Furthermore, former Israelis by the very act of emigration were often regarded by other Jews as disloyal to the nationalist ideals of Zionism and the Jewish people. Thus, by comparing the experience of the different Jewish subgroups during the past 125 years of immigration to one city, Philadelphia, a complex pattern of interaction of historical forces influencing a diverse immigrant group will be charted with other kinds of developments within social life in the United States. Of course American society in the two periods, the turn of the twentieth century and the late twentieth centuries, was a receptacle for the largest waves of immigration in its history. Cultural and social change in those years cannot easily be teased away from the immigrant experience.

I performed the research reported herein between 1981 and 2007. The work consists of ethnographic fieldwork, analysis of historical archival documents, and the study of press reports and secondary sources. The ethnographic research was comprised of participant observation throughout the years, face-to-face interviews using a list of prepared questions in the case of elderly Soviet immigrants in 1981, unstructured recorded conversations in South Philadelphia from 1982 to 1985 and in 1997, recorded Yiddish discussion groups in 1984–1985 and 1997, and a variety of intergenerational education programs involving Drexel University students, community volunteers, and school-age children from 1998 to 2007.[1] In addition, I was a member of the board of directors of HIAS. From 1986 until 1996, I did fieldwork among elderly Jewish children of immigrants in small cities of New England and compared my findings with those from South Philadelphia.

Sticking around the Neighborhood: The Neighborhood Centre

In December 1985 a young arsonist set fire to the building of the Multi-Service Center South, a facility of the Jewish Ys and Centers at Marshall and Porter Streets in South Philadelphia, causing extensive damage to the structure.[2] At the time, I recall that I was not certain that the Center could be guaranteed a future with an elderly clientele for the next several years. However, I was hopeful and deep down inside an optimist, holding the conviction that a few activists can turn community trends around by strengthening the crucial institutions.

Although I had spent the previous year as a participant-observer in neighborhood life, shunning the limelight and certainly not taking on any advocacy positions, in January 1986, while living in Massachusetts, I wrote a letter to the Philadelphia *Jewish Exponent*, agitating for the Jewish community to rebuild the Center:

> My dream is that sometime soon this JCC Center will once again be a cultural center for Jewish children.... The Jewish community must rebuild at Marshall and Porter Sts. It is urgent for us not to forget these elderly Jews. Many center members are in their 60s, and we must provide Jewish communal services for them for decades to come in South Philadelphia.[3]

The Jewish community rebuilt the center. Some eleven years later, I returned to live in Philadelphia and was invited by the center director to facilitate my old Yiddish conversation group. As I perused the membership list of the JCCs Stiffel Senior Center I could only recognize 5 percent of the names. One might expect the disappearance of many names from the rolls of a senior center, but my surprise was at the appearance of new Jewish names. These represented not an influx of new Jewish residents to South Philadelphia, but rather individuals who wished to take advantage of the institution's services.

A visitor to the Stiffel Center in 2008 can still meet members who, in 1928 when the building opened as the Jewish Educational Center #2 (JEC #2), went to Jewish school in the building in the afternoons after attending public school. But the history of the current Stiffel Center goes back much further. It is the descendant of a settlement house, the Young Women's Union (YWU), founded in 1875, in the northern reaches of South Philadelphia, under German Jewish auspices.[4] It served as a model also for non-Jewish social service institutions for children by establishing the first kindergarten, nursery school, and day care center in Philadelphia (Rosen 1983: 200). These institutions served the Jewish immigrant children from eastern Europe. The YWU, at its headquarters at Bainbridge and Fifth Streets, became one of the initial constituents of the newly formed Federation of Jewish Charities in 1901, and was renamed the Neighborhood Centre in 1918. Through a variety of clubs and activities, it served the educational, cultural, and recreational needs of Jewish family members of all ages (Rosen 1983: 200–201; Greifer 1948; Rose 1994; Peltz 1998: 17–19; 1999: 4–5). With time the programming evolved from general education and Americanization classes to include Jewish programs that would strengthen Jewish identification. Although the center of the immigrant population had moved down toward the more southern streets of southeastern South Philadelphia by World War I, the Neighborhood Centre, after discussions as early as 1923, was not able to move its activities until 1947. First it ran teen programs two evenings a week in the Marshall and Porter Streets building, moving its Noar Day Camp to that location in the summer of 1948, expanding its activities there as the South Philadelphia Community Center in 1950, and three years later renaming the institution at that location the Neighborhood Centre South. In 1965, the Neighborhood Centre and the Jewish Ys combined to form the Jewish Ys and Centers (JYC), with the institution at Marshall and Porter called the JYC Multi-Service Center.[5] From the late 1940s through the late 1960s, when the JEC #2 closed, the two institutions (the Neighborhood Centre South and JEC #2) shared the building.

The personal history of contemporary Stiffel Center members intersects the history of the institution at many junctions. When the JEC #2 opened its doors, it was one of the first independently standing formal institutions for educating Jewish children in the city that was free from the supervision of a specific rabbi or synagogue. Some of the members who received their formal Jewish education there later enrolled their own children in the school. These children, the grand-children of the immigrants, also went to day camp and attended religious ser-vices, teen dances, and basketball games in the building. Between the years 1966 and 1976, the Center was transformed into a full-fledged senior center. Starting with only seventeen senior members, it grew to provide an array of nutritional, educational, health, and counseling programs for several hundred elderly first and second generation Jewish Americans (Peltz 1998: 18). The Jewish school was no longer present at the time when some of its first pupils enrolled their parents as charter members of the early senior center.

Such a long-standing and stable, yet forever changing, institution in this immigrant neighborhood has reinforced personal and group identification. Roze recalled learning to sew in the original Neighborhood Centre building before her parents moved south nearer to Marshall and Porter Streets. Beyle remembered teaching at JEC #2 as a teenager and having Eddie Fisher, who would later reach national fame as a singer in the 1950s, as one of her student cantors. He appears front center in the photograph of the elementary school graduating class of 1941.[6] Other children of immigrants conjure up memories of attending high holiday services with their parents in the large main assembly room in the building. Ester-Beyle and Shmuel-Aron told me that their children, of the third generation, grew up in the building, in the Hebrew school upstairs and the center downstairs. As parents of young children, they worked hard to raise money for the multi-service institution by organizing bingo and street parties. Several times, they fought the decisions of central headquarters at Broad and Pine Streets to close the place, as the number of Jewish children in the neighborhood declined. Ester-Beyle had also been an officer of an independent credit union in the building. Both of them reiterated that as adults there was never a period when they did not go to the Center.

The life cycle of the institution has coincided with the personal and family life cycles of the Jews of South Philadelphia. Just as the better known Henry

Street Settlement and Educational Alliance are thriving today on New York's Lower East Side, so too is Philadelphia's Stiffel Center. Neighborhoods of primary immigrant settlement, such as South Philadelphia, last a lot longer than neighborhoods of subsequent settlement (Peltz 2000). Jewish neighborhoods spawned by former residents of South Philadelphia, starting in the early twentieth century, such as North Philadelphia, West Philadelphia, Logan, Strawberry Mansion, Wynnefield, and East Mount Airy, have lasted only a fraction of the time of South Philadelphia (Peltz 1998: 15).[7] Jewish South Philadelphia has provided its residents with a stable home for many years. The daily open door of the Stiffel Center, the descendant institution of the original settlement house, reminds the Jews of South Philadelphia that they are, indeed, the children and grandchildren of east European Jewish immigrants, who are spinning further the stories, rituals, and recipes of their ancestors, for future generations to acquire (JCCs Stiffel Senior Center 1999).

The success of the settlement house in supporting the acculturation of the immigrants and the continued ethnic identification of their children and grandchildren, and in serving as a lynchpin for the permanence of the primary neighborhood, deserves further scrutiny, in order to understand crucial neighborhood factors that may aid different immigrant groups. The first settlement house, Toynbee Hall, was formed in the East End of London in 1884, close to the time of South Philadelphia's Young Women's Union, New York's Lower East Side Neighborhood Guild (founded by Stanton Coit in 1886, later called the University Settlement) and Henry Street Settlement (founded by Lillian Wald in 1893), and Chicago's Hull House (founded by Jane Addams in 1889). All were formed in urban slums to help the urban poor, in those years consisting largely of immigrants. Samuel Augustus Barnett, the founder of London's Toynbee Hall, applied the word "settlement" to the situation in which professionals, at that time from universities, would live in the working-class neighborhood, gain knowledge of the local life, and thus be able to identify with the residents and work to improve their living conditions. He devised this institution as a way of getting people from different economic, social, and educational backgrounds that normally had little contact with each other to learn from each other, improve the lot of the neighborhood, and thereby also enrich the life of the entire nation. In 1911 in the United States, the National Federation of Settlements and Neighborhood Centers was formed (McDowell 1991). Thus, the context for institutional development of South Philadelphia's Neighborhood Centre that I described is part of a contemporaneous movement in the United States and other parts of the world. For the present volume on immigration, the settlement house can serve as a model of a successful community of practice.

I became aware of the concept of a "community of practice" (Lave and Wenger 1991: 100), as I grappled with understanding the role of the group, including my own participation as ethnographer, in stimulating individual and group cultural memory, as an activity that is facilitated by the group practice of Yiddish conversation (Peltz 1998: 216). Although under those conditions, the group practice related to the speaking of and appreciation of the immigrant language by members of the first and second generations, communities of practice operate in settlement houses and in voluntary immigrant associations. Settlement houses are governed by boards that include the public that supports the institution as well as members from the neighborhood. The institution's constituency is all of the neighborhood's residents, not just the members of the settlement (McDowell 1991: 593). These agencies operate with the conviction that the neighborhood environment is fundamental to the development of the life of the individual and the family. The development of children occurs almost exclusively within the confines of neighborhood institutions.

The ideals of the settlement have been championed as the basis for the existence of contemporary American democracy. For example, the life and writings of Jane Addams have attracted the social critic of the democratic tradition, Jean Bethke Elshtain (Addams 1961 [1910]; Elshtain 2002). Some critics have argued for the return to the intimate secondary institutions of the neighborhood, such as the neighborhood bar, if vibrant cultures are to be transmitted in the United States, as contrasted with the culture that is promulgated through bureaucratic centers of power (Hewitt 1989: 46–47; Elshtain 1995: 5–21; Lasch 1995: 117–128; cf. Rose 1989: 8). Crucial to the concept of "community of practice" is the practice of learning that is a democratic give and take for all members of the community. "This collective learning results in practices that reflect both the pursuit of our enterprises and the attendant social relations" (Wenger 1998: 45). Cultural knowledge is situated in the lived-in world, which is socially structured, and learning takes place through participation in the world (Lave and Wenger 1991: 49, 51, 98). Successful communities of practice function and remain alive only when methods are devised for drawing in and teaching (sharing knowledge in both directions) new members. If one posits a settlement house as an institution that shares knowledge of the host society at the same time that it nurtures the specific ethnic group culture, newcomers can benefit from the shared purpose. Such an institution can become the nucleus for the growth of democracy by accommodating immigrants and their descendants in such a learning process. But we can only document its success in the neighborhood of primary immigration.

Philadelphia Farein: Landsmanshaftn, Ideal Communities of Practice

Hometown-based voluntary associations, landsmanshaftn (called *fareins* in Philadelphia), an understudied topic in American history, represent nevertheless the major form of organizational affiliation of the first wave of east European Jewish immigrants to the United States at the end of the nineteenth century and the beginning of the twentieth century (Soyer 1997). The first of these to develop were often synagogues located in the immigrant neighborhood, known as *ansheys* (taken from their Hebrew names, meaning "groups of people from the place ..."). These synagogues also offered mutual aid and financial benefits (Kliger 1988: 148; 1992: 31–32). Another prevalent form aimed at meeting economic needs of the new immigrant was the hometown-based free loan society (Tenenbaum 1993). The number of landsmanshaftn was astounding. In New York City, it was estimated that one in four Jews belonged to one in the first decades of the twentieth century (Kliger 1992: vi). The number of such institutions in that city alone has been estimated to be as high as ten thousand, and a WPA-sponsored study surveyed close to two thousand such organizations in 1938 (Kliger 1992: 145, n. 1; 11). The leader of the survey declared that there were more landsmanshaftn than synagogues in New York City at the time (Ronch 1939). These voluntary hometown associations fulfilled many functions for the immigrants, including health benefits, burial, free loans, providing networks to find employment, teaching organizational dynamics that exist in the United States, opportunities to congregate socially and speak one's language and dialect, and sending aid to the hometown. Kliger (1990) has identified a tripartate axis of activity, dedicated to life in the United States, Israel, and the hometown. In almost all cases the leading amount of energy was directed toward learning to be an American.

The first voluntary Jewish immigrant association to form in Philadelphia was a synagogue, Chevra Bikur Cholim, founded in 1861. The second such group, however, was hometown-based, the Krakauer Chevra Beth Elohim, formed in 1876 and named for the Polish city of Krakow. It first secured a location for prayer and then three years later united with the Krakauer Beneficial Society. The society developed a ladies auxiliary and a federal credit union as well as a bowling league and newsletter (Kliger 1989: 30). A list of Philadelphia synagogues from 1934 includes names containing eighteen European hometowns. Of course, others may not include the town name in the synagogue name (*Seyfer Hazikorin* 1934: 45–47). As more fareins developed, some of them affiliated with national fraternal orders (Kliger 1989: 34, 36). In times of war, the Philadelphia fareins established relief efforts directed toward their hometowns and its survivors. During my fieldwork in South Philadelphia in 1984–1985, I found several residents who belonged to fareins, including a few individuals who were officers. I attended a meeting of one society of members that hailed from Prushin-Shershov. The organization had hundreds of members, including the prominent families of builders, Korman and Orleans. Membership in the grassroots farein seems to cut across socioeconomic dividers.

During most of the years since the beginning of mass immigration in 1882, South Philadelphia was the hub of Jewish organizational, religious, and business life. Included in this flurry of activity were the majority of the buildings used for the meetings of the hometown associations (Peltz 1998: 19–23). Thus, the farein was an intimate secondary institution, to whose headquarters and meetings the immigrants could walk from home. Here the immigrants could hang out, learn about news of relatives in the old country, get tips on employment and housing opportunities, learn how to run a meeting according to *Roberts Rules of Order,* and just shoot the breeze in their homey Yiddish dialect of the northern Ukraine.[8] A survey of the Yiddish immigrant press reveals meeting announcements of the following local South Philadelphia-based fareins: from the pages of the Philadelphia edition of the *Daily Forverts*: United Tarashtsha Rakitner Beneficial Association, Zhitomirer Beneficial Association, Tolner Progressive Society, Tolner-Dubner Brotherhood (Oct. 27, 1946); First Independent Vinkovitser Farein (Nov. 3, 1946); Kaniver Rezishtshiver Beneficial Association (Nov. 10 and 24, 1946); Kaharliker Beneficial Association (Nov. 24, 1946); from the pages of *Di yidishe velt*: Heisiner Independent Young Men's Association, Zhitomirer Beneficial Association, Branch 2 Independent Natsyonaler Arbeter Farband Anshey Zhitomir, Zlatopolyer Beneficial Association and Ladies Auxiliary, Sokolifker Beneficial Association, Voliner Free Loan (Apr. 6, 1941); Tolner Brotherhood (Apr. 13, 1941); Independent Krivozerer Ladies Auxiliary (Apr. 14, 1941); Tolner Ladies Aid Society, Keren Beys Dovid Froyen Farein fun Tolner Rebben shlit"a (Apr. 21, 1941); Makarover Beneficial Association, Congregation Tiferes Yisroel Anshey Zhitomir, Tolner Brotherhood Association, Ostrer mhrsh"a Lodge Ahavas Akhim Beneficial, Voliner Ladies Free Loan (Apr. 27, 1941); Kaharliker Beneficial Association, Independent Anikster Beneficial Association (May 2, 1941); Tolner Dubner Brotherhood Association, Branch No.2 Yidisher Natsyonaler Arbeter Farband Anshey Zhitomir (Oct. 31, 1941); Kaharliker Beneficial Association, Zhitomirer Gmiles Khesed (Nov. 28, 1941).

The Neighborhood Centre in South Philadelphia has demonstrated itself to be tremendously effective as a community of practice, as all settlement houses should be according to design. The partnership of Jewish communal leaders, social work professionals, Jewish educators, and neighborhood residents charted a path that introduced immigrants to the new society and was also able to help support the Jewish identity of three generations of immigrant family members. The farein, a strictly grassroots immigrant-initiated community of practice, directed the immigrants and often their children in developing and balancing their participation and loyalty to three Jewish centers: the new society, the old home, and the new state of Israel. An examination of the theoretical and operational literature on communities of practice reveals the reasons why the farein was such a success in support of immigrant families and what needs of later immigrants might be met by new communities of practice.

Active participation in a neighborhood-based farein, just like "participating in a playground clique or in a work team, for instance, is both a kind of action and a form of belonging. Such participation shapes not only what we do, but also who we are and how we interpret what we do" (Wenger 1998: 4). The theoretical understanding of the efficacy of such associations places the value of the process of learning and knowing in the forefront. An analysis of the functioning of the farein demonstrates that learning the ways of the new society can be coupled with activities that strengthen the immigrant's identity both as a new American and as a Jew. It is the operation of learning about the world in a comfortable environment that builds a firmer individual and group identification. The farein is built on all the principal requirements of a community of practice. Participants develop ways of talking about their changing ability to experience life as meaningful, both individually and collectively. They share and learn about their immigrant experience and their role in the new society. The farein sustains new ways of talking about practice, resources, and frameworks in which immigrants can mutually and actively engage within the new society, and not be alone in such activity. It provides for a community in which to discuss and evaluate enterprises that may be worth pursuing and in which the immigrant's participation may be judged as competent. Moreover, the farein anchors the immigrant's identity by providing ways of talking about the learning which is occurring and which is changing who the immigrant is and helping the immigrant design her personal history as it develops within the context of her new communities (Wenger 1998: 5). Within the farein, the group of hometown alumni in Philadelphia evolve practices that become the property of the community. Owning the joint goals and practices strengthens the individual and group identities of the new immigrants. It is not clear that the new immigrant family not participating in the neighborhood settlement house and farein can acculturate as efficiently and in as satisfying a manner if isolated from the resources of such learning communities (cf. Wenger 1998: 45).

Communities of practice are not new. They span corporations of artisans in Rome, medieval guilds, groups of insurance salesmen today, as well as work-teams in high-tech companies (Wenger et al. 2002: 3, 5; Saint-Onge and Wallace 2003: 13; Wenger and Snyder 2000). Fareins are attractive to members because they value the interactions that take place at their get-togethers, and as they develop over time, the members share information and advice and help each other solve problems. "Over time, they develop a unique perspective on their topic as well as a body of common knowledge, practices, and approaches" (Wenger et al. 2002: 5). The democratic and local nature of the group provides a context for comfortable sharing of ideas and owning of practices. There are, however, a variety of structures for such communities of practice, and they should be cultivated (Wenger et al. 2002: 12–13, 24–29, 43, 51). Is it possible to plan for communities of practice for more recent Jewish immigrant groups in Philadelphia?

Holocaust Survivors Come to Philadelphia

The historic experience of Jewish immigrant families that arrived in Philadelphia starting in the second half of the twentieth century has not been documented to the same extent as the mass immigration of east European Jews at the turn of the twentieth century. That wave of immigrants, numbering more than 100,000, was so large that it overwhelmed the groups of Sephardic Jews that had arrived in colonial times and the German Jews that came in the earlier nineteenth century. By the time Holocaust survivor families, numbering a few thousand individuals, arrived in the late 1940s and early 1950s, Jewish immigration had been at a standstill for almost twenty-five years, because of anti-immigrant legislation. No careful study has been performed on how the acculturation of the Jews was affected by the abrupt cut-off of arrival of new members from the eastern European hometowns and the subsequent decimation of these hometowns of origin of most Jewish families in the United States. The ambivalence of the more established Jews toward the survivors can be associated with the guilt that the American Jews may have felt, for they too were survivors of this culture. Many of them had lost their own parents and loved ones during the Holocaust. Some survivors that arrived had endured the concentration camp experience, being hidden by Christians, or participating in resistance groups. However, most survivors remained alive by crossing borders and being evacuated to the interior of the Soviet Union. Not only was their war experience far different from that of American Jews, but their memories of life in eastern Europe also separated them. Jewish life in Europe between the two world wars had undergone tremendous urbanization and secularization. The hometowns that the older immigrants recalled were a far cry from the ones the Holocaust survivors, largely people in their twenties and thirties, had known.

In 1953, to increase social contacts with one another and to revive Yiddish cultural activity that most American Jews had abandoned, about one hundred fifty families established the Organization of New Americans in Philadelphia. Each year they organized a memorial event to honor the memory of the Jews murdered by the Nazis. This group spearheaded the commission of sculptor Nathan Rapaport, who had produced the Warsaw Ghetto memorial in Warsaw, to erect the first public memorial in the United States in memory of the six million Jewish victims of the Holocaust. In addition, the group was responsible for organizing and hosting the first National Assembly of Delegates of Jewish Survivor Organizations in the United States in 1970, as well as the World Gathering of Jewish Holocaust Survivors in 1985. Many local survivors gave testimony to the Holocaust Oral History Archive of Gratz College, started by Professor Nora Levin in 1979 and currently administered by Josie Fisher, which comprises one of the largest collections of audiotaped testimonies in the United States. In 1980 a branch group of the survivor association was formed, Sons and Daughters of Holocaust Survivors, that later split into two groups and is still in existence. The parent group changed its name to the Association of Jewish Holocaust Survivors (Rosen, Tabak, and Gross 2003: 20–21; epilogue written by Rosen).

The survivors, like the earlier immigrants, were aided in their settlement by the local HIAS. Although the survivors initially settled in several of the Jewish neighborhoods existing in Philadelphia at the time, including South Philadelphia, most of them ended up living in the Northeast and Greater Northeast neighborhoods that were newly developed at the time of their arrival (Blinzen 2003). The territory of this section of Philadelphia, although more spread out geographically than the older neighborhoods, did provide for geographic contiguity of residence for most survivor families.

A perusal of the bulletins of the survivor organization gives an idea of the mutual concerns of this group of immigrants that arrived at a time of no other significant general or Jewish immigration to Philadelphia. A sampling from 1959 through 1977 demonstrates a significant dedication to maintaining an equal number of pages in Yiddish and English. By 1977, there existed only a few American organizations committed to publishing their organizational newsletter in both languages. In fact, in Bulletin No. 3 (April 1959), Dr. Volf Gliksman exhorts his fellow survivors to form a bulwark against assimilation of American Jewry by teaching about the Yiddish culture that had existed in eastern Europe. Not only do the survivors take on the responsibility of remembering the Holocaust, but here they are given the additional task of keeping the thousand-year old-culture of Yiddish going. Two other articles represent diverse topics relating to the children, one calling for a Zionist education and the other teaching tooth-brushing technique. There is also mention of the founding of a children's club and an announcement of a new choir that is led by Yiddish singer, Bina Landau. In Bulletin No. 6 (April 1962), four of the children of these immigrants write their reflections on erecting the Holocaust monument. These children have been taught that it is their obligation to publicly remember the Holocaust, the events that marred their parents' lives forever and sacrificed the grandparents they would never know. At that date, one could ask if there were any other Jewish American children who were focusing on the communal imperative of not forgetting the genocide against their people. The parental organization at this time also started to support a course on Holocaust history at Gratz College.

Only ten years after the establishment of the organization, in Bulletin No. 9 (April 1965), they have taken on themselves initiatives within the greater Jewish community. The impression is not that of an organization of newcomers, but of veterans. How did this happen so quickly? The president, Abraham Shnaper, reviews their achievements this year: "While the monument officially belongs to the city of Philadelphia, its preservation, however, remains the sole responsibility of our organization." They also turned to the Jewish Community Relations Council to launch a mass protest about the oppression of Soviet Jewry. Had the more veteran members of the Jewish community forgotten about European Jewry? The organization also picketed the West German Consulate to protest the German statute of limitations on Nazi war criminals. My impression at first was that the organization was a veteran constituent of the organized Jewish community. But then on page 6, I read a notice that the Jewish Educational and Vocational Service gives guidance and job placement to new Americans. I realized that families that had arrived ten years earlier might still need help adjusting to American society. The notice jolted this reader into appreciating the group not only as activists in public affairs, but also as immigrants with needs. In Bulletin No. 18 (1974), there is once again a report of the formation of a youth group, called the Ben Gurion Chapter. The name connects the second generation to leadership in Israel, not in the United States or eastern Europe. The chapter reports thirty-one members and 125 attendees at a meeting it called. In the fareins, there was rarely an attempt to organize the children, but in this organization there is an expectation that the youth will take on the task of publicly remembering the Holocaust.[9]

The side of the life and concerns of these immigrants that is publicly revealed in the organizational bulletins contrasts with the quality of information that we have about the earlier Jewish immigrants. The publications do not show the pains of adjustment, the psychological struggle to remain resilient after trauma, problems associated with raising immigrant children, or much of the general process of acculturation to a new society. This may indicate that the larger Jewish community was not interested in such issues. Additionally or alternatively, it may demonstrate the fact that the survivors themselves were trying as much as possible to appear "normal," even to the extent of organizing cultural events and initiating the institutionalization in the United States of Holocaust memorial meetings and monuments. Their public initiatives within the organized Jewish community are quite impressive, signifying a higher level of education than the earlier immigrants and previous experience in European political and cultural youth groups. The organization seems more a city-wide public affairs and cultural group than a Jewish neighborhood lodge of east European immigrants. We must also remember that the survivor families are a minority within the Jewish community and neighborhood; the earlier immigrants had in contrast quickly dominated the Jewish population in numbers. Better understanding of the life and activity of survivor families may be sought in the records of the David Neumann Neighborhood Centre that opened its doors in the midst of their Northeast neighborhood on Bustleton Avenue in 1954. Were there activities specifically for these families? The records of the fareins may indicate survivor participation. What will local synagogue records reveal? Perhaps the Holocaust Oral History Archive will make reference to the special acculturation process of this group. From the limited data I have presented, there is little suggestion of the rich neighborhood life of the earlier immigrants or the intimate secondary institutions that developed as communities of practice.

Jews from the Former Soviet Union

Jewish immigrants, most with refugee status fleeing Soviet oppression of Jews, came to Philadelphia over a period of almost thirty years, from about 1970 though the late 1990s. The host Jewish community in Philadelphia, as part of a national and worldwide effort, provided for a variety of services to welcome these newcomers and help in their acclimation. The degree of organization of the host community and the range of services and resources provided the Jews from the former Soviet Union reflect the maturation of the American Jewish community, its acquired self-confidence within American society, its relative affluence, and a politicization with regard to the issue of freeing the Soviet Jews, which had started in the early 1960s. The scale of the organized process of aiding these Jews was far greater than that available to any earlier Jewish immigrants. Philadelphia's HIAS was the first agency contact for the newcomers to the city. The first immigrants settled in Logan and the Oxford Circle area of the Northeast, but by the early 1980s most were living in the Greater Northeast, near the 9000 to 12000 blocks of Bustleton Avenue. HIAS, after helping with the immigration process, provided basic information in Russian about American society, but subsequent stages of settlement and other services were offered by Jewish Family Service, Jewish Educational and Vocational Service, Federation Day Care, and the JCCs, including the David Neumann Senior Center and the Klein Branch. It was largely professional case workers and counselors who steered these Jewish newcomers through English classes, appointments with the Department of Public Assistance for food stamps and medical help, visits to Einstein Northern Medical Center for known illnesses, and free initial memberships at the JCC Klein Branch. From 1976 through October 1978, the Federation of Jewish Agencies, through Jewish Family Service, arranged for grants and loans for one year. Following this, the federal government provided grants of about $2,000 per immigrant per year (Levin 2003: 129). In the late 1980s immigration accelerated tremendously, with many of the new immigrants moving into lower Bucks and eastern Montgomery counties, along with the movement of the rest of the Jewish community (Friedman and Harrison 2003: xix).

The older Yiddish-speaking Jews from the former Soviet Union who arrived before the early 1980s demonstrate differences within the immigrant group and contrast with Philadelphia Jews who had come with their families from Russia and the newly formed Soviet Union in the early part of the twentieth century. Elderly immigrants rarely had financial resources or a source of employment. They arrived accompanying their children and grandchildren, who were busy finding employment, going to school, and establishing a social life. They had little to occupy themselves except attending communal activities for the elderly in Russian and Yiddish. One such individual, Yankl, had become active in the Workmen's Circle headquarters across Bustleton Avenue from the Neumann Centre, because he had been exposed to Yiddish culture as a child in Odessa and could communicate well in Yiddish with the Workmen Circle cultural activists. At the Neumann Centre a visitor would observe two mutually exclusive groups having little contact, the new Soviet Jews and the longtime Americans who derived from Russia. Several of the newcomers complained that the American Jews refused to speak Yiddish and insisted that the Soviet Jews talk English. I was made aware of the dire circumstances of some of the elderly newcomers when I met up with Marye a few years later in South Philadelphia. She entered an arranged marriage with an elderly Jew who had arrived in America fifty years earlier. He treated her like an indentured servant and during almost ten years, Marye had little outside social contact and learned no English (Peltz 1981; 1998: 102–105). Both the Holocaust survivors and the recent immigrants from the former Soviet Union found little in common with the older immigrants and their descendants.

As late as 2001–2002, HIAS was still assisting approximately seventy-seven people to complete Affidavits of Relationship for emigration from the former Soviet Union (FSU), although the major wave of refugees and immigrants had subsided. That year only eighty-seven new refugees arrived in the Philadelphia area under the auspices of the Jewish community.[10] Qualitative information at this time, collected by a sociologist who lived in the Northeast Philadelphia neighborhood settled by Jews from the FSU, demonstrates that these new residents have intensified their identification with Jewish traditional practices. They report that they celebrate holidays, go to synagogue, and give to charity. She found that they shun organizations and forums, based on their experience in the FSU, but do participate more informally in Russian Jewish activities and Russian language and culture clubs, stores, cafes, restaurants, theatre performances, films, and music festivals. In addition, she found little transnational engagement, little home country-directed behavior in relation to the FSU or Israel. All their activity was directed to the host country, to Philadelphia life (Morawska 2004: 1388–1391).

A quantitative survey of the population of Jews from the FSU that was carried out near the end of the immigration period highlights the specific nature of this wave of newer Jewish residents in the Philadelphia metropolitan area. Contrary to the earlier discussion of Yiddish-speakers, the entire profile was based on a Russian-speaking group who emigrated during the previous twenty-five to thirty years. Between August 2000 and February 2001, 542 interviews were conducted in Montgomery, Philadelphia, and Bucks counties. Too few were from Montgomery County; therefore, the tabulated data derived from the latter two counties, an equal number of interviews deriving from each. Although the ethnic subcomposition was varied, the study refers to the entire cohort as "Russian Jewish immigrants." Jews were identified by self-identification; 247 interviews were carried out face-to-face and 294 by telephone (p. 7). Two estimates identify the group as consisting of 31,000 individuals and more than 10,000 households, or 33,700 individuals and 11, 700 households. The latter estimate divides the population into 22,500 individuals in Philadelphia County, 8,700 in Bucks, and 2,500 in Montgomery (p. 9). Thus, Russian immigrants represent at least 14 percent of the Jewish population of 242,000. They are by far the largest group of recent immigrants.

If we compare their residential compactness with the older neighborhood pattern of South Philadelphia, these newer residents, after thirty years, are in four zip codes in Northeast Philadelphia, four in Bucks County, and one in Montgomery County. In 1920, after forty years, 100,000 Jews were in South Philadelphia. It would be much more difficult for the newer immigrants to establish the intense neighborhood life of the earlier immigrants. The Russians are relatively young as compared with the current American Jews, 38 percent of the Americans are older than 55 as contrasted with 28 percent of the Russians. Immigrants are usually younger people. The large size of the recent immigrant group is striking: 68 percent of the Russians arrived after 1990 (p. 17). The transnational connections remain high, since 35 percent of the immigrants still have first-degree relatives in the FSU. The Russian immigrants are far different in regard to their education and training when compared to the immigrants of a hundred years ago. In fact, their education is on a par with current American Jews; 75 percent have computers at home and most are employed in professional, technical, and managerial fields (p. 23). Younger Russians identify less with Judaism than do older immigrants (p. 28). Of the Russian Jewish immigrants, 76 percent say "being Jewish" means feeling and belonging to the Jewish people or nation. American Jews, on the other hand, traditionally consider themselves as a religious group rather than an ethnic group. The Russians view indicators of belonging as knowing and remembering Jewish history, being proud of the Jewish people, and remembering the Holocaust. Eighty-nine percent demonstrate a positive or very positive attitude towards Israel, and 90% attend a religious service at least once a year (pp. 33, 35, 41).[11]

Such a quantitative study offers more information than we have for the earlier waves of immigrants. Historically and demographically, however, it is difficult to compare the refugees and immigrants from the FSU with the large wave of immigrants of a century ago. They have available more communal Jewish resources than during other times in their life in the FSU. However, the ethnic-based identity within the family had withstood many attacks from the unfriendly environs. As newcomers within the larger Jewish community in Philadelphia, they were again a minority. They live in specific neighborhoods that are increasingly suburban, without the intense shared social activity of the earlier wave of immigrants. In addition, although interacting with Jewish communal officials more than in previous periods of history, they form far fewer voluntary associations and experience little organizational life that is characterized by intimate secondary institutions.

Immigrants from Israel

Almost nothing has been published about immigrants from Israel to Philadelphia. This immigration has a long, ongoing history, starting with Holocaust survivor families who went to Israel after World War II and then came to the United States in the mid- and late-1950s. Zionist ideology has looked down upon all Jewish citizens of Israel who leave Israel. Ayelet Palti, director of Habayit Yisraeli[12] in the Philadelphia area, reported to me that the files of the local Israeli consulate identified ten thousand families (25,000 individuals) who derive from Israel. This represents about 10 percent of the local Jewish population, no small number. Actually, this group approaches the size of the Jewish immigrants from the FSU. In her work, Palti found several groups of Israeli immigrants in different regions of the Philadelphia area that have little contact with each other. In the Northeast are families who derive from Asian and North African immigrants to Israel. They are in a relatively lower socioeconomic class and attend services in a few small Orthodox synagogues. On the Main Line is a group consisting largely of academics and professionals who do not affiliate religiously. There is a newer group of young business professionals in Cherry Hill that has formed an organization that convenes in the local JCC. In addition, there are apparel and jewelry storeowners on Market and South streets in Center City, Philadelphia.

Dr. Dina Nevo, a clinical psychologist who has studied local Israeli youth, says directly, "the Israelis have no organizations."[13] Because of the ambivalence associated with leaving Israel, she found that teenage children of Israelis, both those born in the United States and those born in Israel, do not have proper feelings of loss and grieving that is normally associated with emigration. Yet families of former Israelis do, almost exclusively, maintain social ties with other expatriot Israelis. These families maintain the Hebrew language at home, buy Israeli products, and cultivate an appreciation of Israeli culture. An organization of local Israelis has been formed in recent years that maintains a website that lists area cultural events (www.phillyisraelim.com). PhillyIsraelim has organized concerts, summer parties, playgroups in Center City and Wynnewood, Hebrew-speaking evenings, Hebrew language lectures and movie screenings, and parenting workshops in Hebrew.

During intergenerational, educational programs that I have organized as part of the Drexel University Judaic Studies Program, interviews with a parent and child from one family have pointed to very different Jewish experiences and identifications in Israel and after immigrating to the United States. In one family that immigrated in 2003, the eighteen-year-old son missed the intense activity with friends on the street in Israel. Here his friends are largely other immigrant children, not necessarily Jewish. Americans do not realize the special nature of the immigrant experience. In Israel, people went to the synagogue to pray; here, they find that people attend largely for social reasons. The father has a brother who has been in Philadelphia for thirty years, speaks Hebrew at home, but seems American. The younger children have forgotten much of their Hebrew, even though it is spoken at home. In a second case study the son came from Israel eighteen years ago when he was seventeen. He has recently become more religiously observant; in Israel, he did not find that necessary in order to feel Jewish. His mother had a secular upbringing. When they came to Philadelphia, they settled in the Northeast, with a big population of Israelis. However, in order to feel Jewish, she had introduced traditions into her home in Israel and even more so here. They both agree that here they have to work at remembering that they are Jewish.[14]

The limited information on Israelis in Philadelphia points to an immigrant group of diverse religious, socioeconomic, and subethnic backgrounds. They reside in different areas of the Philadelphia metropolitan area. Thus, it is nearly impossible for them to establish neighborhood groups with intense activities. Even after many years of residing in the area, the immigrants report the maintenance of friendship networks with other Israeli immigrants. They also report positive feelings toward their Israeli homeland. At this time, after many years of their presence, the organized local Jewish community is recognizing them as a distinct Jewish subgroup. The absence of strong organizational affiliation within the Jewish community does not allow for meaningful comparison with the groups of earlier Jewish immigrants.

Conclusions

South Philadelphia represents the physical place that has served Jewish immigrants and their descendants as a context for individual and group identification for 125 years. Associated with this neighborhood were two kinds of institutions, one the Neighborhood Centre, a settlement house that has undergone many changes over the years, but continues to serve as an address for Jewish identity. The second institution, the farein, or voluntary European hometown-based group with transnational ties, has afforded its members with ways of becoming American and at the same time maintaining and strengthening their Jewish identification. I analyzed both of these Jewish communal institutions in terms of the model of a community of practice, in order to appreciate their success in fostering the individual and group identifications of Jewish American immigrants, their children, and grandchildren.

As I presented the histories of three other waves of Jewish immigrants to Philadelphia after World War II—Holocaust survivors, Jews from the former Soviet Union, and Israeli Jews—the role of analogous communities of practice could not be identified. In part, this is the case because these immigrant subgroups remain minorities within the local Jewish community, as contrasted with the massive, east European wave of immigration a century earlier. Furthermore, the neighborhood, the place-based locus for the development of such institutions, no longer plays such a major role. But the host American society has also been altered in major ways. The ideology and practices of the isolated individual have replaced those of the community and its voluntary associations (Putnam 2000). Moreover, place within the American landscape, associated in the urban context with the physical and social cues of the neighborhood, was no longer a constitutive aspect of the definition of an American identity, rather it was negotiable, imaginable, or even dispensable (Jacobson 2002: 181–182).

My findings on the legacy of Jewish immigration to the nature of Philadelphia life in general underscore the salience of the contribution of immigrant life to urban affairs. For example, the premier Philadelphia immigrant neighborhood in the nineteenth and early twentieth centuries was South Philadelphia. The residential and institutional framework of the neighborhood, largely established by Jewish, Italian, Irish, and Polish immigrants, gave the neighborhood its identity. In recent years, newer immigrants from Southeast Asia have populated and in turn identified with the neighborhood. Suttles (1972: 27) has noted that neighborhoods primarily identified with single ethnic groups may actually be home to several ethnic groups, and that these neighborhoods can maintain their identities and boundaries despite shifts in ethnic composition. Immigration has given Philadelphia its strong neighborhood composition and identity. In addition, in Philadelphia as elsewhere, it was often the organization serving the immigrants, especially the settlement house, that was the pioneer in social services. Thus, the Young Women's Union, the predecessor of the Neighborhood Centre and the current Stiffel Senior Center, pioneered such institutions as the day care center and foster homes for all of Philadelphia.

The parallel patterns of acculturation for different immigrant groups are striking. The history of the Neighborhood Centre, for example, is similar to that of the German Society of Pennsylvania (GSP; see Pfleger, Chapter 6 of this volume). The wealthier and more Americanized founders tried to clean up the act of their newly arrived brethren, largely serving to teach them English, prepare them for naturalization, and aiding them in shedding their old world ways. Both the Neighborhhood Centre and GSP suffered from staying on in the immigrant neighborhood after the immigrants themselves had moved on. The Neighborhood

Centre, however, eventually transformed itself into a Jewish culture-based organization, serving the newly expressed ethnic interests of a latter day ethnic America. Both organizations, however, competed with the more popular, hometown-based churches and synagogues and social and self-help clubs, the *farein* and *Vereine*, respectively (note the cognate identities of these words).

The new wave of immigration to the United States since 1965 (Waters and Ueda 2007) has much that it can learn from the experience of the primary wave of Jewish immigration to Philadelphia. The cultivation of communities of practice guarantees continual learning and growth for groups in a changing environment. It is possible that the Jewish waves of recent immigrants from the former Soviet Union and Israel may organize their residential settlement to constitute pockets of suburban ethnic enclaves analogous to the former urban ethnic enclaves, such as Jewish South Philadelphia (Alba and Denton 2004: 241, 253). Sociology is dependent on history and vice versa. The creative solutions that previous immigrant groups have evolved for becoming American and maintaining a Jewish identity may yet play a role in the futures of the newer groups.

Notes

1. During 1997 my research was supported by a fellowship from the Center for Judaic Studies at the University of Pennsylvania and a summer grant from the Feinstein Center for American Jewish History of Temple University. Over the years, the archival collections I consulted were located at the Philadelphia Jewish Archives Center, the American Jewish Archives in Cincinnati, the Urban Archives at Temple University, the American Jewish Historical Society, and the Yivo Institute for Jewish Research in New York City. I facilitated a Yiddish discussion group, *A Gleyzele Tey*, at the Multi-Service Center of the Jewish Ys and Centers (later the JCCs Stiffel Senior Center) weekly during 1984–1985 and in the spring of 1997 and monthly after that through 2007.

2. "Fire Ruins a Refuge for Elderly: Arson Suspected in Blaze at South Phila. Jewish Center." *Philadelphia Inquirer*, December 13, 1985, p. 1.

3. *Jewish Exponent*, January 24, 1986, p. 29.

4. "A Glorious Hundred Years of Service: A Centennial Tribute: The History of the Neighborhood Centre." *The Review: Jewish Ys and Centers of Greater Philadelphia* 9, no. 8 (May 1975), 3–4.

5. Ibid.

6. *Bikkurim*, the Record of the Thirteenth Graduating Class, Jewish Educational Center No. 2, a constituent of the Associated Talmud Torahs, Philadelphia, PA, June 1941.

7. By 2007, there are signs of the diminishing nature of the South Philadelphia Jewish institutions. The local meetings of the Masons and Jewish War Veterans had ceased by the mid-1990s. However, from 1984 until 2005, three synagogues functioned in the heart of the neighborhood near the JCCs Stiffel Center. Because of the absence of organizing leaders, two have stopped services. In 2006, Shivtei Yeshuron-Heisiner-Ezras Israel experienced the unexpected death of its "youthful" organizer, who had only been in his mid-sixties. The building had opened its doors ninety years earlier. In April 2007, Adath Shalom at Marshall and Ritner Streets was sold to a Buddhist temple, demonstrating the common ethnic suc-

cession within immigrant neighborhoods. The statues of two Asian felines ceremoniously guard the entrance. Thus ended the more than eighty-year life of a synagogue that started out as *di litvishe shul* (the Lithuanian synagogue), Beis Shmuel. At the time of this writing, only Y.P.C. (Young People's Congregation) Shari Eli at Franklin and Moyamensing Streets convenes in the neighborhood. Its guiding force is a member of the third generation in his mid-fifties who was born in the neighborhood and is the son of one of my informants, a child of immigrants that I interviewed twenty-two years ago. There are four synagogues started by east European immigrants more than a hundred ten years ago that are active on Spruce, Pine, and Lombard Streets; however, that neighborhood, although originally considered South Philadelphia, has been identified as Center City for most of the past century (cf. Peltz 1998: 15–17).

There are reports at the time that I am writing this chapter that the last long-standing Jewish kosher delicatessen and bakery will be closing on New York's Lower East Side, an analogous neighborhood of primary Jewish immigrant settlement, that developed in the same years as South Philadelphia (Salkin 2007). We may be near the end of the maximum lifetimes of urban Jewish immigrant neighborhoods in the United States. However, neighboring Italian South Philadelphia, immediately to the west of Jewish South Philadelphia, whose famed Italian Market has already changed its ethnic composition to Mexican American, remains an Italian American residential neighborhood of primary settlement.

8. The observation that most Philadelphia Jews by dint of chain migration derive from this region was first made by Tabak (1983: 51). My study of Yiddish dialect usage confirmed this (Peltz 1990).

9. MSS 36, 1 box, 3 folders, assorted bulletins, Association of Jewish New Americans in Philadelphia, Philadelphia Jewish Archives Center.

10. Annual Report, Sept. 1, 2001–Aug. 31, 2002, HIAS.

11. "New American Jewish Population Study of Greater Philadelphia: Portrait of Russian Jewish Immigrants in Greater Philadelphia 2000–2001," unpublished study conducted for the Jewish Federation of Greater Philadelphia by The Research Institute for New Americans (RINA). I am grateful to Joy W. Goldstein, Vice-President of Policy, Strategy and Funding, The Jewish Federation of Greater Philadelphia, for making this report available to me.

12. Habayit Yisraeli ("The Israeli Home") is a project of the Israeli Ministry of Immigrant Absorption that promotes educational and cultural programs with the goal of attracting former Israelis to return home. I thank Ayelet Palti for the interview on May 18, 2007, Bala Cynwyd, PA.

13. Phone interview with Dr. Dina Nevo, June 18, 2007.

14. Interviews performed at Society Hill Synagogue Hebrew High School, Philadelphia, PA, in the presence of Drexel University Judaic Studies students, May 2006.

References

Addams, Jane. 1961 [1910]. *Twenty Years at Hull-House.* New York: New American Library.

Alba, Richard, and Nancy Denton. 2004. "Old and New Landscapes of Diversity: The Residential Patterns of Immigrant Minorities." In *Not Just Black and White,* ed. Nancy Foner and George Fredrickson, 237–261. New York: Russell Sage Foundation.

Blinzen, Peter. 2003. "A Place to Live: The Jewish Builders of Northeast Philadelphia." In Friedman, ed., 113–126.

Dubin, Murray. 1996. *South Philadelphia.* Philadelphia: Temple University Press.

Elshtain, Jean B. 1995. *Democracy on Trial.* New York: Basic Books.

———. 2002. *Jane Addams and the Dream of American Democracy.* New York: Basic Books.

Friedman, Murray, ed. 2003. *Philadelphia Jewish Life 1940–2000.* Philadelphia: Temple University Press.

Friedman, Murray, and Andrew Harrison. 2003. "Introduction to a New Edition: The Eighties to a New Century." In Friedman, ed., xv–xxiv.

Gerson, Kathleen, C. Ann Steuve, and Claude S. Fischer. 1977. "Attachment to Place." In *Networks and Places: Social Relations in the Urban Setting,* ed. Claude S. Fischer, Kathleen Gerson, Mark Baldassare, Robert M. Jackson, and C. Ann Steuve, 139–161. New York: Free Press.

Greifer, Julian. L. 1948. "Neighborhood Centre—A Study of the Adjustment of a Cultural Group in America." PhD diss., New York University.

Hewitt, John P. 1989. *Dilemmas of the American Self.* Philadelphia: Temple University Press.

Jacobson, David. 2002. *Place and Belonging in America.* Baltimore: The Johns Hopkins University Press.

JCCs Stiffel Senior Center. 1999. *Memories and Meichels.* Philadelphia: JCCs Stiffel Senior Center.

Kliger, Hannah. 1988. "A Home away from Home: Participation in Jewish Immigrant Associations." In *Persistence and Flexibility: Anthropological Studies on the American Jewish Experience,* ed. Walter Zenner, 143–164. Albany: State University of New York Press.

———. 1989. "In a Common Cause, in This New Found Country: Fellowship and Farein in Philadelphia." In *Traditions in Transition: Jewish Culture in Philadelphia, 1840–1940,* ed. Gail Stern, 28–45. Philadelphia: Balch Institute for Ethnic Studies Press.

———. 1990. "In Support of Their Society: The Organizational Dynamics of Immigrant Life in the United States and Israel." In *We Are Leaving Mother Russia: Chapters in the Russian Jewish Experience,* ed. Kerry Olitzky, 33–53. Cincinnati: American Jewish Archives Press.

———. 1992. *Jewish Hometown Associations and Family Circles in New York: The WPA Yiddish Writers' Group Study.* Bloomington: Indiana University Press.

Lasch, Christopher. 1995. *The Revolt of the Elites and the Betrayal of Democracy.* New York: W. W. Norton.

Lave, Jean, and Etienne Wenger. 1991. *Situated Learning: Legitimate Peripheral Participation.* Cambridge: Cambridge University Press.

Levin, Nora. 2003. "Home and Haven: Soviet Jewish Immigration to Philadelphia, 1972–1982." In Friedman, ed., 127–142.

McDowell, John. 1991. "Settlement House." In *Encyclopedia Americana,* vol. 24, 593–594. Danbury, CT: Grolier.

Morawska, Ewa. 2004. "Exploring Diversity in Immigrant Assimilation and Transnationalism: Poles and Russian Jews in Philadelphia." *International Migration Review* 38:1372–1412.

Peltz, Rakhmiel. 1981. "Yiddish in the Ukraine: A Project with Recent Soviet Immigrants." Unpublished paper. New York: Linguistics Department, Columbia University.

———. 1990. "Spoken Yiddish in America: Variation in Dialect and Grammar." In *Studies in Yiddish Linguistics,* ed. Paul Wexler, 55–73. Tubingen: Max Niemeyer Verlag.

———. 1998. *From Immigrant to Ethnic Culture: American Yiddish in South Philadelphia.* Palo Alto, CA: Stanford University Press.

———. 1999. "Remembering the Center." In *Memories and Meichels,* JCCs Stiffel Senior Center, 4–5. Philadelphia: JCCs Stiffel Senior Center.

———. 2000. "Immigrant Neighborhoods That Never Die." In *Still Home: The Jews of South Philadelphia. Exhibition Catalogue of Photographs by Harvey Finkle,* 6–12. Philadelphia: National Museum of American Jewish History.

Putnam, Robert D. 2000. *Bowling Alone: The Collapse and Revival of American Community.* New York: Simon and Schuster.

Rontch, Isaac. 1939. "The Present State of the Landsmanschaften." *The Jewish Social Service Quarterly* 15:360–378.

Rose, Dan. 1989. *Patterns of American Culture: Ethnography and Estrangement.* Philadelphia: University of Pennsylvania Press.

Rose, Elizabeth. 1994. "From Sponge Cake to *Hamentaschen*: Jewish Identity in a Jewish Settlement House, 1885–1952." *Journal of American Ethnic History* 13:3–23.

Rosen, Phillip. 1983. "German Jews vs. Russian Jews in Philadelphia Philanthropy." In *Jewish Life in Philadelphia: 1830–1940,* ed. Murray Friedman, 198–212. Philadelphia: ISHI.

Rosen, Phillip, Robert Tabak, and David Gross. 2003. "Philadelphia Jewry and the Holocaust." In Friedman, ed., 3–22.

Saint-Onge, Hubert, and Debra Wallace. 2003. *Leveraging Communities of Practice for Strategic Advantage.* Amsterdam: Butterworth Heinemann.

Salkin, Allen. 2007. "Lower East Side Is under a Groove." *New York Times,* June 3, sec. 9, pp. 1, 10.

Seyfer Hazikorin: Souvenir Journal Commemorating the Celebration of the Fortieth Anniversary of the Yeshiva Mishkan Israel and Central Talmud Torah. 1934. Philadelphia: Yeshiva Mishkan Israel and Central Talmud Torah.

Soyer, Daniel. 1997. *Jewish Immigrant Associations and American Identity in New York, 1880–1939.* Cambridge, MA: Harvard University Press.

Suttles, Gerald D. 1972. *The Social Construction of Communities.* Chicago: University of Chicago Press.

Tabak, Robert. 1983. "Orthodox Judaism in Transition." In *Jewish Life in Philadelphia 1830–1940,* ed. Murray Friedman, 48–63. Philadelphia: ISHI.

Tenenbaum, Shelly. 1993. *A Credit to Their Community: Jewish Loan Societies in the United States 1880–1945.* Detroit: Wayne State University Press.

Waters, Mary C., and Reed Ueda, eds. 2007. *The New Americans: A Guide to Immigration since 1965.* Cambridge, MA: Harvard University Press.

Wenger, Etienne. 1998. *Communities of Practice: Learning, Meaning, and Identity.* Cambridge: Cambridge University Press.

Wenger, Etienne, Richard McDermott, and William M. Snyder. 2002. *Cultivating Communities of Practice: A Guide to Managing Knowledge.* Boston: Harvard Business School Press.

Wenger, Etienne, and William M. Snyder. 2000. "Communities of Practice: The Organizational Frontier." *Harvard Business Review* 78 (1): 139–145.

Wireman, Peggy. 1984. *Urban Neighborhoods, Networks, and Families: New Forms for Old Values.* Lexington, MA: Lexington Books.

3

Mapping Memories in Stone

Italians and the Transformation
of a Philadelphia Landscape

JOAN SAVERINO

In October 2004, I attended the eightieth anniversary celebration banquet of the Venetian Social Club in Chestnut Hill, a neighborhood in the northwest corner of Philadelphia (see Figure 3.1). For the benefit of the multigenerational gathering, the second floor hall had been transformed into a mini exhibition of early photographs of the community on the Hill. At one end of the room was a monitor that endlessly replayed a vacation video taken by one of the members during the annual celebration in Poffabro, a northern Italian village in the Dolomite Mountains of the Friuli region, from which this Italian American community originated.[1]

The community marks its beginning in Philadelphia with Maximilian Roman, a stonemason who emigrated from Poffabro to Chestnut Hill in 1890 to work in the booming construction industry. In a classic story of chain migration, Roman supposedly urged his fellow townspeople in a letter to come to Chestnut Hill: "This is a good place to live and work. You would do well to come here." As a result of his invitation, "between 1891 and 1906 nearly 200 families totaling about 1000 persons emigrated from Poffabro and surrounding towns to live and work in Chestnut Hill" (Venetian Social Club 1974).

When the immigrant Friulani arrived on the Hill, they found a landscape dominated by stone quarries and construction taking shape from rock, often being excavated on site. The legacy in stone that is Chestnut Hill is the embodiment of the lived experience of these Friulani. Growing up in

FIGURE 3.1
Contemporary view
of the Venetian Club.
(Photograph by Joan Saverino.)

mountain villages carved from the Dolomia stone, they arrived in Chestnut Hill as experienced stoneworkers and tile setters. They adapted their knowledge of working the stone of the Dolomia to cut and carve the brittle local schist in the Wissahickon Valley. Stone carving was passed from fathers to sons, and as Herbert Lorenzon (2002b: 6), a second generation Friulani who began carving by age ten or eleven, told me, "It's either in your hands or not."

If the ability to carve is in the hands, the emotions tied to place are in the heart. The presence of Poffabro in the midst of the eightieth anniversary celebration of the community's beloved Venetian Club on the Hill was not simply an evocation of a distant past or a faraway landscape. Modern technology allowed the virtual inclusion of a place that has remained real in their lives and in their emotions, a place that has taken on the mantle of the mythical in their imaginations. The evening was filled with public reminiscences as well as privately expressed memories about Chestnut Hill, the Venetian Club, summer homes in Poffabro, and the beauty of that Italian village. Over the many decades in the

United States, the Friulani built a new homeplace while maintaining attachment to the one they had left. Both locales, central to the community's heart, are wrought in stone. It is through stone that people identify who they are and who their families are and their connections to Chestnut Hill and to Friuli.

Approaching the material landscape as an embodiment of memory and a search for meaning, this paper uses this landscape of stone to demonstrate a connection between Italian American ethnicity and place. By using a case study of Italian immigration and settlement, specifically the Friulani to Chestnut Hill, we will see how the relationship between ethnicity and place is complicated, layered, emotionally laden, and intensely personal. The connection must be read in terms of the shifting boundaries of inter- and intra-ethnic social relations and issues of power and class again inscribed in the neighborhood landscape. It involves transnational ties and the home *paese* writ mythical manifested in material locality. We will see how the Italian immigrants transformed the local landscape, and how and why it was the northern Friulani Italian identity that was encoded primarily on the landscape (as opposed to the identity of the southern Italians who lived on the Hill), how ethnic difference was marked spatially during the early first half of the twentieth century, and how it remains and is remembered today. Given the unique state of the physical preservation of the built environment in Chestnut Hill, this neighborhood provides an excellent opportunity to articulate how ethnicity intersects with place, how difference is delineated in space, and how places that once were are kept alive in memory.[2]

Clifford Geertz (1996: 262) has said, "For it is still the case that no one lives in the world in general. Everybody . . . lives in some confined and limited stretch of it—'the world around here.'" Geertz implies that in the past this was even more the case. We will see how it was certainly true for Chestnut Hill in the early twentieth century. In looking at the particularity of place—that is, by attempting to understand how people root themselves to place, transform it, and attach meaning to places they inhabit—we can gain new understanding of how identity is formed and tied to place.[3]

One way of studying identity is by teasing out the boundaries of social relations (Barth 1969) as they are located in space. I am interested in identity formation and in particular the production of interethnic (between Italian immigrants and the Other) and intra-ethnic (between different Italian regional populations) differences that emerged in Chestnut Hill.

To articulate how the Friulani established a different identity, one distinct from both the Anglo and the other Italians on the Hill, requires an articulation of the multilocal and multivocal dimensions of place. As Rodman (1992: 647) indicates, one landscape "shapes and expresses polysemic meanings of place for different users. This is more accurately a multivocal dimension of place, but multilocality conveys the idea that a single place may be experienced quite differently." We shall see how this multilocality and multivocality played out in Chestnut Hill.

Although the literature on place is voluminous, intersecting ethnicity and place is still an understudied area.[4] Recently in Italian American studies, more scholarship has appeared analyzing the interplay of ethnicity, space, and place, although it concentrates primarily on the contemporary landscape.[5] This paper contributes to that growing pool from an ethnohistorical perspective. In general, it is more difficult to look at communities ethnohistorically using a spatial lens. This is due to dual forces (post–World War II urban America's exodus to the suburbs and deindustrialization) that often resulted in a built environment that was decaying and eventually erased. Now decades later, with the landscape devoid of what had existed and the people who had once lived there dispersed, reading the landscape that once was becomes a very difficult endeavor indeed.

As noted previously, although the Italian community was small in Chestnut Hill, because of the good state of preservation of the built environment and because Italians are still living and working in the neighborhood or nearby, there is a unique opportunity to explore ethnicity and difference through the lens of place. This chapter contributes new ground to the emerging discourse of the dynamic interplay of memory, ethnicity, and place, and specifically to place scholarship in Italian American studies.

Scholars have used the term *campanilismo* (within sound of the church bell) to characterize the regionalism of early Italian immigrant urban enclaves. Campanilismo resulted in an early settlement pattern in which the chain migration of networks of townspeople and kin tended to live near one another, resulting in the classic "Little Italies" found in large cities such as New York and South Philadelphia (Yans-McLaughlin 1982; Juliani 1971: 222–223). These enclaves were never totally insular but often had a mix of other ethnicities within the neighborhood. While some attention has been paid to looking at interethnic relationships, very little research analyzes intra-ethnic relationships (among Italians of different regions) on a micro level. Because of the unique situation of northern and southern Italians in Chestnut Hill living in close proximity and the unique state of the preserved landscape, we are afforded such an opportunity.

Methodology

The interpretations in this paper are a result of an ethnohistorical project to research the Italians in Northwest Philadelphia that was funded by the Pennsylvania Humanities Council.[6] Primary source material included oral interviews, family correspondence, census records, and archival documents. Between 1997 and 2002, seventeen tape-recorded open-ended ethnographic oral interviews were conducted with first- and second-generation Italian Americans from ten different families who had once been or were still part of the immigrant

communities in the Germantown and Chestnut Hill neighborhoods of Philadelphia. Follow-up interviews were conducted in eight out of the ten families.
Each interview was conducted at the interviewee's home and lasted from two to
four hours. Questions concerned immigration, settlement, economic and work
life, religious and family life, and ethnic relations. Interviewees were selected
based on advice from the Italian American Advisory Committee that was formed
for the project and followed three criteria: (1) they were immigrants themselves
and therefore could speak from a first-generation perspective; (2) they or their
immigrant families were members who played key roles in the community; (3)
a balance was attempted to select interviewees who represented different structural categories as to gender, education, and economic status.

Immigration and Settlement in Pennsylvania, Philadelphia, and the Northwest

In order to better understand the production of locality in Chestnut Hill, it is
necessary to contextualize the history of Italians within the larger story of immigration and in particular to Philadelphia and its northwest neighborhoods.
Scholars of Italian immigration and ethnicity have focused largely on the dense
enclaves in urban areas. Since South Philadelphia was the earliest and largest
Italian core settlement, the majority of research is focused there.[7] Richard
Juliani's (1971, 1998, 2007) work on Philadelphia has carefully documented the
South Philadelphia community from its beginnings through the period of mass
immigration while noting how and why immigrants settled in other neighborhoods and surrounding suburbs. Caroline Golab's (1977) research on immigrants in Philadelphia, while primarily concentrating on the Poles in Philadelphia, also discussed the Italians. She underlined the centrality of work opportunity
to immigrant destinations and underscored the importance of neighborhoods
in emergent work and settlement patterns.

Because the state of Pennsylvania played a key role in the transformation of
an agrarian nation to an industrial one with an emphasis on the heavy industries
of coal, iron, steel, and rail, as well as cement and glass, it was a huge draw for
the new immigrants looking for jobs in the late nineteenth century. By 1890, so
many Italians headed to Pennsylvania that their population in the state was the
second highest in the country, surpassed only by New York State. It would
remain so until 1960 when the numbers of Italian immigrants in Pennsylvania
dropped to third, behind New York and New Jersey (Golab 1977: 34).[8]

By the mid-nineteenth century, the city of Philadelphia ranked near the top
of large cities in terms of manufacturing. Philadelphia was uncharacteristic
because it offered a larger array of manufacturing jobs than other cities, which
meant greater opportunity for new immigrants. This factor in turn contributed
to the establishment of larger and more stable working-class neighborhoods

than in most cities (Davis 1973: 7–9). Even so, although immigrants found Philadelphia attractive, it attracted fewer proportionally than other large American cities. Between 1870 and 1920, the percentage of foreign-born in Philadelphia was lower than any other large northern city in the United States (Golab 1973: 203).

In spite of these overall state statistics, in terms of demographic trends, Philadelphia has always had one of the largest numbers of those identifying as Italian of any American city. According to the 1990 census, with 497,721, Philadelphia ranked second only to New York City in the number of people identifying as Italian American. Interestingly, in 1870, the ranking was the same as 1990 with Philadelphia second to New York City with 516 Italian-born residents.[9] During the mass immigration period of 1890, Philadelphia's Italian-born population had risen to 6,799. By 1910, it was 45,308 and was almost 12 percent of the foreign-born population, the fourth largest in the city (U.S. Census, cited in Golab 1973).

In the popular imagination, it is South Philadelphia that is thought of as the city's Little Italy, and it had clear boundaries with a well-developed economic, political, and religious infrastructure. The early community was large enough that by the mid-nineteenth century, it warranted its own parish. The first Italian nationality parish in the United States, Mary Magdalen de Pazzi, was founded there in 1852 (Juliani 1998: 163). The earlier arrivals to Philadelphia were primarily from the northern regions of Italy, while the increasing numbers who arrived by the 1880s were from southern Italy and Sicily.

Drawn by work and kin networks, Italians began forming communities in other neighborhoods of the city and the surrounding suburbs (Juliani 1973: 237). Using church records to document that settlement, Juliani (1971: 122) showed that between 1907 and 1932, twenty-three Italian national parishes were founded in the Philadelphia archdiocese. Instigated by the Italian community, Holy Rosary was established as a nationality parish in 1914, but they were large enough to require their own ministry as early as 1894. In that year, a chapel for the Italians was created in the basement of St.Vincent's Seminary at 500 East Chelten Avenue.[10] According to interviews with the second generation, many immigrants did not feel welcomed by the Irish Catholics and wanted a church of their own. In the smaller Italian community of Chestnut Hill, Catholics were mandated by the archdiocese to belong to Holy Rosary in Germantown. Because of proximity, however, many attended Our Mother of Consolation in upper Chestnut Hill, even though older second generation Italians told me their families had not felt welcomed by the Irish congregation.

Italian immigrants intentionally came to Philadelphia, but those arriving in the city directly from the port of entry arrived by train from New York. This was due to the fact that by the period of mass migration, the steamship not the sailing ship was the major mode of transport, and the major port of entry for steamships was New York (Juliani 1971: 111–112). While we have no way of knowing how many immigrants spent an initial period in South Philadelphia and then moved to other neighborhoods, most of my sources indicated that they did not pass through South Philadelphia first but came directly to Northwest Philadelphia. As will be explained below, this was due either to kin networks or because a job was already waiting. Sometime between the mid-1880s and mid-1890s, Italian immigrants were settling in Northwest Philadelphia. Oral interviews point to most who settled in the Northwest neighborhoods coming from the southern regions of Calabria, with a few from Campania and the Abruzzi (now two separate regions, Abruzzo and Molise). The northern Friulani who settled in Chestnut Hill were the exception.

As has been noted, the economic expansion in the city at the time made it easy to acquire a job. The majority found their first jobs as track laborers for the railroads—so many in fact, that by the 1890s, Italians had replaced the Irish as the primary railroad gang. Germantown was one of the destinations that drew them because the Reading and the Pennsylvania railroad companies had large yards there (Juliani 1973: 243–244). Oral history accounts mark the 500 block of East Rittenhouse as the first location Italians settled in Germantown, perhaps as early as the mid-1870s. It was here that the first seven men, who according to oral tradition were the first immigrants to Germantown, lived.[11] Mary D'Agostino Nocella, who grew up in Italian Germantown, noted in her family history that East Rittenhouse, "a dead end street, bordered by a coal yard at one end and cut off by railroad tracks at the other," could never be considered a prime residential area, but it was the area denoted for the Italians.[12] These working-class homes had been built along Haines and Rittenhouse Streets to accommodate the new workers who were attracted there by the spinning mills and other factories that had sprung up from Chelten Avenue to Chew Streets after the Civil War.[13]

As has been documented by other scholars, the situation differed somewhat from city to city, but in general, the *padrone* system, local political bosses, chain migration and kin systems, pre-migration skills, and personal preferences influenced where Italians moved and worked. Such circumstances often required immigrants to move to several different locations and back again in search of work. Some I interviewed told me that family members of the immigrant generation first went to the West Virginia and Pennsylvania coal fields and even to the far western states before settling in Northwest Philadelphia. For instance, unable to find construction work in Poffabro in Friuli, two elder brothers, Charles (Carlo) and Gus (Agostino) Lorenzon, first came to Philadelphia in 1896 in search of work. Unsuccessful in finding any employment in Philadelphia, they traveled west to Silverado, Colorado, where they worked in the silver mines. Before choosing the United States as a destination, one of these brothers had traveled to Egypt to find work building roads. He returned to Poffabro and then left for the United States. Between 1896 and 1902, Charles and Gus returned at least once to Poffabro and then in 1902 settled permanently in Chestnut Hill (Lorenzon 2002a: 21).[14]

Most Italians thought of railroad and construction work as temporary until something better could be found. By Italian social standards, these and other manual labor positions were considered undesirable paid labor jobs, and most intended to move to artisan trades (baker, plasterer, barber, or tailor) or to become a merchant or businessman, occupations they saw as more prestigious (Gabaccia 1984: 62).

In the early boom years in Philadelphia, the switch from unskilled laborer to a more prestigious position was not difficult because jobs were plentiful in large as well as smaller specialized industries. After World War I and the increase in the Italian population in the city, Italians worked in a variety of workplaces including cigar factories, theater bands, restaurants, milk companies, food importing, barber shops, bakeries, banks, insurance firms, streetcar manufacturing, grocery stores, and the government (Juliani 1973: 244–245). As the Italian population grew, the ethnic community could support an expanding infrastructure of merchants and other small businessmen to meet its needs. The Italian community in Germantown, much larger than the one in Chestnut Hill, had its own social and economic infrastructure well in place by the 1930s. Italians owned numerous grocery stores, bakeries, barber shops, other specialty shops, and a funeral home.

Although the Italian ideal was for women to remain at home, economic realities did not necessarily allow it. Women and children in the Northwest found work in clothing manufacturing or the large textile mills, such as Dobson that was located in the East Falls neighborhood.[15] In 1907 at age nine John Fusaro arrived in Germantown with his mother and sister after his father's untimely death in Italy. They came to join his mother's sister and brother-in-law who took them in since the family was destitute. At age fourteen, he began working in the Dobson "spinning mill" located on Wistar Street, joining his mother who was already employed there (Fusaro 1999). Friulani women in Chestnut Hill cleaned houses and did laundry for the wealthy on the Hill (Houseal 2000: 26–27). Due to southern Italian social mores, those women did not go into other people's homes to do such work.

Italians were also arriving in the Delaware Valley to work in the stone quarries, including those in Germantown and Chestnut Hill.[16] The quarries were active places providing the stone for the rapidly developing neighborhoods of Northwest Philadelphia. Contractors and speculators were buying land and building homes for the middle class and wealthy who wanted to take advantage of the newly popularized suburban style of living while still being able to commute to jobs in Center City. Many Italians who immigrated were skilled stonemasons and tile setters who easily found work in the building trades.

Maximilian Roman, who encouraged his fellow townspeople to emigrate from Poffabro to Chestnut Hill, may have been a padrone. A *padrone* was a labor agent who enlisted prospective workers. In the earliest years of Italian immigration, before people had family networks to help them, padroni helped new immigrants get a foothold and guided them through the initial settlement process. The padrone usually charged a fee for the services he performed including providing the fare for the voyage and locating housing. Such agents were very active among construction and railroad workers (Gabaccia 1984: 61–65; 1988: 114–115; Lopreato 1970: 93–95).

Oral documentation indicates that others who arrived in the Northwest also seem to have been recruited from their home villages for the building trades. According to an interview with Jane DeNola (1998), her grandfather Anthony D'Lauro and great-uncle John D'Lauro, both skilled stonemasons, were recruited from Italy in the early 1900s by George Woodward, the son-in-law of Henry Houston, to work for his development company, which was responsible for much of the new construction on the Hill. According to Naomi Houseal (2000: 24), the southern Italians worked for George Woodward but the Friulani did not.

A pattern of finding work illustrates the *paesani* relationship of employment that was common. This occurred when immigrants introduced new arrivals, fellow townspeople or family members, to their employers, thus conveniently providing workers for the growing needs of particular industries (Juliani 1973: 247). Francesco Giorno, arriving from Calabria, found work building the wall around the Grey Towers estate (now Arcadia University), putting his stonemasonry training to good use. Like the Giornos, the Iannuzzis were also stonemasons coming from Luzzi, in the province of Cosenza in Calabria, as were many who settled in Germantown. An excerpt from a family letter demonstrates clearly how a family connection worked well for the Iannuzzis:

> My father [Francesco] and brother Vincenzo were master stonemasons and they worked together with a building contractor. My father later had to retire because he had asthma and couldn't work anymore. My brother Gennarino [diminutive for Gennaro] was a pottery maker by trade. But since pottery jobs were not available at that time, through my brother Vincenzo, Gennarino was hired by the same contractor as a stone mason apprentice. He soon learned the trade and they both worked steady together.[17]

Oftentimes, those who were both skilled and literate could more easily move to supervisory positions. That was the case for Luigi Mercaldo, a stonemason who had come from the city of Naples about 1898. Employed by a local developer, he soon rose to the level of foreman supervising other Italian laborers.

Mercaldo completed the stonework for the Cresheim Valley Fountain at the intersection of Cresheim Valley Road and Germantown Avenue.[18]

The Friulani who immigrated to Chestnut Hill were particularly successful in establishing tile businesses and quarries. For example, Marcolina Brothers, in business since the late 1800s, and Philadelphia Tile became well known businesses and engaged work throughout the region. Pete Marcolina (Fleeson 1995: E10) estimated that more than half of the stone houses in Chestnut Hill were built by his family's business, much of it subcontracted by George Woodward. These ranged from smaller twins and quadruples to mansions in the area, including the former Albert M. Greenfield estate.[19] According to Pat Staffieri, whose parents emigrated from Molise in southern Italy and settled in Chestnut Hill, it was also Italians who laid the streets in Chestnut Hill with Belgian block. Those blocks can still be seen at the intersection of Cresheim Valley Drive and Germantown Avenue (Saverino 2000a: 51–52).

Chestnut Hill and the Spatialization of the Socioeconomic Landscape

In Chestnut Hill, the detailed archival work of identifying the Italian immigrants and verifying the exact number who came in the early years remains to be done. Nevertheless, oral history accounts and archival and secondary sources confirm that a small group of southern Italians, primarily from Calabria and Sicily, and a larger community of Friulani from several small villages (including Poffabro, Maniago, and Frisanco), many of whom were connected by kin networks, settled in Chestnut Hill. Oral interviews show that chain migration continued to draw more Friulani newcomers into the early decades of the twentieth century and the neighborhood received an infusion of new immigrants again after World War II. As we shall discover, it was the Friulani, having arrived as skilled stone carvers and tile setters, who are primarily responsible for transforming the built environment still extant on the Hill today.[20]

When the Italians arrived, they encountered a village atmosphere with a distinct social hierarchy. Since the eighteenth century, Chestnut Hill's main thoroughfare, now known as Germantown Avenue, lined with houses, shops, and stores, operated as a gateway to Philadelphia proper. The Hill developed early economic bonds with Philadelphia; nonetheless, it maintained an autonomous village identity that continued even after its annexation by the city in the mid-nineteenth century (Contosta 1992: 9–13). Chestnut Hill's development accelerated when it burgeoned as a commuter suburb for the wealthy after the first railroad line was built connecting it to the city in 1854. This wealthy stratum were the social elite of the city who built large summer homes in upper east Chestnut Hill, which was located literally at the top of the Hill.

By 1873, industrialist and philanthropist Henry Howard Houston purchased most of the acreage in west Chestnut Hill, and by 1884, he began building the development of St. Martins in southwestern Chestnut Hill. Houston designed St. Martins as a residential development with distinct geographical and social boundaries. The development's design insured its suitability for Houston's own family's social stature, and in 1886, he relocated his family from Germantown to a fifty-two-acre estate within St. Martins (Sies 1987: 272–274). Although Houston sold the larger single homes he built in the development, he rented most houses he built to upper middle-class and professional tenants, effectively retaining control over both the land use and its occupants (Contosta 1992: 94–98).

After Henry Howard Houston's death in 1895, George Woodward, Houston's son-in-law, resumed Houston's suburban development. Woodward was a prominent figure in the Progressive movement, and one of his primary endeavors in Philadelphia was an interest in environmental reform and a goal of making decent housing available for everyone (Sies 1987: 279). While these were his espoused ideals, practice often played out differently.

For instance, between 1909 and 1912, Woodward built new houses in east Chestnut Hill (the Benezet Street project) in his first large real estate venture. Woodward stated in his memoir that he intended to rent this housing to working class families but "when the white collar crowd came along and rented every house in sight," he allowed it to happen although he could have reserved them for the intended group. "They were exactly the people," he wrote, "who pay their bills, and seldom complain" (Contosta 1992: 104, 106). Thus, we see how, through self selection and development design, that within the Anglo population itself, a hierarchy existed that was articulated spatially.

By the mid-1880s, large numbers of laborers were required to support the building boom in Chestnut Hill spurred by Houston and others. It was the labor of these workers that built and supported the neighborhood's economic infrastructure. The workers on the Hill were keenly aware of the Anglo social structure that existed, and mockingly called the middle-class Anglos "half-cuts" ostensibly referring to their "wanna be" status.

The Anglo wealthy maintained both social and physical distance from those they employed. All the working classes, including immigrant workers, were relegated to living in the lower half of the Hill, in designated housing located on both the east and west sides of the main avenue that bisected the village. Those who controlled the neighborhood attempted, in Foucault's sense, to enclose and organize individuals within it (Low 1999b: 113). Since humans tend to resist constraints imposed upon them, we shall see how the elite were not as complete or as successful as they hoped to be.

First, let us situate the southern Italians and the Friulani within Chestnut Hill. By the late nineteenth century when the Italians arrived in Chestnut Hill, they joined the few African Americans and numerous Irish immigrants who were already in service to the Anglo wealthy who controlled the Hill's social and economic life. A social hierarchy segregated by class, ethnicity, and color became clearly mapped in space.

As Gabaccia (2006: 10) points out, Italo-phobia took on particular nuance in English-speaking countries. In the United States by the late nineteenth century, nativist and anti-Catholic sentiment and the association of Italians with racial inferiority caused Italian neighborhoods to be foregrounded in ways that other immigrant settlements were not. After 1899, when Italians came through Ellis Island, northern and southern Italians were identified as different races (Gabaccia 2006: 21). "Little Italies" were stigmatized places. Finding themselves in a social climate that ranged from outright discrimination to at best one of tolerance, and separated from Americans by language issues, Italians reacted with their own insularity. They created a web of community based in the network of extended families and friends that helped to ease the adjustment to life in the United States (Saverino 2003: 10). Juliani (1971: 185–187) has shown the early neighborhood boundaries for South Philadelphia and the inter-ethnic tensions that existed. Many Germantown Italians discussed the discrimination they experienced particularly between the Irish and the Italians. John Fusaro (1999: tape 2, 14) told me, "We weren't accepted very well. No. Not for a while. As I say, they used to call us Guineas and Wop."

Tensions were often demarcated by clear spatial boundaries which at first were not crossed in terms of living space, but that changed over time. In South Philadelphia, Italians began moving into what had been largely Jewish, Irish, and German areas by World War I (Juliani 1971: 186). During the decades characterized by discrimination against the racialized Other, Italians in Germantown and Chestnut Hill were subjected to the informal barriers that could be imposed, such as refusal by some to rent or sell property to them. The spatial boundaries were neither impermeable nor permanent and as soon as they could acquire property, Italians challenged the spatial ordering, sometimes through resistance or subversion. For instance, Joseph Galante, a southern Italian, recalled that in 1917, three years after his family immigrated to Chestnut Hill, they resorted to using straw people to purchase a house on a street that had no other Italians (33 West Springfield Avenue) because the sellers refused to sell to Italians (Galante 1985: 3).

Philadelphia was a city that had some structural factors in place that facilitated the transition from renter to property ownership. Small, well-built single family homes were part of the city's early design. Also, William Penn's establishment of a land rent contractual system that was unique to Pennsylvania enabled a working-class family to invest in a home. Between 1890 and 1930, home ownership in Philadelphia increased from 22.8 percent (a low rate compared to other cities) to 51.8 percent in 1930, the highest among the fourteen largest cities in the United States. While some national characteristics accounted for this rise, a dramatic increase in the number of building and loan associations and their borrowing policies were crucial factors in Philadelphia (Juliani 1973: 248–249). By 1920, Germantown Italians had their own Building and Loan Association with 800 shareholders becoming one of thirty-three such associations in Germantown.

While the example of the Galante family illustrates the intergroup tensions that existed between Anglos and Italian immigrants, intragroup relationships between southern Italians (primarily Calabrians) and the Friulani played out in ways that can also be mapped spatially.

Although Chestnut Hill did not have a large settlement of Italians when compared with neighborhoods such as South Philadelphia, nonetheless, two distinct Italian populations segregated in space evolved.[21] Once again, the extant built environment allows us to trace this self-segregation between the Friulani and the southern Italians, and oral accounts provide interpretive clues about the nature of their relationship.

While southern Italians, such as the Galantes, were for the most part purchasing and adapting homes to their tastes, the Friulani built their own homes, thus attaining the ultimate Italian ideal. Also, several Friulani families who were successful contractors built commercial buildings that they rented. The Venetian Club, originally formed in 1924, was relocated from a small *baracca* built in a quarry off Cheltenham Avenue to Germantown Avenue when the Friulani purchased a former school and built a three-story addition onto it themselves in 1929.[22] Within about a thirty-year span of arrival, the Friulani had mapped physically a distinct identity and aesthetic in the lower part of the Hill.

The Friulani, unlike most southern Italians, had access to a structure of opportunity that allowed some families in particular to gain a firm economic foothold. Given the marginalization of Italians that occurred generally during this period, the relative speed of the Friulani's economic success is all the more surprising. Several factors contributed to this structure of opportunity. The Friulani tended to be highly skilled in stone work and tile setting having been trained in Italy before emigrating. Stone carving and tile setting were trades that were much in demand in the construction business in Philadelphia. While families told me stories of workers walking to worksites on the Main Line, because they could not or did not want to pay the transportation fare, whenever they could workers also found employment on the Hill. Early on, the Friulani used their skills as leverage to move up the economic ladder by establishing their own construction and tile-setting businesses, filling positions in their companies with other immigrants. They hired other Friulani but also southern Italians.

Secondly, because the Friulani had come in such large numbers from Poffabro and surrounding villages, many social networks from the towns that existed prior to immigration were reestablished in Chestnut Hill. This common pattern of chain migration provided new immigrants with an instantaneous network of connections for jobs, housing, and socializing. Anthony Filippi noted, "We had friends here and they came to the house, my father's friends, and they took us under their wing and we had no problems at all. The only problem was learning the language" (Filippi 1985: 6). At another point Filippi commented on the social ties: "We are pretty close knit. There are a lot of relationships too. Even with second and third cousins, there are friendships and relationships. We came from the same town more or less and there had to be a pretty close relationship on the whole."

Two other factors helped the Friulani achieve economic success. The first was that the Friulani tended to have a much higher literacy rate than southern Italians upon arrival.[23] This skill has many obvious advantages and puts such immigrants immediately in the position of serving as ethnic brokers. We know it generally to be true that those who came from the middle class in Italy, or who were better educated or more Americanized than the majority of working-class Italians, often acted as middlemen or "ethnic brokers" between Italians and the dominant society (Di Leonardo 1984: 156). Those who emerged as leaders in the ethnic community became spokespersons for the rest who had no public voice.

Also, the Friulani tended to have lighter skin and hair than their southern Italian counterparts. Some anglicized their names and so, with an appearance that looked more Nordic than stereotypically Italian, they could effectively pass and did. With some derision, one southern Italian I interviewed named a Friulani family whom he knew from school days. They had changed their surname and did not self-identify as Italian at all.

At the height of the immigration period, Italian identity in the United States was a southern Italian one. As has been noted, the idea that southern Italians were racially inferior and prone to criminal behavior was prevalent in the popular imagination in the United States (Messina 2004). Anti-Italian sentiment, often resulting in discrimination, was not unique to Philadelphia but was part of an emergent "ideology of immigration," a widespread xenophobia in the United States that could be felt as the tide of new immigrants from southern and eastern Europe grew larger (Juliani 1998: 315–316).[24] The sheer number of Italians who arrived—people who in appearance, religion, political attitudes, educational standards, behavior, and language were unlike the immigrant groups who had preceded them—fueled fears and prejudice. The nativist attitude against Italians manifested itself both covertly and overtly. Tactics ranging from intimidation to deeds forbidding the sale of property were used in an attempt to keep Italians within the boundaries of "their" neighborhood. Obviously, the Friulani would have an advantage if they could distance themselves from being associated with the negative moniker of "Italian."

Indeed, the Friulani arrived with their own prejudices that existed in northern Italy about southern Italians. Therefore the negative connotations about southern Italians that the Friulani encountered in this country only served to further embed beliefs they already held. In part, this can be explained by referring to Italy's political history. When the immigrants first set foot in the United States, they thought of themselves as natives of the particular town or village from which they hailed, rather than as Italians. Italy itself had been united only since 1861, but more importantly, the government was controlled by northerners, with whom the southerners shared few values or beliefs. Long after unification, Italy remained a country characterized by regional differences. With no sense of an Italian national identity and not yet thinking of themselves as Americans, Italian immigrants, coming from diverse regions and backgrounds, had no uniform, shared past. In a sense, they were a people without history, cut off from the villages they had left, speaking languages so different that a Calabrian could not understand a Sicilian, and living in a new place where they faced an uncertain future.[25]

One example illustrates how the Friulani characterized themselves in contrast to southern Italians. One Friulani told me that they referred to southern Italians as coming from *bassa* [lower] Italy, and they referred to themselves as "brown gravy" Italians because their staple foods were butter and polenta. She said that her grandmother had never seen pasta or red sauce until she met southern Italians who cooked it (Houseal 2000). She commented that "the Friulani weren't snobbish" but that they socialized among themselves (Saverino 2000b: 8). Clearly, it was a separate identity that they cultivated.

We will take a closer look at the Lorenzon family, which was mentioned earlier. By looking at one family's history, we can situate it within the neighborhood economy and the Friulani community. According to Herbert Lorenzon (2002a, 2002b), son of the immigrant Emilio, by 1906 six Lorenzon siblings, their mother, and an uncle had emigrated from Poffabro and settled in Chestnut Hill. The father, a landowner, had died in 1904.[26] Almost immediately upon arrival, they began building a house for themselves. Trained as stone masons and builders, they had worked alongside their father, and by 1898, had built a five-story stone house in their village. They quarried the stone, cut the trees that they used for the wood trim, and even made the tools used in its construction. The father's brother, a cabinetmaker, designed and built furniture for the Poffabro house. By 1914, they had formed their own contracting business incorporating as the Lorenzon Brothers Company. They did not know how to get customers in the early stages of the business, so they would simply bid on subcontracts for the stone work. They soon developed a reputation with several well-known architects who were designing large estates. By the mid-1920s, they were reaping the rewards of the American dream. They had purchased cars and built their own architect designed-homes as well as commercial and apartment buildings that they rented.

Transforming the Landscape

Because of such advantages in opportunity, the Friulani, were able to effectively establish a hierarchy of their own in stone. I am offering an analysis of the social production of space, that is, the material aspects of the environment, as divided into three categories on the Hill. First, are the designs that the Friulani were hired, generally as subcontractors, to build. These include public buildings, private residences, and smaller structures.

Some of these buildings, such as the public library and the Presbyterian church, are landmarks on the Hill. Others were large estate houses designed by nationally renowned architects such as Robert McGoodwin, with whom the Friulani developed relationships. This category of building realizes the aesthetic tastes of the Anglo community but demonstrates the technical skill of the immigrants. Their contribution in this realm is virtually undocumented but it lives on in the collective memory of the Friulani community and in the memories of the families who did the work.

It is in the realm of the buildings that they built for themselves and the transformation of the land itself that the innermost desires and emotions of the Friulani are played out. Although the gardens and landscaping have for the most part disappeared, the buildings remain. They built commercial structures that line the lower part of Germantown Avenue and homes that radiate from either side of it onto the neighborhood streets defining the lower half of Chestnut Hill. Their own construction allowed expression of cultural values and aesthetic tastes in a way that mere adaptation did not. The houses they constructed were often a curious hybridization of contemporary American tastes and old world cultural values and aesthetic ideals.

The most successful Friulani built substantial middle-class single homes on the lower east side of Chestnut Hill.[27] Emil Lorenzon's house (see Figure 3.2) was built in 1926. He served as his own contractor and hired the well-known architect H. Louis Duhring to design his two and one-half story house. Its design, a classic center hall colonial, is in keeping with contemporary American tastes of the period, but if closely surveyed, certain features indicate the skills and values of Italian craftsmanship. Although the tile roof is not uncommon to this period, when various kinds of classical architectural styles had been popularly revived, the roof is also typical of the landscape of the Italian folk past. The cut stone quoining and cut stone windows and door surrounds are a testament to the workers' fine skills. The gargoyle on the front portico, the arches on the sun porch, are elements that reflect the owner's aesthetic.

By the mid-1920s, many families were beginning to live the American dream if on a lesser scale than the Lorenzons. Although most Italian immigrants could not afford to build a home of the grand nature of the Lorenzon house, their modest homes are hybridizations on a more moderate scale.

FIGURE 3.2 Built in 1926, Emil Lorenzon served as his own contractor but hired architect H. Louis Duhring to design this stone classic center hall colonial that features Italian aesthetic ideals and craftsmanship. (Photograph courtesy of Herbert Lorenzon.)

Some adopted the twin housing construction, so typical of Philadelphia, and a more economical way to build than a free-standing single structure. Frugality and practicality had been a way of life in Italy. Immigrants Alberiglio Roman, a carpenter, and Sante Marcolina, a tile setter, are one example of Friulani friends who cooperated to build a house together on East Moreland Avenue (Roman 2002: 1–2, 4, 8). They built a two and one-half story stucco over concrete block dwelling because it was cheaper than brick or stone (see Figure 3.3). They moved there in 1929, but it took Roman until 1942 to finish the house, reflecting the family's financial capabilities during the Depression Era (Roman 2002: 2–3, 11).

Many of the buildings, both commercial and residential, incorporate architectural and decorative elements that mark them as Italian built and owned. Two of the most common are the arch and balcony. While the arch is a neoclassical feature not uncommon in contemporary buildings of the period, in Chestnut Hill it seems to be used almost exclusively by Italian builders. An apartment building, built in 1925 by the Lorenzon brothers, memorializes their own name in stone on its cornice and incorporates wrought iron balconies and an arch at the peak of the roof.[28]

Several Friulani established tile setting businesses. The Philadelphia Tile Company, owned by Friulani immigrants, was located on Germantown Avenue (7904–7906).[29] Still extant, one can view through the exterior window examples of the tile work from which customers could choose. (See Figure 3.4.)

FIGURE 3.3 Alberiglio Roman and Sante Marcolina built these twin homes of stucco over concrete block in 1929. (Photograph by Joan Saverino.)

FIGURE 3.4 Multicolored tile detail from the former showroom of The Philadelphia Tile Company, located at 7904–7906 Germantown Avenue. (Photograph by Joan Saverino.)

The Roanoke Garage was built in 1922 by Antonio Roman from Poffabro. He spelled out the name of his garage in a decorative brick design. In the Marcolina/Roman twin mentioned previously, Sante Marcolina used his tile-setting expertise to pave his front porch in tile. Tile setters' work still embellishes exteriors, entrances, and foyers throughout the neighborhood.

These embellishments are sometimes small and are often hidden, but within the Friulani community they are valued and regarded as elements of beauty. They identify the Friulani to themselves and the nooks and crannies and objects resonate with stories of the past; yet they are probably unnoticed and unknown by outsiders.[30] They certainly had been to me until their location and significance were revealed to me as I got to know people.

When I interviewed Gisella Roman, Alberiglio's widow, she brought me onto her front porch to show me Sante's adjacent tiled front porch. She relayed to me how, when the children were small, she and her neighbor would fill the porch, which had cement sides, with water and allow the children to use it as a shallow pool. Another widow told me how her husband, a tile setter, had made large planters for her and decorated them in tile. She had them filled with flowers in her front garden and had them there for years. A few years ago someone stole the planters. In retelling the story, the distress she still felt at recalling the incident was palpable. A middle-aged granddaughter told me where her grandfather's tile setting business office had been. The building was extant but it had been transformed into an upscale antique shop complete with a weathervane on the roof. The owners of the shop had not appreciated the original front of the building which had been covered in the tile that the family sold—as a sort of advertisement of their trade—and so the current owners had it plastered over and painted it blue. So even as the stories remain, some of the physical landmarks are erased.

The Venetian Social Club was the largest and most important monument the Friulani built. The Club is the central symbolic location of the community's collective dual identity as Chestnut Hillers and Friulani. This building situates the identity of the Friulani to themselves, intra-ethnically with the southern Italians, and in relationship to the larger Anglo community.

The Venetian Club was officially founded in 1924 when it purchased a school building that was located on Germantown Avenue. In 1929, to accommodate increased membership, members raised funds and constructed a three-story addition onto the front of the original building. The members completed much of the interior and exterior decorative work themselves. The craftsmen's aesthetic tastes are reflected in the brick addition with its stone ground floor, center arched two-story stone entrance with terrazzo floor, stone lintels and sills, tile roof, and the stone caps with a winged lion sculpture, the mascot of Venice, at the top.

By crowning the stately façade with the symbol of the Venetian republic, the Friulani aligned with a Renaissance past. Such a move was not uncommon by Italian immigrants of the period who wished to publicly distance themselves from their peasant past. By positioning the Club on the main thoroughfare, they symbolically laid claim to the realm of Anglo public space.[31] Because they all lived on nearby streets, they walked to and from the Club regularly. Through this very act of routinization, they created and normalized the paths from house to Club, marking them as Friulani. On warm nights when a band played and the windows were open, the noise that emanated from the Club extended ownership of space to the surrounding street.

The Club was the one central gathering place for the entire Friulani community where they could reinforce local ties and maintain and renew memories of their beloved *Val Colvera*, the Colvera Valley. While the card room was a sacrosanct area for the men, multigenerational families used the bowling alleys, game room, and lounge.

Privately, in the interior of the Club, they ate polenta and brown gravy, spoke Friulani, and sang and danced to Friulani music. Through acting, speaking, and remembering, they engaged in a group dynamic that engendered and reinforced cohesiveness intergenerationally. Such social behaviors renewed their feelings of what it meant to be Friulani in Italy and connoted a new Friulani identity situated in Anglo Chestnut Hill. One member remarked on how the second generation grew up at the Club: "That was the hubbub. The life was the Venetian Club" (Houseal 2000: 13). These second-generation Friulani wax nostalgic when they recall the weekly socializing. This is how cultural values and memories were passed on in the effortless way that enculturation occurs. These acts, highly symbolic, also reinforced a difference in feeling from the Anglos who never fully accepted them and the southern Italians with whom they felt little affinity and from whom they wished to distance themselves.

The impact of the Friulani on this urban neighborhood is not recognized or even known by most residents of Chestnut Hill. But for the Friulani themselves, although many no longer live on the Hill, a remembrance of their past is inscribed and constituted in the landscape. The production of the local that once was lives on in memory now and is re-enacted on special occasions at the Venetian Club, an evocative imagined landscape merging two stone villages, one of many-colored Dolomia and another of mica-flecked Wissahickon schist.

Notes

Acknowledgments: Much of the research for this article took place between 1998 and 2002 when I was the resident scholar at the Germantown Historical Society. The research was supported in part by two grants from the Pennsylvania Humanities Council, the

Federal-State Partner of the National Endowment for the Humanities. Versions of this paper were presented at the American Folklore Society, the Organization of American Historians, and the American Italian Historical Association annual meetings. I wish to thank the editor of the *Germantown Crier,* Judith Callard, for allowing me to use portions of two previously published articles I authored (see References). I especially want to express my gratitude to all the community members in Chestnut Hill and Germantown who opened their hearts, their homes, and shared their memorabilia and memories so willingly. Thanks go as well to David Contosta and Liz Jarvis, who shared some of their own research so generously. Finally, thanks are extended to the editors of this volume, the anonymous reviewers, and Richard Juliani, Alex Loeb, Joseph Sciorra, and especially to Nancy Watterson for their helpful comments and critique of versions of this paper.

1. It is now the Friuli-Venezia-Giulia region.

2. Chestnut Hill has been designated a National Historic District, ensuring its unique state of physical preservation.

3. See Web site by Bruce B. Janz, "Research on Place and Space," at http://pegasus .cc.ucf.edu/~janzb/place/placesense.htm, for a good overview of the history of place studies and pertinent bibliographies from anthropological, historical, and other disciplinary perspectives. Sociologist Jerome Krase (2006: 80) has called the transformation of place and the changed meanings that result "spatial semiotics."

4. See 2005 Conference Proceedings, "Reconceptualizing the History of the Built Environment in North America," available at http://www.fas.harvard.edu/~cwc/builtenv/, for recent discussion on reconsidering race and ethnicity in the built environment. For a bibliography on race and space, go to http://cdms.illinois.edu/pages/Research_CDMS/Critical Whiteness/Race_and_Space.htm. Cultural geographer Wilbur Zelinsky (1990) rejected the idea that any connection of real substance between ethnicity and place can be made.

5. In Italian American studies, see Harney and Baldassar 2006, Buzzelli 2001, Del Giudice 1993, Helzer 2001, Krase 1997, and Sciorra 1999.

6. The research was conducted under the auspices of the Pennsylvania Humanities Council project "Raising Our Sites: Community Histories of Pennsylvania" local scholar grant, 1998–2001, and the PHC visiting scholar grant, 2002–2003.

7. For book-length and dissertation studies, see Luconi 2001, Mathias 1974, Passero 1978, Stanger-Ross 2005, Varbero 1975, and numerous articles by these and other authors.

8. Interestingly, according to Golab (1977: 3–5), although the two largest cities, Pittsburgh and Philadelphia, had large numbers of Italians, 71 percent of the Italians who immigrated to Pennsylvania settled in midsize and smaller industrial towns scattered throughout the state.

9. In 1870, New York had 2,793 Italians. Boston was ranked third with 263 (Juliani 1998).

10. "The Story of St. Vincent's Seminary" (unpublished manuscript, Germantown Historical Society, 1988), 17, 30; Norman Giorno-Calapristi, "A Brief History of Holy Rosary Church" (unpublished manuscript, Germantown Historical Society, 2000).

11. On Haines and High, streets that are north and parallel to Rittenhouse, the block equivalent is the 400 block. It is unclear why the numbering is different for Rittenhouse. According to Mary Nocella (personal communication, 20 July 2000), among the first arrivals are said to be Francesco Iannuzzi, Gennaro LaGreca, Beniamino DiTommaso, Pasquale Altomare, and Totonno Amoroso. This information was relayed to her by her aunt, Margaret Cupo LaGreca, whose husband was Frank LaGreca, the son of Gennaro LaGreca, listed above. Margaret Cupo LaGreca died in 1997 in her nineties.

12. Mary Nocella, "The D'Agostinos and the LaGrecas: A Family History" (unpublished manuscript, Germantown Historical Society), 15.

13. "The Germantown Settlement: A Short History" (unpublished manuscript, Germantown Historical Society), 1.

14. Personal communication from Herbert Lorenzon indicates the town was Silverado. A printed family history lists the town as Silverton, Colorado. It is unclear which is correct, since both towns exist and both had silver mines.

15. Dobson Mills was located at Scott's Lane and Ridge Avenue in East Falls. In 1895, it had 1,400 looms and employed approximately 5,000 workers (Scranton and Licht 1986: 266).

16. According to Pete Marcolina, whose family was from the Friuli region, and who owned a contracting business in Chestnut Hill, there were at one time more than six quarries in the Chestnut Hill area alone (Fleeson 1995: E10).

17. Pasqualina's letter in Vincenza Iannuzzi Cerrato file, Germantown Historical Society.

18. Mary Anne Mannino, personal communication, 27 April 1999.

19. The Greenfield Estate was then purchased by Temple University to become a conference center. It was recently purchased by Chestnut Hill College.

20. Javier Grossutti's (2007) research begins to document the Italian mosaic and tile workers in the United States.

21. Juliani (1971: 184–185) discusses intragroup relationships in South Philadelphia.

22. Venetian Social Club history papers, Germantown Historical Society.

23. Due to the complexities of the political and economic system in Italy, the educational system in northern Italy was far more advanced than in the southern regions.

24. For more on nativism and xenophobia, see John Higham 1998.

25. Eric R. Wolf (1982: x) uses the phrase "the people without history" in reference to the common people—peasants, laborers, immigrants, minorities—who were "as much agents in the historical process as they were its victims and silent witnesses." It is used here in a different sense, to indicate Italians who were cut off from their historical past through the process of emigration.

26. The Lorenzon siblings were Carlo, Agostino, Emilio, Vittorio, Alberto, and Marina. Their parents were Maria and Vincenzo. The uncle who immigrated was Valentino.

27. Lorenzon Brothers continues to operate as a commercial contracting company with offices in Chestnut Hill.

28. Luisa Del Giudice (1993) discusses the use of the arch by Italians.

29. The original owners of Philadelphia Tile were John Marcolina, Louis Roman, Angelo Rosa, and Joe Peraglia (Naomi Houseal, personal communication, 1 July 2003).

30. An outsider would be anyone, including southern Italians, who were not Friulani.

31. See Low 1999a, 8, for use of the term "white public space."

References

Barth, Fredrik, ed. 1969. *Ethnic Groups and Boundaries. The Social Organization of Culture Difference.* Boston: Little, Brown.

Buzzelli, Michael. 2001. "From Little Britain to Little Italy: An Urban Ethnic Landscape Study in Toronto." *Journal of Historical Geography* 27 (4): 573–587.

Contosta, David. 1992. *Suburb in the City.* Columbus: Ohio State University Press.

Davis, Allen. 1973. "Introduction." In *The Peoples of Philadelphia: A History of Ethnic Groups and Lower-Class Life, 1790–1940,* ed. Allen F. Davis and Mark H. Haller, 3–12. Philadelphia: Temple University Press.

Del Giudice, Luisa. 1993. "The 'Archvilla': An Italian-Canadian Architectural Archetype." In *Studies in Italian American Folklore,* ed. Luisa Del Giudice, 53–105. Logan: Utah State University Press.

DeNola, Jane. 1998. Interview by *Chestnut Hill Local* [newspaper], 3 September.

Di Leonardo, Micaela. 1984. *The Varieties of Ethnic Experience: Kinship, Class, and Gender among California Italian-Americans.* Ithaca, NY: Cornell University Press.

Filippi, Anthony. 1985. Interview by David Contosta, 26 June.

Fleeson, Lucinda. 1995. "Philadelphia's Stone Age." *Philadelphia Inquirer,* 16 June: E1, E10.

Fusaro, John. 1999. Interview by author, 25 May, tape 2, 2–6, 14, Germantown Historical Society.

Gabaccia, Donna R. 1984. *From Sicily to Elizabeth Street: Housing and Social Change among Italian Immigrants, 1880–1930.* Albany: State University of New York Press.

———. 1988. *Militants and Migrants: Rural Sicilians Become American Workers.* New Brunswick, NJ: Rutgers University Press.

———. 2006. "Global Geography of 'Little Italy': Italian Neighbourhoods in Comparative Perspective." *Modern Italy* 11 (1): 9–24.

Galante, Joseph. 1985. Interview by David Contosta, 25 February.

Geertz, Clifford. 1996. "Afterword." In *Senses of Place,* ed. Steven Feld and Keith H. Basso. Santa Fe, NM: School of American Research Press, 1996.

Golab, Caroline. 1973. "The Immigrant and the City: Poles, Italians, and Jews in Philadelphia, 1870–1920." In *The Peoples of Philadelphia: A History of Ethnic Groups and Lower-Class Life, 1790–1940,* ed. Allen F. Davis and Mark H. Haller, 203–230. Philadelphia: Temple University Press.

———. 1977. *Immigrant Destinations.* Philadelphia: Temple University Press, 1977.

Grossutti, Javier. 2007. "Italian Mosaicists and Terrazzo Workers in New York City. Estimating the Size, Characteristic and Structure of a High-Skill Building Trade." Available at http://www.Italianacademy.Columbia.edu/publications/working_papers/2007_2008/paper_fa07_Grossutti.pdf (accessed 4 October 2008).

Harney, Nicholas DeMaria, and Loretta Baldassar, eds. 2006. "Italian Diasporas Share the Neighbourhood." *Modern Italy* 11 (1, Special Issue).

Helzer, Jennifer J. 2001. "Old Traditions, New Lifestyles: The Emergence of a Cal-Ital Landscape." *APCG Yearbook* 63:49–62.

Higham, John. 1988. *Strangers in the Land: Patterns of American Nativism, 1860–1925.* 2nd ed. New Brunswick, NJ: Rutgers University Press.

Houseal, Naomi. 2000. Interview by author, 30 June, tape 16, Germantown Historical Society.

Juliani, Richard N. 1971. "The Social Organization of Immigration: The Italians in Philadelphia." PhD diss., University of Pennsylvania.

———. 1973. "The Origin and Development of the Italian Community in Philadelphia." In *The Ethnic Experience in Pennsylvania,* ed. John E. Bodnar, 237. Lewisburg, PA: Bucknell University Press.

———. 1998. *Building Little Italy: Philadelphia's Italians before Mass Migration.* University Park, PA: Penn State University Press.

———. 2007. *Priest, Parish, and People: Saving the Faith in Philadelphia's "Little Italy."* Notre Dame, IN: University of Notre Dame Press.

Krase, Jerome. 1997. "The Spatial Semiotics of Little Italies and Italian Americans." In *Industry, Technology, Labor and the Italian American Communities,* ed. Mario Aste, Jerome Krase, Louise Napolitano-Carman, and Janet E. Worrall. Staten Island, NY: American Italian Historical Association.

———. 2006. "Seeing Ethnic Succession in Little Italy: Change despite Resistance." *Modern Italy* 11 (1): 79–95.

Lopreato, Joseph. 1970. *Italian Americans.* New York: Random House.

Lorenzon, Herbert. 2002a. Interview by author, 19 June, tape 28, Germantown Historical Society.

———. 2002b. Interview by author, 26 June, tape 30, Germantown Historical Society.

Low, Setha M. 1999a. "Introduction: Theorizing the City." In *Theorizing the City: The New Urban Anthropology Reader,* ed. Setha M. Low. New Brunswick, NJ: Rutgers University Press.

———. 1999b. "Spatializing Culture: The Social Production and Social Construction of Public Space in Costa Rica." In *Theorizing the City: The New Urban Anthropology Reader,* ed. Setha M. Low. New Brunswick, NJ: Rutgers University Press.

Luconi, Stefano. 2001. *From Paesani to White Ethnics: The Italian Experience in Philadelphia.* Albany: State University of New York Press.

Mathias, Elizabeth Lay. 1974. "From Folklore to Mass Culture: Dynamics of Acculturation in the Games of Italian-American Men." PhD diss., University of Pennsylvania.

Messina, Elizabeth G. 2004. "Psychological Perspectives on the Stigmatization of Italian Americans in the American Media." *Psychotherapy Patient* 12 (1–2).

Passero, Rosara Lucy. 1978. "Ethnicity in the Men's Ready-Made Clothing Industry, 1880–1950: The Italian Experience in Philadelphia." PhD diss., University of Pennsylvania.

Patusky, Christopher, and Johnny Ceffalio. 2004. "Recent Trends in Immigration to Philadelphia, Pennsylvania: Who Came and Where Do They Live?" Philadelphia: Fels Institute of Government, University of Pennsylvania. Available at https://www.fels.upenn.edu/sites/www.fels.upenn.edu/files/Philadelphia_Immigration_Trends_0.pdf (accessed 11 May 2007).

Rodman, Margaret C. 1992. "Empowering Place: Multilocality and Multivocality." *American Anthropologist,* New Series, 94 (3): 640–656.

Roman, Gisella. 2002. Interview by author, 18 April, tape 20, Germantown Historical Society.

Saverino, Joan. 2000a. "The Italians of Northwest Philadelphia: Remembering a Community's Past." *Germantown Crier* 50 (Fall): 44–70.

———. 2000b. "Naomi Houseal." Fieldnotes.

———. 2003. "Memories in Artifact and Stone: Italians Build a Neighborhood." *Germantown Crier* 53 (Fall): 48–64.

Sciorra, Joseph. 1999. "'We Go Where the Italians Live': Religious Processions as Ethnic and Territorial Markers in a Multi-ethnic Brooklyn Neighborhood." In *Gods of the City: Religion and the American Landscape,* ed. Robert A. Orsi, 310–340. Bloomington: Indiana University Press.

Scranton, Philip, and Walter Licht. 1986. *Work Sights: Industrial Philadelphia, 1890–1950.* Philadelphia: Temple University Press.

Sies, Mary Corbin. 1987. "American Country House Architecture in Context: The Suburban Ideal of Living in the East and Midwest, 1877–1917." Vols. 1 and 2. PhD diss., University of Michigan.

Stanger-Ross, Jordan. 2005. "The Choreography of Community: Italian Ethnicity in Postwar Toronto and Philadelphia." PhD diss., University of Pennsylvania.

Varbero, Richard A. 1975. "Urbanization and Acculturation: Philadelphia's South Italians, 1918–1932." PhD diss., University of Pennsylvania.

Venetian Social Club. 1974. *50th Anniversary Celebration*. Philadelphia: Germantown Historical Society.

Wolf, Eric R. 1982. *Europe and the People without History*. Berkeley: University of California Press.

Yans-McLaughlin, Virginia. 1982. *Family and Community: Italian Immigrants in Buffalo, 1880–1930*. Urbana: University of Illinois Press.

Zelinsky, Wilbur. 1990. "Vision, Culture and Landscape—Seeing beyond the Dominant Culture." *Places* 7 (1).

4

Pan-Latino Enclaves in Philadelphia and the Formation of the Puerto Rican Community

Victor Vazquez-Hernandez

According to the U.S. Census Bureau's 2005 American Community Survey, the Puerto Rican population of Philadelphia was 97,689 out of a total Latino population of 146,856. While the Puerto Rican portion of the Latino population was still large (66.5 percent), the survey found a steady increase in and diversification of the Latino presence in the city.[1] This supposedly "new" phenomenon of a growing varied Latino community is actually not so new—a diverse Latino population in Philadelphia was evident as early as the 1890s. This chapter describes how these early pan-Latino enclaves made up of Spaniards, Cubans, Mexicans, and other Latin Americans, through the building of religious and social organizations, established during the first half of the twentieth century a Puerto Rican community in the city of Philadelphia. The chapter also briefly outlines the post–World War II experience of Puerto Ricans and the incorporation of a growing diversity and dispersal of non–Puerto Rican Latinos in the Quaker City.

Puerto Ricans were present in Philadelphia in the early twentieth century, numbering less than one hundred in 1910; they resided among the several thousand Latinos in the city. These Spanish-speaking residents often shared neighborhoods with other immigrants of the period. In this regard the reader will note that their community building experiences have many similarities to those of other groups like the Italians, Jews, and Chinese discussed in this section of the book. As the immigration restrictions of the

1920s cut off the immigration of Spaniards, labor recruiters focused on attracting Puerto Ricans who, since 1917, were U.S. citizens. The number of Puerto Ricans in the city progressively increased. By the 1950s, Puerto Ricans were the premier Latino group in the city and represented the bulwark of the Latino community's organizational structure. Not until the early 1960s, when Philadelphia began to receive large numbers of Cuban refugees, did the proportionate numbers of Puerto Ricans experience a decline. The influx of Dominicans after 1965 and refugees from Central America and Colombia in the 1970s and early 1980s, as well as Mexicans after the 1990s, contributed to a pan-Latino diversification not seen in the city since the 1930s. Community-based organizations founded and headed mostly by Spaniards and Cubans gave way to a growing Puerto Rican leadership in the 1950s, 1960s, and 1970s. The trend in the early twenty-first century is that although many organizations in the community are still led by Puerto Ricans, increasingly more non–Puerto Rican Latinos are taking over leadership positions within those groups.[2]

Beginning in the early twentieth century, Puerto Ricans and other Latino residents of the city of Philadelphia initiated a community development process, which gestated throughout the 1920s and 1930s and came to fruition during the 1940s. Before World War I, Puerto Ricans and other Latinos had founded the Hispanic American Beneficial Association, "La Fraternal," a mutual aid society, and a Spanish-language Catholic chapel, Our Lady of the Miraculous Medal, "La Milagrosa." In the 1920s and 1930s, the number of organizations serving the needs of Latinos increased as Puerto Ricans, Cubans, and Mexicans founded a Spanish-speaking Protestant church, the First Spanish Baptist Church. By the beginning of World War II, Puerto Rican and other Latino-based groups in Philadelphia were operating across enclave boundaries and sponsoring events that served to unite the different nationality and class groups into a Spanish-speaking colonia. It was within the population shifts and economic restructuring in Philadelphia in the early twentieth century that Puerto Ricans and other Latinos organized and built the community institutions to sustain them as they incorporated into the city.

Puerto Rican Migration and the Creation of Pan-Latino Working Class Enclaves

During the late nineteenth and early twentieth centuries, many Puerto Ricans were attracted to Philadelphia by contacts made through informal networks developed by earlier Spanish-speaking immigrants. These networks served to get the word out to the island about the existence of Spanish-speaking enclaves in the city as well as about the employment opportunities that existed at the time. This was especially true for cigar makers, who were accustomed to traveling throughout the United States and the Caribbean in search of work. The continuous business transactions between the island and Philadelphia, especially in the sphere of sugar and tobacco, helped promote the city as a point of attraction for Puerto Rican migrants. Communication between Puerto Rico, Cuba, New York, Tampa, and Philadelphia among Spanish-speakers, as well as the increased migration of Cubans and Spaniards to the city in the early twentieth century, also helped consolidate this group in the city. Finally, the recruitment efforts of companies, such as the Pennsylvania Railroad, attracted Spanish-speaking workers to the region. Many of these migrants eventually settled in Philadelphia.

By the early 1890s, Spanish-speakers, especially Cubans and Spaniards, were well represented among Philadelphia's cigar makers and cigar manufacturers. Cigar makers were an important group that contributed a significant number of Puerto Rican migrants to Philadelphia during the late nineteenth and early twentieth centuries. Throughout the second half of the nineteenth century, cigar makers migrated to the principal centers of cigar manufacturing in the United States. Among these centers were Tampa, Philadelphia, New Orleans, and New York.[3] Cigar makers, many of whom were political activists, were well known for their keen sense of organization. They founded some of the earliest Spanish-speaking mutual aid societies in the United States.[4] Cigar makers also played a pivotal role in the development of late nineteenth-century labor movements in the United States, Cuba, and Puerto Rico. As early as 1877, cigar makers had established a Spanish-speaking local of the Cigar Makers International Union (CMIU) in Philadelphia.[5]

During the first years of the twentieth century, Puerto Ricans in Philadelphia became increasingly concentrated in three enclaves located in the neighborhoods of Spring Garden, Northern Liberties, and Southwark. They shared these communities with Italians, Poles, Russian Jews, and African Americans, who were overwhelmingly working class. The settlements were located in these three areas because of inexpensive housing and work available nearby. The earliest Spanish-speaking migrant enclaves depended on the availability of work, and the formation of a subsequent community depended on the accessibility of cheap housing, good transportation, and shopping. Driven by these demands, the movement of Puerto Ricans into the aforementioned geographic areas and the conversion of them into distinct enclaves increased during the late 1920s and 1930s.[6]

Initially, Puerto Rican residency in Philadelphia was dispersed, but it became more concentrated after World War I. This concentration was due to the influx of wartime workers and the establishment of community institutions. Puerto Ricans settled in areas in which Spaniards, Cubans, and Mexicans were the predominant Latino groups. These enclaves, which in the 1950s became major

Puerto Rican neighborhoods, developed around work and church. Enclaves like those that evolved in Southwark, Spring Garden, and Northern Liberties contained the bulk of Spanish-speaking residents in Philadelphia in the years between 1910 and 1945. This community existed even though not always visible to scholars or contemporaries.[7]

Puerto Rican migration to Philadelphia accelerated during the interwar period. It occurred at a time when the city's population shifted, and housing policies implemented during this time made Philadelphia one of the most segregated northern cities. These population and housing shifts had a tremendous impact on Puerto Rican migrants and established long-term residential patterns that influenced where they went to live when they arrived in greater numbers in the post–World War II period. The shift in population in this period, the move of native-born whites to the suburbs and outer rims of the city, and the substitution of the outbound groups by new immigrants, like Puerto Ricans, contributed to the concentration of Spanish-speaking enclaves in the city. Local and federal housing policies further restricted these newer migrants, especially African Americans and Puerto Ricans, to those specific neighborhoods in Philadelphia.[8] In the post–World War II period, housing patterns in Philadelphia continued to shift and contributed to the concentration of Puerto Ricans and other Latinos in neighborhoods that became increasingly segregated by race and ethnicity. The housing experience that Puerto Ricans confronted in this period in part shaped the future formation of their community and the long-term legacies that these earlier years bequeathed.[9]

Puerto Ricans who migrated to Philadelphia during the first half of the twentieth century were overwhelmingly working class. In the early twentieth century, workers in Philadelphia invariably lived near their jobs, and most walked to work. This had a tremendous impact on the location of the particular industries that hired African Americans and Puerto Ricans. Where industries that hired blacks and Puerto Ricans were located had an impact on where these two groups resided. Housing segregation often meant that African Americans and Puerto Ricans were relegated to lower blue-collar jobs. Initially, semiskilled workers like cigar makers and others were more representative of these migrants. Progressively, however, in the 1920s, 1930s, and 1940s, more diverse displaced laborers from the island joined in the migration to Philadelphia. Possessing few industrial skills, many Puerto Ricans joined other "new" immigrant workers as well as African American migrants from the South in the City of Brotherly Love.

Puerto Rican migrants in Philadelphia experienced a segmented labor market in the interwar period. Increasingly, the better paying white-collar and professional jobs were occupied by whites, while African American and foreign-born laborers, including Latinos, were stuck in the unskilled sectors. Puerto Ricans and other Latinos experienced the initial wave of deindustrialization that solidified following World War I. Philadelphia had become a premier industrial center in the last quarter of the nineteenth century, but by the 1920s, the city had begun to experience the flight of industries to other parts of the country. Puerto Rican labor force participation in the city reveals their proletarianization; a process begun in Puerto Rico that continued in Philadelphia. For the most part, though, Puerto Ricans and other Latinos' occupational patterns in the city reveal that they labored largely in the blue-collar sectors of the city's economy. The occupational pattern of Puerto Ricans, in the earlier period, is also an indicator of their plight in postindustrial Philadelphia. The postindustrial poverty and economic dislocation of Puerto Ricans and African Americans in Philadelphia after 1945 has its roots in the economic transformation of the city during the previous decades.

While the Southwark enclave developed around the cigar-making shops, the piers, and economic activity along South Street, the Spring Garden enclave also grew and expanded during the period from 1920 to 1940. Poplar and Vine streets bounded the enclave on the north and south, and 23rd and Broad Streets on the west and east. For many Spanish-speakers, the allure of jobs, especially at the giant Baldwin Locomotive Works, was reason enough to live in Spring Garden. But one of the most important reasons why Spring Garden attracted so many Puerto Ricans in this period had to do with the establishment of La Milagrosa in the heart of this enclave. La Milagrosa moved from Southwark to Spring Garden in 1912 to a location at Spring Garden and 19th Streets. The chapel's facilities began to expand beyond religious services to include charity work as well. Institutions like La Milagrosa were central to their neighborhoods in attracting settlers, as hubs of activity and as institutional centers.

The arrival of Puerto Ricans in the first decades of the twentieth century enhanced efforts of Latinos in developing the small but significant organizational network of mutual aid and labor groups that connected the Spanish-speaking enclaves in the city. These enclaves that evolved during the first decades of the twentieth century assumed the characteristics of the colonia, defined by sociologist José Hernandez Alvarez as "an urban nucleus, which provided for . . . social identity and way of behavior," strengthening the bonds of community "by frequency of internal activity and dependence." Language, in this case Spanish, cultural identity, and institutional development characterized the formation of a Puerto Rican/Latino colonia in Philadelphia by 1945. The intricate organizational network and leadership of this colonia played a decisive role in the development of the Puerto Rican community in the city during the 1950s and 1960s. The next section discusses how four institutions, in particular, were built up by Latinos simultaneously as they consolidated the respective enclaves in sections of Spring Garden, Northern Liberties, and Southwark into a vibrant pan-Latino colonia.[10]

The Spanish-Speaking Colonia:
From Enclaves to Pan-Latino Colonia

The three enclaves in Southwark, Spring Garden, and Northern Liberties developed organizations and leadership across the city, which helped them consolidate into one interconnected colonia. Although many Spanish-speaking organizations contributed to this unification, four major religious and social groups had the greatest impact on the consolidation of Puerto Ricans and other Latinos in Philadelphia between the early twentieth century and the end of World War II. Institutions like the Catholic Chapel Our Lady of the Miraculous Medal (La Milagrosa), the Hispanic-American Fraternal Association (La Fraternal), the First Spanish Baptist Church, and the International Institute formed the core institutional support to these enclaves, and provided the rising Latino leadership a variety of locations from which they organized many social and charity events. This evolving colonia also relied on a diverse but increasingly Puerto Rican leadership, like Dr. Jose DeCelis, president of the Latin American Club during World War II, the Reverend Enrique Rodriguez of the First Spanish Baptist Church, Cesar Arroyo, leader of the Spanish Catholic youth groups, and Domingo Martinez, member of La Fraternal and founder of a business association. These leaders helped form many inter-enclave organizational ties in the 1930s, 1940s, and 1950s.

The period from 1910 to 1940 served as the incubator for several pan-Latino organizations around which the enclaves in Southwark, Spring Garden, and Northern Liberties flourished. Two of these institutions began in Southwark, the oldest Spanish-speaking enclave in the city. La Fraternal was founded around 1908 and La Milagrosa began as a Catholic mission in 1909; both were established within one year and two blocks from each other. Together, these two organizations proved pivotal not only in the evolution of the pan-Latino enclave in Southwark, but of the other two enclaves as well.

La Fraternal came about as the result of a mass meeting of a pan-Latino group representing the diversity of Spanish-speakers. It is unclear exactly when and how this meeting was organized, but writing his first report on La Milagrosa in 1910, Father Antonio Casulleras, the priest in charge, noted that the "gathering . . . led to the formation of a . . . well known society . . . for all Spanish-speaking people."[11] The headquarters of La Fraternal were established at 419 Pine Street, the heart of the Southwark Latino enclave. For Puerto Ricans and other Spanish-speaking residents of Southwark, the formation of La Fraternal, essentially as a mutual aid society providing some banking, death insurance, and employment referrals and sponsoring many well attended social events such as plays, discussions, dances, and festivals, marked a turning point in the development of their communal emergence in the city.[12]

The Latino group that met in 1908 realized that they needed spiritual as well as social organizations that could help them achieve greater benefits and success as a community. This group, which included Puerto Ricans, Spaniards, Cubans, Mexicans, and other Central and South Americans, strove for this goal. One of their first successful projects was the creation of La Milagrosa, with the help of the Archdiocese of Philadelphia. The establishment of a Catholic chapel staffed by Spanish-speaking priests and other religious services helped bring Latinos together from around the city into this unique institution. Initially located in the schoolhouse of Old St. Mary's Catholic Church in Southwark during its first three years of existence, La Milagrosa quickly developed into a full-fledged chapel. The chapel priests often served as employment agents referring newcomers to jobs around the city and, on occasion, acting as translators for immigrants.[13]

In the 1920s, the increasing numbers of Puerto Ricans and other Latinos in the city also brought greater religious diversity. Spanish-speaking Protestants, though smaller in number than their Catholic brethren, began to organize their own church. Initially interdenominational in nature, Spanish-speaking Protestants founded the First Spanish Baptist Church in 1929. The fruits of this effort added another organization to the Spanish-speaking enclaves in the city, especially for those residents of Spring Garden, where the Spanish Baptist Church was first housed.[14] According to Puerto Rican theologian Edwin David Aponte, at this particular time there appeared to be little religious partisanship among Latino Protestants in Philadelphia. The group was made up of Puerto Rican, Cuban, and Mexican families, some of whom had moved to Philadelphia from New York. They met more or less regularly, and in 1933 Oscar Rodriguez, a Puerto Rican, took up the ministerial duties of the group and leadership of the mission. At the time, Rodriguez was a student at the Eastern Baptist Theological Seminary. The First Spanish Baptist church, through the efforts of its pastor and members, often collected winter clothes and distributed them to newcomers, especially to farm workers who decided to stay in Philadelphia once their contracts on South Jersey farms had expired.[15]

The local chapter of the International Institute was the fourth organizational entity that had a major impact on the consolidation and development of pan-Latino groups in Philadelphia in the 1920s and 1930s. The Institute, a part of a national network of groups initially started by local YWCAs in New York City, supported both cultural and ethnic pluralism, while at the same time seeking "a better integration of immigrants and their children in American society." Beginning in the 1920s, the Philadelphia-based chapter of the International Institute took a special interest in the local Spanish-speaking community especially in Spring Garden.[16] The International Institute was located in Spring Garden on Fifteenth Street near Mount Vernon. The services provided by the Institute's social workers to immigrants, especially to Spaniards, Cubans, Mexicans, and Venezuelans, added to the organization's attraction for Spanish-speakers in the vicinity. Newcomers could learn English at the Institute as well as take a general American civics course, but the institute also believed that immigrants should maintain some of their native culture, so the staff encouraged Latinos to form social and cultural groups, including Anahuac, a Mexican dance group, and the Club Juventud Hispana, a predominantly Puerto Rican group made up of youth from La Milagrosa. Other groups representing Cuba, Spain, and Venezuela were organized during the 1930s. Once a year, during the month of May, these groups came together to hold a folk festival at the institute.[17]

These four organizations, among others, were representative of pan-Latino and working class individuals and families living in Philadelphia at this time. The leadership of La Fraternal was most reflective of the diversity of the enclaves. Led mostly by Spaniards or persons of Spanish descent, the leadership group tended to be made up of professionals or small shop owners who lived in one of the pan-Latino enclaves. Yet their events seemed to gather persons of all classes, including cigar makers. By the late 1930s and early 1940s, La Fraternal's leadership had passed into the hands of Cuban tampenos and Puerto Ricans, a reflection of the increase of these two groups in the city. "Tampenos" was a popular name given to Latinos, especially Cubans and Puerto Ricans, who originated from Tampa, Florida, and migrated north to Philadelphia and other cities in the 1920s and 1930s. A key feature of the leadership of La Fraternal throughout this period is that it included people who continued to live within the enclaves in Spring Garden, Northern Liberties, and Southwark.

By the 1930s and 1940s, La Milagrosa had developed into a hub of activity for the community. The chapel organized an Association of La Milagrosa, which handled many of the social aspects of the services provided. The association was responsible for organizing English classes, recreational activities, and picnics. The acquisition of the property around the corner from La Milagrosa at 1836 Brandywine Street, known as the Spanish Catholic Club, helped the chapel expand its range of activities. This location was used primarily for social functions such as dances and graduations. However, the facility was also rented out for weddings and baptism parties. Social functions at the club attracted many Latinos from the other enclaves as well.[18]

By the early 1940s, a Spanish-speaking, interconnected colonia had begun to take shape in Philadelphia. An affirmation of ethnic and religious belief contributed to consolidated links between the different enclaves. Spanish-speaking churches and the International Institute were strongest institutionally and had the greatest long-term impact on the evolving colonia. Language, culture, and an increasing organizational network characterized the colonia across the three enclaves. The consolidation of the colonia was particularly helped by the work of La Fraternal in Southwark, La Milagrosa in Spring Garden, the First Spanish Baptist in Northern Liberties, and the community-wide work of the International Institute.

World War II: From Pan-Latino to a Puerto Rican Colonia

World War II was a defining period in the evolution of the Puerto Rican community of Philadelphia. Two meaningful components of this development were (1) a significant increase of the Puerto Rican population in the city, particularly made up of migrant wartime workers, and (2) a notable increase in social activity of the various pan-Latino organizations in the city. During World War II, the diverse pan-Latino groups would often sponsor events to foster their language and cultural presence even further and to support the war effort. The efforts of Spanish-speaking residents solidified their colonia and poised it for further community development, which occurred in the ensuing decades of the second half of the twentieth century. The evolution of a Puerto Rican colonia in Philadelphia by the end of World War II, then, was an indication that the diverse Spanish-speaking enclaves had been transformed. An increase in the level of activity during the war, coupled with a major increase in Puerto Rican migration, enhanced the organizational developments of the period. There was also a proliferation of Puerto Ricans who moved from New York City to Philadelphia. Along with the efforts of men like contract labor recruiter Samuel Freedman and the Reverend Enrique Rodriguez, who preached to Puerto Rican farm workers in their barracks, the Puerto Rican colonia in Philadelphia grew during and immediately after World War II.

In the early 1940s, the First Spanish Baptist Church under the leadership of the Reverend Enrique Rodriguez became an important religious and community center. The church later branched out, moving north into the heart of North Philadelphia in the ensuing decades. Reverend Rodriguez frequently preached to Puerto Rican migrant workers on New Jersey farms and to industrial workers at Campbell Soup Company in Camden, New Jersey, in their respective barracks. Many of these workers sought out Reverend Rodriguez once their contracts were expired. They moved to Philadelphia to the neighborhood where his church stood. These new members of the Spanish Baptist Church, once established in Philadelphia, oftentimes sent for their respective families, thus contributing to the expansion of the colonia.[19]

By 1945, the former enclaves of Southwark, Spring Garden, and Northern Liberties were a complex web of social, cultural, and religious fervor, poised to give birth to a new community in Philadelphia. There was a Puerto Rican colonia in Philadelphia comprising Spring Garden and Northern Liberties, straddling

Broad Street, as well as Southwark, which was connected to Northern Liberties through the tenderloin section. This greater enclave-plus area was evident for its Spanish-speaking settlement density and display of social identity denoted by its organizational output and regularity of activity. The community served as the necessary link for Puerto Rican migrants and their dispersal.

The International Institute continued in its support of Latino groups throughout in the 1950s and 1960s. The Mexican Association Anahuac continued functioning in this period and still exists even today. Even when Spanish-speaking groups discontinued, the institute continued to invite former members, like those of the Club Juventud Hispana, to its events. In 1939, the Juventud Hispana was reorganized by the youth of La Milagrosa. They met until 1942, when some of the most active members married and moved away. The relationship between the institute and other more established Spanish-speaking organizations, like La Fraternal, also were sustained all through this period.[20]

The work of the International Institute was noted even in Puerto Rico. In 1946, Clarence Senior, American sociologist and research director of the Social Science Research Center of the University of Puerto Rico and soon-to-be-appointed head of the U.S.-based Puerto Rican Migration Division Office in New York, an office of the Puerto Rican government's Department of Labor, wrote to the International Institute of Philadelphia. In his letter to Marion Lantz, director of the institute, Senior inquired about the local Puerto Rican community. At the time, Senior was preparing a manuscript on the Puerto Rican migration experience, a study that was published a year later. Senior's interest, however, denotes the institute's prestige as an agency that served immigrants in the city, especially Puerto Ricans, and that amassed reliable data on these groups.[21]

The marked expansion in the social activities among Latinos during the war years was evident in the flyers and other promotional materials used for these events. One interesting feature of these materials is that they were produced in English, probably to attract a wider audience beyond the colonia, as well as some second-generation migrants who may have increasingly used English as their primary language. The use of English and American war symbols may have been intended to appease the larger Philadelphia society, much like the immigrant patriotic rallies that were organized in Philadelphia during the First World War. Events sponsored by Spanish-speaking organizations invariably promoted and sold war bonds. The promotion and sale of war bonds illustrates a degree of patriotism for the new land on the part of Spanish-speakers.

Puerto Rican migration to the United States increased dramatically during World War II. Despite limitations in transportation facilities during the war, the number of Puerto Rican migrants increased in each fiscal year between 1941–1942 and 1945–1946. Evidently, military service accounted for some of the growth, but it was wartime employment, together with economic hardships already existent on the island, that fueled emigration in this period. During 1943 and 1944, the inclusion of Puerto Ricans in the labor recruitment efforts of the War Manpower Commission accounted for the thousands of island laborers who came to the Philadelphia region. Invariably, a great many of these wartime laborers found their way to the increasingly notable Puerto Rican colonia in the city. Some of the laborers were drawn to the city by the ministerial work of the Reverend Enrique Rodriguez, as well as by the increasingly active and diverse cultural and social organizations. This made the influx of Puerto Rican migrants during the war all the more impressive.[22]

The locations at which events were held during the war included not only those spots within the pan-Latino colonias like the Boslover Hall (7th and Pine Streets) and the Musical Fund Hall (8th and Locust) in Southwark, but also locations outside of the colonia. For example, the Grand Rally Dance was held in 1943 at the Ambassador Hall, 1701 North Broad Street, in a heavily Jewish section of North Philadelphia. This event is illustrative of the period for several reasons. First, it was promoted as a "United War Chest Rally" and was sponsored by the "Spanish Committee." The Spanish Committee was made up of three of the most prominent Latino organizations at the time: La Fraternal, the Mexican association Anahuac, and the Latin American Club—a reflection of the pan-Latino nature of the enclaves. Highlighted in the program of this event was the American flag, and in large bold letters the words "Buy War Bonds." Clearly, events such as the Grand Rally Dance reflected not only the coming together of members of the different Latino groups—an important accomplishment in its own right—but of greater significance, the establishment of the colonia as a part of the larger Philadelphia community. Undoubtedly, the American war symbols were not lost on those outside the colonia who attended the event or saw the promotional materials.

The connection between the enclaves was also cemented as reported numerous times in *La Prensa*, an important Spanish-language daily published in New York City during the interwar period and distributed in Philadelphia. This was a reflection of the continuous connection between the Philadelphia colonias and those in New York City. By the early 1950s, this newspaper had established a regular column entitled *En Filadelfia*, which was written by Philadelphia Puerto Rican community leader Domingo Martinez. Even before then, La Prensa had been reporting regularly on social and cultural events among Latinos in Philadelphia. Family ties between New York and Philadelphia were also very important in connecting both cities. Puerto Rican migrants like Mary Rodriguez, Domingo Martinez, and Juan Canales all cited New York City–based relatives as their first point of contact in the United States as one of their reasons for migrating to New York, and later, to Philadelphia. Mary Rodriguez had immigrated initially to New York City in 1933 but soon relocated in Philadelphia where an old boyfriend lived. Domingo Martinez moved to Philadelphia in 1941 after first having lived with relatives in the Big Apple. Juan Canales who moved to New York during World War II, came to the Philadelphia area in 1944 to take a job at the Campbell Soup Company located in Camden, New Jersey.[23]

Puerto Rican labor migrants, who came to work in the Philadelphia area during World War II, found the Spanish-speaking social, cultural, and religious ambiance of the city a welcome relief from the doldrums of barracks-style living of the South Jersey farms or the Campbell Soup factory. Labor shortages in the United States brought thousands of Puerto Ricans to the area during the war, but a lack of social and cultural activities could not keep them on the farm or in the factory. Also, labor conditions, including meager, plain living quarters, unfamiliar food, and a lack of Spanish-speaking personnel, were often cited as reasons for Puerto Ricans leaving their employment and moving to Philadelphia. Some Puerto Ricans returned to the island when their contracts expired, but many more came following the "ambiente" (ambience) in Philadelphia.[24]

Toward the end of World War II, individuals like Puerto Rican–born Samuel Freedman capitalized on the labor shortage situation, especially on the farms of southern New Jersey, to establish a company of labor recruitment on the island. His knowledge of the local language and customs, as well as his relationship with the growers in the New Jersey region placed him in a unique situation to promote this endeavor. His contribution in bringing thousands more Puerto Rican laborers to the Philadelphia region has not been fully studied, but his relationship with the Reverend Enrique Rodriguez helped him channel many Puerto Ricans to his church in the immediate postwar years. Freedman's organizing efforts also led to the establishment of a division of the Puerto Rican Migration Office in Glassboro, New Jersey, in the late 1940s, ascribed to the island's Department of Labor. Eventually, this office was moved to Philadelphia and became a cornerstone of social services to Puerto Rican migrants and their families.

Post–World War II: A Synopsis

Between 1945 and 1970, the Puerto Rican community of Philadelphia blossomed into the third largest concentration in the United States. Many Puerto Ricans also migrated first to other cities, such as New York, and then found their way to Philadelphia. Between 1940 and 1950, the Puerto Rican population in Philadelphia increased from 854 in 1940 to 7,300 in 1950. As the Puerto Rican community grew during the 1950s and 1960s, so did its organizational efforts. Supported by leaders from La Milagrosa, the First Spanish Baptist Church, and La Fraternal, new groups began to evolve, especially town-based social clubs representing the migrants' hometown back on the island.[25]

In 1953, two events led to public recognition of the previously invisible Puerto Rican community in Philadelphia. On the night of July 17, 1953, a fight between Puerto Rican and white residents of the Spring Garden neighborhood led to rioting and street fighting that lasted more than a week. Although it was fairly evident that racist attitudes of white neighbors led to the conflict, the city's newly created Human Relations Commission treated the matter as a conflict and as a lack of understanding between old established (white) residents and the newly arrived Puerto Rican (foreign) neighbors. The incident prompted the first study of the Puerto Rican community by a city agency and led to the creation of the Puerto Rican Affairs Committee of the Health and Welfare Council, made up primarily of leaders of the Puerto Rican community and city officials.[26]

On July 25, 1953, the Puerto Rican community marked the first anniversary of the establishment of the Commonwealth of Puerto Rico. Celebrated during the backdrop of the street fighting of the previous week, the event was in stark contrast, orchestrated by local Puerto Rican leadership and members of the Philadelphia official political arena. A speech by Puerto Rico's Governor Luis Munoz Marin was broadcast on a loudspeaker at a local park where the celebration took place.

These two events marked an important step in the evolution of the Puerto Rican community in Philadelphia because of the attention they brought to themselves through local media and political officials. This was the first time the city paid this much attention to the Puerto Ricans in their midst.[27] Throughout the 1950s, leaders of the Puerto Rican Affairs Committee like Carmen Aponte, who had come to Philadelphia in 1947, Domingo Martinez, and the Reverend Enrique Rodriguez, among others, struggled to get the city to address the many needs of the Puerto Rican community. Their efforts led to the formation of the Council of Spanish Speaking Organizations, El Concilio, in 1962. The Concilio, currently the oldest Puerto Rican/Latino social service agency in Philadelphia, initially brought together many diverse Latino community groups under one pan-Latino organization made up mostly of Puerto Ricans, but inclusive of all Latinos in La Fraternal. In 1968, the Concilio became the first full social service agency funded by city and federal funds.[28]

Beginning in the 1970s, during the height of the black liberation and anti–Vietnam War movements, elements in the Philadelphia Puerto Rican community began to organize direct-action groups. Made up of the sons and daughters of the pioneer Puerto Rican migrants of the 1930s, 1940s, and 1950s, this second generation of "Philly-Ricans" began to protest conditions in the community and, in some cases, to confront the established community leadership—accusing them of being conservative and conformists. Two such groups, the Philadelphia chapter of the Young Lords Party (YLP) and the Puerto Rican Socialist Party, led protest marches to demand city services for the Puerto Rican community in the early 1970s and 80s.[29]

During the mid to late 1970s, after the disappearance of the YLP chapter, other radical groups emerged to take up the mantle of the community struggle for empowerment. Among these, the most successful was the Puerto Rican

Alliance. The efforts of this group to seek better housing, health care, and education for Puerto Ricans in Philadelphia garnered it the respect of the community and the ire of the older leadership and of then-Mayor Frank Rizzo's administration. In addition, the alliance was instrumental in leading campaigns against police brutality and racial violence against Puerto Ricans in the city.[30]

The campaigns of the Puerto Rican Alliance bore fruit in the decade of the 1980s. In 1981, attorney and Temple Law School graduate Nelson A. Diaz was appointed judge of the Court of Common Pleas. In 1985, Mayor W. Wilson Goode, the first African American mayor of the city of Philadelphia, appointed Dr. Christine Torres Matrullo as the first Latina to serve on the Philadelphia School Board. In the electoral arena, the Puerto Rican community celebrated the election of Ralph Acosta as state representative in 1984 and Angel L. Ortiz as city councilman in 1985. However, despite these important political gains, a Temple University study on the Puerto Rican community in Philadelphia published in 1985 found that community lagged behind blacks and whites in terms of economic status, educational attainment, labor force participation, and housing segregation in the city.[31]

During the summer of 1990, for instance, the Philadelphia Human Relations Commission conducted public hearings regarding the concerns of the Philadelphia Latino community. Prompted by incidents of racial violence from the previous summer, dozens of Puerto Rican residents testified to the lack of adequate city services to Puerto Ricans in the areas of health and human services, the judicial system, employment and economic development, fire and police departments, and recreation, among others. According to the testimony provided by Councilman Ortiz, who was the first speaker at the hearings, "Puerto Ricans still do not play a role in the City government . . . there is a strong feeling in the community that City government has consciously maintained institutional barriers to prevent Latinos from securing employment and obtaining city services." For his part, Judge Diaz added, "We are continually abused and used by the political process."[32]

Conclusion

The small but significant organizational network that sprang up within the Spanish-speaking enclaves of Philadelphia became, by the end of World War II, a rich cultural mosaic representing Puerto Rican and other Spanish-speaking national groups in the city. Using a combination of mutual aid, labor, social, and cultural organizational formats, Philadelphia Puerto Ricans and other Latinos established the parameters for the appearance of a colonia. It was this colonia, made up significantly of many Latinos and some Puerto Ricans, which served as a welcome mat for the large numbers of Puerto Ricans who arrived in Philadelphia after 1945. The network of religious, social, and cultural groups that evolved between 1910 and 1945 formed the backbone of the Puerto Rican community that existed in the 1950s and 1960s. The roots of the present-day Puerto Rican community in Philadelphia can be traced directly to the community-building efforts of the pioneer groups in the interwar period.

During the 1990s, the Latino community continued to grow, yet the Puerto Rican population, still dominant in terms of numbers, began to cope with an increase in diversity among other Spanish-speakers. Prominent among the new groups were Dominicans, Colombians, Venezuelans, Peruvians, and Mexicans. Members of these respective groups reflected this growth in the establishment of a variety of organizations. The Dominican Community Cultural Center, founded to provide social services, was initially set up in the basement of the Incarnation Catholic Church in Olney and later moved to more permanent quarters at El Concilio in Northern Liberties. Meanwhile, the Colombian community experienced unprecedented growth as many left the war-torn country. Along with pioneers who had lived in Philadelphia for decades, Colombian immigrants formed business and social organizations such as the Colombian Coalition and two weekly Spanish-language newspapers, *Al Dia* and *El Sol Latino,* among others. During this period there was also a marked increase in the number of Central Americans, especially Guatemalans. Places like La Iglesia de Cristo y San Ambrosio, a Spanish-speaking Episcopal church in Hunting Park, opened its doors to this group with the Proyecto Sin Fronteras, an adult basic education program.

Certain sectors of the Puerto Rican community, especially in North Philadelphia, began to show signs of an increasingly diverse Latino population. Gone were the days of a dominant presence of Puerto Rican grocery store owners. Dominicans purchased those grocery stores, many financed by their Asociación de Bodegueros Dominicanos, a mutual aid and business association made up of Dominican grocery store owners. This organization played an active role in the Latino community in support of Democratic mayoral candidate Michael Nutter (May 2007).[33] Nutter won the Democratic Party primary and the general election. Mexican farm laborers, who had begun to replace Puerto Rican laborers in the outlying areas of Philadelphia, surpassed them in the 1990s. By the year 2000, Mexican farm workers, especially from Michoacan, constituted the absolute majority of laborers in Philadelphia's outlying areas and in southern New Jersey. Subsequently, as Puerto Ricans did before them, these Mexican laborers discovered better-paying jobs in the restaurants and hotels of the burgeoning Philadelphia hospitality and tourism industry. This opportunity lured them to the city. Currently, the biggest Mexican enclave is located in South Philadelphia, where the majority now lives. There, the local community has organized Casa Guadalupe, a multi-service, nonprofit entity. Also, through the help of the local consulate, a Mexican cultural center has been formed.

Just as in the early 1900s, organizations such as the Concilio and the Congreso de Latinos Unidos in the early twenty-first century reached out to Mexican residents in South Philadelphia and to Colombians and Dominicans in the northern sections of the city, providing them with needed social services. In this regard, although Puerto Ricans continue to predominate as a group, the pan-Latino nature of the community has once again provided the backdrop for working across national lines in the interest of all Latinos in the city of Philadelphia.

Notes

1. The survey found that there were 12,217 Mexicans residing in the city, making them the second largest Latino group. Cubans come in fourth with 3,040. The "other" Latino groups number 33,910, marking a continuing diversification of the Latino population of Philadelphia. See U.S. Census Bureau, 2005 American Community Survey (available at http://factfinder.census.gov: data set 2005 American Community Survey; data profile for Philadelphia County, Pennsylvania; table of General Demographic Characteristics, 2005).

2. The current executive director of the Congreso de Latinos Unidos, for instance, the largest Latino community-based organization in Philadelphia (2007), is Colombian and the president of its Board of Directors is Mexican American. The Congreso was founded by Puerto Ricans in 1981.

3. German Delgado Pasapera, *Puerto Rico: Sus Luchas Emancipadoras, 1850–1898* (Rio Piedras, Puerto Rico: Editorial Cultural, 1984), and Cesar Andreu Iglesias, ed., *Memoirs of Bernardo Vega: A Contribution to History of the Puerto Rican Community in New York* (New York: Monthly Review Press, 1984), are two good sources on the collaboration between nineteenth-century Puerto Rican and Cuban revolutionaries, especially their efforts from bases within the United States, particularly in New York, Boston, Philadelphia, and New Orleans.

4. A fair number of books and articles document cigar makers' organizational abilities and the many mutual aid societies they built in the United States. See Iglesias, *Memoirs of Bernardo Vega*, especially Chapters 6, 7, and 8; Gary R. Mormino and George E. Pozzetta, *The Immigrant World of Ybor City: Italians and Their Latin Neighbors in Tampa, 1885–1985* (Urbana: University of Illinois Press, 1987), Chapter 6; and Dorothee Schneider, *Trade Unions and Community: The German Working Class in New York City, 1870–1900* (Urbana: University of Illinois Press, 1994), Chapter 3. For essays on this subject see Gary R. Mormino and George E. Pozzetta, "The Reader Lights the Candle: Cuban and Florida Cigar Workers' Oral Tradition," *Labor's Heritage* 5, no. 1 (Spring 1993): 4–27; Susan Greenbaum, "Economic Cooperation Among Urban Industrial Workers: Rationality and Community in an Afro-Cuban Mutual Aid Society, 1904–1927," *Social Science History* 17, no. 2 (1993): 173–193; Nancy A. Hewitt, "The Voice of Virile Labor: Labor Militancy, Community Solidarity, and Gender Identity Among Tampa's Latin Workers, 1880–1921," in *Work Engendered: Toward a New History of American Labor,* ed. Ava Baron (Ithaca: Cornell University Press, 1991), 142–167; Durward Long, "La Resistencia: Tampa's Immigrant Labor Union," *Labor History* 6 (Fall 1965), 193–213; and Manuel Martínez, *Chicago: Historia de Nuestra Comunidad Puertorriqueña* (Chicago: Reyes and Sons, 1989).

5. *The Cigar Makers Official Journal (CMOJ)* "reported a union of Spanish and Cuban cigar makers in Philadelphia in 1877." See *CMOJ* 1 (December 1877), cited in Patricia Cooper, *Once a Cigar Maker: Men, Women and Work Culture in American Cigar Factories* (Urbana: University of Illinois Press, 1987).

6. Sam Bass Warner, *The Private City: Philadelphia in Three Periods of its Growth* (Philadelphia: University of Pennsylvania Press, 1987). The concentration of Puerto Rican and other Spanish-speakers' residential patterns in the period leading up to the Great Depression resembles the form of the letter "S." Beginning at the bottom of the "S" (Grays Ferry and Southwark), the pattern snakes along an eastbound direction to include parts of Society Hill, Chinatown, and East Poplar, then moves along a northwesterly direction to include parts of Northern Liberties, Spring Garden, Strawberry Mansion, and West Kensington. In addition, there was another concentration in West Philadelphia, especially in Parkside, with a smattering representation in the areas of Tioga and Hunting Park, north of Lehigh Avenue, and in the east in Port Richmond.

7. Kenneth L. Kusmer, *A Ghetto Takes Shape: Black Cleveland, 1870–1930* (Urbana: University of Illinois Press, 1976), 41–45. In his study of the black community in Cleveland, Kusmer found that a similar residential pattern evolved relative to segregation of black and ethnic communities. Although some segregation of blacks in Cleveland existed before World War I, the pace quickened after migration of that period. Also, not all ethnic groups were dispersed throughout the city in this period. Yet blacks became more segregated into communities clearly defined as "Negro sections" while, progressively, white ethnics were able to disperse throughout the city. The Philadelphia experience in this period also points to increased segregation for blacks, and though Latinos had similar experiences as other ethnic groups such as Italians, Polish, and Russian Jews, as the city became more racially segregated, the residential experiences of Puerto Ricans and other Latinos took on characteristics of black neighborhoods: deplorable housing, concentrated unskilled labor, and poverty.

8. Douglas S. Massey, "American Apartheid: Segregation and the Making of the Underclass," *American Journal of Sociology* 96, no. 2 (September 1990), 331; and Carmen T. Whalen, *From Puerto to Philadelphia: Puerto Rican Workers and Post War Economies* (Philadelphia: Temple University Press, 2001), 227. Massey argues that an increase in a group's poverty rate, blacks and Puerto Ricans in the case of this essay, inevitably produces a concentration of poverty when it occurs under conditions of high segregation. Following this argument, Whalen, in her study of the Puerto Rican community in the post–World War II period, argues that in U.S. urban centers, blacks and Puerto Ricans were the only groups who simultaneously experienced high levels of segregation *and* sharp increases in poverty. My focus in this chapter is to broadly outline how residential segregation of blacks and Puerto Ricans in Philadelphia was evident in the changing residential patterns of the city during the period between 1910 and 1930.

9. Carolyn T. Adams, David Bartelt, David Elesh, Ira Goldstein, Nancy Klenieswki, and William Yancey, *Philadelphia: Neighborhoods, Division and Conflict* (Philadelphia: Temple University Press, 1987), 17.

10. Jose Hernández Alvarez, "The Movement and Settlement of Puerto Rican Migrants within the United States, 1950–1960," *International Migration Review* 2, no. 2 (Spring 1968): 41.

11. Antonio Casulleras, C.M., *First Annual Report of the Spanish-American Colony* (Philadelphia: Pamphlet Collection, 1910), 1–2, St. Charles Borromeo Archives, Archdiocese of Philadelphia (STCA).

12. Many of these events were held in Boslover Hall, which was located at Seventh and Pines Streets, and in Garden Hall, which was located at Seventh and Morris Streets, *La Prensa* (8 January 1926), 2 (Center for Puerto Rican Studies Archives [CEPRA], Hunter College, New York).

13. Casulleras, *First Annual Report*, 1; and William Rickle, "Interethnic Relations in Hispanic Parishes in the Archdiocese of Philadelphia" (PhD diss., Temple University, 1996), 40.

14. Edwin David Aponte, David Bartelt, Luis A. Cortez, Jr., and John C. Raines, *The Work of Latino Ministry: Hispanic Protestant Churches in Philadelphia* (Philadelphia: Pew Charitable Trusts, 1994), 38; and Joan D. Koss, "Puerto Ricans in Philadelphia: Migration and Accommodation" (PhD diss., University of Pennsylvania, 1965), 64–65.

15. Aponte et al., *The Work of Latino Ministry*, 35–38; and Koss, "Puerto Ricans in Philadelphia," 65.

16. Raymond A. Mohl, "Cultural Pluralism in Immigrant Education: The International Institutes of Boston, Philadelphia and San Francisco, 1920–1940," *Journal of American Ethnic History* (Spring 1982): 37, 41; and Eleanor Morton, "How the International Institute Operates to Bring About a Feeling of Friendliness Among the City's Many Foreign-Born Groups," *Philadelphia Inquirer*, 15 July 1936, 39, YWCA Collection, Box 26, Temple University Urban Archives (TUUA).

17. Morton, "How the International Institute Operates," 39.

18. *Polk Philadelphia City Directory, 1935–36*, 2004; and interview with Jesse Bermudez, February 6, 1999.

19. Aponte et al., *The Work of Latino Ministry*, 38; and Koss, "Puerto Ricans in Philadelphia," 65.

20. Q. Fereshetian, "Spanish Community, 1951," Nationalities Services Center [NSC], folder 13, TUUA; Virginia Sanchez Korrol, *From Colonia to Community: The History of Puerto Ricans in New York City* (Berkeley: University of California Press, 1983), 18–19; and Centro de Studios Puertorriqueños, *Sources for the Study of Puerto Rican Migration* (New York: Research Foundation of the City University of New York, 1982), 4–5.

21. See invitation list of former members of the "Spanish Club" (Club Juventud Hispana), 1942; letter from Isabel Moreno, events secretary of La Fraternal to Marion Lantz, International Institute, inviting the agency to an event dated March 8, 1945; and letter from Clarence O. Senior to Marion Lantz, November 26, 1946, *Spanish Historical Developments, 1940–1957* (selected years), NSC, TUUA.

22. The five-year period, 1941–1946, accounted for 47 percent of the total Puerto Rican migration to the United States in the thirty-eight-year period beginning in fiscal year 1908–1909. More than 50,000 Puerto Ricans moved permanently to the United States in this period. Clarence O. Senior, *Puerto Rican Emigration* (Rio Piedras, Puerto Rico: Social Science Research Center, University of Puerto Rico, 1947), 7.

23. See *La Prensa* throughout the 1950s and 1960s; Mary Rodriguez, interview, March 7, 1999; and Juan Canales, interview, February 20, 1999.

24. Koss, "Puerto Ricans in Philadelphia," 65. In this ethnographic study on Puerto Ricans in Philadelphia, the author found that sixty-five Puerto Ricans who came to work at the Campbell Soup Company in 1944 were still employed there in 1961.

25. Carmen T. Whalen, "Puerto Rican Migration to Philadelphia, Pennsylvania, 1945–1970: A Historical Perspective on a Migrant Group" (PhD diss., Rutgers University, 1994), 420.

26. Arthur Siegel, Harold Orlans, and Lloyd Greer, *Puerto Ricans in Philadelphia: A Study of Their Demographic Characteristics, Problems and Attitudes*, Philadelphia Human Relations Commission (April 1954; reprint, New York: Arno Press, 1978); "7 Hurt in Fight of 300 at 15th and Mt. Vernon," *Philadelphia Evening Bulletin*, 18 July 1953, 3; and "7 Hurt as 1000 Clash in Riot," *Philadelphia Inquirer*, 18 July 1953, 5.

27. Whalen, *From Puerto Rico to Philadelphia*, 204–205.

28. Ibid., 216–217.

29. Ibid., 221; Juan D. Gonzalez, "The Turbulent Progress of Puerto Ricans in Philadelphia," *CENTRO Journal* 2, no. 2 (Winter 1987–1988): 17. For a full discussion of the presence of the Young Lords Party in Philadelphia, see Carmen T. Whalen, "Bridging Homeland Politics and Barrio Politics: The Young Lords in Philadelphia," in *The Puerto Rican Movement: Voices from the Diaspora*, ed. Andres Torres and Jose E. Velazquez (Philadelphia: Temple University Press, 1998), 107–123.

30. Gonzalez, "The Turbulent Progress of Puerto Ricans in Philadelphia," 38.

31. Ibid., 41; Eugene P. Ericksen, David Bartelt, Patrick Feeney, Gerald Foeman, Sherri Grasmuck, Maureen Martella, William Rickle, Robert Spencer, and David Webb, eds., *The State of Puerto Rican Philadelphia* (Philadelphia: Institute for Public Policy, Temple University, 1985), iv–vi.

32. Philadelphia Human Relations Commission, "Report to the Mayor W. Wilson Goode on Public Hearings Regarding Concerns of Philadelphia's Latino Community," September 1991, 1–3; sections II-1 and III-1.

33. Telephone interview with former City Councilman Angel L. Ortiz, May 16, 2007.

5

Opportunity, Conflict, and Communities in Transition

Historical and Contemporary Chinese Immigration to Philadelphia

Lena Sze

A report produced by the University of Pennsylvania's Fels Institute of Government notes: "The Philadelphia area generally attracts around 2% of Vietnamese and Chinese immigrants each year. Chinese have remained remarkably consistent at that level" (Patusky and Ceffalio 2004 [cited hereafter as "Fels Report"]). Among foreign-born nationalities, the Chinese population, excluding those from Hong Kong and Taiwan, ranks number three in Philadelphia following immigrants from Vietnam and Ukraine, respectively (Fels Report: 24). In a city otherwise struggling to attract and retain residents, what, then, helps to explain the steady immigration of Chinese to the Philadelphia region? How does Philadelphia's particular spatial configuration and economic landscape represent a unique challenge and opportunity for incoming Chinese migrants?

This article alternates between examining trends in contemporary Chinese immigration to the United States and describing historical Chinese immigration and Chinese immigrant life as evoked and recalled by the oral histories of twenty-two Philadelphians who participated in a Chinatown oral history project from 2002 to 2004.[1] It seeks to do so by situating contemporary Chinese immigrant life in a specific place, Philadelphia, and emerging out of particular historical contexts. As Mary Osirim and Ayumi Takenaka assert in the introduction to this book, Philadelphia's current stance with respect to immigration is to view it as an opportunity for economic revitalization. This approach follows a contemporary neoliberal paradigm in which diverse urban sites compete globally using similar mechanisms of privatization, deregulation, and a reliance on "creatives" in capital-intensive cores.[2] However Philadelphia is not New York, London, or Tokyo. The epitome of a post-industrial city, Philadelphia resists certain key elements apparently intrinsic to the continued economic success of those global cities. For example, "Philadelphia and Detroit, the only top 10 [U.S.] cities to lose population in the 1990s, were also the only top 10 cities to have less than 10 percent foreign-born overall" (Fels Report: 14). However, from 2000 to 2005, the county of Philadelphia saw a notable increase of 3,149 Chinese people, from 17,390 to 20,539.[3] Current Chinese immigration to Philadelphia, then, resists the smaller immigration rates that are typical of the city's post–World War II profile, yet concurs with broader immigration flows from China to the primary U.S. "gateway" cities (New York, Los Angeles, etc.).

In this article, I suggest that the global Philadelphia of today, at least as far as Chinese immigrant communities are concerned, the Philadelphia whose "resurgence" is often tied by policy-makers to a much-needed influx of immigrants, has roots in prior periods of Philadelphia's history and earlier global economic and political shifts. Thus I outline these recurring themes that both contextualize the historical experience of Chinese immigrant lives in Philadelphia and help produce the experience of contemporary Chinese immigrant Philadelphians: spatial density and dispersion across Philadelphia and issues of urban space; the important role of community institutions; diversity within the Chinese community; and the place of the "transnational" within local sites and processes.[4]

Density, Dispersion, and Questions of Space

Born in 1920 and a veteran of World War II, Joseph Eng, a Chinese Philadelphian, recalls his family's personal history:

> Because of the Depression, nobody was able to get work, money was so tight. We settled down in Camden [New Jersey] and we walked. We got two pair of shoes, one was good—to go to church [in Philadelphia's Chinatown], one was bad—to walk on the bridge. Back and forth, back and forth. Wintertime, it didn't make any difference. (Sze 2004: 28)

Mr. Eng's story not only evokes the poverty of the Depression with its haunting description of the preciousness of his one pair of good shoes, but also demonstrates how Chinese residents in Philadelphia at varied historical moments built community across much of Philadelphia's urban space and even the surrounding region. In this section, I examine how the space of Philadelphia was and is lived by Chinese Philadelphians to illuminate how these immigrants have helped to shape that space.

Historian John Kuo Wei Tchen has pointed out that "the history of Penn-sylvania's earliest Asian settlement [Philadelphia's Chinatown] has yet to be written" (2004: 11). It is certainly true that the details of the lives of these very early Chinese migrants and settlers, probably sailors, are unknown to us, but what we can glean is that Chinese people, cultural objects, and ideas were cir-culating in complex ways in colonial America and in Philadelphia in particular.[5] Jonathan Goldstein, for instance, argues that Philadelphia's colonial and early nineteenth-century dominance of the "China trade," in which Chinese objects and products were imported on long sea journeys from China for American consumption, had significant effects on Philadelphians' and Americans' atti-tudes toward the Chinese.[6] He writes: "By 1785, Philadelphia was not only the most populous but probably the most cosmopolitan city in the United States, with a significantly large and intellectual French émigré community, and an ethnic diversity that embraced Chinese and East Indians as well as the inhabit-ants of European ancestry, not to mention blacks" (1978: 11).

In the mid-nineteenth century, intellectual and philanthropist Nathan Dunn even built "the 'Chinese Museum' in Philadelphia at Ninth and George (now Sansom) Streets, open to the public from 1839–1842," at the time one of the West's few museums dedicated to Chinese culture (Goldstein 1978: 77). The former site of this museum sits just south of Philadelphia's current Chinatown, a neighborhood on the western fringes of the oldest part of the city (adjacent to the Delaware River). Although no physical remnant of the museum or these very early Chinese migrants exists, the fact of Philadelphia's predominance in the China trade helps us situate Chinese immigrant communities in a historical continuum within the city's collective memory.

Why is it critical to understand Chinese Philadelphians' history regionally, to know that Chinese immigrants were moving across the Delaware Valley region, including Southern Jersey and what is now suburban Philadelphia? Thinking more broadly about space in regional terms and the Chinese immi-grant lives in and around Philadelphia complicates our understanding about their patterns of settlement as well as the spatial and social consequences of cultural assimilation then and now. Mary Waters and Tomás Jiménez (2005) as well as Nina Glick Schiller et al. (2006), for instance, usefully interrogate the ethnic succession, gateway city, and ethnicity-based models of immigration studies and reveal their limitations. The traditional measures of immigrant assimilation (socioeconomic status, residential patterns, linguistic patterns, intermarriage) were pioneered by Chicago School sociologists, who were espe-cially formative in trying to make cultural claims about immigrants by studying the residential patterns of the city (spatial assimilation in which immigrants were thought to be more assimilated when they were generally more dispersed, i.e., not residing in "ethnic enclaves"). Although underscoring that Chinese immigrants have settled across the greater Philadelphia region for more than a century, it is also important to understand the crucial role that historic China-towns like Philadelphia's have held in the context of substantive social, legal, and economic barriers present in dominant U.S. society.

Moving forward in time, the recent Fels Report asserts that currently the Chinese in Philadelphia are more dispersed than their Vietnamese and Cambo-dian counterparts. If the Chinese tend to congregate in any one area, it is in Center City's Chinatown. Additionally, as the boom in Chinese home-buyers indicates (Bahadur 2005), Northeast Philadelphia is fast becoming a new hub for Philadelphia's Chinese community.[7] Chinese immigrants are also located in South Philadelphia where many Vietnamese (and Vietnamese Chinese) reside, including near Washington Avenue south of Center City, a strip notable for its high concentration of immigrant businesses and restaurants. The oldest organ-izations serving Philadelphia's Chinese community tend to be sited in China-town (the various family, name, and district associations as well as churches), but their program participants and parishioners are a mix between Chinatown residents and residents of Northeast and South Philadelphia as well as the Phila-delphia suburbs. Thus the places contemporary Chinese Philadelphians reside and work follow historical patterns of Chinese individuals and small communi-ties living and laboring across a broad swath of the Philadelphia region, with movement between relatively porous spatial boundaries.

Continuing this trend, the 2002–2004 oral history interviewees lived and worked across the city, although nearly all had some regular social, work, or recreational appointments in Chinatown. Lisa Cancelliere, the principal of Holy Redeemer Chinese Catholic School, a central institution in Chinatown, observes: "On their days off, you'll see our students playing here if their parents are work-ing in Chinatown and they're waiting for them to get off work" (Sze 2004: 18). Similarly Catharine Fan, a Chinatown parishioner and police officer, describes the importance of the central gathering place, the psychic core of the Philadel-phia Chinese community, Chinatown: "Though my parents lived in West Phila-delphia, they socialized here. If you wanted to eat Chinese food, there was only one place to go. All their friends socialized, worshipped, did grocery shopping in Chinatown" (Sze 2004: 30).

Scholars generally attribute the establishment of Philadelphia's Chinese (and Asian) community and the founding of its Chinatown to be the opening of Lee Fong's laundry at 913 Race Street in 1870.[8] Ninth and Race Streets remain in the heart of Philadelphia's relatively small but thriving twenty-first-century Chinatown.[9] Although the community is dispersed across the city, precisely because it is Chinese immigrants' "psychic core" in Philadelphia, Chinatown is a good place to note the ways in which Chinese immigrants have shaped the landscape of the city. For instance, Cecilia Moy Yep and Mitzie MacKenzie, two important leaders of Philadelphia's Chinatown, both describe the physical and social impact of Chinese immigrants on Philadelphia (Sze 2004: 48, 58). The built environment of downtown Philadelphia has literally been reshaped by the organization that Yep founded in 1966, the Philadelphia Chinatown Development Corporation (PCDC). Resistance to urban renewal, which I detail in the next section, gave way to a vision of Chinatown that included several housing developments. Perhaps most visually noticeable in the landscape of Chinatown are PCDC's 1984 development of On Lok House, a Section 8 development for Chinatown senior citizens, and the 1984–1985 China Friendship Gate on Tenth and Arch Streets in the heart of Chinatown. On Lok House incorporates Chinese-style architectural elements into its design, and the China Friendship Gate is advertised as the "first authentic gate built in America by artisans from China."[10] The PCDC and its efforts to integrate Sinitic architectural and design elements into the Philadelphia landscape are a useful place for us to examine the role of community institutions in the making of Chinese immigrant Philadelphia.[11]

Community-Making:
The Role of Community Institutions

In this section, I argue that community institutions have significantly shaped the contours of Chinese immigrant life in Philadelphia. A number of articles have documented the relatively recent struggle of Philadelphia's Chinatown against the dictates of urban renewal and development policies over the last forty to fifty years (Auyang 1978; Guan 2002). I too spend some time highlighting these formative events. However, too often does the narrative of Chinese immigrant life in Philadelphia begin with a few historical references to individuals, only then to proceed to a discussion of institutions during this most recent historical period (1960s–present). Rather, it may be more useful to ask what forms of participation constitute community institutional life for Chinese immigrant Philadelphians historically and in the present moment.

Grace Auyang has importantly pointed out that Lee Fong's laundry, signaling the start of Philadelphia's Chinatown in 1870, was no mere commercial enterprise.[12] These relatively informal social networks among immigrants as well as the more established organizations together formed an institutional lattice that in the nineteenth and early twentieth centuries could theoretically serve in the place of the state, which then was mostly absent for Chinese Americans except in disciplinary forms. Through these oral histories, it is even still possible to identify the kind of active participation among immigrants and Chinese Americans in Philadelphia that allowed a continuous Chinese community to exist in place for over a hundred and forty years to this day.

For example, Chun Moy Lee, an oral history interviewee now in her nineties, came to Philadelphia's Chinatown from Guangdong in the 1960s. Regarded by many in the community as a grandmother figure, she has volunteered at Holy Redeemer Church and School for more than twenty-four years because, as she says, "my granddaughter wanted somebody to be the lunch lady to help the cafeteria. But my granddaughter said there's no salary and I said, 'That's okay.' I wanted to help because that would make me feel more happy and comfortable" (Sze 2004: 40). Holy Redeemer, as we shall see, is one of the keystone institutions of the Chinese in Philadelphia, around which there has been much community organizing. But each community institution is comprised of the efforts of individuals such as Lee to make community a cohesive idea.

Neighborhoods where Chinese or ethnically Chinese immigrants settled themselves changed as stores, residences, eating establishments, places of religious worship, and social gathering places emerged to accommodate the needs of the newest Philadelphians. Changes in American immigration and foreign policy caused new ethnic organizations to flourish, as occurred in the plethora of newly founded organizations of Chinese following World War II (Zhou and Kim 2006: 236–237). The influx of Chinese immigrants that transformed New York's Chinatown in the 1960s, due to the historic immigration acts of the 1960s, affected Philadelphia to a lesser but still significant extent. A number of the interviewees or their parents immigrated or re-immigrated to Philadelphia during this decade, with one long-time Chinatown advocate and the only non-Asian American interviewed for the Oral History Project, Mitzie MacKenzie, declaring that "Chinatown needed housing in the 1970s, desperately" (Sze 2004: 48). This comment suggests that the services and housing that were adequate for the older Chinese immigrant and Chinese American populations of the city, represented by the old-timers with long family roots in America, such as Joseph Eng, were no longer sufficient with the substantial numbers of Chinese arriving on U.S. shores by the 1970s.

With new populations of Chinese immigrant communities entering the United States, it becomes imperative to consequently analyze the new dynamics and the institutions that mediate between these old and new social actors. For Philadelphia, in particular, the institutional level of social change is important to underscore, since Philadelphia has a very active group of Chinese ethnic and Chinese immigrant organizations. In fact, the history of Chinese Philadelphians and Philadelphia's Chinatown is intricately intertwined with its institutions. In addition to local chapters of the most common family, district, and name associations, and merchants' associations that characterized almost all major Chinatown communities, including the original Six Companies, or Chinese Consolidated Benevolent Association (CCBA), churches played a formative role in community life. Following the repeal of the Chinese Exclusion Act in the 1940s, and with the steady trickle of women into the formerly male-dominated community of Chinese immigrants, "A number of churches were founded in Chinatown during and after the war, such as the Holy Redeemer Chinese Catholic Church and School (1941), Chinese Christian Church and Center (1941), and Chinese Gospel Church (1952)" (Historical Society of Pennsylvania Web site).

Historian Nayan Shah (2001) has described the ways in which Chinese Americans in San Francisco's Chinatown sought to recuperate an image of middle-class respectability after decades of racialization of Chinese as unhealthy bearers of disease and subjects undeserving of citizenship. The community institutions sited in place worked in tandem with state organs to construct precisely this image. So, too, in Philadelphia by the twentieth century, and certainly after World War II, did Chinese Philadelphians participate in activities and build institutions that were primarily "pro-American," establishment, and favoring the middle class. Chinese American churches in Philadelphia played a particularly dominant role in the initial push for acceptance into mainstream society. Mitzie Mackenzie, the former director of the Chinese Christian Church and Center who influenced generations of Chinese Philadelphian youth, comments on the process of "Americanization" in 1941:

> I was given the key to 1006 Race Street which used to be a Chinese mission Sunday school. . . . My mission was to make them Americans. The first thing we did was have a girls club where they learned how to cook American dishes to introduce to their parents. Their parents were from China and they were American. Some of the girls won the American Legion award in their schools. (Sze 2004: 48)

Of religious institutions, Holy Redeemer Catholic Church and the Chinese Christian Church and Center (CCCC) are the most important for the Philadelphia Chinese community. The current director of the CCCC, Harry Leong, recalls the church's role in his own youth: "The Chinese Christian Church and Center playground is where I grew up. My parents' building was adjacent to the playground so we would pretty much go everyday, whenever it wasn't rainy. As far back as I can remember, my family has been attending this church" (Sze 2004: 46). Thus this memory suggests that religious institutions, although they may have served as mechanisms for assimilation and the construction of certain idealized subjects, are an important means by which larger religious, cultural, and ethnic identities are formed.

Over the course of the Chinese community's century and a half in Philadelphia, other important organizations besides the CCBA include the Chinese Young Men's Christian Association (YMCA), Chinese Cultural and Community Center, the Greater Philadelphia Overseas Association, and such pan-Asian organizations as Asian Americans United, Asian Arts Initiative, Asian American Women's Association, and the Community Youth Organizing Campaign (CYOC) Collective. These organizations' activities range from the aesthetic and purely cultural (cooking classes and demonstrations for non-Chinese) to the explicitly political (organizing, protests, and demonstrations), often with an eye to the preservation of some perceived past, such as "traditional" architectural motifs or the celebration of Chinese New Year and its attendant traditions.[13] The most important established community institutions for Philadelphia Chinese and Chinese American communities (CCCC, Holy Redeemer, CCBA, and PCDC) have traditionally been focused on developing thriving local Chinese communities by providing a number of social and cultural services to their constituents. The CCBA and Holy Redeemer, as well as Chinese Gospel Church, are religious-cum-community centers of Chinese life. Much of their orientation is to service the manifold, complex needs of Chinese immigrants alongside the more explicitly missionary components of their spiritual goals (Historical Society of Pennsylvania Web site). The CCBA, as the main Chinese associational organization in Philadelphia's Chinatown, like other chapters of the historically influential associations, arose out of a need to protect the interests of politically and economically vulnerable Chinese immigrants, especially in the pre-1965 period.

Peter Kwong, however, argues that working-class Chinese live under a "dual form of oppression" in that both mainstream American society and "uptown Chinese" maintain social control over and economically exploit them through ownership of businesses and control of certain community institutions and associations (1987: 9). This phenomenon holds true for documented as well as undocumented immigrants. In fact, the potential for social control (or, in some cases, mobility) within Chinese immigrant communities is heightened by the great class and ethnic diversity present among Chinese immigrants. In the oral histories of KeKe Wang and Bihong Guan, we learn that both were graduate students at Temple University before settling down in Philadelphia. Philadelphia, with its density of colleges and universities, attracts both educated Chinese (Chinese academics and students) with high income potential and poor and working-class immigrants laboring, sometimes to provide income to family back in Asia, in restaurants as waiters or as take-out deliverymen or in factories and stores in Chinatown (Moran 2006). As Wei Yew Lee, a waiter who recently emigrated from Malaysia, concludes: "In the States, it's difficult, twelve hours. The restaurants require, you have to work twelve hours. In order to get into them, you have to work overtime" (Sze 2004: 44).

Of the thirteen oral history interviewees who are immigrants, six immigrated to Philadelphia since the late 1980s. At least half that number (KeKe Wang, Bihong Guan, Shi Xing Zeng) are involved in a community organization or community activities, reflecting their desire to establish a foothold in Philadelphia's Chinese community as well as their desire to perform community service. As Shi Xing (Happy) Zeng notes: "There are many people who just arrived who don't speak English. They need a place to live, but when they apply for electricity, water, gas, these kinds of things, they need help. They can't read the forms, they don't know where to get this done, they don't know any of this. I regularly do things in Chinatown, helping people who need help" (Sze 2004: 60).

The influx of Fujianese (and other mainland Chinese) to Philadelphia, both inside Chinatown and elsewhere in the city, which I outline in the next section, has meant a corresponding institutionalization of Fujianese community life, as evidenced by the fact that "five Fujianese business associations have been created in Philadelphia in the last five years [2000–2005]" (Bahadur 2005). Thus, not only class distinctions, but new immigrant status may be a spur to the development of new community organizations to fill a void that prior institutions leave.

The classic example in Philadelphia of Chinese immigrant institutional life not addressing the needs of a portion of its constituency occurred at the beginning of the "Save Chinatown" movement. In 1966, when the Pennsylvania Redevelopment Authority (RDA) threatened to demolish a central Chinatown and Chinese Philadelphian institution, the Holy Redeemer Church and School, to build the Vine Street Expressway, the traditional associations in Philadelphia's Chinatown floundered. Holy Redeemer, an important site for the Chinese community in Philadelphia, became a rallying cry for diverse sets of younger leaders who established their own organizations to deal with the crisis. As founding member of the Philadelphia Chinatown Development Corporation, Cecilia Moy Yep relates: "I organized a town meeting. . . . Basically Chinatown was a bachelor society, and there were no women in the organizations at that time. The elders said, 'We can't fight City Hall,' because of the language barrier. 'If you want to fight, you will have to do it on your own'" (Sze 2004: 58). The "Save Chinatown" movement in Philadelphia during 1966–1986 was responding not just to the dramatic proposal to raze Chinese Philadelphia's cultural center (Holy Redeemer), but emerged out of the context of a number of other city, state, and private projects that proposed to hem in Chinatown's residential and retail space. Due to Chinatown's location on prime real estate in Center City, Philadelphia's main commercial downtown area, many of these projects were built, including the Convention Center to Chinatown's west and a shopping mall to its south. Even though the Vine Street Expressway was constructed, "Save Chinatown" activists saved Holy Redeemer and forced certain structural concessions from the state, such as sound barriers (Guan 2002: 132–135).[14]

Another formative moment for Chinese Philadelphians occurred when Mayor John Street proposed to build a baseball stadium in Chinatown in 2000 (Guan 2002: 135–137). A successful coalition of Chinese immigrant, Chinese American, Chinatown, and Asian American community institutions called "Stadium Out of Chinatown" held public protests and testified at hearings. Whether due to the coalition's pressure or to the proposal's economic unfeasibility, the latest incarnation of public protest for Chinese Philadelphians represented a rare moment that radical political activists worked with business and tradition-minded associations. This event sets in stark relief the predicament of Chinese in Philadelphia and, in particular, Philadelphia's Chinatown. State schemes to "renew" and reinvest in Philadelphia's core in response to the flight of manufacturing and industry so key to the city's economic health until the 1950s have had significant material and physical impacts on the space of Philadelphia's small Chinatown community. The frequency and seriousness with which China-town and Chinese institutional life have been impacted, first by urban renewal and now by spatial, development, and design "upgrades" leading to fears of gentrification and displacement, demonstrates how Philadelphia's Chinese pop-ulation has been disproportionately affected given Chinatown's relatively small size in relation to the city. However, as a consequence, so too is the effectiveness of Chinese immigrant and Chinese American community institutions in Phila-delphia disproportionate to the numbers of Chinese in Philadelphia.

All these disparate institutions, although focused on working directly with Philadelphia Chinese on specific local goals and projects, are part and parcel of larger historical movements (e.g., the relationship between American mission-ary churches and Chinese communities in the United States and China; the prevalence of nineteenth- and early twentieth-century anti-Chinese sentiment and the emergence of the Chinese immigrant association in diasporic China-towns; and the rise of the local development corporation as a means to com-munity revitalization in the 1970s and forward). These institutions have much to tell us about the meaning of Chinese immigrant life in Philadelphia and how that life is experienced, constructed, and contested.

Diversity of Chinese Philadelphians, or What Does It Mean to Be "Chinese"?

There are many insights to be gleaned from the information organized and dis-tributed by the U.S. Census Bureau; coupled with the flesh-and-blood portraits provided by the oral histories, however, these insights begin to take on added meaning and demonstrate the depth of diversity even within the ethnic Chinese communities of Philadelphia. In 1990, 2.7 percent of Philadelphia's total popu-lation was Asian or Pacific Islander; in 2000, 4.5 percent was Asian; and in 2005, 5.4 percent was Asian (including those of mixed race). In fifteen years, then, the number of immigrants from Asia has increased significantly, with the percentage of Asians in relation to the total population doubling in that period. The num-ber of Chinese alone in 2005 comprised nearly half the county's entire 1990 Asian population.[15]

What the fantastic growth of Chinese in Philadelphia over the last decade and a half obscures, however, is a true sense of the difference (material as well as emotional) among those who are categorized together by their nation of ori-gin or ethnicity. As noted above, recently immigrated oral history interviewees have noted that Philadelphia has its fair share of wealthy, professional Chinese. KeKe Wang, the president of Asia America Travel Group in Chinatown, asserts that "young Chinese are different because they're more involved in different aspects of society. So many of them have a good education, university or higher degree, like Master's or PhD" (Sze 2004: 54). But with a median annual household income at $24,227 in 1999, there were also 979 Chinese Philadelphian families and 5,418 Chinese individuals living below the poverty level.[16] In addition to stark disparities in income, the historical moment at which Chinese immigrants arrive and settle is often crucial to their lives as new immigrants.

Elderly Chinatown resident Joseph Eng describes his experience working and living in his father's laundry, and in so doing portrays a particular moment in time when laundry work was the major occupation for early Chinese migrants to the United States who otherwise had extremely limited employment opportunities. Restaurant work, too, was and continues to be an important industry for Chinese immigrants. As interviewee Wai Lum Chin describes, "It's easier to manage a restaurant. Sometimes starting other businesses is difficult since I wasn't experienced and not too educated" (Sze 2004: 22). Romana Lee, a second-generation biracial Chinese American, shares her frustrations about the difficulties of restaurant work and the trope of the Asian restaurant worker:

> Watching my father really helped me to see how Asian Americans are pigeonholed into doing one kind of work. In Chinatown, there aren't too many different opportunities. Just open a restaurant, accumulate capital from family, friends, borrow money. What really drove me nuts is that my dad . . . had to revert to the only way he knew how to make a living that was stable. It's hard for me to watch him. (Sze 2004: 42)

As these oral histories demonstrate, the Chinese population in Philadelphia is wide ranging in terms of class, income, educational attainment, age, and occupation, as well as in levels of assimilation characterized by the traditional markers of spatial concentration (in Chinatown) and language (bilingualism). However, as Lee's quotation suggests, although there are multiple avenues open to many Chinese immigrants and notable differences within the community itself, there are also ways in which occupational and life choices are sometimes circumscribed by social forces outside Chinese communities, thus forcing her father, for example, into the restaurant industry, a stereotyped profession for Chinese immigrants. Whereas restaurant work is an option that has been open to Chinese immigrants in the United States for several generations, the kinds of restaurants that Chinese immigrant entrepreneurs have opened have changed with larger changes in immigration policy from storied Chinese American fare such as chop suey to Southeast Asian, regional Chinese, and pan-Asian cuisine.

Perhaps even more transformative for the landscape of Philadelphia's Chinese communities than the 1965 Hart-Cellar Immigration Act were developments following the Vietnam War. Refugees from Vietnam moved into Philadelphia's Chinatown and other areas in the 1970s and 1980s, reviving the lifeblood of the community. Peter Kwong notes about Manhattan's Chinatown during this same period: "At the end of the Vietnam War thousands of Vietnamese, Laotian, and Cambodian refugees of Chinese descent, who spoke Chinese and originally came from Kwangtung, came to Chinatown" (1987: 40). In Philadelphia, Wai Man Ip, a long-time small businesswoman, comments on the phenomenon and her reaction to it:

> At the end of the Vietnam War, many Vietnamese Chinese immigrated here. At that time, Chinatown was very prosperous because the Vietnamese Chinese were used to shopping in the streets. When they first came here, they didn't know English, so on Saturdays and Sundays, they all rushed to Chinatown—to buy groceries, buy rice or flour, in bags of all sizes. I was really happy when I saw this happening. There were so many Chinese. All of Chinatown started to change. (Sze 2004: 34)

The Southeast Asian refugees that ended up in Philadelphia, aided by various religious (e.g., Quaker) organizations servicing refugees, came to a city/region where the Asian community was still relatively small, unlike the experiences of those who settled in New York, California, or the Northwest. Although Chinese Philadelphian communities existed, the local economies could accommodate and indeed thrive, as Ip describes later in her interview, with the arrival of these new ethnic Chinese. Thus, the impact of the post–Vietnam War Asian immigration on Philadelphia, although nowhere near the numbers of Vietnamese Chinese to immigrate to New York's Chinatown, may have been disproportionately greater, not just in Chinatown, but in large sections of South Philadelphia where many Vietnamese, Lao, and Cambodian Chinese Philadelphians live to this day.

The entry of Vietnamese and other Southeast Asian Chinese into Philadelphia's Chinatown in the 1970s and 1980s was, however, not to be a unique phenomenon in the history of Philadelphia's Chinese community. According to the U.S. State Department, "Today, the majority of [Chinese] emigrants departing for destinations around the globe originate in an area the size of Delaware (2,396 square miles or about 6,133 square kilometers) in China's Fujian (Fukien) Province."[17] In fact, for scholars and policy analysts tracking Chinese immigration to the United States, it is widely known that the most important development over the last twenty years has been the arrival of phenomenal numbers of Fujianese documented and undocumented immigrants and their transformation of older, primarily Cantonese- or Toisan-speaking Chinese communities in the Americas: "As a result of the large volume of immigrants from Fujian to the New York area, the Fujianese population and community have quickly emerged and challenged the traditional dominance of immigrants from Guangdong. Fujianese have a dense social network, speak their own dialects, and have their own lawyers who help them get green cards and resolve other legal matters" (Liang and Ye 2001).

The Fujianese presence in Chinese immigrant communities is echoed in Philadelphia by the anecdotal evidence offered by the oral histories. Benny Lai, a successful Vietnamese Chinese restaurant owner, asserts: "Today in Chinatown it reminds me of back then when we got flooded by the Vietnamese community—now we have Chinese immigrants called Fuzhou, from Fujian province. They've almost taken over the whole of Chinatown because there's so many of them. That's why you see a lot of businesses and new stores popping up" (Sze 2004: 36). Lai makes a crucial connection between the high numbers of Vietnamese, Cambodian, and Lao refugees in the 1970s and 1980s and those Fujianese arriving in Philadelphia today because, with their arrival, both sets of immigrants have significantly impacted the established Chinese immigrant culture of Philadelphia with its Toisan-, Cantonese-, and Chinatown-specific focus.[18]

Indeed for most of the history of Chinese immigration to the United States, Toisan- or Cantonese-speaking immigrants from Guangdong province predominated. The Hart-Cellar Act of 1965, passed during the Cold War, effectively allowed entry only to highly educated immigrants from Taiwan and—because of its family reunification clause—Cantonese relatives of Chinese Americans, often from Hong Kong: "One of the cornerstones of the 1965 Immigration Act was to shift admission procedures from unskilled laborers to skilled professionals, since America was moving toward a post-industrial economy" (Kwong 1987: 77). But by the early 1990s, the shift to the Fujianese and other mainland Chinese brought a significant number of new features to the Chinese communities of the diaspora, including changes related to language (the new immigrants speak Mandarin or Fujianese rather than Cantonese) and ideology (the new immigrants tend to reject the pro-Taiwan/Kuomintang outlook held by the Chinese old-timers in U.S. Chinatowns).

Two Chinese immigrant Philadelphians interviewed reflect some of the changes that these mainland immigrant populations have effected on traditionally Chinese immigrant communities. KeKe Wang, a prosperous businessman, notes that "In 1989, I was the first one from mainland China to start a business in Chinatown. It was followed by a printing press, run by a Mr. Lee. Then there was the New China Bookstore, followed by a number of newspaper stands. I don't speak much Cantonese because I'm not from Guangzhou. At first, I felt like I was being excluded. But the situation is different now" (Sze 2004: 54). Bihong Guan, an acupuncturist and real estate developer, puts it this way:

We thought during that time it was strange here that the old residents, the Chinese, Chinatown, nobody celebrated the National Day of the People's Republic of China—the People's Republic of China was founded

October 1, 1949. I come from mainland China, Communist China. Here they only celebrate Ten Ten Day, shuang shih [Taiwan's independence day].... We think this situation should be changed.... So in 1997 we had some friends, got together, and first thing on October 1st, we had a big celebration at Independence Park, raised the flag of the People's Republic, and had a parade. (Sze 2004: 32)

Philadelphia's ethnic Chinese community includes immigrants and refugees from all parts of mainland China, Hong Kong, Taiwan, Vietnam, Cambodia, Laos, and Indonesia who may or may not identify as Chinese. Because each immigrant identifies so differently with being ethnically "Chinese," the content of each immigrant's experience of being Chinese in Philadelphia also differs. Identification with a culturally coherent group known as Chinese is an especially difficult to classify but significant marker of diversity and difference among Chinese immigrants and Chinese Americans in Philadelphia. For instance, Iwan Santoso, a refugee from Indonesia, states:

I am actually an Indonesian of Chinese descent. My great-grandmother was native Chinese but we lived in Indonesia for decades.... We had problems because of that issue—race—and the economy was down too. In Indonesia after 1964, Chinese schools and culture were no longer allowed.... We look Chinese, people say we are Chinese, but Chinese people themselves are sometimes wary of us, because we don't speak Mandarin, and our names are different. (Sze 2004: 50)

The pragmatic understanding of cultural identity based primarily on pheno-typical appearance and external perception that frames Santoso's perspective is quite different from that of Vietnamese Chinese Khai Tang's parents. He describes how their habits and aesthetic choices are inflected with a sense of a remembered past of being Chinese in Vietnam: "[My parents] don't do anything really Americanized. They just do their usual things, traditional way. My dad, you know, got all these lanterns in the house. The whole house is pretty much traditional, I would say.... My parents would probably call themselves Chinese from Vietnam" (Sze 2004: 52). Later in his oral history, he states that, in contrast to their parents, he and his siblings are "definitely Philadelphians ... and we're Chinese Americans" (Sze 2004: 52).

With the recent influx of Chinese immigrants to Philadelphia, we have seen and will continue to see the evolution of communities from small numbers of mostly Toisan immigrants to the full breadth of ethnic Chinese coming from a whole range of geographical areas and economic circumstances. Over the last thirty years, Vietnamese Chinese and now Fujianese have remade what it means to be a Chinese Philadelphian. Other factors that figure into the diversity of Chinese immigrant populations in the city/region are more difficult to measure, including levels of social and cultural assimilation, generational difference, and ethnic identification. Historian of immigration Mae Ngai has elaborated on the ways in which U.S. immigration policy has frequently dovetailed with prevailing attitudes about Asian (and Latino) immigrants to create subjects that are "illegitimate, criminal, and unassimilable" (2004: 2). Understanding that these subjects are diverse and emerging out of manifold histories helps situate the processes that construct them as particularly complex and multi-sited.

Siting the Transnational

In an oral history mentioned earlier, Bihong Guan describes how he and other mainland Chinese students and immigrants founded the Greater Philadelphia United Chinese American Chamber of Commerce in the 1990s. This organization's pro-mainland orientation and its lack of rootedness in the historic core of the Chinese community (Chinatown) caused a certain level of distrust among older leaders and organizations in Chinatown: "In 2000 . . . we fought inside Chinese community because it is not so united. A big fight in the newspapers because I wrote an article against [Philadelphia mayor] Street's decision to build a baseball stadium in Chinatown. Some people said, 'You cannot represent us.' I said, 'I represent my organization. I didn't represent you.' So we had a big fight in our newspaper, our community" (Sze 2004: 32). Just as the Yellow Seeds, a radical Asian American activist group, and PCDC held perspectives and initiated approaches quite different from those of existing associations in the 1960s and 1970s, so now with the increase in mainlanders and Mandarin-speakers does a level of productive tension exist between old and new.

The perceived and real conflicts between the "old-guard" or established institutions serving Philadelphia Chinese and Chinese Philadelphia's newer organizations may best be apprehended by the difference in their precise relationship to extra-local forces. Whereas CCCC, Holy Redeemer, CCBA, and PCDC all have as their emphasis serving local Philadelphia Chinese communities, these new organizations, such as the Greater Philadelphia United Chinese American Chamber of Commerce co-founded by oral history interviewee Bihong Guan or the China Trade Center of Philadelphia, whose president is interviewee KeKe Wang, have made more explicit partnerships, especially commercial and business ones, with mainland China.[19] Wang's China Trade Center and its affiliate Asia America Group are particularly interested in the idea and practice of exchange, primarily for economic and cultural reasons. Of the major programs of the China Trade Center of Philadelphia, whose mission statement describes hosting a China exposition in Philadelphia, all involve the movement of ideas, objects, and peoples, such as trade missions, educational exchange, import/export business, cultural exchange, and tourism and hospitality. Even PCDC—with the bulk of its history oriented to Philadelphia Chinatown-specific projects—forged alliances in 1984 and again in 2008 with Philadelphia's sister city in China, Tianjin, for economic and cultural purposes.[20] These multiple transnational endeavors involving actors from China and Philadelphia work very well with popular current strategies of municipal and regional economic development, including attracting global business partnerships and encouraging tourism.[21]

I do not mean to suggest that the key difference between the historic Chinese and Chinese American organizations in Philadelphia and the newly established ones simply maps the degree to which the organizations are transnational or not. This simplistic binary distinction between the local versus transnational focus of earlier as compared to more recent organizations must further be complicated, for instance, in a discussion of how the current incarnation of economic globalization evidences itself in more performatively transnational ways, or of how Chinese institutions in Philadelphia historically articulated their missions and projects on local, regional, and diasporic terms. It may be no accident that in contemporary Philadelphia, people are attempting to build a healthy commercial connection between China and the United States, for Philadelphia appears to have thrived during the colonial era into the nineteenth century during which its dominance of the "China Trade" was the city's greatest commodity.

In addition to the Hart-Cellar Act, the explosion of Chinese refugees and immigrants from Southeast Asia in the 1970s and 1980s following the wars in Southeast Asia, and the huge numbers of Fujianese Chinese immigrants arriving in the United States since the 1990s (discussed above), it is crucial to understand that foreign policy and events in other nation-states have had important effects on local Chinese immigrants in Philadelphia, extending even farther back than the pivotal 1960s. Hostile American foreign policy attitudes toward China during the height of the Cold War in the 1950s led to the strict scrutiny of Chinese immigrants arriving in the United States (Ngai 2004: 206–212); federal immigration policy barred the immigration of nearly all Chinese to U.S. shores, beginning with the 1882 Chinese Exclusion Act among other legislation, until the 1940s–1960s (Ngai 2004: 201–204; Lin 1998: 24–26); and the spatial and social organization of Chinatowns dominated by a mix of commercial businesses and residents is evidenced by the presence of street vendors, locally owned and operated banks, and tenement dwellers (Lin 1998: 76–78, 95–98, 114–115). Also, in the oral history interview with Joseph Eng, he describes how he was able to bring his new wife to Philadelphia because of the War Brides Act (1945), which legally permitted the immigration of spouses of U.S. service members to the United States, as well as China's new (and temporary) status as American ally: "The immigration law did not open until 1946 when the Second World War was over and my wife was the first group who was free to come over as a G.I. bride" (Sze 2004: 28).

Even for Lee Fong's laundry, which "established" Philadelphia's Chinatown in 1870, anti-Chinese feeling, circulating nationally and responding to imperialist attitudes toward the Chinese state, took an inauspicious local form: "The police, in response to complaints from the neighbors, raided the establishment on the evening of August 13, 1882, and arrested Lee Fong and Lee Wang. It was charged that they were running an illegal gambling house" (Auyang 1978: 5). It is important to note here that the racial animus and violence against Chinese workers and immigrants, emanating most strongly from California and other parts of the West Coast, resulted in the passage of the Chinese Exclusion Act the very same year as Lee Fong's arrest, 1882.

Despite immigration legislation targeting them, there has historically been a fluid movement between Chinese communities in Asia and the United States. Both oral history interviewees Joseph Eng and Wai Lum Chin, for instance, describe being born in the United States, spending at least part of their childhood in China, moving back to Philadelphia as young men, and having fathers who were U.S. citizens who traveled back and forth between China and the United States most of their working lives. Thus the transnational is sited not only in economic processes that emerge out of particular historical contexts, but also in social practice and identity that continue to have a significant effect on Chinese immigrant Philadelphians.

Conclusion

Only a few of these oral histories give an account of the Chinese immigrant narrative to the United States described in terms of a single here and there, a place from which one comes (China) and to which one arrives (Philadelphia). But, more frequently than not, especially in this age of constant global flows of capital, labor, and culture, the immigrants interviewed spoke of an evolving story of immigration, one with pit stops, accidental destinations, and evolving itineraries.[22] To be sure, Philadelphia is attempting to develop economically using the standard neoliberal economic development strategies popular among policy makers, and a straight-arrow, simplistic narrative of immigration and achievement of the "American Dream" may even be useful. However, Philadelphia and its Chinese communities are no mere satellites to larger New York's, and the stories that populate Chinese immigrant Philadelphia are much more textured and complex.[23]

Philadelphia is able to offer unique opportunities to its Chinese immigrants: a tight-knit Chinatown community, increasingly diverse and effective community institutions, more affordable homes and rents, a lower cost of living than many East Coast cities, and the capability to carve out a commercial and residential niche and have greater impact more rapidly than in larger cities. Ironically, the opportunities the city provides can also be seen to be in danger as Philadelphia develops its core and certain neighborhoods gentrify (Chinatown in Center City) or become more expensive (parts of Northeast Philadelphia). The city's economic development and strategies for attracting immigrants, then, may be ultimately at odds with the continued possibility of such Philadelphia-specific opportunities and amenities for immigrants.

As we have seen from these oral histories, Philadelphia's Chinese immigrant community is by no means monolithic. Of various ethnicities, genders, nationalities, sexual identities, classes, ages, education, abilities, political affiliations, and degrees of documentation, the community is a veritable polyglot.[24] It is also a community in transition, between old-timers and those recently immigrated, from Cantonese- or Toisan-speaking Chinatowners to Mandarin- and Fujianese-speaking residents spread across the city and suburbs, to those for whom there existed significant racial barriers to equal employment to a generalized increased access to professions and acceptance by mainstream society. The most generative periods for Philadelphia's Chinese community, both economically and socially, are those in which there is substantial flux and change, opportunity as well as conflict. Such periods include the introduction of women and families to Philadelphia's Chinatown following the opening up of immigration laws in the 1940s–1960s, the huge surge in Southeast Asian Chinese invigorating an aging Chinese community, and the urgent, recent transformations by the Fujianese to the Philadelphia landscape.

Joseph Eng, the octogenarian, perhaps puts it best when he links the demographic fact of increasing Chinese immigration to Philadelphia to the materialization of his specific dream, the growth of the "heart" of Chinese immigrant communities, Chinatown, past its present bounds: "So many Chinese come to Philadelphia. . . . And I would like to see more homes on the north side of Vine Street for the youngsters to see some dream—something started on the other side" (Sze 2004: 28). What is instructive about Mr. Eng's dream of the "other side" is that it is not the fantasy of a return to an imagined Chinese homeland, as earlier migrants might have formulated. Rather, here he specifically links the changing and growing populations of Chinese immigrants and the evolution of a troubled American immigration policy toward "Chinese" people with a rootedness in a local place: Philadelphia. Specifically, he describes a uniquely compelling dream of a "home" in Philadelphia, an understudied but critically important place within the larger map of the Chinese diaspora, a place for Chinese immigrants where material and imaginative opportunities and conflicts both lie.

Notes

Acknowledgments: Thanks to John Chin and Betsy Self Elijah for their assistance with research requests, and to participants, volunteers, and administrators of the Asian Arts Initiative's Chinatown Oral History Project. A thank you is also due to the editors Mary Osirim and Ayumi Takenaka, whose hard work and good cheer brought together the essays in this volume.

1. The ethnographic data informing this chapter are derived from the oral histories collected from 2002 to 2004 during the Chinatown Oral History Project, a project of the Asian Arts Initiative, a Philadelphia-based community arts center. This project attempted to provide an intimate portrait of the lives of people integrally involved in Philadelphia's Chinatown community. As such, many of the interviewees worked and/or lived in Chinatown, but still others, although living outside Chinatown, participated through informal connections and associations in Chinatown, a neighborhood located in the city's central commercial district known as "Center City Philadelphia." The staff and board members of the Philadelphia Chinatown Development Corporation helped generate the initial list of interviewees for the Project along with Asian Arts Initiative staff members. This sample was expanded with the efforts of staff and volunteers of the Asian Arts Initiative who visited a number of stores and establishments in Chinatown where they met other interviewees. Those interviewed generally tended to speak English, although a number of interviews were conducted in Cantonese and Mandarin; they were ethnically Chinese or Chinese-identified even if their families had immigrated from Vietnam or Indonesia; they tended to be upwardly mobile, although levels of education and income varied; and they consisted of documented citizens or residents, although one woman we spoke with was in the process of seeking asylum. Those for whom public exposure was an issue, such as undocumented immigrants and workers paid below the minimum wage, generally did not want to be interviewed for obvious reasons.

Twenty-one of the twenty-two interviewees were Asian American or biracial Asian American, twenty identified as Chinese American or ethnically Chinese from an Asian country, twelve interviewees in our sample were male, and the interviewees ranged in age from seventeen to ninety-two, with the largest number of interviewees in their twenties to forties. Many of the interviewees were involved in Chinese American and/or Chinatown organizations, retired, and/or the staff of nonprofit organizations or working in the commercial businesses serving Chinatown residents. To be clear, this collection of oral histories was not intended to comprehensively represent the various populations within a very diverse community, but rather to offer a number of reflective oral histories that shed light on historical circumstances and political, cultural, and economic developments in Philadelphia. Throughout this chapter, whenever I take direct quotations from the oral history interviews of the Chinatown Oral History Project, I will be citing *Chinatown Live(s): Oral Histories from Philadelphia's Chinatown,* edited by Lena Sze (2004).

2. Geographer Jamie Peck (2005) elaborates on the ways in which the "creatives" of Richard Florida's creative class thesis participate in "neoliberal development agendas."

3. These numbers are taken from U.S. Census Bureau data for Philadelphia County from the 2000 U.S. Census (available at http://factfinder.census.gov: data set Decennial Census, Census 2000 Summary File 1 (SF 1) 100-Percent Data; table PCT5, Philadelphia County, Pennsylvania) and the 2005 American Community Survey (available at http://factfinder.census.gov: data set 2005 American Community Survey; data profile for Philadelphia County, Pennsylvania; table of General Demographic Characteristics, 2005).

4. In addition to the specific sources cited in the text, the following readings have helped me develop my understanding of Philadelphia's Chinese and Chinese immigrant community: Anderson 1991; Chacón and Davis 2006; Chun 1996; Laguerre 2000; Logan, Alba, and Stults 2003; Louie and Omatsu 2001; Passel, Capp, and Fix 2004; Rosaldo 1997; Sinn 1998.

5. For a fascinating account of how the attitudes of colonial and nineteenth-century Americans simultaneously expressed and produced notions of China and the Chinese through encounters with Chinese objects, people, and images, see Tchen 1999.

6. According to Jonathan Goldstein, "between 1783 and 1846 Philadelphia may have controlled as much as one-third of United States trade with China, and one-ninth of China's total maritime commerce with the West" (1978: 67).

7. According to Jun Li, "These new ethnic centers could be the suburbs, as Northeast Philadelphia was repeatedly brought up as a place with an increasing population of Asians. . . . They could also be other areas of the city—such as South Philadelphia, which was not only the top alternative neighborhood for Chinatown's business owners, but also frequently brought up as a place for Asian congregation" (2007: 57).

8. See, for example, Auyang 1978. By emphasizing the dispersion of Chinese immigrants, I do not mean to especially tout the Chinese of the nineteenth century as being particularly mobile actors with an ability to move through borders seamlessly. Rather, we must remember that Chinatowns were frequently communities that arose out of limited opportunity, racial violence, and group stigmatization and inability to settle in great numbers elsewhere.

9. Estimates from PCDC and other commentators range from 3,000 to 5,000+ residents in Philadelphia's Chinatown.

10. For a description of PCDC's various projects and accomplishments, see the organization's Web site at http://www.chinatown-pcdc.org/accomplishments_timelines.htm (accessed 18 August 2008).

11. Greg Umbach and Dan Wishnoff (2008) have written a provocative piece in which they suggest that Manhattan Chinatown elites engaged in self-orientalizing promotion efforts in concert with official planners of Chinatown in a series of urban renewal and development projects during 1950–2005.

12. In Auyang's account, Lee Fong's laundry played the role of a community center since it was one of relatively few Chinese immigrant spaces in the city/region. This function was similar to other central businesses in early Chinatowns. See, for example, John Kuo Wei Tchen's description of Wo Kee's store at 34 Mott Street in Manhattan's Chinatown (1999: 236–238).

13. For a more detailed description of what services different Chinese voluntary and community organizations provide in Philadelphia, see Toll and Gillam 1995.

14. Grace Auyang argues that PCDC was itself radicalized by the presence of an even younger generation of Philadelphia activists inspired by the nationwide Asian American movement (1978: 41–43).

15. The following figures are taken from U.S. Census Bureau data for Philadelphia County. In 1990, there were 43,522 persons in the Asian or Pacific Islander category, or 2.7 percent of the total population of 1,585,577 persons. In 2000, there were 67,654 persons in the Asian Alone category, or 4.5 percent of the total population of 1,517,550 persons. In 2005, there were 75,574 persons in the Asian category (including race alone or in combination with one or more other races), or 5.4 percent of the total population of 1,406,415 persons. In 2005, the Chinese population alone totaled 20,539 individuals. Specific data sources:

1990 U.S. Census (available at http://factfinder.census.gov: data set Decennial Census, Census 1990 Summary Tape File 1 (STF 1) 100-Percent Data; table P006, Philadelphia County, Pennsylvania), the 2000 U.S. Census (available at http://factfinder.census.gov: data set Decennial Census, Census 2000 Summary File 1 (SF 1) 100-Percent Data; table QT-P5, Philadelphia County, Pennsylvania), and the 2005 American Community Survey (available at http://factfinder.census.gov: data set 2005 American Community Survey; data profile for Philadelphia County, Pennsylvania; table of General Demographic Characteristics, 2005).

16. Data are taken from the 2000 U.S. Census (available at http://factfinder.census.gov: Fact Sheet for a Race, Ethnic, or Ancestry Group; population group Chinese Alone; Philadelphia County, Pennsylvania; table of Census 2000 Demographic Profile Highlights).

17. From U.S. State Department, "Chinese Human Smuggling: Where Do the Migrants Originate?" Available at http://usinfo.state.gov/eap/east_asia_pacific/chinese_human _smuggling/originate.html (accessed 4 January 2007); alternatively, see http://beijing .usembassy-china.org.cn/human_smuggling.html. See also Liang and Ye (2001).

18. The continual addition of new immigrants to Chinatown communities contributes to the relatively robust economies of these ethnic enclaves as assessed by Min Zhou (1992).

19. See the China Trade Center of Philadelphia Web site: http://www.ctcp.org.

20. From the PCDC Web site: http://www.chinatown-pcdc.org.

21. The increasing importance of understanding processes through transnational frameworks lies at the heart of Saskia Sassen's (2005) argument about immigration policy.

22. Recent work in diaspora studies is at the forefront of this thinking. Seeing im/ migration as a highly complex and contingent (political, economic, and cultural) set of processes allows scholars to explore various sites of literary and expressive culture, political history, and collective memory in a more multivalent, nuanced representation of im/migration. See Gopinath 2005 and Siu 2005 for more.

23. According to a recent *New York Times* article (Pressler 2005), Philadelphia has become an attractive alternative for upwardly mobile, young, and artistic New Yorkers. Extending this thesis that Philadelphia's relative proximity to New York provides an affordable option for aspiring individuals, not just to recent graduates but also to immigrants, Philadelphia is rendered a place once again fully within the orbit of metropolitan New York. Although New York is clearly integral to Philadelphia's development, economy, identity, and culture, I believe that Philadelphia, Philadelphia's Chinatown, and neighborhoods in Philadelphia, in which many Chinese immigrants settle, should be conceived of less as traditional satellite communities related to the core (New York) than as communities enjoying alternative (and alternatively rich) immigrant cultures.

Generally satellite communities arise around urban spaces in which there is overcrowding, congestion, and other factors such as rising rents causing people to move outside the core community into a nearby area. The classic satellites of Manhattan's Chinatown are Flushing in the borough of Queens and Sunset Park in Brooklyn. Philadelphia, however, although exhibiting for Chinese immigrants some of the same characteristics as those satellite communities, including affordability and a perceived higher "quality of life," is quite different. New York's metropolitan area can broadly be said to cover many areas outside of the city including parts of New Jersey, Connecticut, and upstate New York, whereas the city of Philadelphia, although part of the same Northeast Corridor dominated by New York, creates a similar, smaller orbit centered around the city and extending outward to its many diverse working-class, middle-class, and wealthy suburbs in Pennsylvania, New Jersey, and Delaware. In my opinion, one especially crucial difference between the satellite communities of Manhattan's Chinatown within New York City and Philadelphia is that the Chinese immigrant community in Philadelphia, whether in the Northeast or in Chinatown, is small in both relative and absolute terms. Thus the city may offer something that New York City or San Francisco cannot provide—a tight-knit community. In fact, what is startling about Philadelphia's established Chinese community concentrated in Chinatown is the extent to which residents know and know of each other, through participation in associations or through years of living in Chinatown. As teenager Eric Law puts it in his oral history, "[Outsiders] come in [to Chinatown] to eat, but it's just like any other neighborhood in Philadelphia—we just have a lot more restaurants. But underneath that it's people growing up, their daily lives" (Sze 2004: 38).

24. David Parker writes the following about British Chinese identity formation, which is useful to us here, "A conception of identity as composed of fluid and moveable affiliations was a precondition for having multifaceted identifications and multiple commitments" (1998: 104).

References

Anderson, Kay J. 1991. *Vancouver's Chinatown: Racial Discourse in Canada, 1875–1980.* Montreal: McGill-Queen's University Press.

Auyang, Grace. 1978. "Structural and Processual Change in Philadelphia's Chinatown and among Suburban Chinese." PhD diss., Temple University.

Bahadur, Gaiutra. 2005. "Chinese Immigrants Reshape a Neighborhood." *Philadelphia Inquirer,* 8 September, sec. A.

Chacón, Justin Akers, and Mike Davis. 2006. *No One Is Illegal: Fighting Racism and State Violence on the U.S.-Mexico Border.* Chicago: Haymarket Books.

Chun, Allen. 1996. "Fuck Chineseness: On the Ambiguities of Ethnicity as Culture as Identity." *boundary 2* 23 (2): 111–138.

Glick Schiller, Nina, Ayse Caglar, and Thaddeus C. Gulbrandsen. 2006. "Beyond the Ethnic Lens: Locality, Globality, and Born-Again Incorporation." *American Ethnologist* 33 (4).

Goldstein, Jonathan. 1978. *Philadelphia and the China Trade, 1682–1846: Commercial, Cultural, and Attitudinal Effects.* University Park: Penn State University Press.

Gopinath, Gayatri. 2005. *Impossible Desires: Queer Diasporas and South Asian Public Cultures.* Durham, NC: Duke University Press.

Guan, Jian. 2002. "Ethnic Consciousness Arises on Facing Spatial Threats to Philadelphia's Chinatown." In *Urban Ethnic Encounters: The Spatial Consequences,* ed. Aygen Erdentug and Freek Colombijn, 126–141. New York: Routledge.

Historical Society of Pennsylvania Web site: "Philadelphia's Chinatown: An Overview." Available at http://www.hsp.org/default.aspx?id=190 (accessed 18 August 2008).

Kwong, Peter. 1987. *The New Chinatown.* New York: Hill and Wang.

Laguerre, Michel S. 2000. *The Global Ethnopolis: Chinatown, Japantown, and Manilatown in American Society.* New York: St. Martin's Press.

Li, Jun. 2007. "Philadelphia's Chinatown: An Ethnic Enclave Economy in a Changing Landscape." Undergraduate thesis, University of Pennsylvania. *College Undergraduate Research Electronic Journal.* Available at http://repository.upenn.edu/cgi/viewcontent .cgi?article=1094&context=curej (accessed 18 August 2008).

Liang, Zai, and Wenzhen Ye. 2001. "From Fujian to New York: Understanding the New Chinese Immigration." In *Global Human Smuggling: Comparative Perspectives,* ed. David Kyle and Rey Koslowski, 187–215. Baltimore: Johns Hopkins University Press.

Lin, Jan. 1998. *Reconstructing Chinatown: Ethnic Enclave, Global Change.* Minneapolis: University of Minnesota Press.

Logan, J. R., R. D. Alba, and B. J. Stults. 2003. "Enclaves and Entrepreneurs: Assessing the Payoff for Immigrants and Minorities." *International Migration Review* 37 (2): 344–388.

Louie, Steve, and Glenn Omatsu, eds. 2001. *Asian Americans: The Movement and the Moment.* Los Angeles: UCLA Asian American Studies Center Press.

Marcuse, Peter, and Ronald van Kempen, eds. 2000. *Globalizing Cities: A New Spatial Order?* Oxford: Blackwell Publishers.

Moran, Robert. 2006. "For Takeout Operators, Dreams Undaunted by Danger." *Philadelphia Inquirer,* 6 September, sec. A.

Ngai, Mae. 2004. *Impossible Subjects: Illegal Aliens and the Making of Modern America.* Princeton, NJ: Princeton University Press.

Parker, David. 1998. "Emerging British Chinese Identities: Issues and Problems." In *The Last Half Century of Chinese Overseas,* ed. Elizabeth Sinn, 91–114. Hong Kong: Hong Kong University Press.

Passel, Jeffrey S., Randy Capp, and Michael Fix. 2004. "Undocumented Immigrants: Facts and Figures." Urban Institute Immigration Studies Program. Available at http://www.urban.org/UploadedPDF/1000587_undoc_immigrants_facts.pdf (accessed 31 May 2007).

Patusky, Christopher, and Johnny Ceffalio. 2004. "Recent Trends in Immigration to Philadelphia, Pennsylvania: Who Came and Where Do They Live?" Philadelphia: Fels Institute of Government, University of Pennsylvania. Available at https://www.fels.upenn.edu/sites/www.fels.upenn.edu/files/Philadelphia_Immigration_Trends_0.pdf (accessed 17 January 2007).

Peck, Jamie. 2005. "Struggling with the Creative Class." *International Journal of Urban and Regional Research* 29 (4): 740–770.

Pressler, Jessica. 2005. "Philadelphia Story: The Next Borough." *New York Times,* 14 August. Available at http://www.nytimes.com/2005/08/14/fashion/sundaystyles/14PHILLY.html?ex=1281672000&en=c2dde94c3019c7d8&ei=5088&partner=rssnyt&emc=rss (accessed 21 January 2007).

Rosaldo, Renato. 1997. "Cultural Citizenship, Inequality, and Multiculturalism." In *Latino Cultural Citizenship: Claiming Identity, Space, and Rights,* ed. William V. Flores and Rina Benmayor, 27–38. Boston: Beacon Press.

Sassen, Saskia. 2005. "Regulating Immigration in a Global Age: A New Policy Landscape." *Parallax* 11 (1): 35–45.

Shah, Nayan. 2001. *Contagious Divides: Epidemics and Race in San Francisco's Chinatown.* Berkeley: University of California Press.

Sinn, Elizabeth, ed. 1998. *The Last Half Century of Chinese Overseas.* Hong Kong: Hong Kong University Press.

Siu, Lok. 2005. *Memories of a Future Home: Diasporic Citizenship of Chinese in Panama.* Palo Alto, CA: Stanford University Press.

Sze, Lena, ed. 2004. *Chinatown Live(s): Oral Histories from Philadelphia's Chinatown.* Philadelphia: New City Community Press/Asian Arts Initiative.

Tchen, John Kuo Wei. 1999. *New York before Chinatown: Orientalism and the Shaping of American Culture, 1776–1882.* Baltimore: The Johns Hopkins University Press.

———. 2004. "Here the Local Struggles Truly Are Global: Philadelphia's Feisty Chinatown." In *Chinatown Live(s): Oral Histories from Philadelphia's Chinatown,* edited by Lena Sze. Philadelphia: New City Community Press/Asian Arts Initiative.

Toll, Jean Barth, and Mildred S. Gillam, eds. 1995. *Invisible Philadelphia: Community through Voluntary Organizations*. Philadelphia: Atwater Kent Museum.

Umbach, Greg, and Dan Wishnoff. 2008. "Strategic Self-Orientalism: Urban Planning Policies and the Shaping of New York City's Chinatown, 1950–2005." *Journal of Planning History* 7 (3): 214–238.

Waters, Mary, and Tomás Jiménez. 2005. "Assessing Immigrant Assimilation: New Empirical and Theoretical Challenges." *Annual Review of Sociology* 31:105–125.

Zhou, Min. 1992. *Chinatown: The Socioeconomic Potential of an Urban Enclave*. Philadelphia: Temple University Press.

Zhou, Min, and Rebecca Y. Kim. 2006. "The Paradox of Ethnicization and Assimilation: The Development of Ethnic Organizations in the Chinese Immigrant Community in the United States." In *Voluntary Organizations in the Chinese Diaspora*, ed. Kuah-Pearce Khun Eng and Evelyn Hu-DeHart, 231–252. Hong Kong: Hong Kong University Press. Available at http://www.sscnet.ucla.edu/soc/faculty/zhou/pubs/Zhou_Kim_Paradox.pdf.

PART II

The Role of Institutions

Religious, ethnic, and social service institutions played a major role in the experiences of immigrants from the First and Second Great Waves, as well as for those who came after the passage of the Hart-Cellar Act of 1965, opening the door to populations from Global South nations. Such organizations facilitated the adaptation of these groups to their new "host" society, helped them establish communities and ultimately to "become American." While such associations generally assisted immigrant populations in their quest for social mobility in Philadelphia, their effect was somewhat tempered by the time period in which these newcomers arrived in the city and the development of the urban/regional economy at that time. Although the services provided by these organizations were often similar across groups, they also engaged in activities that addressed the specific needs of the population they were serving.

Dating back to the colonial period, the German Society of Pennsylvania (GSP), founded in 1764, was one of the earliest ethnic organizations in the city. Unlike some of the other German and Irish associations that would follow, the GSP was not a social club. Rather, as discussed by Pfleger (Chapter 6), it played a pivotal role in providing language and cultural literacy training and assisting in poverty alleviation for German émigrés for nearly 200 years. Beginning with providing assistance to indentured laborers in the colonial period, to establishing German and English language courses and U.S. naturalization classes for later immigrants, to creating scholarships for German American students and helping families survive the Great Depression, the GSP united Germans across generations, religions, and social classes. Their unity was particularly noted during the two World Wars when the U.S. government's surveillance of this community led them to question their sense of "belonging."

Like the Germans, the Scotch-Irish can also trace their ancestry back to the colonial period in the United States. Prominent Irish institutions, however, were largely created in response to the major migration of Irish Catholics after the potato famines in the early and mid-nineteenth century. As illustrated by Farley and Kilbride (Chapter 7), Irish ethnic-based and fraternal organizations, such as the Ancient Order of Hibernians and the Philadelphia Donegal Association, played major roles in providing educational and employment opportunities for immigrants as well as in maintaining Irish culture in the New World, similar to the activities of the GSP. In the mid-twentieth century, the Irish Center, now called the Commodore Barry Club, was the major organization engaged in celebrating Irish culture and traditions. In many ways, however, the greatest institutional legacy of the Irish in Philadelphia, as well as in many other cities in the United States, is the establishment of Catholic schools. Such schools, which were part of Catholic parishes, were very inclusive communities that provided not only education, but also met migrants' needs for health care and family counseling. These educational institutions, from the elementary level up to and including universities, not only educated the daughters and sons of Irish immigrants, but their primary and secondary schools today continue to address the needs of urban residents, who are increasingly non-Catholic populations of color.

Unlike the immigrants of the First Great Wave, such as the Germans and the Irish, many of whom arrived in Philadelphia during our Industrial Revolution, today's immigrants face an entirely different urban economy. Over the past thirty years, many of the former smokestack industries and their blue-collar occupations (which provided some opportunities for social mobility) have vanished and been replaced by service-sector activities in health care, education, finance, and hospitality. For those without university degrees, most available positions in these fields are concentrated in low-wage services. This is the Greater Philadelphia area to which recent Mexicans have migrated. They have encountered racism, problems in obtaining jobs that pay a living wage, and lack of access to essential services. In the midst of a broader national and to some extent local public opinion that has reflected anti-immigrant views, the daily lives of Mexicans and their children, especially of those without documents, have become exceedingly difficult. In Chapter 8, Atlas explores these issues with particular reference to Mexican immigrants' access to healthcare institutions. How does the structural blockage that Mexicans experience in the Philadelphia area affect their prospects for social mobility and the formation of viable communities?

6

German Immigration to Philadelphia from the Colonial Period through the Twentieth Century

BIRTE PFLEGER

The journey of the *Charming Molly* from Rotterdam to Philadelphia in the fall of 1773 ended catastrophically for the family of Jacob Uleckinger. After a stopover in Portsmouth, England, the *Charming Molly* took ten weeks to cross the Atlantic.[1] Jacob and three of his five children died on route before reaching the New World. His wife succumbed just as the ship arrived in Philadelphia. Jacob's brother-in-law, George Seess, survived but had to be brought to the sick house, where he reported that money his late sister had given to a fellow passenger to exchange for local currency had disappeared. It was not clear whether Jacob and his family had paid their fare or if they had planned to sell their labor to the highest bidder upon arrival to pay for the voyage. Regardless, the two surviving children, Peter, age thirteen and handicapped by a malformed hand, and Andrew, age nine, would have to enter some kind of servitude to earn their keep now that both of their parents were gone. An unnamed weaver offered to pay twelve pounds for Andrew, and Nathaniel Witmore was reportedly "willing to take the eldest lame Boy without paying any thing for him."[2] Negotiating the boys' indentures as well as recovering the missing money and Jacob's chest, which was still aboard the *Charming Molly*, required inquiry and supervision.

Over a century and a half later in 1928, Josef Uhl arrived from Germany in New York on board the steamship *Albert Ballin* and moved to Philadelphia. A year later his wife of seven years, Clara, and their infant daughter followed. Hard hit by the Great Depression, Josef had difficulties finding steady employment and paying the $25 monthly rent for the modest apartment on Westmont Street in West Philadelphia. Most of their working class neighbors, young native-born families and some eastern European immigrants, were also renters. By 1934 the Uhl family had moved to Reese Street in South Philadelphia and Josef worked intermittently as an electrician's assistant, making $18 a week, barely enough to support his family. But life had improved tremendously from just a year earlier when Clara had been hospitalized for over six weeks with a serious yet undiagnosed illness and the family had relied on charity to survive. In July 1934 the Uhls were able to splurge on a one-day excursion to River View Beach in New Jersey. This was the first time they had left the city since their arrival five years earlier. By 1936 Josef's weekly wages increased to $24 a week and with the additional income from weekend work the family managed to obtain a mortgage for the house on Reese Street. Located in a narrow alley the house was probably rather modest. But home ownership ended their worries over increasing rent. With Clara's health restored and enjoying a regular income, the family was, in Clara's words, "happy and content, that we can see the path before us again."[3]

Although separated by 155 years, these two German immigrant families share more than their ethnic origin and their choice of Philadelphia as their home in America. Both families appear in the vast records of the German Society of Pennsylvania (GSP), the oldest German immigrant aid organization in the western hemisphere. Sixty-five well-to-do German-speakers founded the GSP at Philadelphia's Cherry Street Lutheran Schoolhouse in 1764 to assist newly arriving ethnic brethren. The GSP quickly became an advocate for newly arrived German-speakers. With the establishment of its library in 1817, the creation of an employment agency in 1842, and the hiring of a full-time paid agent who distributed cash and vouchers for transportation, food and lodging as well as referrals for medical and legal advice, the GSP turned into a cultural broker and virtual clearinghouse for Germans in Philadelphia. In many ways the GSP served as an example of immigrant aid organizations in Philadelphia and the nation as a whole. The GSP differed from other, older ethnic societies in Philadelphia in that its primary purpose lay not in fostering "social intercourse and mutual attachments" among their countrymen, as for example the Welsh Society of Pennsylvania did. To ensure that the quarterly meeting would not turn into gregarious occasions for drinking and conversation among men, the original GSP rules prohibited the meetings from being held in taverns. The GSP was not a social club.

The GSP played a leading role in uniting the regionally, religiously, and economically diverse group of German-speakers who arrived in Philadelphia from the colonial period through the twentieth century. The organization's importance declined briefly in the 1830s when most members were second or third generation Germans and when few German-speakers immigrated to the United States. The GSP was revived by the second large wave of German-speakers arriving in Philadelphia in the mid-nineteenth century. By the early twentieth century the organization's importance weakened again as a uniting force for German-speakers in the city. This time the decline was due to the emergence of many competing German ethnic organizations in the Philadelphia area and to the general growth of public amusements that vied for people's leisure time and spending money. All German organizations in the United States experienced severe hardships during World War I. The GSP survived the war and grew again, but was never again able to regain its status as *the* German organization in Philadelphia.

This essay offers an overview of German immigration to Philadelphia from the colonial period to the twentieth century and highlights the importance of the German Society of Pennsylvania in creating a sense of community among German-speakers as well as the organization's role in shaping public perception of Germans in America. The GSP played a crucial role in transforming newly arriving German-speakers into loyal British subjects before the American Revolution and into good citizens of the nation after 1776 (Pennsylvania's constitution of 1776 defined citizenship in terms of support for the Revolution, and GSP leadership included a number of famous and ardent supporters of independence). During the eighteenth century the GSP's legal and financial assistance to many German redemptioners (indentured servants) facilitated these newcomers' experience with the Anglo legal system and language.[4] Later the GSP had a threefold mission: assimilating newly arrived Germans through education, assisting immigrants in finding employment and providing charity for those unable to work, and lastly, preserving and celebrating German language culture among its members. In many ways the history of German immigration to Philadelphia parallels the story of the GSP: whenever German immigration increased, the organization's role as community center grew; when the number of German-speaking newcomers declined, the GSP's influenced weakened.

The essay draws on GSP meeting minutes, account books, and library records to offer a glimpse into the lives of countless ordinary German immigrants who arrived in Philadelphia until the twentieth century. Together with German language newspapers, census records, and other sources, this essay argues that colonial German immigration to Philadelphia served as a model for immigrants from other ethnic groups who came later. German-speakers were among the first non-Anglo immigrants to arrive in British North America in large numbers, relying on increasingly sophisticated transatlantic trade networks. Push and pull factors, which historians have identified for other ethnic groups who arrived in the nineteenth century, brought about the first wave of mass immigration of German-speakers to Philadelphia in the mid-eighteenth century. Pushed by war and religious and political turmoil as well as high taxes and military conscription, tens of thousands of German-speakers, especially from the Palatine region, sought new homes in the American colonies. Pull factors that attracted Germans to Pennsylvania included the colony's famed religious tolerance, the availability of farmland, and high wages for skilled craftsmen. Colonial German immigration was also characterized by the first chain migration in which not only whole families migrated but large segments of entire villages or regions in Germany settled in the Philadelphia area.

Pennsylvanians of German descent have a long history in the Mid-Atlantic region and particularly in Philadelphia. Starting with the arrival in 1683 of the first thirteen Krefelder families led by Daniel Francis Pastorius to found Germantown, over 100,000 German-speakers came to British North America before the American Revolution.[5] Germans made up 10 percent of all colonists, constituting the largest group of immigrants to the colonies in this period, second only to Africans. The steadily growing influx reached its peak between 1737 and 1754 when more than 55,000 German-speakers arrived in Philadelphia.[6] During the same period a mere 16,000 people emigrated from England to the city.[7] By 1790 German-speakers made up 33 percent of Pennsylvania's population, while 35 percent were of English descent. Eleven percent were Scotch-Irish; 9 percent were Scottish. The remainder were of various other European ethnic backgrounds, some Native Americans and African Americans.[8] These striking demographic realities left visible markers in colonial Philadelphia, ranging from German language street signs to German-style farming techniques to architectural styles.

German immigration dwindled to a trickle between 1790 and 1830.[9] The renewed influx of Germans after 1840 and the tremendous increase after 1846, when between 100,000 and 200,000 Germans entered the United States annually, revived German immigrant culture.[10] While only a fraction of the estimated 5.5 million Germans who came to the United States between 1816 and the beginning of WWI in 1914 chose to live in Philadelphia, they nevertheless shaped especially the northeastern section of the city. German-speakers were most visible in Philadelphia during the second half of the nineteenth century when well over six hundred German mutual aid institutions, singing societies, and *Vereine* (German for "association," "club," or "society") vied for members and organized parades and festivals which attracted large numbers of Philadelphians of all ethnic backgrounds. The impact of German influx into Philadelphia lasted until the 1960s when parts of northeastern Philadelphia were almost entirely populated by German-speakers whose butchers and bakeries as well as other businesses dominated the landscape.

German immigration in the twentieth century was not only influenced by U.S. immigration restrictions but more importantly by the two world wars that found Germany and the United States on opposing fronts. Although the anti-German hysteria of the late 1910s was not repeated during the Second World

War, hundreds of Philadelphia Germans were interned, and many more were questioned by federal authorities. While the decade after 1945 witnessed another large influx of German new arrivals, German immigration to the Philadelphia area and the United States in general essentially ceased in the 1960s. This resulted in a dramatic disappearance of German shops and restaurants and the end of Philadelphia's last German-language newspaper as well as a steep decline in the number of German *Vereine*. A revival of interest in the German language and culture over the past decade has been largely limited to Philadelphia's academic circles and small groups of younger German-speakers. While the GSP has survived the turbulences of the twentieth century, its public appeal is marginal in a time and place where German immigration has virtually come to an end.

The continued existence of the GSP as a cultural and social institution is dependent on its ability to continue to cast its net wider for new members and its willingness to broaden its cultural and social programs. These challenges are not too different from the struggles encountered by the Irish Center, as discussed in Chapter 7 by Noel Farley and Philip Kilbride.

Eighteenth-Century German Immigration

The large number of German-speaking newcomers in the eighteenth century resulted in the first attempts to legislate immigration and to regulate assimilation, giving rise to xenophobia and eventually the emergence of uneasy cultural pluralism. Benjamin Franklin's critical commentary depicting German-speakers as permanent and undesirable outsiders was just the most famous expression of widespread fears that these newcomers would change the character of the city of brotherly love:

> [W]hy should the Palatine Boors be suffered to swarm into our Settlements, and by herding together establish their Language and Manners to the Exclusion of ours? Why should Pennsylvania, founded by the English, become a Colony of *Aliens,* who will shortly be so numerous as to Germanize us instead of our Anglifying them, and will never adopt our Language or Customs, any more than they can acquire our complexion.[11]

Although Franklin and Pennsylvania lawmakers in general were not proponents of restrictive laws, legislative means to address immigration to Pennsylvania were nearly as old as immigration to the colony itself. Periodic discussions to limit immigration into Pennsylvania offer some evidence of hostility and disdain toward Germans that Franklin had publicly expressed. At the same time, these discussions were never enacted into law. Quite the opposite was true—when Parliament passed the naturalization act of 1740, the Pennsylvania assembly allowed non-Quaker aliens to become naturalized by affirming allegiance instead of swearing an oath, thus aiding many Anabaptists, Moravians, and other Germans to claim the rights of Englishmen. Like Quakers, these religious groups objected to swearing oaths, and this provision extended to them a right of religious conscience that Quakers already enjoyed in Pennsylvania, without which these Germans would have had a religious obstacle to being naturalized. An examination of the *Votes and Proceedings of the Pennsylvania Assembly* shows that instead of restricting the rights of non-Anglo Europeans in Pennsylvania, colonial lawmakers responded to the growing influence of German-speakers in particular by considering and eventually passing laws to protect immigrants.

The GSP, founded in response to the growing number of poorer Germans arriving as indentured servants who had often endured terrible conditions on board ships, was instrumental in getting the first protective legislation passed in 1765, which specified the minimum space allotted for each passenger at three feet and nine inches (two feet and nine inches for steerage). The new law also covered other rules and regulations that would be strictly overseen by GSP officers who dedicated much time and financial resources to this task. The passing of this bill marked the first legislative victory for GSP members. In the eleven years prior to the American Revolution more than 8,000 Germans arriving in Philadelphia would benefit from this new supervision.[12] As GSP records indicate, however, the Society was never at a loss for cases and people that needed their attention.

Providing money, food, lodging, medical care, and legal counsel to "poor, sick and otherwise needy" newly arrived Germans was among the most important activities of the GSP in the eighteenth and nineteenth centuries. The Society's officers carefully evaluated each application for help, noting when the petitioner had arrived in Pennsylvania. Generally, anyone who had been in the New World for more than a year was no longer considered a newcomer and was thus ineligible for GSP assistance.

While the Society acted quickly to help those in immediate need, there was also a limit to how long the officers were willing to lend their support. On September 13, 1770, for example, they agreed to house and feed the passengers of a ship owned by James Pemberton that had just arrived from London. At their next meeting nine days later, they resolved that "it must be made known to these people that they should settle in this land so that they are no longer a burden" on the GSP.[13] The Society wanted to protect newly arriving Germans from abuse but did not intend to serve as a permanent almshouse. GSP members were convinced that hardworking, pious Germans would succeed in Pennsylvania. After all, they themselves had been able to attain considerable wealth and prestige in their new homeland.[14]

German immigrants who suffered misfortunes during the transatlantic voyage or immediately upon arrival were usually eligible for GSP assistance. Simply being of German birth or descent and in need of help did not necessarily make a person eligible for GSP support. This became quite clear to John Andrews, who asked the GSP to assist a German-born doctor in Yorktown. The doctor, Andrews had reported, suffered from "a great and universal Tremor of his nerves" and was unable to work. In describing the doctor's worthiness, Andrews highlighted his intellectual accomplishments, which had included an appearance at the Philosophical Society. But despite Andrews's lengthy explanation of his needy friend's medical condition, the GSP denied the request for financial assistance. Henry Kammerer, the Society's vice president, noted that "according to our fundamental Articles, the German Newcomers only come under [our] Notice" and thus his hands were tied.[15]

When it came to offering help in legal matters, the GSP was more generous in its definition of who qualified as a "newcomer."[16] Judging by the large number of cases it took on, the Society clearly had a particular interest in immigrants who were unable to pay for their passage. Any German-born redemptioner who had been wronged, physically abused, or persuaded to sign an indenture that was not in accordance with customary practice in Pennsylvania could apply to the GSP for help and be assured that it would do everything in its power to secure him or her redress. Depending on circumstances, the Society might try to resolve such conflicts informally or would pursue action in the courts. This assistance in legal matters facilitated German newcomers' assimilation into Anglo society and its common law culture.

Some ship captains tried to raise the price of passage from Europe upon arrival in Pennsylvania. Women whose husbands had died during the transatlantic voyage were especially vulnerable to this form of abuse. The GSP must have seemed like a godsend to the widow Mary Christina Martin, who arrived in Philadelphia with her six children on the *Minerva* in the fall of 1772. Martin reported to the Society's officers that her husband had agreed to pay "Nine Guineas a Freight" and had paid "40 Guilders Hollandish" up front. Martin's husband died en route. The captain subsequently sold the services of three of her sons for thirty pounds Pennsylvania currency each, and Martin's brother-in-law paid ten pounds Pennsylvania currency to cover the passage of the two youngest children.[17] Despite having received 100 pounds (Pennsylvania), the captain also sold the forty-six-year-old widow's service for a term of five years for twenty-two pounds (Pennsylvania). Although it is now difficult to calculate a meaningful conversion rate between Dutch guilders, the British pound, and the Pennsylvania pound, the GSP's officers recognized that Mary Christina Martin had been overcharged. They sent an officer to the ship's owners "to desire to know of them whether the Facts alleged by the said Woman are true, And whether the Gentlemen would be pleased to favour us with a Copy of the Amount of that Woman as it stands in their Books."[18] While the dispute was eventually resolved in Martin's favor, it illustrated the importance of the GSP: Mary Christina Martin, a poor widow only newly arrived in Philadelphia, sought the GSP's help, indicating that the Society had become very well known within the city.

German redemptioners suffering violence at the hands of their masters could turn to the GSP for assistance. In August 1785, for example, Johannes Öttinger complained that his master Friedrich Kistelman (or Kesselmann) had "treated him barbarically [by] hitting him with the thick end of a whip, smashing a shovel on his head resulting in blood flowing from his ears" and had also threatened further physical abuse. Öttinger suffered from "lameness in the hip," but he did not know if that was the result of the beatings he had suffered or from having fallen. Three GSP officers formed a committee to ask Chief Justice McKean what might be done. The committee was also authorized to hire an attorney if necessary. A fourth GSP board member was in charge of taking care of the injured man and advancing money to cover whatever costs became necessary.[19] Three weeks after receiving Öttinger's petition, the board approved an agreement whereby Öttinger would be transferred from a local inn to a hospital at his master's expense. He was to be discharged from the hospital only after GSP president Christoph Wengman had been notified.[20] The minutes of a meeting three weeks later indicate that the board expected that Öttinger would soon be released from the hospital; if his master did not voluntarily pay his hospital fees, the board would take the master to court. Since there is no further mention of the case in the Society's records, Kistelman (Kesselmann) most likely paid.[21]

Öttinger's experience was not typical, nor was it unique. Barbara Ham arrived in Philadelphia in the fall of 1792 and entered into an indenture with Nathan Eyre. Seven months into her term of service, Ham sought refuge with her local alderman on the grounds that her master had treated her "inhumanly." The alderman took Ham to a physician and may well have helped her when she filed charges against Eyre. The court, ruling in Ham's favor, imposed fines that came to nearly four pounds Pennsylvania currency and ordered him to post ten pounds security for his good behavior. But it also ordered Ham to return to Eyre's service. It was at this point, in March 1793, that the GSP stepped in and resolved to help get Ham released from her indenture.[22] The GSP's board decided to extend Ham a loan of five pounds so that she could pay off her obligation to her master and get free of him.[23] Eyre, however, apparently wanted much more than five pounds; only after he was paid twenty pounds for Ham's indenture was she finally free of her violent master.[24]

Indentured servitude was on the decline by the 1790s. As Aaron Fogleman has shown, the proportion of European immigrants who sold their labor to the highest bidder upon arrival in the New World decreased dramatically after 1776. In the years 1700–1775, more than 40 percent of the estimated 255,000 European immigrants to British North America came as indentured servants or redemptioners. The combination of wartime social disruptions and the revolutionary ideology of freedom and equality helped bring about a rapid change: between 1776 and 1809, only 8 percent of voluntary immigrants from Europe, 18,300 out of 253,900, entered into indentured servitude. The percentage was cut in half again between 1810 and 1819, after which the practice of indentured servitude had essentially ended for white Europeans.[25] In Philadelphia, 255 indentures were registered in 1819. The number fell to thirty-five the next year, and the total for the years 1821–1831 was thirty-four.[26] Although the demise of unfree white labor in Pennsylvania can be attributed in part to economic change, historians also emphasize that the erosion of established hierarchies after the Independence made the idea of white men in bondage "anomalous and anachronistic."[27]

Many German-speakers were not enthusiastic about the American Revolution, at least initially. While Americans of German descent today often point out proudly that the first printed version of the Declaration of Independence came from the press of German printer Henry Miller on July 5, 1776, scholars have shown that German-speakers in Pennsylvania were rather reluctant supporters of the Revolution. Pennsylvania Germans understood liberty primarily as negative freedom, namely freedom from oppression. Many Germans were not familiar with English conceptions of liberty and did not see British imperial policies as reason to revolt. To Lutherans in particular, "the possibility that liberty and property could justify rebellion against legitimate authority seemed utterly preposterous."[28] Philadelphia's Germans did not on the whole play prominent parts as either Patriots or Loyalists. Some did, of course, take sides. The Pietist Germantown printer Christopher Sower (Saur), for instance, was arrested as a Loyalist and his press confiscated.

The American Revolution also affected the GSP as an organization. While the meeting minutes for the years leading up to 1776 do not mention the political turmoil at all, the war and the British occupation of Philadelphia disrupted the Society's meetings, charitable activities, and plans to construct its own building. A substantial number of GSP leaders actively supported the Revolution in various capacities ranging from baking bread for the Continental Army to soldiering. The most famous GSP supporter of the American cause was Frederick Muhlenberg who later became the first Speaker of the House of Representatives and served as GSP president from 1790 to 1797.

When the war ended the GSP resumed its charitable activities and joined German-speakers in Philadelphia in heralding the new nation as their own. Since Pennsylvania's constitution had bestowed citizenship on any free person who supported the Revolution, most Germans and the GSP grasped the opportunity and considered their consent to the new republic as the end to ethnic discrimination.

A German-language newspaper suggested a definition of citizenship that solved the problem of being German in the American nation. The *Philadelphische*

Correspondenz noted that "Americans are a people (*Volk*) which originated from many nations." What bound settlers together was the fact that they were better off here than in Europe and that they loved "their country, their people and their government." Prejudice and hatred based on ethnic and national differences, nurtured only by monarchical forms of government, were not acceptable for a "true American" since his "worthy and upright neighbor" might be a descendant from another nation. Being American was also inextricably tied to a representative government in which the majority ruled. Accordingly, a "true American" must also be "a true Republican. He must believe that the Republican form of government is the best. He must not grumble against the will of the majority."[29] Violent rebellion against the government was perpetrated by ignorant or malicious people who either never read or who were so blinded by their own ideas that they simply used profanities and rage instead of valid argument.

Another installment in the definition of a "true American" predicted that as long as the United States offered untilled soil and high wages, industrious people from Europe would continue to come, much to the advantage of American citizens. A "true American" would welcome strangers with hospitality and friendship since those who stayed and became citizens "increased the strength of the Republic . . . and the wealth of the land."[30] In other words, American citizenship was a matter of ideology, attitude, and economic prosperity. The United States could not, however, use ethnicity as a criterion for exclusion.

This pluralistic conception of the nation and of American citizenship stood in marked contrast to the Anglo-American elite's assessment of ethnic diversity. Thus Oliver Wolcott, the Connecticut-born and Yale-educated Secretary of the Treasury in Washington's and Adams' administrations, remarked that "Pennsylvania is the most villainous compound of heterogeneous matter conceivable. Though there are many good men and good things, yet as a state it is bad in the extreme."[31]

Pennsylvanians, on the other hand, began to celebrate their heterogeneity, proudly proclaiming that ethnic origin no longer mattered.

> What is it to me, when I am about to vote, whether the great grandmother of the candidate came from Germany or from Ireland—from the banks of the Rhine, or the Lake of Calarney—whether he and his ancestors have dined oftenest on cabbage or potatoes? . . . I don't think one of those vegetables is calculated to make an honest man or a rogue than the other.[32]

By 1792, this York newspaper portrayed non-Anglo Americans of European descent as acceptable political candidates whose ethnic differences could literally be boiled down to preferences for certain foods. German immigration to Philadelphia during the nineteenth century benefited from this emerging cultural pluralism. At the same time, second and third generation Germans and the GSP had to confront the decline of their language and other cultural traditions. Only the influx of new German immigrants, especially those who fled Germany after its failed revolution in 1848, allowed Philadelphia's German community to preserve its cultural and linguistic heritage.

Language, Culture, and German Immigration in the Nineteenth Century

As part of its ongoing effort to secure its standing as the voice of Germans in the Mid-Atlantic region, in 1781 the GSP began efforts to preserve the German language in Pennsylvania by sponsoring deserving male German students at the University of Pennsylvania. The university had earlier created a professorship for instruction in the classical languages "through the medium of the German tongue."[33] The first two holders of the position—Johann Christoph Kunze and Justus Heinrich Christian Helmuth—were both Lutheran clergymen and GSP members. They were also the driving forces behind the GSP's decision to sponsor students at the university. Lamenting that "only crafts and commerce find fertile grounds" in the United States, Kunze argued "we must begin to turn the poor into scholars."[34]

Ultimately the GSP's attempt to preserve the German language by creating an educated German-American elite failed.[35] By 1810, the GSP was sponsoring only one or two students at a time, and some years it had none. Stipend recipients in the early nineteenth century were exclusively students of theology, which suggests the GSP and leading German ministers were eager to ensure the supply of German-speaking clergymen. The GSP stopped sponsoring students after 1833. At that point, the so-called German department at the university was essentially defunct, and the GSP itself was experiencing a decline in membership as a result of the fall in German immigration. Likewise, nothing came of plans to conduct an annual essay contest on the theme "how best to preserve and expand the German language in Pennsylvania."[36]

The GSP's faltering support of German-language education in the early nineteenth century perhaps reflected its members' increasing preference for English over German. In 1818, the Society made English its official language.[37] That decision was partially reversed in 1842, when members voted that "all the records and proceedings of this society shall be kept and conducted in the english [sic] Language excepting the minutes of the society which may be kept in the english [sic] and German Languages."[38] The GSP thereupon recorded its minutes in German for the next three years; both English and German were used between 1845 and 1848, and after that English predominated. It was not until the 1860s, after recent immigrants had come to play a leading role in the GSP, that German was again used consistently for record keeping.[39]

Ironically, as the GSP was wavering in its attachment to the German language and in its efforts to foster a German-American elite, it finally decided to take action on a long-standing pledge to create a German library in 1817.[40] Two years later the library committee, "understanding it to be the wish of a large number of the members of the Society that a part of the Library should consist of works written in the English language," began to purchase books in English as well.[41] Before long, there were more titles in English than German: in 1826, the library contained 853 English and 798 German books.[42] By 1842, the collection had grown to 2,355 books in German and 3,369 in English.[43] The GSP would continue to add more books in English than in German to its collection—and its members would continue to borrow English works more often than German—until recently arrived immigrants came to dominate the GSP in the 1860s.[44] Works in German then began to account for an ever-larger share of the more than 10,000 loans the GSP's library recorded annually in the decades after the Civil War.[45] The decline in the number of English books GSP members borrowed was especially marked after 1894, when the Free Library of Philadelphia opened its doors to the general public. Given the expansion of the city's public library system at the end of the nineteenth century, which broadened access to works in English, the change in members' use of the GSP library should not be seen as a sign of increased ethnic identification, but merely as a shift in where they went to read books in the two languages.[46]

The recent immigrants who began to assume leadership positions in the GSP in the 1850s and 1860s were exasperated by the Society's lack of "Germanness," and they largely failed to recognize the distinctly German-American culture that had emerged in Philadelphia by then.[47] The newcomers reinstated German as the GSP's official language and tried to revive the organization as a promoter of German culture.[48] GSP leaders deemed only highbrow German literature and music as worthy. The centenary of Schiller's birth in 1859, for instance, provided an occasion to celebrate a German literature hero. The so-called Pennsylvania Dutch traditions that had developed by the mid-nineteenth century were, by contrast, generally looked upon with disdain by the Forty-Eighters, the largely middle class Germans who had fled Germany after the failed democratic revolution. They saw the dialect of the Pennsylvania Dutch and their adherence to traditional ways of life and farming as perhaps quaint, but refused to recognize them as authentically "German." The two groups by and large stayed far apart. When the Pennsylvania Dutch created their own organization, the Pennsylvania German Society, in 1891, they limited membership to those of Pennsylvania German ancestry and denied admission to anyone born in Germany.[49] While the society shared a few members with the GSP, most notably Pennsylvania Governor Samuel Pennypacker, the two groups remained distinct from and politely distant toward one another.

The nineteenth century saw a steady increase in the number of Germans immigrating to the United States. Although only a small percentage arrived in Philadelphia, and fewer still chose to settle in the city, the demand for the GSP's services grew, leading it to hire a full-time paid agent. Besides administering poor relief, the agent was in charge of providing information and advice to newly arrived immigrants, ensuring that the ill received medical care, and referring those with legal problems to the Society's attorneys. The influx of German immigrants continued to grow in the decades following the Civil War. Anywhere from twenty to seventy-one steam ships brought as many as 10,000 immigrants to Philadelphia every year, and between 17 to 50 percent of them were German-speakers. After the Red Star Line steamship company began to offer service between Antwerp and Philadelphia in 1873, German immigrant traffic increased so much that the GSP appointed an immigration committee. Members of the committee spent countless hours every month manning a desk at Philadelphia's port of entry for immigrants and, handing out free or discounted train tickets, as well as vouchers for lodging, food and clothing. In this capacity the GSP served as a travelers' aid organization and officers turned into much-needed interpreters of the English language for newly arriving Germans.

In addition to the professional agent, the most interesting innovation in the GSP's efforts to aid immigrants was the employment agency it created in response to the mid-century revival of German immigration. Ever since the disappearance of indentured servitude, newly arrived immigrants often required assistance in finding ways to make a living. The number of job referrals the GSP's employment agency made fluctuated widely over the years, ranging from 1,302 in 1847 to 117 in 1855. On average, it placed about 450 immigrants in jobs each year through the end of the century.[50]

As the number of German immigrants increased, so, too, did the number of those seeking the GSP's assistance. The records of the Society's poor relief efforts make clear that the dream of America as the land of opportunity often turned into a nightmare.[51] New and recent immigrants were vulnerable to shifts in Philadelphia's economy. During the economic crisis of 1873, for example, 1,380 men and women turned to the GSP for help; the year before, the figure had been 838.[52] In the absence of government welfare programs, private charitable initiatives like the GSP's were the only source of aid to America's poor. Many immigrants must have found it embarrassing to ask the GSP's help and to undergo its scrutiny.

The growing number of newly arrived German-speakers in Philadelphia also stood behind a program that contributed substantially to a change in the character of the GSP. More than ever before the GSP aimed to ensure that German immigrants would be held in high esteem by Americans. A major part of this effort involved teaching immigrants the English language. In 1867, the

Society began operating a night school that offered courses in English. Thousands of immigrants, mostly but not exclusively men, took advantage of the school. This renewed involvement in education was notably different from the GSP's earlier support of a few talented students at the University of Pennsylvania. Instead of trying to foster a homegrown German-American elite, the Society now concentrated on uplifting the huddled German masses. Its school committee noted with satisfaction that the students would "give honor to the German name" as they overcame not only their lack of English language skills but their more general educational deficiencies as well.[53]

Although the GSP's English classes usually had a few adult students who had been living in Pennsylvania for a decade or longer, newcomers who had been in the country less than a year typically accounted for as much as half of each class. In 1871, for example, 192 students enrolled in the GSP's classes, of whom ninety-one had been in the United States for less than one year, fifty-one for less than two years, and thirty-one for less than three years.[54] That same year, the city of Philadelphia began to fund the GSP's school, which allowed the Society to begin offering German language courses. The enrollment in the German courses was low, however, and the program did not survive long. Demand for instruction in English remained strong, and total enrollment reached over one thousand students annually. Most were skilled workmen ranging in age from thirteen to thirty.[55] Women generally made up less than 10 percent of the students.[56] As German immigration declined in the late nineteenth century, enrollment decreased accordingly. In 1915, the GSP converted its English language courses into naturalization classes for German immigrants, which illustrates that the GSP recognized that English language skills alone were not enough to turn Germans into American citizens.[57]

The revival of German immigration in the mid- and late nineteenth century transformed not only the GSP's activities but also Philadelphia's German-American communities. The new arrivals founded a variety of social clubs and associations that reinforced German regional identities. Some of these *Vereine* can be compared with the *farein* and *landsmanshaftn* founded by eastern European Jewish immigrants around the same time, as discussed by Rakhmiel Peltz in Chapter 2. The GSP was in competition with at least half a dozen other associations engaged in highlighting German contributions to American history, organizing social events, and offering charity to poor Germans. The *Cannstatter Volksverein,* for example, was named after the southwestern German city of Cannstatt and founded in 1873 with the express purpose of providing traditional German entertainment. For most of its history, it could boast a larger membership than the GSP.[58] A few prominent German-speakers, such as John File and Pennsylvania Governor Samuel Pennypacker, were members of both the GSP and the Cannstatter Volksverein.[59] Part of the Cannstatters' appeal, no doubt, stemmed from their three-day festival every September. All Philadelphians were invited to have a good time eating, drinking, and dancing in the city's parks during the festival. But Cannstatter members were concerned with more than just having a good time. Within seven years of its founding, the organization was contributing more money to charity annually than the GSP.[60] Concentrating on socializing, singing, dancing, and, of course, beer drinking, a number of Vereine surpassed the GSP in membership. It is ironic that just when their German fatherland was being united as a nation-state, Germans abroad deliberately cultivated the regional and religious distinctions that had divided them in the Old World.

Contemporary observers divided Germans in America into "soul Germans" and "stomach Germans." "Soul Germans" asserted the superiority of German *Kultur* and the German language and were often attracted to organizations such as the GSP; German cultural influence, they insisted, could help make America the greatest civilization on earth. "Stomach Germans," on the other hand, limited their ethnic identification to partaking of certain culinary delights, engaging in social activities, and perhaps reading a German-language newspaper.[61] Members of this latter group were more likely to join institutions such as the Cannstatter Volksverein.

While this contemporary assessment may be rather simplistic, it does highlight the diversity among ethnic Germans in America in the late nineteenth and early twentieth centuries. As many as one-third of German-speakers in America were not active in any sort of German institution or organization.[62] The principal institutions that attracted German Americans were churches (above all Lutheran, Reformed, and Catholic) and Vereine (associations). Particularly in the Midwest, *Kirchenvereine*—church-affiliated charitable associations—were sometimes established even before parishes or congregations were organized.[63] Vereine that were not church-affiliated attracted secularly oriented, mainly urban Germans who were "possessed by an almost missionary eagerness to propagate and spread their particular *Weltanschauung*," which rested in large measure on the belief that Germans were culturally superior to native-born Yankees.[64]

In 1892, the GSP was just one of 642 German organizations, including nearly three hundred mutual-aid institutions and over two dozen singing associations, in the Philadelphia area.[65] The city was home to approximately 160,000 first and second generation Germans, who made up 15 percent of the population.[66] The GSP attracted middle class Germans who aspired to be the elite of their ethnic group. Although the GSP was officially unaffiliated with any religious denomination, its members were more often than not Protestants. A number of Lutheran and Reformed ministers held leadership positions within the GSP over the years; Catholic priests, by contrast, appear not to have been active in the Society.[67] Even if German Americans were not directly affected by the confessional tensions aroused by Bismarck's anti-Catholic *Kulturkampf,* Catholic Germans in the United States tended to avoid German organizations that were not church affiliated.

The GSP aimed to be a neutral ground where the different German communities within Philadelphia could come together to express, create, defend, and celebrate their *Deutschtum*. But due to the GSP's middle class character and values, working class Germans rarely set foot within its hall except to apply for assistance or to take advantage of its evening English courses. Working class Germans appear to have looked beyond ethnicity and were bound to their counterparts of other ethnic backgrounds by their shared class interests. During Philadelphia's general strike in March 1910, for example, thousands of German workers joined their Irish and Anglo-American colleagues on the picket line.[68] For middle class Germans, ethnic identity generally remained more important than class consciousness in the decades before World War I. Ironically, the outbreak of war in Europe did more than any of the efforts of organizations like the GSP or the National German-American Alliance to unite Germans in America across class lines.[69]

German associations of all varieties increasingly had to compete with other forms of entertainment and leisure activity in the decades around 1900. Recent scholarship on German-American institutions dates the beginning of their decline to the 1890s rather than the First World War, as had long been assumed.[70] With the proliferation of inexpensive mass entertainment—ranging from sporting events to vaudeville and amusement parks—and the emergence of a new consumer culture, Americans had increasingly less time and money for participation in social or charitable groups. This shift in habits was reflected in the membership figures of organizations like the GSP. In 1911, for example, the GSP lamented a 30 percent decline in its membership since 1902.[71]

Another factor in the decline of ethnic associations was a change in the conception of "race." By 1900, the once-derided Irish could at last claim to be "white," for example, but Eastern and Southern Europeans, who were entering the United States in large numbers, could not. In Philadelphia the percentage of Italians, Russians, and Poles in the city's total foreign-born population rose from 16 percent to 33 percent between 1900 and 1910.[72] Adding to the multi-cultural mix was the increasing migration of African Americans from America's South to the Mid-Atlantic region; in the first two decades of the twentieth century, more than 50,000 blacks settled in Philadelphia.[73]

World War I

The struggle for membership and survival among German ethnic organizations became exponentially more difficult when war broke out in Europe in 1914. While the war united Americans of German descent initially in their effort to assist their brethren abroad, these activities and the United States' entry into the war brought suspicion and the charge of disloyalty to German-speakers and their organizations. In response to the war, the GSP and the National German-American Alliance, an organization founded in 1899 to combat the decline of the Vereinswesen, embarked upon an ambitious effort to "preserve the prestige of the German name . . . against malice and ignorance." Both organizations, closely linked in membership, leadership, and goals, urged German Americans to organize local aid societies to collect donations for wounded German soldiers and the widows and children of soldiers who died, thereby demonstrating to the American public at large that "blood is thicker than water."[74] "[E]very German *Verein*, every German association, German societies and churches of all denominations everywhere" were exhorted to collect donations on behalf of the National Relief Fund Committee for the Wounded and Destitute in Germany and Austria-Hungary.[75] The appeal was extremely successful: within weeks, well over $100,000 had been collected.[76]

The fundraising and relief efforts undertaken by the GSP and other German-American organizations were seen by many Anglo-Americans as evidence of "extravagant partisanship for Germany," even though they "were not necessarily representative of the masses of German Americans."[77] In a message to Congress in December 1915, President Woodrow Wilson insinuated that German Americans' support of Germany was disloyal to the United States. There were, Wilson said, "citizens born under a different flag and admitted and welcomed to the privileges of citizenship and opportunities of this country who have infused into the veins of this country the poison of disloyalty."[78] In the presidential election of 1916 German Americans voted for the first time as a recognizable ethnic block in an effort to defeat Wilson.[79] Still, in February 1917, Wilson broke off diplomatic relations with Germany in response to Germany's resumption of unrestricted submarine warfare. On April 2, at the president's request, Congress declared war on Germany.

The National German-American Alliance, meeting in the GSP's hall, decided in February 1917 that it would hand over donations collected for the survivors of German war dead to the American Red Cross in the event of war between Germany and the United States. By then it had become clear, however, that German Americans were widely seen as a special class, as a threatening postcard the GSP received demonstrates. The postcard had been sent by the Patriotic Sons of America, an anti-Catholic and antiradical organization.[80]

If the sympathy of your Society is with the United States, place the stars and stripes outside of your building, as you did of the German colors. This is a friendly tip. The Society of the Patriotic Sons of America is only one short square from your building on 6th and Spring Garden Streets. So get the flag out at once. If you do not do so and anything happens you know you have been warned.[81]

The head of the GSP House Committee reported that the Society had followed this menacing advice.

Following Congress's declaration of war, GSP president Mayer issued a statement that was carried in several Philadelphia newspapers. Mayer renounced German Americans' identity as hyphenated Americans, insisting that "we do not want to be put in a special class and called German-Americans. . . . We protest most emphatically such a term in a crisis like this," he declared. "We are Americans, nothing but Americans, loyal through and through." Americans of German descent, he emphasized, "will do their duty."[82] Rudolph Blankenburg, who had earlier served both as mayor of Philadelphia and as president of the GSP, went a step further and exhorted "all citizens of German birth or descent to declare their unflinching allegiance to the country of their adoption and to show by word and deed that they are true and unfaltering Americans."[83]

Before long, everything associated with Germany came under attack in the U.S. In the fall of 1917, for example, the Philadelphia orchestra banned German music from its repertoire.[84] Sauerkraut became liberty cabbage, and the public burning of German books was considered a demonstration of American patriotism in some communities.[85] German Americans in Philadelphia and nationwide became the targets of suspicion and wild accusations.[86] Some were victims of anti-German violence; one German immigrant in Illinois was hanged by an angry mob.[87]

In August 1917, President Wilson signed an executive order requiring the registration of all aliens over the age of fourteen. They were also barred from transportation hubs and other strategic locations considered vital for the war effort. Some commercial properties belonging to aliens were confiscated, and thousands of German aliens were interned.[88] The German-language press came under close government scrutiny, and several socialist German-language newspapers were charged with criminal offenses under the Espionage Act of 1917.[89]

The GSP endeavored both to aid Germans caught up in the anti-German hysteria and to demonstrate its patriotism. It supplied those in need with job referrals or relief aid, and it did what it could to provide German aliens with legal advice.[90] Although the GSP opted not to call attention to itself—deciding, for example, to cancel its annual German Day celebration in 1917 and foregoing the commemoration of the 400th anniversary of Martin Luther's posting of his Ninety-Five Theses—it also tried to demonstrate its patriotism. It invested $1,000 in Liberty Bonds; paying 4 percent interest, the bonds were not the best investment, but the purchase was intended to send a signal.[91] In similar spirit, the GSP's board suspended its usual Monday evening meetings when the Wilson administration introduced "heatless Mondays" to conserve coal. Noting that it "wished to avoid all possible conflicts with the authorities," the board decided in early 1918 to turn down almost all requests from other organizations to use its hall. More importantly, the GSP became an intermediary

between government officials and Philadelphia's noncitizen Germans by assisting police officials in cities and postmasters in rural areas to register noncitizen
Germans as enemy aliens.[92]

The GSP's efforts to adapt to the new situation did not prevent it from coming under suspicion. In April 1918, the Philadelphia *Evening Bulletin* reported
that the GSP's library held "many books carrying the most bitter form of German propaganda." When the board met to discuss the allegations, a member of
the library committee dismissed the attack, explaining

> these pro-German books . . . undoubtedly came to us merely through
> ordinary commercial channels. They were not specifically ordered. . . .
> If there is the slightest objection to the circulation of some of the books
> named in the report, I am sure the objection would be honored. The
> members of this society are loyal to America, . . . We have added during
> the year a large number of books that might be styled intensely anti-
> German. There has not been the slightest thought of propaganda, and
> there will not be, in connection with the library.

The board decided to limit library access to GSP members only. Previously, nonmembers had been allowed to use library materials during business hours.[93]

Shortly before the GSP's run-in with the *Evening Bulletin*, the National German-American Alliance disbanded. The decision came in response to a U.S.
Senate investigation launched by Senator William King of Utah. The Congres-
sional hearings determined the Alliance had "fostered racial separatism and
foreign allegiance among German-Americans" but had done nothing illegal.[94]
Although cleared of actual wrongdoing, the Alliance could not withstand the
animosity bred by anti-German hysteria. On April 11, 1918, the leaders of the
Alliance voted to dissolve the organization.

The GSP inadvertently became entangled in the investigation of the National
German-American Alliance. Some of the Alliance's records were stored at the
GSP and a reporter told federal investigators that the Alliance's files contained
"a list of German sympathizers within draft age . . . and statistics of value to the
German cause." A subsequent search of the premises turned up documents
belonging to Alliance in the furnace room. Some allegedly connected the Alliance to Philadelphia liquor interests and Sinn Fein, the radical Irish party.[95]
Within hours of the search, GSP leaders made their way to the federal investigators' office on Ninth and Market Streets, just a few blocks from the GSP's building and "admitted being favorable to Germany before the entrance of the United
States into the war."[96] This interview appears to have brought the government's
investigation of the GSP to a close.

The investigations of the Alliance and the GSP testify to the prevailing climate of suspicion. The neighborhood around the GSP's building was swarming

with federal agents searching for German spies. One agent, for instance, responded to reports about a German man who lived "alone, with a helmet, some army clothes and various documents" at 728 Green Street, literally around the corner from the GSP. The man's neighbors had reported that he came and went at all hours and carried a cane that some thought might be a weapon. When the agent found that no one was officially registered as residing at the address and learned that the house had recently been offered, unsuccessfully, at a sheriff's sale, he decided to turn the matter over to the U.S. Attorney.[97] Although it is not clear who the mysterious man living in the abandoned house might have been, he was certainly not a dangerous German spy.

Anyone of German descent could easily come under suspicion. Long-time GSP board member Frank Sima was accused by his neighbors of celebrating German victories "with beer, wine and German patriotic songs."[98] Similarly, Harry J. Smith, the Pennsylvania Dutch manager of the Allentown Branch of the State Employment Bureau, came under official scrutiny after he sang a German song during a social gathering at the posh Adelphia Hotel. The agent investigating Smith brought the case to a close only after receiving ample evidence of Smith's patriotism—evidence that ranged from his father's military service during the Civil War to his own purchase of $800 worth of Liberty Bonds. Even then, the agent cautioned Smith against "engaging in singing any more songs of a German character."[99]

No accusation, no matter how unlikely or trivial, went unchecked. Investigators were sent out to the Hillside Cemetery just outside of Philadelphia in response to a report that it housed "a life statue of a German soldier carrying a German flag." The offending statue turned out to be a monument honoring the veterans of Germany's war against France in 1870. The investigators learned that the memorial had been erected at the turn of the century by the German Veterans Association and decided that it could stay where it was, since most members of the association "were good loyal citizens with sons with the colors overseas."[100]

The best way for both individuals and organizations to combat allegations of disloyalty was to buy war bonds. Failure or refusal to do so raised serious suspicion. As the U.S. Attorney in Philadelphia explained,

> Of course it is a man's right to refuse to subscribe to either Liberty bonds or the War Chest, and there is no legal obligation to subscribe to either. Of course, a refusal to subscribe to the Loan, coupled with disloyal remarks, might be evidence to be considered with other matters in determining a man's loyalty.[101]

As this outlook was tantamount to official policy, it is not surprising that the GSP purchased $3,500 worth of Liberty and Victory Bonds, even though they did not yield as much as its other investments.[102] GSP vice president Franz

Ehrlich proudly wrote to Philadelphia U.S. Attorney Francis Fisher Kane in the spring of 1918 to report how much money Americans of German descent had contributed to the annual war bond drive. Perhaps tired of the pointless investigations and futile hunts for German spies, Kane took the time to reply and praised a "splendid showing" that "ought to make German Americans of this city proud of what they have done."[103]

The war and anti-German sentiment took a toll on German-American associations. Some suspended their activities for the duration of the war.[104] Struggling to survive, some changed their names or merged with others. Many were forced by circumstances to close their doors for good. The GSP was among those that tried to ride out the wave of anti-German hysteria by publicizing their patriotic efforts.

The GSP continued to tread a careful path following the armistice of November 1918, tentatively trying to reestablish itself as a visible German presence in Philadelphia while still underscoring its American patriotism. In June 1919, it began to discuss the possibility of organizing relief for Germany; it decided three months later that it would work with the Religious Society of Friends rather than establish a German aid organization under its own leadership.[105]

The GSP was careful in the public image it presented in the early postwar period. At Philadelphia's Fourth of July parade in 1919, the representatives of all non-German ethnic organizations marched in traditional outfits and carried national symbols; the GSP contingent, by contrast, wore everyday street clothing and waved American flags. Later that year, the all-male social Verein *Schlaraffia* asked to use the GSP's building for its weekly meetings; the board turned down the request on the grounds that Schlaraffia opened its meetings by singing the German national anthem.[106] In 1920, the GSP's school committee decided to resume free classes to prepare German-speaking aliens for naturalization.[107] The GSP's efforts to Americanize newly arrived German immigrants stand as evidence of its goal to be 100 percent American. They also reflect the self-perception of the GSP's leaders; as "old stock" Americans, they saw themselves as fully qualified instructors in what it meant to be American.[108]

By 1920, the GSP's board apparently thought hostility toward all things German had abated sufficiently for it to back away from one of its more demonstrative wartime displays of patriotism. It decided to trade some of its Liberty Bonds in order to invest in mortgages that paid one and a half percentage points more than the government securities. Clearly, the GSP no longer considered it necessary to hold war bonds as proof of its patriotism.[109]

Having survived wartime anti-German hysteria, the GSP found itself confronted with a different sort of challenge in the postwar period. The neighborhood around its headquarters at Spring Garden and Marshall Streets had changed considerably since the GSP had moved there in 1888. German immigrants and German Americans were moving to northern sections of the city.

Large numbers of Eastern European and Russian immigrants, above all Russian Jews, had moved into the neighborhood, establishing businesses and religious institutions of their own. Whereas about half the residences and businesses in the area had been German-owned at the turn of the century, only about a quarter were still in German hands by the mid-1920s. Some German organizations and institutions, recognizing the demographic shift early on, had already relocated to other parts of the city.[110]

It was not only the GSP's immediate neighborhood that was changing. The number of German-born Philadelphians was declining and would fall from approximately 40,000 in 1920 to fewer than 28,000 by the end of the decade.[111] The interwar years would also see an increasing divide between new and recent arrivals from Germany and long-settled German Americans. During the 1920s, some 400,000 German immigrants entered the United States, and they felt largely alienated from the majority of Germans who had arrived before 1895.[112] More recent immigrants had little interest in preserving the *Deutschtum* and did not like what they saw as an outdated version of German culture cultivated in German ethnic organizations. Those organizations, many already having struggled for survival during the war, were dealt a serious blow by the enactment of the Eighteenth Amendment in January 1920. Prohibition not only put an end to the beer-fueled sociability that was central to many Vereine, but also put a core constituency of the Vereins' life out of work, namely brewery owners and workers.[113] Many of the German Americans who had identified themselves as hyphenated Americans before 1914 ceased to do so after the war, opting instead to call themselves "Americans of German descent" or simply "Americans."[114] Steadily fewer German Americans could speak German or were interested in German culture. The generation of German Americans who came of age between the two world wars was characterized, in the words of Frederick Luebke, by "a sort of cultural amnesia."[115]

The Great Depression, WWII, and Beyond

While organizations such as the GSP did not effectively rekindle interest in Germanness, its role as a charity organization increased once again as the so-called roaring twenties gave way to the Great Depression. Philadelphia's public and private resources to assist those in need were stretched thin in the wake of the crash of 1929. By the end of the year, more than 10 percent of the city's wage earners were without jobs. The unemployment rate rose to 15 percent during the first five months of 1930, and by the end of that year it was clear the Depression had come to Philadelphia.[116] Over a nineteen-month period stretching from late 1930 through the summer of 1932, Philadelphia's wealthy elite contributed $14 million toward alleviating the hardship many of their fellow citizens were suffering, but the funds were quickly exhausted. Tens of thousands of destitute people relied on family, friends, and neighbors to survive. Local merchants and landlords extended credit even when it became evident the debts would likely never be paid. In 1933 unemployment skyrocketed when 11.5 percent white, 16.2 percent black, and 19.2 percent foreign-born Philadelphians were out of work. In other words, Josef and Clara Uhl together with their daughter, with whom this essay began, were simply among the fortunate few who escaped the misery of the Great Depression with the assistance of the GSP as well as Josef's fortuitous employment as an electrician. The decade of the 1930s also marked the steep decline of the GSP's ability to assist those in need. Plagued by questionable political sympathies, declining membership, increased government scrutiny during the Second World War, and financial problems, the Society barely survived the 1940s.

The GSP did not turn into a quasi-Nazi organization during the 1930s. However, some leading American Nazi sympathizers were influential Society members and might have contributed to the decline in membership. While the GSP tried its best to demonstrate its American patriotism during the war by once again purchasing war bonds, the organization was put on the defensive when the U.S. government investigated it. With a declining and aging membership, financial problems, and a divide between leadership and rank and file members, the GSP emerged from World War II with less resolve and support than after World War I. Only the influx of German refugees, a fortuitous monetary bequest, and the challenge of sending aid to Germany made it possible for the Society to survive this crisis.

After the war Philadelphia became once again an important point of entry for many German immigrants. Of the nearly 600,000 German refugees entering the United States between 1946 and the late 1950s, thousands came to the Delaware Valley.[117] Although many refugees established their own organizations, a sizable number of the most active and dedicated GSP members today are former refugees and their children.[118] These expatriate families had endured terrible hardships and had little interest in dealing with German atrocities or questions of culpability. Instead they focused on their own ordeals, which helped to shape the Society for the next sixty years.[119] Some Americans of German descent may have been put off from joining the organization because of its failure to address Germany's and its own recent past. Perhaps this partially explains low membership numbers through the early 1970s. Yet the GSP's troubles extended far beyond the membership within its walls: postwar economic and social changes radically altered the landscape and politics of Philadelphia and other urban centers, transforming the neighborhood in which the GSP was located, and therefore the GSP itself. With the building of a federal housing project directly adjacent to the GSP building in 1969, the organization and the German community that it had created, preserved, and housed, crumbled until it nearly disappeared. While Jewish immigrants still see South Philadelphia as the physical place that has served their community, German Americans can no longer identify a distinctly German neighborhood today. This may be another reason why the GSP building on Spring Garden Street represents the German heritage of many Americans of German descent in the Philadelphia area, explaining further why the building is so dear to many.

In many ways, the history of the German Society of Pennsylvania and German immigration to the city are tied to the history of Philadelphia. In the colonial period, Philadelphia was the nation's largest city. It remained preeminent as the country's industrial center until the early twentieth century, and during this entire time period Philadelphia attracted a large share of German newcomers. When the city's fortunes declined steadily from the 1940s through the 1970s, the brief wave of German refugees arriving during the postwar era did not often choose Philadelphia as their new home but instead moved to the surrounding suburbs. For the past two decades the city has experienced an uneven renaissance, attracting especially Latin American immigrants, raising concerns that are reminiscent of the apprehensions voiced about German newcomers in the colonial period. While the days of German immigration to Philadelphia are over, if we look and listen carefully, the lessons of their experiences may help us to understand the city's present and future immigrants.

Notes

This essay incorporates material from Birte Pfleger, *Ethnicity Matters: A History of the German Society of Pennsylvania,* published by the German Historical Institute, Washington, DC, in 2006 (available at http://webdoc.sub.gwdg.de/ebook/mon/2008/ppn%20561484260 .pdf). I thank the German Historical Institute for permission to make use of the material here.

1. Information about the ship from Marianne Wokeck, *Trade in Strangers; The Beginnings of Mass Migration to North America* (University Park: The Pennsylvania State University Press, 1999), Appendix "German Immigrant Voyages, 1683–1775," 248.

2. German Society of Pennsylvania Minutes, November 1, 1773 (hereafter GSP Minutes), German American Collection at GSP.

3. Information based on *New York Passenger Lists, 1820–1957* (online database maintained by Ancestry.com; available at http://search.ancestry.com/iexec/?htx=List&dbid=7488 &offerid=0%3a7858%3a0); U.S. Census 1930; and letters from Clara Uhl to Bertha Schweizer dated May 17, 1933, July 17, 1934, August 17, 1934, December 13, 1935, and December 18, 1936, Women's Auxiliary Records, uncatalogued, German Society of Pennsylvania.

4. Eighteenth-century German immigration transformed the indentured servitude system that most immigrants had relied on since the earliest English New World settlements, providing a much needed labor force for the Mid-Atlantic region. Indentured servants, generally from the British Isles, contracted themselves for a fixed number of years before embarking upon the transatlantic voyage and were sold off to the highest bidder upon arrival. On the other hand, redemptioners, typically of German and Swiss birth, agreed with the captain on a specific sum for their freight to the New World but did not learn how long they would have to serve a master who agreed to pay for their passage until they were auc-

tioned off. Thus German-speakers often felt that they had little control over the length of their bondage and other terms of their servitude. The arrangement seemed to leave many Germans at the mercy of their masters, even more so than people with indentures. While most early German-speakers arrived in Pennsylvania through their own means, those who came after the 1740s increasingly relied on the redemption system to pay for their voyages.

5. I use the terms "German-speakers" and "Germans" interchangeably to avoid repetition. Before a German nation state existed in 1871, German-speakers could include people from a variety of areas that did not become part of the nation. For an excellent recent study on the formation of German ethnic identity among eighteenth-century immigrants to New York, see Philip Otterness, *Becoming German: The 1709 Palatine Migration to New York* (Ithaca, NY: Cornell University Press, 2004).

6. Marianne Wokeck's study has the most accurate numbers based on ship lists. Aaron Fogleman's estimates are slightly lower. Aaron Fogleman, *Hopeful Journey: German Immigration, Settlement, and Political Culture in Colonial America* (Philadelphia: University of Pennsylvania Press, 1996), 2. A contemporary German almanac attributed Germans' preference for Pennsylvania to the great religious and civil freedoms in the colony, the quality of the soil, and the climate, all of which were best suited for German agricultural practices. See *Neu-Eingerichteter Americanische Geschichts-Calendar, Auf das Jahr 1750,* German American Collection at GSP.

7. See Fogleman, *Hopeful Journeys,* 2.

8. See also Sally Schwartz, *"A Mixed Multitude": The Struggle for Toleration in Colonial Pennsylvania* (New York: New York University Press, 1987). And see Forrest McDonald and Ellen Shapiro McDonald, "Ethnic Origins of the American People," *William and Mary Quarterly* (3rd series), vol. 37 (April 1980), 179–199; and Thomas Purvis, "The European Ancestry of the United States Population," *William and Mary Quarterly* (3rd series), vol. 41 (January 1984), 102–119.

9. A. G. Roeber estimates that about 32,000 German-speakers arrived in the United States between 1790 and 1820. About 5,753 Germans came during the 1820s. "But from 1830 to 1840, this number jumped to over 124,000 arrivals." A. G. Roeber, "Readers and Writers of German in the Early United States," in *A History of the Book in America,* vol. 2, *An Extensive Republic: Print, Culture, and Society in the New Nation, 1790–1840,* ed. Robert Gross and Mary Kelley (Chapel Hill: University of North Carolina Press, 2010, forthcoming).

10. Based on U.S. Immigration and Naturalization Service data, 1991. Between 1816 and 1914 an estimated 5.5 million Germans immigrated to the United States, making them "the largest immigrant group." Klaus J. Bade, "From Emigration to Immigration: The German Experience in the Nineteenth and Twentieth Century," in *Migration Past, Migration Future,* ed. Klaus J. Bade and Myron Weiner (Providence, RI: Berghahn Books, 1997), 5. For a brief overview of nineteenth-century German immigration to the United States, see also Kevin R. Ostoyich, "The Transatlantic Soul: German Catholic Emigration during the Nineteenth-Century" (PhD diss., Harvard University, 2006), 2–5.

11. Benjamin Franklin, "Observations Concerning the Increase of Mankind, Peopling of Countries, etc.," in *The Papers of Benjamin Franklin,* vol. IV, ed. Leonard Labaree (New Haven: Yale University Press, 1961), 234.

12. Number according to Wokeck, table 2, p. 45.

13. GSP Minutes, September 13, 1770, and September 22, 1770.

14. These paragraphs are part of chapter 1 of my dissertation, "Between Subject and Citizen: German-Speakers in Eighteenth-Century Pennsylvania" (PhD diss., University of California Irvine, 2003).

15. GSP Minutes, December 18, 1788. See also original rules of GSP stating, "No one should receive money from our treasury but those poor German people who arrived here this last fall from Germany and those who will arrive here in similar fashion in the future." Oswald Seidensticker and Max Heinrici, *Geschichte der Deutschen Gesellschaft von Pennsylvanien, 1764–1917* (Philadelphia: Neudruck von Graf & Breuninger, 1917), 141.

16. Wokeck (p. 148) even argues that the GSP "was chartered and organized primarily as a legal aid society."

17. Guineas were often used by European immigrants upon arrival in the New World. Pennsylvania pounds were gradually phased out after 1796 until the more available U.S. dollar designated American currency. In 1800, $5 were equal to 20 guineas. Five pounds Pennsylvania currency were equal to $70 in 1804. However, no complete currency conversion table exists for all three currencies for this time period. For a discussion of currency issues in the late eighteenth century, see Farley Grubb, "The Constitutional Creation of a Common Currency in the U.S. 1748–1811: Monetary Stabilization Versus Merchant Rent Seeking," Working Paper Series, Department of Economics, Alfred Lerner College of Business and Economics, University of Delaware, Working Paper No. 2004-07.

18. GSP Minutes, October 24, 1772.

19. GSP Minutes, August 10, 1785.

20. GSP Minutes, September 2, 1785.

21. GSP Minutes, September 21, 1785.

22. GSP Minutes, March 23, 1793.

23. GSP Minutes, March 28, 1793.

24. GSP Minutes, March 28, 1793. Statement in minutes book dated March 29, 1793.

25. Aaron Fogelman, "From Slaves, Convicts and Servants to Free Passengers: The Transformation of Immigration in the Era of the American Revolution," *Journal of American History* (June 1998): 43–76; table 1, p. 44.

26. Numbers according to Seidensticker, 93. Thanks in large part to the GSP's lobbying, indentures in Philadelphia had to be registered by bilingual officials starting in 1785.

27. Gordon Wood, *The Radicalism of the American Revolution* (New York: Alfred Knopf, 1992), 184.

28. A. G. Roeber, *Palatines, Liberty and Property: German Lutherans in Colonial British North America* (Baltimore: Johns Hopkins University Press, 1993), 284.

29. *Neue Philadelphische Correspondenz,* January 1, 1799, Historical Society of Pennsylvania.

30. Ibid., January 15, 1799.

31. Oliver Wolcott to Frederick Wolcott, April 2, 1799, in *Memoirs of the Administrations of Washington and John Adams,* vol. II, ed. George Gibbs (New York: Burt Franklin, 1971 reprint), 230–231.

32. *Pennsylvania Herald and York Advertiser,* October 3, 1792 (York, PA: Edies and Willcocks).

33. As quoted by Seidensticker, 187.

34. Kunze as quoted in Seidensticker, 188.

35. The decline of the German language became the subject of a legal dispute between two factions of St. Michael's and Zion Lutheran Church in 1816. Friederike Baer, *The Trial of Frederick Eberle: Language Patriotism, and Citizenship in Philadelphia's German Community, 1790–1830* (New York: New York University Press, 2008).

36. GSP Minutes, November 1788.

37. GSP Minutes, March 25, 1818.

38. GSP Minutes, March 26, 1842.

39. Starting January 30, 1860, Society minutes were written in German. This lasted for over a century when in 1958, without any minuted discussion, the recording secretary kept the minutes in English. The board had already debated the issue of language four years earlier in 1954, but decided not to switch to English at that time (GSP Minutes, May 3, 1954). When GSP secretary Max Pohl resigned for health reasons, his successor, a Mr. Schlegel, recorded the minutes in English without discussion (GSP Minutes, October 27, 1958).

40. GSP Minutes, March 25, 1817.

41. GSP Minutes, March 25, 1819.

42. Numbers based on Seidensticker, 204.

43. GSP Minutes, December 26, 1842. In 1849, the Society began to make library subscriptions available to nonmembers for $5 annually. The records indicate that usually few people took advantage of this offer. Only in the late 1890s did the number of library subscribers reach into the sixties, with a high of eighty-one in 1899. After that the librarians no longer recorded the actual number of individuals using the library but instead counted the number of visits made by members, library subscribers, and by "strangers"—nonmembers who were allowed to read library material but could not check it out. This allowed less affluent people to read current newspapers, magazines, and other reading material imported from Germany.

44. In December 1862, the library committee reported that the Society owned 5,812 German and 5,574 English books. That year 210 readers, of whom 196 were GSP members, borrowed 2,341 German and 1,791 English books (GSP Minutes, December 26, 1862). By 1875, the gap between English and German books had grown when the Society owned 8,929 German but only 6,935 English books. Numbers based on Seidensticker, 205.

45. A detailed study of the library is necessary. For an analysis of German Americans' nineteenth-century reading habits, see Roeber, "Readers and Writers of German in the Early United States." For a history of the GSP library and Oswald Seidensticker's role in it, see Frank Trommler, "The Library of the German Society of Pennsylvania and Its Consolidation under Oswald Seidensticker," in *Atlantic Understandings: Essays in Honor of Hermann Wellenreuther,* ed. Claudia Schnurmann and Hartmut Lehmann (Münster: LitVerlag, forthcoming). Also see Frank Trommler, "Die Bibliothek der German Society of Pennsylvania; Volksbücherei und deutschamerikanisches Archiv," *Imprimatur: Ein Jahrbuch für Bücherfreunde,* Neue Folge XIX, 2005: 85–102.

46. In 1895, GSP readers borrowed 3,943 English language books. Three years later that number was down to 1489. Charles Hexamer, chair of the library committee in 1896, reported that "the purchase of English works, especially English novels, has been limited this year; also because the creation of free public libraries in all parts of the city has made the need for such books superfluous" (GSP Annual Report 1896).

47. For the best scholarship on Pennsylvania German culture and folklore, see Don Yoder, *Discovering American Folklife: Essays on Folk Culture and the Pennsylvania Dutch* (Mechanicsburg, PA: Stackpole Books, 2001).

48. For a general history of German Forty-Eighters as immigrants to the United States, see Bruce Levine, *The Spirit of 1848: German Immigrants, Labor Conflict and the Coming of the Civil War* (Urbana: University of Illinois Press, 1992).

49. The Pennsylvania German Society changed its membership rules in 1966. There were individuals who were active in both the GSP and the Pennsylvania German Society, notably Governor Samuel Pennypacker (1843–1916; term of office, 1903–1907).

50. Numbers based on Seidensticker, 164. The number of job referrals in the twentieth century was much lower.

51. Zimmermann highlights this aspect of the thirteen volumes of the GSP's records of its employment agency. Manfred Zimmermann, "Quellen zur deutschen Einwanderungsgeschichte in der Bibliothek der German Society of Pennsylvania," *Yearbook of German-American Studies* 34 (1999): 133–140.

52. Seidensticker, 140.

53. GSP Minutes, September 21, 1871.

54. GSP Minutes, September 21, 1871.

55. GSP Minutes, March 19, 1874.

56. For example, 402 male and only thirty-nine female students made up the spring classes in 1881, while of the 733 students only fifty-two were female during the fall classes that year (GSP Minutes, December 15, 1881).

57. GSP Annual Report 1915.

58. The Canstatter Volksverein rarely had fewer than one thousand members and often had more. See Russell A. Kazal, *Becoming Old Stock: The Paradox of German-American Identity* (Princeton, NJ: Princeton University Press, 2004), 99–100.

59. This fact can be seen from the last names on the late nineteenth-century membership list.

60. In 1881, the GSP spent $3,381.65 on its charity work, which included funding the evening school, while the Cannstatter Volksverein gave $4,250. The following year the GSP included the agent's salary in its charitable contribution expenses, which totaled $3,954.83, while the Cannstatter Volksverein spent $4,763. By 1885 and 1886, the Verein spent over $2,000 more on charity work than the GSP. For GSP numbers see *Jahresberichte der Deutschen Gesellschaft,* 1881–1896, German American Collection at GSP. For the Cannstatter Volksfestverein numbers, see Cannstatter Volksfest-Verein Annual Reports for 1886. GAC Pamphlet, AE 1265.2 v. 1886.

61. Frederick C. Luebke, *Bonds of Loyalty: German-Americans and World War I* (DeKalb: Northern Illinois University Press, 1974), 27–28.

62. Historian Frederick Luebke estimates that a third of Germans in America were not affiliated with or were perhaps even overtly hostile to both ethnic churches and secular societies (Luebke, *Bonds of Loyalty,* 44–45).

63. This was true for some Kirchenvereine in Milwaukee, for example. See Anke Ortlepp *"Auf denn, Ihr Schwestern!" Deutschamerikanische Frauenvereine in Milwaukee, Wisconsin, 1844–1914* (Wiesbaden: Frank Steiner Verlag, 2004), 49–54.

64. Frederick C. Luebke, *Germans in the New World: Essays in the History of Immigration* (Urbana: University of Illinois Press, 1990), 15.

65. Kazal, 31.

66. Kazal, 19. The U.S. Census of 1890 counted 74,974 Philadelphia residents who were born in Germany. Kathleen Neils Conzen, "Germans," in *Harvard Encyclopedia of American Ethnic Groups,* ed. Stephan Thernstrom (Cambridge, MA: Harvard University Press, 1980), 413, table 4.

67. Joseph Bernt, GSP agent from 1893 to 1916, was the rare exception: not only was he Catholic, he also served as editor for the Catholic newspaper *Nord Amerika* for twenty-five years.

68. See Kazal, 146.

69. Within days of the start of the war, German newspapers, Vereine, and churches condemned "the English-American press" for favoring the Allied side.

70. Kazal, especially pages 79–94. See also James M. Bergquist, "German Communities in American Cities: An Interpretation of the Nineteenth-Century Experience," *Journal of American Ethnic History* 4 (Fall 1984): 9–30. German women's organizations did not follow this trend of declining membership as explained in Pfleger, *Ethnicity Matters*, Chap. 3.

71. GSP Annual Report 1911.

72. Lloyd M. Abernethy, "Progressivism, 1905–1919," in *Philadelphia: A 300-Year History*, ed. Russell F. Weigley, Nicholas B. Wainwright, and Edwin Wolf 2nd (New York: W. W. Norton, 1982), 527.

73. Pulled by economic opportunities and pushed by increasing racial violence and agricultural catastrophes such as the boll weevil infestation of the cotton crop, more than 50,000 blacks moved to Philadelphia from 1900 to 1920 (Kazal, 214).

74. Charles Hexamer press release, August 3, 1914, quoted in Georg von Bosse, *Dr. C. J. Hexamer: Sein Leben und Wirken* (Philadelphia: Graf & Breuninger, 1922), 58–59.

75. Von Bosse, 59–61.

76. By the end of 1915, calls for supporting the German Empire by the Alliance, together with other German-American organizations, had resulted in more than $10 million worth of war loans to Germany. See La Vern J. Rippley, *The German-Americans* (Lanham, MD: University Press of America, 1984), 182.

77. Luebke, *Germans in the New World*, 34.

78. December 7, 1915, Protokollbuch der Vereinigten Sänger von Philadelphia [Minutes of the United Singers of Philadelphia], German American Collection at GSP.

79. Luebke, *Bonds of Loyalty*, 190–192.

80. The PSA had been founded in the late nineteenth century in Pennsylvania and became known for its antiradicalism and anti-Catholicism. Nativism and racism were added to their cause after World War I. See Kazal, 237.

81. GSP Minutes, March 26, 1917.

82. *Evening Bulletin*, April 3, 1917.

83. Rudolph Blankenburg, quoted in Lucretia L. Blankenburg, *The Blankenburgs of Philadelphia* (Philadelphia: The John C. Winston Company, 1929), 87–88.

84. Luebke, *Bonds of Loyalty*, 249.

85. Luebke, *Bonds of Loyalty*, 249; Kazal, 176.

86. For a discussion of how the anti-German hysteria affected German Americans in Philadelphia and beyond, see Kazal, 171–190.

87. Luebke, *Bonds of Loyalty*, 3–24.

88. Ibid., 255–256.

89. Among them was Philadelphia's left-leaning *Tageblatt*, which had its second class mailing privilege revoked and its editor brought to court. Although the GSP did not usually champion the socialist cause, members regarded the editor as an innocent victim who had been attacked essentially only for the Germanness of his newspaper.

90. Examples include the case of Heinrich Neese, who was interned in New Orleans (GSP Minutes, June 25, 1917); the case of the widow Schrader and her five children; and the case of Paul Winter from Sicklerville, NJ, who had emigrated to the United States under a false name (GSP Minutes, December 27, 1917).

91. See the article in *New York Staatszeitung*, September 27, 1917, which criticized the GSP for letting the day pass without acknowledgment. For the decision to cancel a planned Martin Luther celebration and to buy the war bond, see GSP Minutes for October 29, 1917.

92. See GSP Minutes for January 29, 1918, and February 25, 1918. Eventually 6,481 German aliens were registered in Philadelphia (Kazal, 181).

93. The newspaper report appeared in the *Evening Bulletin*, April 29, 1918. For the GSP board discussion of the report, see GSP Minutes for April 29, 1918.

94. Phyllis Keller, *States of Belonging: German-American Intellectuals and the First World War* (Cambridge, MA: Harvard University Press, 1979), 158.

95. Historians' examinations of the federal investigation of the Alliance cast doubt upon many of the allegations. Most would agree that the Alliance did have close ties to liquor interests nationwide and was involved in the opposition to Prohibition, as were many other German organizations. Yet there is no evidence the Alliance had any connection to Sinn Fein. The alleged list of names of Germans eligible for the draft was probably a list that the Alliance did compile. However, the list was supposed to demonstrate the patriotic and numeric strength of German Americans for the American military rather than assist imperial Germany.

96. Report made by W. F. McDevitt, Philadelphia, June 10, 1918, Precedent Case Files, 1911–1943, Records of the United States Attorney for the Eastern District of Pennsylvania, Records of U.S. Attorneys and Marshalls, Record Group 118, box 39, file 3432 Restricted, National Archive, Philadelphia (NAP).

97. W. S. Carman, Philadelphia, June 25, 1918, Record Group 118, box 39, file 3432 Restricted, NAP.

98. This anecdote was recorded by GSP member and historian Max Heinrici. See Max Heinrici, "Die ereignisreichen zwanzig Jahre, 1915–1935 der Geschichte der Deutschen Gesellschaft von Pennsylvanien," unpublished manuscript, page 6, GAC, uncatalogued.

99. R. L. Hagele, Conshohocken, PA, May 31, 1918, Record Group 118, box 39, file 3432 Restricted, NAP.

100. W. S. Carman, Philadelphia, October 31, 1918, Record Group 118, box 39, file 3432 Restricted, NAP.

101. U.S. Attorney to Mr. William Clark, October 1, 1918, Record Group 118, box 38, folder 6, NAP.

102. GSP Annual Report 1919.

103. Ehrlich to Kane, May 21, 1918, and Kane to Ehrlich, May 23, 1918, Record Group 118, box 38, folder 6, NAP.

104. The Pennsylvania German Society, for example, founded in 1891 as an amateur historical society dedicated to writing the history of the Pennsylvania Dutch and keeping its folklore alive, suspended its annual meetings between 1916 and 1920. See Homer Tope Rosenberger, *The Pennsylvania Germans, 1891–1965* (Lancaster: The Pennsylvania German Society, 1966).

105. See GSP Minutes for June 30, 1919, and September 29, 1919.

106. Schlaraffia was originally founded in Prague in 1859 as an all-male social club that made fun of the aristocracy. The Philadelphia chapter was organized in the 1890s and finally had its *Burg* at the GSP from the early 1960s until 2002. For the GSP board meeting discussion about Schlaraffia, see GSP Minutes for October 27, 1919.

107. GSP Minutes, February 23, 1920.

108. For a discussion of the Americanization movement, see Edward George Hartmann, *The Movement to Americanize the Immigrant* (New York: Columbia University Press, 1948).

109. GSP Minutes, May 31, 1920.

110. St. Paul's Independent Lutheran Church decided to move to Olney after more than fifty years at its Northern Liberties location, for example (Kazal, 217).

111. Kazal, 198.

112. Luebke, *Bonds of Loyalty,* 69.

113. For a more detailed discussion of the effects of Prohibition on German brewers in Philadelphia, see Kazal, 202–204.

114. Even George Beichl, GSP President from 1974–1993, whose newsletters are full of almost militant Germanness, did not consider himself German American during the 1920s and 1930s. See Kazal, 234.

115. Luebke, *Bonds of Loyalty,* 329.

116. Margaret B. Tinkom, "Depression and War, 1929–1946," in *Philadelphia,* ed. Weigley et al., 609.

117. One study estimates that 888,303 Germans emigrated to the United States between 1946 and 1970. Most arrived between 1946 and 1957. Between 1957 and 1965 an average 22,000–32,000 came each year. After that German immigration steadily declined to an average of 10,000 per year by 1970. See Wolfgang J. Helbich, *Alle Menschen sind dort gleich* (Düsseldorf: Schwann, 1988), 152. I am indebted to Frank Trommler for pointing out this source to me.

118. In 1955, there were some concerns within the GSP that newly arriving Germans were not joining "the old associations" and were thus constituting a loss for "the established German-American movement." Speech by former GSP President Louis Schmidt at the Pastorius Celebration, October 2, 1955, GSP Box 1957–58.

119. Decorations in the Ratskeller of the German Society are a good example of how World War II refugees shaped the Society's image of Germany and its past. A huge map in the hallway to the Ratskeller, for example, depicts the "Deutschland in den Grenzen von 1937," which does not recognize the postwar borders of Poland or the existence of the German Democratic Republic from 1948 to 1989. The map itself was drawn by Wilhelm Neufeld and Martin Kornrumpf and published by the Müller and Kiepenheuer Verlag, 1953, 1954. It is not clear when the map was put up by the GSP.

7

Changes in the Behavior
of Immigrants

The Irish in Philadelphia

Noel J. J. Farley and Philip L. Kilbride

Irish immigration to the Philadelphia area has a long and diversified
history. Two thousand Irish Quakers came to Pennsylvania between
1682 and 1750. By the early eighteenth century in the mid-Atlantic
region, the Presbyterian Scotch-Irish became the predominant group of
Irish immigrants and this pattern continued until about 1815.[1] Most of our
attention is given to the still later Catholic Irish who with the Great Famine
made the United States their prime destination and were the main immigrant group there in the mid-nineteenth century.

One hundred fifty-two years have passed since the Great Famine was an
unwelcome visitor to Irish shores. In those years many things have happened
to Ireland and its population and emigration has helped to shape many of
the highlights of Irish history. Reciprocally, immigrant experiences in Philadelphia have been diversified over time in terms both of the events involved
and their causes and effects. Thus, we focus our eyes on the events at the
beginning and end of our period of study and we examine some of the factors in between, causing the still pictures of the 1850s and 1990s to be so
different from one another. To this task, we bring some of the analytical tools
of the anthropologists, economists, and economic historians. In the process,
we hope to answer questions about the causes and consequences of migration patterns among the Irish in both Ireland and Philadelphia. Our following statement focuses us on the questions and the boundaries of our work:
in the course of the nineteenth and twentieth centuries, political, economic

and social changes in Ireland, Philadelphia, and Pennsylvania made it inevitable that the level of Irish immigration as well as its characteristics and geographical distribution would go through a significant transformation. There were effects on Irish immigration produced both by the changing operations of the Irish-Philadelphia labor market over time and by the evolving character of U.S. and Western European immigration policies. What followed was that there was a tremendous change in the settlement patterns of the Irish-born and their descendants through Pennsylvania, as well as in the nature of the economic and social institutions these immigrants created to guide their lives.

To quote Dennis Clark,[2] writing in 1982, "Whether it [i.e., the Irish Center in Philadelphia—our comment] can continue to sustain itself in the 1980s, when Irish immigration to the city is likely to be reduced to a trickle, is a question that can be answered only by conjecture about the future of immigrant and ethnic organizations in the life of the country as a whole." Writing in 2007, we intend to assess the degree of validity of these speculations about immigration patterns and judge their consequences, if correct, for the condition and future of Irish social organizations, with a particular focus on the Irish Center in Philadelphia.

In handling these hypotheses, we have recourse to both qualitative and quantitative data that deal with Ireland, Philadelphia, and Pennsylvania, including the level and distribution of the Irish-born and the Irish stock in Pennsylvania through time. We are led to examine a process of change in the pattern of Irish migration to Philadelphia as well as transformations over time in the institutions and organizations (the Institutional School) at the center of Irish and Irish-American life. We hypothesize that this pattern had, as its basis, a process of economic, social, religious, and political change, built on historic circumstances that produced a particular pattern of Irish behavior that had an impact on the character of the economy and society in Philadelphia and Ireland.

The Location of Irish Immigrants in Pennsylvania

There is the general impression that nineteenth century Irish immigrants had a tendency to be highly concentrated in geographical space. It was based on the idea that many of the Irish went to major cities in the east such as Boston, New York, and Philadelphia as well as to particular neighborhoods of those cities. Clark[3] has told us that in 1860 there were four major areas of Irish concentration around the periphery of the city of Philadelphia—Southwark-Moyamensing and Grays Ferry-Schuylkill in South Philadelphia, and Lower Kensington and Port Richmond in North Philadelphia. For those seeking employment in manufacturing and wholesale trade, Kensington, Schuylkill, Manayunk, and South Philadelphia were the places they worked, close to the places where they lived.[4]

Let us broaden our perspective and focus on Philadelphia in the framework of the state of Pennsylvania. There are sixty-seven counties in Pennsylvania and we have most of the data for the Irish population of each county for each decade over a period of 140 years. In examining these data, we must distinguish between the Irish-born and the Irish stock. The Irish-born are those born in Ireland, and the Irish stock is the sum of the first and second generations of Irish. The U.S. Census Bureau specifically defines the second generation of Irish as the children of a marriage where both parents are Irish-born as well as the children of a mixed marriage where the father is Irish. For all census years except 1970, we have data for Irish-born across the counties. For that year, we have data on the Irish-born for the city of Philadelphia and for the whole state. However, we do have the 1970 data for the foreign-born across the counties of Pennsylvania. The ratio of the foreign-born to the foreign stock in each county is the mean for each county of the foreign-born to the foreign stock. We have the number for each county in 1970. We use these results to handle the Irish case and construct the new Irish-born series for 1970 as a substitute for the Irish stock series that we have at hand.

We now examine the means and coefficients of variation at various dates for the Irish-born in Pennsylvania (see Table 7.1). Changes in the coefficient of variation speak to either the growing or lessening dispersion of the Irish born across the counties of Pennsylvania. Our findings for the Irish-born provide numbers for population levels, means and coefficients of variation. In the year 2000, there were 1,359 Irish-born immigrants in Philadelphia and 6,687 in the state. These numbers contrast sharply with the counts of 201,929 for Pennsyl-

TABLE 7.1   DATA FOR IRISH IMMIGRANTS FOR THE STATE OF PENNSYLVANIA AND PHILADELPHIA

Year	Irish in Pennsylvania	Irish in Philadelphia	Mean numbers of immigrants per annum	Coefficient of variation
1860	201,939	95,548		
1880	236,505	101,000	3,530	
1890	243,836	110,935		
1900	205,909	98,427		
1910	165,091	83,187	2,464	4.279
1920	121,601	64,590	1,815	4.497
1930	97,600	51,941	1,457	3.848
1940	67,826	36,063	971	4.236
1950	56,378	24,896	669	4.614
1970	21,153	8,076	398	3.699
1980	14,887	3,707	188	3.295
1990	7,712	2,004	115	3.129
2000	6,687	1,359	100	2.819

Sources: U.S. Department of Commerce, Bureau of the Census, *Census of Population, Economic Characteristics* (Washington, DC: Government Printing Office, census years as indicated), data for state of Pennsylvania. Data for 2000 are available on the Web, specifically from the Bureau of the Census (http://www.census.gov).

vania and 95,548 in Philadelphia in 1860[5] and 494,850 in Britain in 2001.[6] The means for the counties had fallen. It is clear that this diminution in the Irish role in immigration had been coming on for a long time. Just as dramatic a change is shown by the behavior of the coefficient of variation. In this case, the outcomes are also very low in the family of numbers after 1950 as contrasted with the numbers between 1860 and 1940. They have been falling persistently in the last 50 years. The reason for this is the drastic fall in the numbers of Irish-born in large urban areas such as Philadelphia and Pittsburgh. What were the causes and consequences of these changes?

The American Economy: Irish Labor in the Second Half of the Nineteenth Century

Rostow[7] tells us that the industrial revolution in America started around the 1840s. Robust growth occurred and continued through the period that followed the Great Famine in Ireland (1845–1850). After Rostow's "take-off," the American economy continued its growth, going through economic cycles and speeded along by generations of new technologies. These developments had an influence on the occupational structure of both the labor force and the new, primarily Irish (and European) migrants who entered. The particular characteristics of the industrial revolution were that while techniques of production became more capital intensive and machines became central to the pacing of operations in many of the workplaces, this opened up primarily unskilled jobs at the factory level in a range of manufacturing industries. Cities were becoming more important in economic activity, and immigrants settled there. In addition, industrial infrastructure based on construction was linked to the development of a transportation system with the steam ships and the railroads. Two classes of labor became important in economic activity. The first was skilled operatives who could manage the machines used in the factory system and the second a much larger pool of laborers who could do the tough manual work in manufacturing, mining, and construction. Men and women laborers entered many of these low-skilled occupations, and women became predominant particularly in the textile industry but also in a range of domestic services.

By 1900, the employment structure of the Pennsylvania economy, as well as that of Philadelphia, could be described as an industrial economy. The early Irish migrants had been succeeded by a second generation that began to climb up the economic and social ladders. Manufacturing had taken its expected dominant position in the structure of economic activity. Domestic and personal services were contained inside other statistical classifications and, after manufacturing, dominated the occupations of women. Manufacturing, and specifically textiles, provided the second source of female employment. There were some highly educated skilled Irish people in America's labor force, but their numbers were dwarfed by the numbers of the semi-skilled and the unskilled. Many of these highly skilled people were in the ranks of occupations known as "professional services."[8]

There were similarities in the nineteenth century economies of Philadelphia and Pennsylvania, but there were also important differences. Philadelphia was the home of the textile industry. As early as the 1840s, Kensington was a key area where weavers often worked at home. As the years passed, what had been true when artisan production was prevalent remained true under modern industrialism. Outside of Philadelphia the location of metals dictated the placement of the mining industry and the iron and steel industry took on importance in such places as Bethlehem and Pittsburgh.

It is often said that the Irish played a key role in the creation of the infrastructure of America and in the development of the new industries of the U.S. industrial revolution. This was true of the development of the infrastructure in the city of Philadelphia and in Philadelphia County. The construction of a regional and continental transportation system was an essential prerequisite to the industrial revolution in the United States generally and in the mid-Atlantic region particularly. In the Philadelphia area, such a system was essential to the expansion of markets for final output, the exploitation of broader markets for inputs of industry, and the increased access of foreign and domestic labor to the Philadelphia labor market. The labor for these developments came from the natural increase of the indigenous population and from inter- and intrastate movements of labor and immigration.

The Irish famine immigrants crossed the Atlantic in the second half of the 1840s and for many years after that. Irish immigration to the United States was at its historical peak in the 1840–1860 period.[9] It was the freak coincidence of history that the Irish Famine and the American industrial revolution occurred at about the same time. Through much of this time period, the movement of migrants into the United States was, in the view of many Americans, a very good thing for economic development. America was a land of abundance, but a labor scarce economy with enormous potential for both the exploitation of its natural resources and technological change. Nevertheless, there were those, including residents of Philadelphia, who objected to Irish immigrants on cultural, social, and religious grounds.

Conversely, there was very little industrial activity in Ireland until the 1930s. In 1850 Ireland could be identified as a preindustrial economy even though, at that moment, there were the beginnings of modern industrialism with factories created in Belfast and its suburbs, as well as in Dublin and in Cork, particularly in the textile and dairy product industries. Ireland's industry was geared to artisan works attached to the home or to property in the local village rather than to factory operations in the nearest town. On the surface of things, while Ireland

and Pennsylvania had some of the same industries, Ireland was more involved in providing the finishing touches to products and it lacked significant heavy industry. In other cases, such as the chemical industry, the goods produced reflected the old rather than the new technologies. Examples of this were the soap and candle industries within the chemical industry. The big handicap of the Irish migrant was that most of the Irish labor force lacked experience working in a factory system. They came from artisan, family, and agricultural traditions in production. The famine debacle left them with no desire to enter American agriculture, which few in fact did. It also left them with no thoughts of returning to Ireland, and caught with no other choice than to stay at their American destination. The question for the new Irish arrivals was how to make the best of their opportunities and provide themselves with a better future in America. They had engaged in forced migration, and many of them thought that they faced the ultimate choice between survival and death.

The statistical picture adds to this understanding. The Irish Census of Population of 1851[10] has statistical tables relating to the occupations of Irish emigrants in the years 1851–1855. First, we note that 49.4 percent of emigrants had farming occupations, whereas up to 97 percent of total occupations of Irish migrants could be characterized as unskilled. The compilation of the emigrants by occupations left much to be desired. Of the 747,999 Irish migrants between 1851 and 1855, 200,145 were in a group that did not specify their occupation and 70.8 percent of these were women. In light of the importance of agricultural activities in the lives of Irish emigrants as well as the gender components of migrants, we judge that many of the "unspecified" were relatives assisting in Irish agriculture. This is consistent with all we know about the basis of Irish emigration in that it was "forced" after the Great Famine. Overall, at their point of destination, these migrants were undoubtedly people with limited skills and no industrial experience.

Let us examine the Philadelphia labor history of Irish men and women at the end of the nineteenth century. In light of our discussion, it goes without saying that most Irish immigrants in Philadelphia were seeking employment in unskilled occupations in modern manufacturing, construction, transportation, and government service. For Irish men the construction and shipping industries provided opportunity, as did a range of government service jobs, such as the fire, police, and sanitation departments. Heavy physical work and dangerous jobs in the smelting and mining of metals were other positions occupied by Irish immigrants. Pennsylvania provided all of these kinds of jobs, as well as occupations that involved old artisan skills for migrants such as leather workers and those who worked at metal forges. For women, domestic service and textiles provided a great deal of opportunity. At a much later stage, as literacy became more prevalent, women entered the teaching and nursing professions.

Clark[11] notes that Irish leaders in economic activity began to appear. This was particularly true in construction, in recreational activity built around the Irish pub, and in local fire and police departments. At the same time, women began to experience occupational mobility by moving from positions in domestic and laundry services and similar occupations to teaching, wholesale and retail trade, and nursing late in the century.[12]

Two Economies: Irish Labor at the End of the Twentieth Century

The telling issue at the other end of the historical spectrum is the economic condition of Ireland during the 1990s. Ireland's economic growth was the highest in Europe and the Celtic Tiger bellowed its loudest roar. The Irish owed a great debt to the European Union for the Structural Funds that had been provided to create infrastructure and to maintain agricultural prices under Common Agricultural Policy establishing prosperity in the Irish countryside. Multinational firms entered the island and contributed to the Irish economy's participation in the global economy. A consequence of these outward-looking policies was that Ireland's agriculture was responsible for only 10.6 percent of employment there.

The growth stimulating sectors of the economy were chemical and metal groupings, including telecommunications and computers, as well as banking and other financial services. For Ireland, of course, the important changes were that it had gone through its industrial revolution after 1960. By 1990, it was a semi-postindustrial economy and had become an integral part of the European economy, its front door so to speak. Ireland became "high tech" in its vision and the labor supply came to mirror the highly skilled labor that was required. As a result, the Irish government initiated significant educational reforms in the 1970s. "The world had become flat," said Thomas Friedman.[13] These changed perceptions opened the door to global communication, led to the spread of knowledge, fostered technological diffusion, permitted a division of labor in the manufacturing of goods, where different stages of production were done at different geographical locations across the world, and improved factory productivity wherever this technological innovation touched economic activity. Significantly, the back door to the Americas, once its front door, became a magnet for the return of the Irish to America, the so-called "new Irish."

An examination of these results for 1996 produces telling findings.[14] While the educational reforms of the 1970s required that teenagers had to be at school until age fifteen, 58.2 percent of the total population in 1996 had completed the secondary level of education. Three-quarters of the fifteen-plus age group had completed their education beyond the primary level, and 21.7 percent had completed their education at the third level. What a contrast to 1841 when 53 percent of the Irish immigrants could neither read nor write English and another 20 percent of the fifteen to twenty-six age group had not attended school. The Celtic Tiger had indeed become a literate "animal"!

How would we characterize the Philadelphia and Pennsylvania economies in the second half of the twentieth century—always best seen, to some extent, in interaction with Ireland as far as Irish America is concerned? Examining the data for Philadelphia County, we note that between 1950 and 1990, total employment had fallen from 827,243 to 651,621 and then to 584,957 in 2000.[15] Over this period Philadelphia became a postindustrial economy. Its path to this outcome was straight and clear. Not only did total employment fall, but so also did manufacturing employment from 291,312 in 1950 to 51,394 in 2000. Employment in construction had also fallen from 46,926 to 23,090. To complete the picture of decline, the services sector had fallen from 530,691 to 509,713, although some areas, such as entertainment and recreation, were growing. The growth stimulating high tech sectors were going elsewhere, and New York was providing employment opportunities in financial services. New products and methods of doing things had eaten somewhat into Philadelphia's old advantages.

These are important results. They provide essential background findings about the population group in which the Irish immigrants either placed themselves or were permitted into the United States, according to the Hart-Cellar Immigration Act of 1965 and later amendments to it. A top preference was given to the children of U.S. citizens. The other top preference was given to people with skills required for jobs in the United States where there were no local workers to fill them. Events in Philadelphia had lessened the jobs available for the semi-skilled and unskilled, and the accumulation of Irish skill in high tech industries found very limited outlets in the new structure of the Philadelphia economy. The financial services sector provided some potential opportunities but did not compete well with New York and other financial centers. This was discouraging for an immigrant group only 16.8 percent of whom had less than a high school education.

The English labor market had always been open to Irish immigrants, and since 1972 so had the E.U. market. They did see opportunity in the United States, but given the signals from many locations for their attention, they saw problems with engagement in the U.S. labor market. They wondered about the bureaucratic challenges of going through the U.S. Naturalization and Immigration Service. Those with few skills thought that opportunities in Europe offered better prospects. In addition, the family provisions of the Hart-Cellar Act were no longer the avenue along which many Irish immigrants would enter the United States. The most urgent problems lay elsewhere.

Explanations of Changes in the Level and Geographic Distribution of Irish Immigrants

Our analysis has pointed to reasons for the emerging low levels of Irish immigration over the last 150 years. Irish immigrants of the mid-nineteenth century were unskilled, low wage laborers, and progressed to become high tech and skilled with improving education and growing per capita incomes in the late twentieth century. Migration contributed to closing the wage rate gap, but it was not alone in wielding its influence. The process of industrialization led to the introduction of new technologies, which increased the demand for labor wherever the industrial revolution occurred. Over the 150-year period considered in this study, there was a significant decline in the wage gap. Therefore, today Ireland has a per capita income at the top end of countries in Western Europe.[16]

How can we understand changes in the level and geographical distribution of Irish-born immigrants since the Great Famine? First, very compatible economic conditions existed in the nineteenth century in the United States, Philadelphia, and Ireland resulting in significant Irish migration to the United States, but that changed by the end of the twentieth century. Previously, a country going through an industrial revolution would match up well with a preindustrial economy subject to severe hardship conditions in achieving labor migration between them. As Douglas Massey has pointed out, economic factors, such as we have noted here, are at work historically in the global flow of immigration.[17] Second, the most recent Irish immigrants were seeking economic opportunity and had greater financial resources than their counterparts in earlier times. They could survive for lengthier periods without Irish and other charitable institutions both because of their own financial positions and the local, state, and federal policies that were in existence before the 1990s but not in place in the mid-nineteenth century.[18] Thus, the Irish today are more likely to have the financial resources to assure their own self-sufficiency and enhanced educational achievement in Ireland that we noted above. Third, the decline in immigration in the 1920–1950 period contributed to the decline in the friends and neighbors effect in the post-1945 period. Contacts weakened between the potential Irish migrants at home and friends and neighbors abroad. Fourth, recently there has been a fundamental change in the traits of the Irish-born immigrant and his or her view of the world during the last forty years. The result of the recent Irish economic transformation is that the Irish migrant is mobile in the world economy. The prestige of the Irish has been enhanced by the successes of Irish and Irish-American residents in climbing the business and professional ladders in the United States and elsewhere. The search for economic opportunity has become prevalent among Irish migrants, and the Irish have developed a positive reputation in the world economy. They come to the United States presuming that they will be geographically spread and are led to this by the location of economic activity.

They now inject themselves into cosmopolitan communities and less into Irish ethnic enclaves than in the past. They now have dual loyalties as citizens of the world as well as of Ireland and, if they remain in the United States, many of them seek American citizenship. On all of these grounds, including the small numbers entering the United States, it is no wonder that the geographic spread of the Irish migrant in Pennsylvania and in Philadelphia has increased and that many are outside the large urban area where they had previously settled.

There are still the very few with limited educational backgrounds and poor occupational skills who enter the United States. Some arrive to join relatives; others additionally seek employment opportunity. For a long time, many entered as tourists and worked temporarily in the U.S. economy. In recent years, and until 9/11, it is also suggested that the unskilled went back and forth between the United States and Northern Ireland, working in construction and other industries for lengthy periods on these visits, before returning to Ireland. At present, the estimate is that there are approximately 50,000 illegal immigrants in the United States from Ireland but it is very difficult to gauge the credibility of such a number.[19] There are also those with limited skills who enter the United States legitimately, making up about 25 percent of the Irish-born immigrants. However, their numbers are extremely small. Our guess is that the number of the less skilled in Pennsylvania in 2000 might have reached 1,700, while the figure for Philadelphia was about 350. We conclude that the story of Irish immigration to the United States, Pennsylvania, and Philadelphia has changed dramatically in recent years.

Changing Functions of Irish Urban Enclaves in the Nineteenth and Twentieth Centuries

We turn to the diaspora experience of the Irish in Philadelphia and the state of Pennsylvania. With the change in the number, character, and propensity to wander of the Irish immigrants over the last century and a half, we focus on what has happened to the functioning of the first and later generations of Irish in the United States. In particular, we examine the Irish immigrant's choice of social and cultural institutions, the impact of those institutions on the behavior of the Irish immigrants and their descendants, and the forces behind the ultimate redefinition of these institutions.

It is important to realize that most of the traditional Irish had been dispossessed farm owners whose families had taken possession of Irish lands in the sixteenth and seventeenth centuries. With British control of the new official institutions and organizations, the structure of political, social and economic human interactions in Ireland changed. In earlier times, Irish society had been ruled by the clans and their chieftains and had its own institutions and organizations. The Brehon laws and those that preceded them created a hierarchical structure of people by class, spelled out the use of the land and the qualifications for occupation, established criminal, civil, and contract provisions that controlled human behavior, provided for the enforcement of law and the adjudication of conflict, and laid down penalties for proven misbehavior.[20] In the terminology of the Institutional School of Economics,[21] this is a picture of a sophisticated system of institutions to direct, discipline, and limit human interactions, including those based on production and consumption of goods and services. Institutions for early Irish society comprised a set of rules and procedures that reflected pagan cultural values and ultimately local rules that were the result of weaving together of both pagan and Christian thinking. Ultimately, British plantations disturbed this system, and into the nineteenth century, the British system of codified law and the old Irish laws were in conflict. In addition, the old traditional holders of land under the Brehon laws had responsibilities to their families, to the clan chieftain and his followers, and to their neighbors that would have fallen under the headings of altruism, generosity, and hospitality.[22] The British landlord, often an absentee, did not accept the obligation to adhere to any of the old Irish customs. The traditional Irish found themselves without the land or the social capital that bonded together the Brehon precolonial community.

Slowly with time, the Catholic Church took over the leadership role from both the clan chieftains of old and the Anglican Church of Ireland that aspired to that role. As the nineteenth century unfolded, the Catholic Church involved itself in directing the lives of their parishioners and leading them to make provision for the construction of churches, provide education and medical services, play peacemaker in the local community, and arrange for generosity between them and their neighbors. The formal practice of charity for the parish member was taken over by Catholics and the development of a caring sense of community was their concern. Although with time the Catholic clergy came to own land and property in Ireland, they were not producers of material income and wealth. Instead the clergy played the role of pulling together resources from the community to finance the achievement of social goals that were part of the church's mission. To that extent, they replaced clan chieftains. In the language of the Institutional School, in the face of political revolts, old institutions that normally involved rules that had become habits of behavior were replaced by new organizations that brought about new revised institutions.[23]

Where institutional economists and economic historians believed institutions to be locked in,[24] the traditional Irish showed them to be open to transformation. Whereas many perceived the famine as likely to be the death knell for them of the old traditional Ireland and of all their dreams for an independent Ireland, they now had in mind the end of the plans for the return of the old Ireland with its traditional institutions and organizations in political, social, and economic matters. The realization was bitter because, on a daily basis, they were getting evidence of the British system of governance's lack of concern with their current survival and their future fate. The landlord class and the British government, prisoners of their ideological bent, neglected them. There were some exceptions to this, such as Lord Sligo of Mayo and, for a time, Dennis Mahon of Roscommon. The postfamine emergence of the Catholic Church witnessed the rise of a Catholic presence in formal education, a dramatic rise in missionary activities, and American parochial schools that were Irish dominated well into the twentieth century in the United States, especially through the roles of Irish leaders and nuns in the classroom and in church governance.[25]

The broader question was how were these immigrants going to survive in their foreign homes? The answer was that the famine had persuaded many of them that they had lost their homeland forever. They saw the task before them as not only survival on foreign soil, but also the formation of a "New Ireland"[26] at their new home. There would be the Irish in Ireland as well as the Irish in the United States, and Irish institutional practices dictated that both interests be served.

The Irish Americans, through funding efforts, were deeply involved in various movements in Ireland, resisting British colonial policy there.[27] The Irish in Ireland made institutional innovations in the face of the new challenges. Where House of Commons hearings and the Devon Commission Report had considered but rejected state aid for Irish emigrants, the British government also rejected these proposals, and the Irish created self-financing through friends and neighbors. This not only permitted Irish migrants to cross the Atlantic but created the friends and neighbors effect between the Irish migrants and those at home, stimulating migration and creating clusters of Irish migrants in American cities including Philadelphia. They built their churches and schools, created their clubs, and set up their pubs in the local districts. Their own institutions and organizations, particularly their own social clubs, were a response to the political, social, and economic necessities in their lives. What the state did not provide, the Irish did for themselves. Federal, state, and local governments[28] had highly limited concern for social policies for the immigrants. The need for job opportunities was taken care of by Irish neighbors and the Irish social club which was always there to help. The church was there to provide family counseling, basic education, and banking services, and where religious orders were concerned, hospital services.

The work of individual Catholic Irishmen was important in the provision of Catholic religious and social services. Francis Kenrick, born and reared in Dublin, was educated at the Urban College of the Propaganda Fide in Rome. He was imbued with the Catholic spirit of restoration reform. He started his missionary work in Kentucky in 1821 and in 1830 came to Philadelphia. He saw his task as Romanizing the church in its administrative practices, in its doctrines, and in its liturgical rituals. Besides aiming to create a universal restoration

Roman Church, he set out to establish the authority of the bishops over the laity and saw the future of the church in terms of a middle class contributing to the spiritual wellbeing of this religious body. He was an able and controversial leader until his departure in 1851. The controversies that he faced had a number of sources, the most important being that he disliked, as did Rome, separate and independent nationality-based Catholic parishes, but that did not sit well with European immigrants. Old traditional Irish priests did not welcome his interfering authority over parish affairs, even though many middle class Irish Catholics did. Paul Cullen, another famous Irishman of the Irish College of Propaganda in Rome, played out a similar hand. As archbishop of Armagh, he worked to bring the restoration church to Ireland in the 1850s. John Hughes, still another Irishman, looked after Rome's interests in the Archdiocese of New York. The three knew one another well and collaborated in work. They were a significant team in the reconstruction of the nineteenth-century Catholic Church in Philadelphia.[29] Their influence has been a lasting one.

Fraternal orders within the police and fire departments were key institutional support networks where the Irish were employed in large numbers. Ultimately, generosity toward one's neighbor was an essential quality of the behavior of the Irish immigrant, who was sometimes on the doorstep of starvation and in need of immediate sustenance. It is clear that, quite imaginatively, the Irish created a system of institutions and organizations conceived in a state of calamity and fostered by a communal spirit that permitted them to recover, survive, and produce another generation of Irish who could emphasize improvement in their lives in the years that followed. The ingenuity of the Irish in sustaining the flow of immigrants, through the friends and neighbors effect, had a central role in the story of the arrival of the traditional Irish in Philadelphia. Their actions reflected a refinement of the communal spirit that went back to Celtic Ireland and that, by the time of the famine, had been a habitual guide to Irish behavior for centuries.

In the case of both men and women in recent years, the majority of the modern Irish immigrants are highly educated. Because of globalization and instant communication, entrepreneurs choose production techniques that are similar in Ireland and Philadelphia. In accord also are the same educational opportunities needed to participate in the world economy. We notice that 1980 seems to be a dividing line in observing the educational achievement of Irish immigrants.[30] The limited numbers entering after 1980 had higher educational achievements than those entering before. The passage of time showed the impact of new technologies and new thinking about the nature of the organization of production that was changing the character of the labor force. The key factor in competing in the national and global economies had become knowledge capital.

This is well illustrated by the structure of economic activity into which the Irish immigrants could place themselves in the Philadelphia area in 1990. Looking at the employed people in Philadelphia County, we see that the sum of managerial and professional specialty occupations, technical, sales and administrative support occupations, and services make up 76.3 percent of the employed labor force. In these three groupings, we find those who are skilled in the practices of the financial sector and those who have scientific and technical training. High levels of educational attainment are also required for those in medical services, education, social services, and legal, engineering, and other professional services, making up 29.5 percent of employment in Philadelphia County.[31] We conclude that the Irish immigrants in Philadelphia have the appropriate skills and background to fit into the Philadelphia economy as it is presently constituted.

Some Irish Institutions in the Philadelphia Region

Education

In the second half of the nineteenth century, Catholic elementary schools in the Philadelphia Archdiocese (post-1868) became an important part of the training of Irish immigrants including the Irish-born. These were generally attached to the Catholic parish. For the Irish in particular this was an important attribute of the Roman Catholic Church. In 1842, the Augustinians founded Villanova University and its importance grew dramatically in the twentieth century. Saint Joseph's University was established in 1851, and La Salle College came along in 1868. Initially, these institutions primarily trained secondary level students for college. Saint Joseph's and La Salle were not to become important to Irish-born immigrants until later in the century and today are very important to Irish Americans in providing higher education.

The inspiration for the development of Catholic school systems came from the Irish-born. John Hughes, who became Bishop of New York in 1841, was familiar with the conflicts between Protestants and Catholics in Ireland regarding the curriculum in Irish national schools and was present when the Holy See established the Archdiocese of New York. In education, Bishop Hughes had a big hand in the abolition of the Public School Society, a Protestant-dominated body that had received state money for the running of a state school system. The result was the creation of elected school boards which proceeded to forbid religious teaching in the public schools. Bishop Hughes withdrew and created a Catholic school system in New York that became the model for Catholic schools in the United States. In Philadelphia, there was a long dispute about the use of the King James Version of the Bible in the public schools, which involved Bishop Kenrick on the Catholic side. Finally, Saint John Neumann developed a Catholic educational system attached to the parishes when he was a bishop in the Philadelphia Archdiocese.

For the Irish, Catholic education provided that blend of spiritual and secular training of the mind that created the good Christian, the good citizen, and the vocationally trained person that could fit into the modern economy. The message was always there for the observer to see that Catholic education provided the right return to assure its adherents that this institution of the Irish immigrants would remain in place for them, but more importantly for Irish Americans. In the present generation of Irish Americans, the pursuit of a university education is a persistent and robust one. This is seen in registrations at the college level. More in trouble, however, is the parish school in the Philadelphia community and in some of its immediate surroundings.

The reasons for this are not hard to find. The major one is that the mix of population in Philadelphia has changed significantly. Irish Americans in Philadelphia number just over 209,000 now out of a population of 1,517,550 or 13.8 percent. The Irish-born are a mere 1,359. The Catholic Education Office of the Philadelphia Archdiocese reports that today its system contains 194 elementary schools, twenty-one high schools, and five schools of special education.[32] The emerging disparity between the paucity of the Irish-born and the size and spread of the school system points to the changes in both the geographical location and ethnic and racial backgrounds of the parishioners at the parish level (see Table 7.2). There is no doubt that Catholic education has had its problems at the pre-university level. Changing geographical patterns of population, new ethnic compositions of population in different neighborhoods, and the decline in total population have put many schools at the elementary level under stress in terms of numbers and under pressure in terms of their finances. On top of this, the clergy scandals of the last few years have put a severe financial strain on all of the operations of the Roman Catholic Church. Undoubtedly, this has affected the amount of resources that go into Catholic education. Nevertheless, old institutional commitments have been maintained and elementary education has remained an important focus. At the high school level, eleven schools were opened between 1890 and 1950. We estimate that a total of thirty high schools and schools of special education are currently in operation. The institutions pertaining to education are evolving with much more emphasis now on the high school and university levels.

We should note that these numbers refer to the educational policies that apply in the Philadelphia Archdiocese. This is a religious jurisdiction that covers not only the city of Philadelphia, but also Philadelphia County, Bucks County, Chester County, Delaware County, and Montgomery County. The scope of the effort that the diocese has made in its Catholic education system can be seen in Table 7.2. Included are elementary schools, high schools, and schools of special education. Colleges and universities in the diocese are run by religious orders. The Web site for the Catholic School System of the Philadelphia Archdiocese provides a list of the names of the schools in the diocese. In Table 7.2, we have

TABLE 7.2   SCHOOLS IN THE ARCHDIOCESE OF PHILADELPHIA, 2000

Location	Total	High schools	Special education	Elementary schools
Bucks County	31	4	1	26
Chester County	17	2	0	15
Delaware County	42	4	1	37
Montgomery County	46	5	0	41
Philadelphia North	51	6	1	44
Philadelphia South	36	6	0	30
Total	223	27	3	193

Source: 2000 The Catholic Directory: Official Directory of the Archdiocese of Philadelphia (Philadelphia: The Catholic Standard and Times, 1999).

assembled the numbers of institutions for four counties of the diocese, as well as a split of Philadelphia County into Philadelphia North and Philadelphia South.

The scale of the enterprise is demonstrated in the results. Philadelphia North and Philadelphia South are responsible for just 38.3 percent of the elementary schools as well as 44.4 percent of the high schools. This reflects the flight to the suburbs in the post-1945 period. The scope of activities is enormous, and in the midst of all this, the diocese has succeeded in maintaining seventy-four elementary schools and twelve high schools in the city. In the diocese, where there are 284 parishes, there are 193 elementary schools. This is stunning coverage for Catholic elementary education.[33]

Catholics have set their sights on increasing their participation in the economic and social life of the community. They have accepted the challenge of diversifying the backgrounds of their student bodies, and this was a necessary and justified response to the changing demographic and social realities. From the earliest inspirations of Irish practices, the Catholic educational system is alive and as well as can be expected in the light of the economic, political, and social changes of the last sixty years and in the perspective of the catastrophic consequences of the clergy scandals that have traumatized the operations of the Church in the last decade. Irish institutional evolution, in terms of the thinking of Catholic clergy, many of whom are Irish-born or of Irish descent, is alive and resilient in the light of all the doom and gloom that has followed the church in recent years.

Cultural Identity: Irish Institutions and Organizations

Today, Irish American identity is a matter of self-chosen identity. Previously, under an older institutional regime when the Irish lived together in neighborhoods and parishes and when the public at large had a somewhat negative view of the Irish, an ethnic label was more difficult to avoid. Being Irish today is primarily a matter of cultural taste through choice.[34] Although dispersed today in the Philadelphia suburbs and in the city, and now a small number, the Irish-born join with many of their Irish American counterparts to enjoy and celebrate such activities as Irish festivals, sports competitions, including hurling, musical performances and dances, including the Ceili and step dancing, social occasions at Irish pubs, and Saint Patrick's Day parades throughout the region.

The immigrants of the 1850s needed the Irish clubs. They were often attached to the Catholic parish, especially when they dealt with education, social life, and employment services. Others were attached to religious orders. Ethnic-based associations included the Ancient Order of Hibernians and the Friendly Sons of Saint Patrick. Others came later such as the Mayo Association of Philadelphia, the Philadelphia Donegal Association, and the Cavan Society of Philadelphia.[35] Of interest in the present age of geographical dispersion of Irish immigrants, these organizations chose a point in space to which they drew their Irish compatriots from distant locations. Such can be said of the Irish Center, the youngest of the organizations. Formed in 1958 as the Commodore Barry Club, its institutional commitment is to foster Irish culture and traditions in the Delaware Valley area. At the time of their creation in the nineteenth century, all of the older organizations were in place to help the new immigrants entering the country. All of them were engaged in charitable activity and provided a place away from home where the Irish could congregate, enjoy, and help one another. Besides providing essential social services, they helped to maintain a pride in Irish identity and to give support to Irish causes in Ireland. Most of them were Irish and, except for the Friendly Sons, exclusively Roman Catholic. The Irish Presbyterians and the Irish Anglicans also had their parish and other organizations. History tells us that the Orange Order developed lodges in Ireland as the place of origin and then in such diverse places as South Africa, Canada, Australia, New Zealand, and the United States. Pennsylvania was also one of its locations.

Let us illustrate some of the work of these organizations. Organized in Philadelphia in 1771, the Friendly Sons of Saint Patrick, whose membership encompassed many prominent Americans, included members of Congress, the cabinet, and the military, as well as Protestants, especially Presbyterians. That membership is notable as is its comparative wealth and upper class achievement and privilege. After the Great Famine, the Friendly Sons promoted benevolence, especially for disadvantaged Catholics in Ireland and the United States. Many non-Irish were helped also as victims of national disasters through donations to ethnic relief societies, such as the Russian Jewish Relief Fund. Local Catholic colleges and Irish graduate students in academic programs in the United States have also benefited as have American students studying in Ireland. As an example, we are aware of Gerald Quinn, Irish born and a graduate of University College Dublin, who was awarded a Friendly Sons fellowship to do graduate study in Economics at the University of Pennsylvania in the 1950s. He later joined the economics faculty at University College Dublin.

The Irish Center was founded to assist Irish immigrants, although it was of appeal also to Irish Americans, whereby "the disposition of the Irish population, paradoxically, led to a concentration of its activities. . . . soon the Barry club was humming with . . . bar patronage . . . meetings . . . and a cycle of Irish society balls and dances."[36] As we stated earlier, Clark had wondered if the Irish Center would persist beyond the 1980s when Irish immigration would virtually have disappeared.[37] It turned out that the optimists were right in noting that the dispersal of the Irish into the suburbs over time would not necessarily result in a loss of heritage. In fact, in one sense demographic dispersal promoted its concentration and continuation. Clearly, however, an Irish identity is now a matter of self-choice to a greater degree than previously when demographic concentration and poverty were pronounced in the Irish experience in Philadelphia and benefits provided by clubs were crucial.

The cosmopolitan, citizen-of-the-world Irish individual, both American and Irish-born, is now among us in large numbers. He or she is English-speaking, likes modern music to which Irish brothers and sisters have made a contribution, is very much integrated into Irish society, and values patriotism for America. This raises questions for today's Irish institutions in Philadelphia. Should they broaden their focus to a wider interest in world cultures and the needs of the disadvantaged in American society? The members of the Irish Center answer yes. Among them are Irish Americans in search of their roots and looking for enduring Irish qualities with which to associate. They, like the new Irish-born immigrants coming to the United States, embrace a more global perspective and outreach to the less privileged. With this new perspective and the changed characteristics of the new Irish immigrants, the Irish societies have new purposes while continuing to appreciate the Irish Americans in their traditional ways of enjoying themselves, earning a living and showing business expertise, engaging in storytelling, gregariously expressing themselves with humor and zest, and showing the same charity and generosity that has prevailed among the Irish for many generations.[38] They are the focus of attention of the Irish societies and the new migrants, who are so small in numbers, and necessarily much less noticed than those who came before them. The broadened mission of the Catholic Church in the area of education is another reflector of these changes in Irish institutions and organizations.

Final Reflections

To a degree, the pattern of Irish immigration to Philadelphia that we have examined can be generalized as a case in which both sending and receiving countries experienced specific religious, economic, social, and political changes, as well as faced revisions in government migration policies. We call it the "European Migration Model of Change" in that changed characteristics of social, economic, and political life for both national peoples helped to determine the size and characteristics of the population movements between them. We have some tentative conclusions about the impact of Ireland-Philadelphia migration on both locations. There seems little doubt that Irish migration to the United States in general, and to Philadelphia in particular, helped create an environment in which the Irish in Ireland enjoyed economic improvement through the direct effects of labor migration and migrants' remittances. Success in religious, social, and cultural activities among Irish Americans stimulated social, political, and economic improvements for Ireland which reverberated in the city of Philadelphia.

Probably as important as the social effects was the role that the Irish clergy and laity had in strengthening the hand of the Catholic Church and shaping its character in the Archdiocese of Philadelphia. Depending on your perspective, Irish Catholics either led or at least accommodated the "Restoration Reform" in Catholicism brought about by the universalizing of Christian doctrine, the Romanizing of Episcopal authority, the new practices of the Devotional Revolution, and the strengthening and modernization of the traditions of social action. The lasting imprint of Irish figures of the Catholic Church on Philadelphia life in such areas as education, medicine, and social services is astounding in light of the small size of Ireland and its population.

We conclude that the migration process was a major factor in placing the Irish economy where it is today. However, for reasons discussed above, few new Irish migrants now come to Philadelphia, and the influence of new generations of Irish immigrants, while present, are less obvious. We see the last result in very positive terms. No doubt, the Irish migration process contributed to the progress of the Irish in Ireland, to Irish born everywhere, and to all living in Philadelphia and across the United States. Economists often build models that distribute the benefits of international migration among migrants and donor and host countries. The outcomes of these models include the possibility that one or more of the actors in the migration experience may fail to gain very much or anything at all from the process. The Irish experience shows the opposite, as the Irish economy ultimately overcame its barriers to progress, the Irish migrant group prospered, and Philadelphia, America, and other receiving countries gained from their presence.

Ireland and its immigrants share a number of similar experiences with many other previously colonized territories. It went though occupation from England over many centuries and won its battle for independence. The twentieth century was the time when a number of important outcomes happened simultaneously. The Irish leaving Irish shores prospered in the new homelands. They helped with the development of the Philadelphian and American economies, as well as the Catholic Church and its institutions. Meanwhile, the island of Ireland, bolstered by emigrants' remittances until the mid-twentieth century, ultimately went through and completed its own industrial revolution. We know that there are many, either Irish-born or of Irish ancestry, who think that in moving from a preindustrial to a modern economy, the Irish experience should be examined as a model that has lessons to offer contemporary, preindustrial countries which hope that their migration patterns will contribute to the wellbeing of their native peoples both at home and abroad.

Notes

1. Albert Cook Myers, *Immigration of the Irish Quakers into Pennsylvania, 1682–1750, with Their Early History in Ireland* (Swarthmore, PA: The Author, 1902), 82. The following is also an excellent article on the early Irish immigrants: Joseph S. Kennedy, "The Irish Ventured to Pennsylvania in Several Waves," *Philadelphia Inquirer,* March 17, 1966. For a history of nineteenth-century emigration from Ireland, see Noel J. J. Farley, "Irish Emigration in the 19th Century" (mimeographed, 2006), Chap. 4; available from the author, Noel J. J. Farley, Bryn Mawr College.

2. Dennis Clark, *The Irish Relations: Trials of an Immigrant Tradition* (London: Fairleigh Dickinson University Press, 1982), 218.

3. Dennis Clark, "The Philadelphia Irish: Persistent Presence," in *The Peoples of Philadelphia: A History of Ethnic Groups and Lower Class Life, 1790–1940,* ed. Allen F. Davis and Mark H. Haller (Philadelphia: Temple University Press, 1973), 136–137; Clark, *The Irish Relations,* 145–146.

4. Clark, "The Philadelphia Irish"; Clark, *The Irish Relations.*

5. Carolyn Adams, David Bartelt, David Klesh, Ira Goldstein, Nancy Kleniewski, and William Yancey, *Philadelphia Division and Conflict in a Post-Industrial City* (Philadelphia: Temple University Press, 1991), Chap. 1.

6. The British figure is taken from "Born Abroad: An Immigration Map of Britain" posted by BBC News at http://www.bbc.co.uk/bornabroad.

7. W. W. Rostow, *The Stages of Economic Growth: A Non-Communist Manifesto* (Forge Village, MA: Cambridge University Press, 1960), Chap. 4.

8. U.S. Department of Commerce and Labor, Bureau of the Census, *Special Reports: Occupations at the Twelfth Census* (Washington, DC: Government Printing Office, 1904).

9. The data are taken from U.S. Department of Commerce, Bureau of the Census, *Bicentennial Edition: Historical Statistics of the United States: Colonial Times to 1970* (Washington, DC: Government Printing Office, 1976).

10. U.K. Government, *The Census of Ireland for the Year 1851,* Part VI, *General Report, Statistical Appendix* (Dublin: Alex Thom & Sons, for Her Majesty's government, 1856).

11. Dennis Clark, *The Irish in Pennsylvania: A People Share a Commonwealth,* Pennsylvania History Studies, no. 22 (University Park: Pennsylvania Historical Association, 1991), 26.

12. Clark, *The Irish Relations,* Part 2; Clark, "The Philadelphia Irish."

13. Thomas L. Friedman, *The World Is Flat: A Brief History of the Twenty First Century* (New York: Farrar, Strauss and Giroux, 2006).

14. Central Statistics Office of Ireland, *Census '96: Principal Economic Status and Industries,* Vol. 5 (Dublin: The Stationery Office, 1998).

15. U.S. Department of Commerce, Bureau of the Census, *Census of Population, 1950, Characteristics of the Population* (Washington, DC: Government Printing Office, 1952); U.S. Department of Commerce, Bureau of the Census, *Census of Population, Social and*

Economic Characteristics, Pennsylvania (Washington, DC: Government Printing Office, 1993). We gathered the 2000 year figures electronically from the U.S. Bureau of the Census Web site (http://factfinder.census.gov). We should note that there was some recovery in the services sector of the Philadelphia economy between 1980 and 2000. It was not enough, however, to overcome the dismal picture of regression that we have drawn.

16. On the wage gap, see Jeffrey G. Williamson, "The Evaluation of Global Labor Markets since 1830: Background Evidence and Hypotheses," *Explorations in Economic History* 32 (1995): 141–196. Recent publications on Irish and European income per capita can be found in EU, Commission of the European Communities, *European Economy,* Statistical Appendix (various issues).

17. Douglas Massey, Joaquín Arango, Graeme Hugo, Ali Kouaouci, Adela Pellegrino, and J. Edward Taylor, "New Migrations, New Theories," and "Contemporary Theories of International Migration," Chap. 1 and 2 in *Worlds in Motion: Understanding International Migration at the End of the Millennium* (Oxford: Oxford University Press, 1998; reprinted in 2002).

18. For examples of discussions of American social policy. see Michael B. Katz, *In the Shadows of the Poorhouse: A Social History of Welfare in America,* 10th Anniversary Ed. (New York: Basic Books, 1996). This work contains much detail on Philadelphia. See also Edith Abbott, *Historical Aspects of the Immigration Problem* (Chicago: University of Chicago Press, 1926); O. A. Pendleton, "Poor Relief in Philadelphia, 1790–1840," *Pennsylvania Magazine* 70, no. 1 (January 1946): 161–172; and Priscilla Ferguson Clement, "The Philadelphia Welfare Crisis of the 1820s," *Pennsylvania Magazine* 105, no. 2 (April 1981): 150–165. For a comparison of the "poor laws" in America and Philadelphia on the one hand and in Ireland on the other, read the above together with John O'Connor, *The Workhouses of Ireland: The Fate of Ireland's Poor* (Dublin: Anvil Books, 1995).

19. At this point we do not have an official estimate for undocumented Irish immigrants. For what it is worth, there is an estimate of 50,000 from the Irish Lobby for Immigrant Reform; available at http://www.irishlobbyusa.org.

20. See Fergus Kelly, *A Guide to Early Irish Law* (Dublin: School of Celtic Law, Dublin Institute for Advanced Studies, 2001).

21. See, for example, Douglass C. North, *Institutions, Institutional Change and Economic Performance* (Cambridge: Cambridge University Press, 1990). Another example is Geoffrey M. Hodgson, "The Approach of Institutional Economics," *Journal of Economic Literature* 36 (March 1998): 166–192.

22. See Kelly, *A Guide to Early Irish Law.* Also, on the existence in Irish life of hospitality, generosity, and charity, see Philip L. Kilbride and Noel J. J. Farley, *Faith, Morality, and Being Irish: A Caring Tradition in Africa* (Lanham, MD: University Press of America, 2007). For previously published writings on these matters, see Conrad Arensberg, *The Irish Countryman* (Garden City, NY: American Museum Science Books, The Natural History Press, 1937); and Daniel Corkery, *The Hidden Ireland* (Dublin: Gill and Macmillan, 1924). There is an Irish historical novel that deals with issues of Irish hospitality and generosity: Liam O'Flaherty, *Famine* (Dublin: Wolfhound Press, 1992).

23. North, *Institutions,* Chap. 9.

24. North, *Institutions,* Chap. 11.

25. See Andrew Greeley, *The American Experience: An Interpretation of the History of American Catholicism* (New York: Doubleday, 1967), 28–29. For a more extensive and detailed account of the dispute, see Donald Akenson, *The Irish Education Experiment* (Toronto: University of Toronto Press, 1970).

26. For a volume on the Irish ascendancy, see Michael McConville, *Ascendancy to Irish Oblivion, The Story of the Anglo-Irish* (London: Phoenix Press, 1986). For a volume on nineteenth-century Irish history, see Cormac O'Grada, *Ireland: A New Economic History 1780–1939* (Oxford: Clarendon Press, 1994). The notion of the Protestant State is discussed on video tapes produced by Walt Disney Studios in association with WGBH Boston, *The Irish in America: Long Journey Home* (Lennon Group Productions, 1998).

27. There are many possible sources, and we list one dealing with this issue in Philadelphia: Noel Ignatiev, *How the Irish Became White* (New York: Routledge, 1995).

28. See Katz, *In the Shadow of the Poorhouse,* Part 2.

29. See Dale Light, *Rome and the New Republic* (Notre Dame, IN: University of Notre Dame Press, 1996); Jay P. Dolan, "The Irish Parish," *U.S. Catholic Historian* 25, no. 2 (Spring 2007): 13–24; and Emmet Larkin, "The Devotional Revolution in Ireland, 1850–1875," *American Historical Review* 77, no. 3 (June 1972): 625–652.

30. Various issues of U.S. Department of Commerce, Bureau of the Census, *Census of Population, Economic and Social Characteristics, Pennsylvania* (Washington, DC: Government Printing Office).

31. U.S. Department of Commerce, Bureau of the Census, *Census of Population, Economic and Social Characteristics, Pennsylvania* (Washington, DC: Government Printing Office, 1990).

32. In Table 7.2 there is a minor discrepancy between my estimates from the findings lists of schools and archdiocesan estimates. Mild differences in definitions are involved and the differences in the numbers are not a cause of any confusion or ambiguity. We did the exercise, however, to look at the geographical distribution of the schools.

33. See *The Catholic Directory* (Philadelphia: *Catholic Standard and Times,* Archdiocese of Philadelphia, 2000).

34. Erin McGauley Heberd, "Irish-Americans and Irish Dance," in *Encounters with American Ethnic Cultures,* ed. Philip L. Kilbride, Jane C. Goodale, and Elizabeth R. Ameisen, in collaboration with Carolyn G. Friedman (Tuscaloosa: University of Alabama Press, 1990).

35. There is information on all of these bodies on the Web sites for the Irish Center (http://www.theirishcenter.com) and the Friendly Sons of Saint Patrick (http://www.friendly sonsofstpatcin.org).

36. Phrases taken from Clark, *The Irish Relations,* 213.

37. Clark, *The Irish Relations,* 213.

38. In the modern context among Irish Americans, this tradition is very much reflected in the actions of Irish societies and clubs in America.

8

Healthcare Access for Mexican Immigrants in South Philadelphia

Jennifer Atlas

T he number of Mexican immigrants in Philadelphia has increased rapidly over the past decade. In 2000, the U.S. Census estimated that there were approximately 6,220 Mexican immigrants in Philadelphia.[1] Just three years later, the Mexican Consulate estimated that over 12,000 Mexican immigrants called the city of Philadelphia home, making the Mexican population the second largest Latino immigrant group after Puerto Ricans.[2] The recent growth of the Mexican population in Philadelphia has far outpaced the social services available, with the shortage of services manifesting itself most acutely in the area of health care.

Healthcare services that are both culturally competent and accessible to the Mexican immigrant population must encompass a variety of characteristics. The majority of Mexican immigrants nationwide speak mostly Spanish, making the supply of bilingual providers or language services essential in the delivery of health care. Additionally, most Mexicans work in blue-collar jobs, making low-cost health services important. Further, many Mexicans come to the United States with their own cultural beliefs about healing and folk remedies, making knowledge of these beliefs and cultural sensitivity on the part of healthcare providers a matter of great importance.[3] Finally, many Mexican immigrants who come to the United States are undocumented, making citizenship an issue of chief concern in the seeking and delivery of healthcare services.

The rapid growth of the Mexican population over the past five to seven years has created a burgeoning need for healthcare services. While grassroots organizations exist within the Mexican community in Philadelphia, there are no large, formal institutions that specifically target this population and provide health services. Instead, existing organizations tend to focus their efforts on education, advocacy, and the promotion of Mexican culture. While Philadelphia's Mexican population is rapidly expanding, the absence of a healthcare infrastructure for this population makes the city's situation different from that of cities in Arizona, Texas, New Mexico, and California, where well-established health programs, health coalitions, and bilateral health agreements with Mexico exist to meet the needs of these cities' larger and longer-established Mexican communities.

It is important to examine healthcare access because it is an essential need, the absence of which profoundly affects the daily life (and often the very survival) of those lacking it. Even though health care has been declared a human right by the United Nations,[4] many Mexican immigrants in Philadelphia are undocumented and lack access to health care because of their legal status. The immigration status of many in this community complicates healthcare access and makes the study of it even more vital and multifaceted.

This chapter will use published studies and interviews[5] with leading immigrant advocates and health professionals to examine why health care has emerged as an important issue in the Mexican community in Philadelphia. Additionally, this chapter will explain why there are not enough healthcare services for the Mexican population, focusing on the inaccuracy of demographic data on the Mexican population, national legislation that has hindered immigrants' access to public benefits, and the absence of formal institutions within the Mexican community providing healthcare services. Finally, this chapter will explore some of the implications of the failure to provide adequate healthcare services to Philadelphia's Mexican community.

Mexicans in Philadelphia: The Past and the Present

Although the influx of Mexicans in Philadelphia has largely occurred since the year 2000, Mexicans have worked in Philadelphia since as early as the turn of the nineteenth century.[6] Before and during World War II, many Mexicans were contracted by the U.S. government to work on the railroads in Philadelphia. During World War II, many Mexicans also worked in agriculture in the area surrounding Philadelphia. Mexicans were not the only Latino group to be heavily recruited during wartime; as Victor Vazquez-Hernandez describes in Chapter 4 of this volume, large numbers of Puerto Ricans took over wartime jobs and established community institutions in Philadelphia during this era.

Most Mexican migration to Philadelphia started to occur between the mid- to late 1990s, reaching a peak after the year 2000 that continues to this day. The literature explaining Philadelphia's immigration patterns is largely incomplete and does not explain what triggered such significant influxes in this particular decade. However, there are a number of hypotheses. One hypothesis is that economic crises occurring in Mexico between the years of 1986–1987 and 1994–1997 spurred massive emigration from Mexico to the United States. During this first recession, inflation in Mexico rose from 74 percent to 153 percent, and during the second recession, inflation rose from 7 percent to as high as 41 percent.[7] Statistics show that during the 1990s, the number of Mexicans living in the United States rose by nearly five million people but traditional Mexican destinations, such as Texas and California, had become less popular.[8]

Another hypothesis is that Mexican migrants—some first-time migrants coming directly from Mexico and some secondary migrants coming from New York and New Jersey—came to Philadelphia because of the affordable cost of living and housing as compared to other cities like New York, Boston, and Washington DC.[9] This was not only true for the Mexican population but for many other immigrant populations as well. In Chapter 9 of this volume, Garvey Lundy also highlights how many Haitian immigrants relocated from New York to Philadelphia because of lower housing prices in the latter city. A third reason is the large expansion of the restaurant, hospitality, and hotel industries in the late 1990s, which provided jobs to many Mexicans in Philadelphia.[10] Finally, the initial influxes of Mexican immigrants to Philadelphia in the first part of the decade has resulted in the selection of Philadelphia as a destination by more recent immigrants desiring to be in the presence of family and friends.

Today, some Philadelphia-area Mexican immigrants live in the suburb of Norristown and some are located on Fifth Street in North Philadelphia.[11] However, the majority of Philadelphia's Mexican population is located in South Philadelphia near the Italian Market. Peter Bloom, the former director of the Mexican advocacy organization JUNTOS/La Casa de los Soles, estimates that the Mexican immigrant population is comprised of more males than females and is mostly between the ages of 18 and 35.[12] He estimates that approximately half of the Mexican immigrants are from Mexico City and its surrounding areas, while the remaining half are predominantly from the region of Puebla, as well as the cities of Tlaxaca, Oaxaca, and Guerrero. In terms of health care, it is particularly important to note that the majority of Philadelphia's Mexican immigrant population do not have more than a middle school education, speak limited—if any—English, and have undocumented legal status.[13]

Healthcare Services Available to Mexican Undocumented Immigrants in Philadelphia

To date, there have been no extensive studies published on the healthcare access that Mexican immigrants have in Philadelphia. However, a comprehensive examination of this population's demographic profile and existing healthcare services in Philadelphia, as well as interviews with healthcare providers and leaders of NGOs engaging with this population and with these issues, strongly indicates that there are not enough services to meet the needs of the burgeoning undocumented Mexican population. In discussing the healthcare services available for the Mexican immigrant population, it is necessary to make distinctions among three different types of health care: primary care, emergency care, and chronic care. These distinctions are important because each of these three categories is associated with different national and state policies that in turn affect Mexican immigrants' access to existing resources.

Primary Care

In 1978, the World Health Organization defined primary health care as "the first level of contact of individuals, the family and community with the national health system, bringing health care as close as possible to where people live and work."[14] At the fundamental level, primary health care should seek to combat the main health problems in the community by providing "promotive, preventive, curative, and rehabilitative services,"[15] especially in, but not limited to, the areas of maternal and child health; the prevention and control of infectious, nationally common, and locally endemic diseases; treatment of injury; adequate supplies of safe water and basic sanitation; the promotion of food supply and proper nutrition; and the provision of essential drugs. In essence, primary care centers should be the patient's healthcare home, a place where they should be able to come to seek health information and diagnosis, counseling, and treatment.

In Philadelphia, very few Mexican immigrants utilize primary healthcare providers because of a multitude of barriers that will be explained throughout this chapter.[16] Because the majority of Mexicans in Philadelphia are undocumented and speak very little—if any—English, most have low-wage labor jobs where they do not have access to health insurance. Typically, males work in restaurant, hospitality, landscaping/gardening, and construction industries while females work as housecleaners, nannies, and as mothers and homemakers.[17] This leaves little opportunity for them to have employer-based insurance.

Without employer-based or government-provided health insurance, undocumented Mexican immigrants are greatly limited in their options for seeking primary health care. The most commonly conceived and used options will be referred to here, but a comprehensive listing of all health services that immigrants in the state of Pennsylvania can access is available on the Pennsylvania Health Law Project Web site.[18]

Philadelphia has federally qualified health centers (FQHCs) and district health centers—designated as "FQHC look-alikes"—that are required to treat all patients, regardless of immigration status. In accordance with Section 330 of the Public Health Service Act, FQHCs are marked by their presence in medically underserved areas; their governing boards composed of a majority of health center patients who represent the underserved; their provision of comprehensive primary care services; their provision of supportive services such as education, translation, and transportation; their provision of services to all with fees adjusted based on ability to pay; and their meeting of other performance and accountability requirements set by the federal government.[19] In exchange for meeting these qualifications, FQHCs are provided with federal funding, malpractice insurance, and through Section 340B of the Public Service Act, drug purchasing discounts.[20] FQHCs are located throughout Pennsylvania.

Philadelphia's District Health Care Centers are funded through a mix of local taxpayer dollars and federal and state Medicaid funds.[21] There are eight healthcare centers located throughout Philadelphia. These District Health Care Centers have the federal status of FQHC look-alikes. Like FQHCs, FQHC look-alikes receive 340B drug purchasing discounts and government cost-based reimbursement for their services but they do not receive malpractice insurance and cannot apply for certain federal grants. According to the Philadelphia Department of Health Web site, the District Health Centers were established beginning in the mid- to late 1960s when the city experienced a decline in the availability of primary care for its residents. The Philadelphia Department of Public Health saw the creation of these District Health Centers as "a way to decentralize an administration which had become too large to effectively provide public health services in a traditional centralized manner."[22]

Both FQHCs and Philadelphia's District Health Centers service the Mexican immigrant population, particularly the Southeast Health Center and Philadelphia Health Care Center #2. The Southeast Health Center, a FQHC established in 1979 and sponsored by Greater Philadelphia Health Action (GPHA), is located right in the heart of the Mexican community at 800 Washington Avenue. This health center provides adult medicine, pediatrics, geriatrics, podiatry, nutrition, OB/GYN services, family planning, case management, immunizations, HIV/AIDS testing and treatment, and access to convenient dental care and pharmaceuticals.[23] The District Health Centers most likely to be frequented by Latin American immigrants are the three that are advertised as having Spanish-speaking providers or Spanish language services available. Of these three District Health Centers, Philadelphia Health Care Center #2 on South Broad Street is located in closest proximity to the Mexican community in South Philadelphia. This particular health center offers all of the services that the Southeast Health Center does, in addition to podiatry, radiology, tuberculosis testing, and other advanced lab tests such as EKGs.[24]

Observing these particular care centers reveals that they see hundreds of patients per day. District Health Care Center #2 acknowledges this even in its informational handout, stating that "because of the many services and the large number of patients that we service, at times, you may experience waiting times longer than expected and we also ask that you be patient and understanding."[25] As current director of the Health Federation of Philadelphia Natalie Levkovich told me in our interview in December 2008, "there are a finite number of health centers in Philadelphia that have the capacity and are geographically proximate to those [immigrant] populations and they provide a lot of services," causing the existing health centers to be overburdened.[26]

Mayor Michael Nutter's executive order No. 9-08 of June 2008 required that all city departments, agencies, boards, and commissions—regardless of whether they are recipients of federal financial support or are supervised by the managing director—"have a language access plan in place to provide both policy direction and the necessary protocols to carry out the provision of language access services to limited English proficient residents and visitors."[27] The executive order is useful to the Mexican immigrant population because it attempts to lessen language barriers. However, the executive order does not mean that all healthcare providers in public clinics are fluent in Spanish. This translates into long wait times for Spanish-speaking patients who want to see the limited number of Spanish-speaking healthcare professionals or longer clinic visits for patients who must use a language line to communicate with their healthcare provider.

All of these issues are compounded by the fear that many Mexican undocumented immigrants have of being deported if they access healthcare services. In a memorandum released in 2003, the city solicitor of Philadelphia clarified that "no person shall be denied any City services or benefits because of his or her immigration status."[28] Furthermore, the city solicitor declared that "a city officer or employee, other than law enforcement officers, shall not inquire about a person's immigration status unless such a person's immigration status is necessary for the determination of program, service or benefit eligibility."[29] A subsequent memorandum released by the Philadelphia City Department of Public Health in 2004 stated that to qualify for District Health Care Center clinics, "there is no requirement that a patient be a citizen or have a certain immigration status."[30]

In spite of this, many immigrants still fear accessing government health services. According to immigrant expert and Pennsylvania Health Law Project associate Leonardo Cuello, "[The immigrant] mantra is 'I just don't want any problems' and they are not going to do anything to put themselves in jeopardy."[31] For this reason, Cuello has noted immigrants are more likely to seek care from smaller clinics within their own communities that they can trust or not access services at all because they think of preventive care "as something that they could put off."[32]

One of the organizations that has arisen to meet the needs of the Mexican immigrant population in South Philadelphia is Puentes de Salud. Started by the innovative leadership of Steven Larson, Matt O'Brien, and Rebecca Bixby,

Puentes prides itself on "high-quality clinical care services, innovative education opportunities, and participation in peer-to-peer health programs."[33] Puentes first established itself in south Philadelphia by holding town meetings, attending health fairs, and starting ESL classes in the community. In 2006, Puentes de Salud opened its free clinic in the basement of St. Agnes Hospital. Open every Thursday night, Puentes provides entirely bilingual health care to Spanish-speaking immigrants, who are predominantly Mexican, through a staff of volunteer healthcare professionals and undergraduate and graduate students. Puentes strives to engage the immigrant community in multifaceted ways, be it through the provision of ESL classes, public health literature in Spanish, legal presentations on immigrant rights in the waiting room, exercise classes, or community-based participatory research involving health promoters—"*promotoras*"—in the community. Puentes has tried to expand its services by forming community partnerships with the Children's Hospital of Philadelphia, Latina Community Health Services (a new Spanish-speaking clinic open two days a week to service the OB/GYN needs of Latinas), and the Maternity Care Coalition. In spite of the great services that Puentes provides and the comfort that it gives immigrants of every legal status, the organization is constrained by its limited budget, its lack of space, and its ability to be open only once a week.

Thus, Mexican immigrants' abilities to access primary care services in Philadelphia are constrained by a lack of healthcare insurance, largely due to their undocumented status. This forces immigrants to turn to other options, such as public clinics and community-based health programs. Even with the myriad of different services available, long wait times, insufficient numbers of Spanish-speaking personnel, and lack of funding prevents these clinics and organizations from being the full healthcare homes that immigrants need.

Health Care for Emergency Conditions

Under Section 1867 of the Social Security Act, known as the Emergency Medical Treatment and Labor Act (EMTALA), all Medicare- participating hospitals are required to provide treatment and stabilize emergency medical conditions, including active labor, regardless of the patient's ability to pay. If the hospital is unable to do so, the patient must be transferred to a different facility.[34]

If a Mexican immigrant who is undocumented has a medical emergency and is hospitalized, one of four things can happen: the immigrant could apply for emergency medical assistance, become a charity care case of the hospital, set up a payment plan with a hospital, or not pay the bill and have it become uncompensated care for the hospital.

Emergency Medical Assistance (EMA) is a type of medical insurance operated by the Medicaid program that covers an emergency medical condition, which is defined by Pennsylvania state law as "acute symptoms of such severity, including severe pain, that without immediate attention, the result may be that the patient's health is in serious jeopardy, serious impairment to bodily functions, or serious dysfunction of any body part or organ."[35] Emergency Medical Assistance coverage varies by state. The state pays for Emergency Medical Assistance and the federal government is supposed to reimburse the state through federal matching funds. Unlike general Medicaid requirements, Emergency Medical Assistance does not require verification of a social security number, alien status, or the signing of a citizenship/alienage declaration form.[36] It does, however, require meeting all of the other Medical Assistance eligibility requirements. In Pennsylvania, these requirements include being a Pennsylvania resident, fitting into a Medicaid category—pregnant, permanently or temporarily disabled, child under age 18, elderly ages 59 and up, using health-sustaining medication, adults ages 21–58 working at least 100 hours per month, or having breast or cervical cancer—and being within the income and asset limits required for Medicaid.[37] In addition, according to Pennsylvania state law, being able to qualify for EMA requires a written statement from a healthcare provider that will "identify the emergency medical condition, specify that the medical treatment was necessary because of the medical condition, [and] provide a date on which the emergency is expected to end."[38]

The Pennsylvania immigrant who is submitting a claim for Emergency Medical Assistance must receive this letter from his or her doctor (in some areas, doctors can fill out a simple form) and fill out the regular application forms for Medical Assistance. The claim is then submitted to the County Assistance Office. A caseworker reviews the application and notifies the applicant within 30 days about whether EMA coverage has been awarded. Health insurance coverage is not lost within this time period.

According to Leonardo Cuello of the Pennsylvania Health Law Project, the problems with applying for Emergency Medical Assistance are many and occur on both a macro and a micro level. One of the biggest problems has been the interpretation of what comprises an emergency medical condition. Depending on the political environment, the term "emergency medical condition" has either been interpreted strictly or broadly, causing problems at the macro level by the lack of a consistent standard.[39] At the micro level, this ambiguity causes numerous problems for physicians who must fill out the EMA applications. For example, labor and delivery qualifies as an emergency medical condition but prenatal care does not unless it is for a high-risk pregnancy.[40] Although many doctors might not consider a small malignant tumor an emergency, it could be considered an emergency under EMA because of the serious jeopardy to one's health that it poses without treatment.[41] Because applying for EMA is so complicated, it is critical that immigrants have an advocate, not only to make them aware that they have an emergency condition that could qualify, but also to assist them with the relatively complex application process and appeals process if necessary.

Besides difficulties about what comprises an emergency medical condition, applying for EMA itself is a daunting task. Because emergency room doctors do not establish the same rapport with their patients that primary care physicians do, it may be difficult for the immigrant to recall which doctor they saw to ask for the EMA physician's letter. It may also be difficult for the doctor to remember the particular case. This is especially problematic, given that doctors must write down either the specific dates of the emergency medical treatment if the EMA application follows the emergency retroactively, or forecast the dates that the treatment will end if the treatment is proactive, such as for a tumor.

With special regard to the Mexican population in Philadelphia, Cuello says that the most common claims for Emergency Medical Assistance are due to work-related accidents among men and labor and delivery and cervical cancer among women.[42] Cuello has seen a fear among undocumented Mexican immigrants in applying for Emergency Medical Assistance, though he is trying to combat that fear by raising awareness about EMA through his provision of training to healthcare providers and through resources available on the Pennsylvania Health Law Project Web site. Although some Pennsylvania hospitals are successful at getting patients to apply for emergency medical assistance, Cuello acknowledges that generally hospitals could do much better. He recounted in our interview: "it's pretty often that I deal with clients who could have been told and just weren't."[43]

Pennsylvania Emergency Medical Assistance trends mirror those of other states. One study on emergency medical assistance utilization in North Carolina conducted in 2004 revealed that, as in Pennsylvania, the greatest spending for EMA was in pregnancy and birth complications (82 percent), followed by injury and poisoning (approximately 33 percent), and then digestive (16 percent), genitourinary (12 percent), and circulatory system diseases (11 percent).[44] The study also revealed that only 5 percent of North Carolina's undocumented population—estimated to be at 300,000 in 2004—was being covered by EMA. Although no large studies on Emergency Medical Assistance coverage have been published for Philadelphia, undocumented immigrants who receive EMA are still probably a fraction of the total population who could be eligible for coverage.[45]

If immigrants are unable to obtain EMA, hospitals should apply to make the immigrant a recipient of charity care. Pennsylvania hospitals receive millions of dollars through federal, state, and private funds to provide free, uncompensated care to patients—in many cases regardless of immigration status—with outstanding medical bills.[46] Although hospitals should be making every effort to enroll immigrants into EMA and then into charity care, what Cuello says is that, more often than not, hospitals—many times unknowingly—"put an immigrant straight into a payment plan even if they would be eligible for emergency medical assistance or charity care."[47] Immigrants generally do want to pay their medical bills, so if they are given the option of a payment plan, they are likely to follow through with this option. Ultimately, some emergency care for immigrants still remains uncompensated. These costs are covered through a pot of federal and state funds reserved for each hospital.[48]

Chronic Care

Chronic care is defined as including both chronic illness, "the presence of long-term disease or symptoms," and impairments, "a physiological, psychological, or anatomical abnormality of bodily structure and function."[49] Examples of chronic conditions include but are not limited to AIDS, arthritis, cancer, heart disease, diabetes, hearing impairment, and mental retardation.

According to Cuello, immigrants who are undocumented have the least access to chronic care. EMA does not cover chronic conditions and although public clinics do provide treatment for chronic conditions, the degree of comprehensive follow-up that is needed for management of such conditions proves challenging when dealing with patients who do not speak English as their first language and cannot afford much.[50]

Chronic conditions are particularly salient among Mexican immigrants nationwide. The Pan American Health Organization did an analysis of diabetes on the Texas-Mexico border and found that the incidence of diabetes was 31.9 percent of the total population in the border region as compared to 24.9 percent of the total population for the state and for the nation.[51] According to information released by the University of California at Berkeley, the incidence of hypertension, a condition that leads to heart disease, is as high as 9 percent among Mexican adults ages 18–64 nationwide.[52] These trends are not specific to Mexican immigrants but to Hispanics as a whole. The top four leading causes of death for Latina females in 2001 were heart disease, cancer, stroke, and diabetes respectively.[53] These four conditions plague the Hispanic immigrant community because the stress of working long hours contributes to high blood pressure and eating unhealthy fast food,[54] living in crime-ridden neighborhoods discourages physical activity, and undocumented legal status means largely being unable to access the primary healthcare services essential for earlier remedying of unhealthy behaviors and detection of cancers.[55]

In 2004, the Pennsylvania Department of Public Welfare issued an Operations Memorandum stating that some chronic care conditions, including dialysis, could be considered EMA conditions.[56] However, for the majority of chronic conditions, especially developmental ones, Mexican undocumented immigrants in Philadelphia have little recourse.

Explanations for the Absence of
Healthcare Services

Thus far, this chapter has described the areas in which there are not enough healthcare services to meet the needs of the burgeoning Mexican immigrant population in Philadelphia. There are three reasons that one can attribute to Mexicans' lack of healthcare access: lack of demographic data on the Mexican immigrant population, laws that have limited immigrants' access to public benefits, and the lack of formal institutions serving health needs within the Mexican community.

Lack of Demographic Data

Because the Mexican population in Philadelphia is largely Spanish-speaking, undocumented, fearful of the government, and transient in their constant movement between the United States and Mexico or between different locations in the United States, it can be very difficult to ascertain accurate data.[57] Much of public health programming is data driven, so without accurate data on the Mexican population, it can be hard to establish future services.

The 2000 U.S. Census determined that there were 6,220 Mexican immigrants in Philadelphia, and the 2007 American Community Survey estimated that there were 4,900 Mexican immigrants in Philadelphia.[58] These numbers are respectively 41 percent and 52 percent of the 12,000 proposed by the Mexican Consulate in 2003. In my interview with Natalie Levkovich, current director of the Health Federation of Philadelphia, she said that "data follows the money . . . if there's no source of reimbursement, if there's no claim generated, if there's no bill, there's likely to be inadequately sorted data."[59]

According to Levkovich, the Philadelphia Department of Public Health uses data to drive its priorities. Mayor Michael Nutter acquiesced to this upon receipt of the results of a 2008 study conducted by the Brookings Institution on the state of immigration in Philadelphia. In a press conference that celebrated the study's findings, Nutter promised that the data would be used to implement further public policy initiatives in Philadelphia.[60] Without accurate data to begin with, there can be no creation of public policy initiatives to address the unmet healthcare needs of the Mexican population in Philadelphia.

National Healthcare Legislation and Its Impact on
Healthcare Access for Mexican Immigrants

Federal policies also serve to explain why many Mexican immigrants in Philadelphia lack healthcare access. The 1996 Personal Responsibility and Work Opportunity Reconciliation Act (PRWORA) was responsible for severely hindering immigrants' access to health care and to other public welfare benefits nationwide. Even though the Legal Children's Health Improvement Act of 2009—signed into law by President Obama on February 4, 2009[61]—revoked many of the provisions of PRWORA for pregnant women and children, it is still essential to discuss PRWORA in order to understand the healthcare barriers that have affected Mexican immigrants nationwide.

PRWORA was born out of a sentiment that public services should not be "an incentive for immigration to the United States" and that "individual aliens not burden the public benefits system."[62] The law prohibited immigrants who did not have a qualified immigrant status[63] or had a qualified status but had not been in the United States for at least five years, from accessing "any retirement, welfare, health, disability . . . or any other similar benefit for which payments or assistance are provided to an individual, household, or family eligibility unit by an agency of a State or local government or by appropriated funds of a State or local government."[64] Immigrants had previously been entitled to these benefits, causing this law to institute major change. Immigrants who did not meet PRWORA's stipulations could still receive immunizations, testing and treatment for communicable diseases, and treatment for emergency medical conditions under the law.

Health insurance is most commonly obtained through one of two ways—either through the provision of employer-based coverage or through the provision of public insurance programs, such as Medicare and Medicaid. PRWORA left qualified immigrants who had not been in the United States for at least five years and undocumented (nonqualified) Mexican immigrants with only the former option. Previous studies have demonstrated that the average lower levels of educational attainment among many immigrants, particularly those from Mexico and Latin American and Caribbean nations[65]—compared to the native-born population—makes it difficult for immigrants from these regions to find jobs where employment-based healthcare insurance benefits will be offered to them.[66] Undocumented immigrants are particularly likely to find themselves in such positions, as numerous studies have demonstrated that such immigrants have lower levels of education than documented immigrants.[67] Statistics on health insurance coverage for Pennsylvania released by the Urban Institute and the Kaiser Commission on Medicaid and the Uninsured reflect this fact, as well as reflecting existing racial disparities in healthcare access. As shown in Table 8.1, among those in Pennsylvania who have employer-based health insurance coverage, only 3.6 percent are Hispanic; in contrast, those with coverage are 85.0 percent white and 8.3 percent black.

PRWORA's effect has been studied in detail in states with large immigrant populations. According to a 2005 Kaiser Report,[68] only 38 percent of undocumented Latino adults in Fresno and Los Angeles counties combined had an annual visit to a physician in the United States, compared to 67 percent of all

TABLE 8.1   DISTRIBUTION OF THE NONELDERLY WITH EMPLOYER-BASED
HEALTH INSURANCE COVERAGE BY RACE/ETHNICITY

	Pennsylvania (2007–2008)		United States (2008)	
	Number	%	Number	%
White	5,893,200	85.0	113,047,300	72.1
Black	572,000	8.3	15,636,000	10.0
Hispanic	250,800	3.6	17,391,400	11.1
Other	213,200	3.1	10,785,500	6.9
Total	6,929,200	100.0	156,860,100	100.0

Note: The nonelderly are those aged 0–64 years. The numbers reported are the numbers of individuals in each group who have employer-based health coverage (*not* absolute numbers of individuals in the population). The percentages given indicate the percentage of employer-based health insurance coverage that is held by each group (*not* absolute percentage of each group that has employer-based coverage).

Source: Web site of statehealthfacts.org: http://www.statehealthfacts.org/profileind.jsp?ind=148&cat=3&rgn =40. Data derived from Urban Institute and Kaiser Commission on Medicaid and the Uninsured estimates based on the U.S. Census Bureau's March 2007 and 2008 Current Population Survey (CPS: Annual Social and Economic Supplements).

Latinos nationwide and 75 percent of all adults nationwide. Over 90 percent of these undocumented Latino immigrants in Fresno County were Mexican immigrants, and 80 percent in Los Angeles were Mexican as well. Similarly, a 1994 study[69] in New York City revealed that undocumented Mexican migrants who had come to the United States before 1997 were more likely to report access to a regular healthcare provider than Mexican migrants who had come to the city in subsequent years. The authors of this study speculated the 1996 PRWORA legislation might have contributed to these findings.

PRWORA was the main legislation that had an impact on healthcare access for immigrants in the United States. Although its impact in Philadelphia was not quantified, Philadelphia was subject to this federal law and it is likely that Philadelphia's Mexican population was affected similarly to other Mexican populations nationwide. Now that states have the option of eliminating PRWORA's five-year waiting period for children and for pregnant women through recent reforms by the Obama administration, it will be interesting to observe if the number of immigrants enrolled in public health insurance programs rapidly increases or if PRWORA's legacy has left immigrants hesitant of receiving public benefits.

Absence of Formal Institutions within the Mexican Community That Provide Health Care

A third reason that explains the lack of healthcare access among Mexicans in Philadelphia is the way in which community building has occurred within this population and within the Latino community. There are large, long-standing, and well-respected Latino social service organizations, such as the Council of Spanish Speaking Organizations Inc. (CONCILIO) and Congreso de Latinos

Unidos Inc. (CONGRESO), in Philadelphia. However, these organizations' primary focus is on Philadelphia's Puerto Rican population, the oldest Latino population in Philadelphia. Teen parenting programs, HIV/AIDS education and counseling programs, and alcohol and drug abuse programs, among others run by CONGRESO and CONCILIO, are specifically targeted at Latinos living in North Philadelphia, where these agencies are located.[70] Although some Mexican immigrants from South Philadelphia do travel to North Philadelphia to access the quality services these agencies provide, the majority of Mexican immigrants in South Philadelphia do not leave their community to access these services.[71]

Organizations that predominantly service the Mexican community include JUNTOS/Casa de Los Soles and the Mexican Cultural Center. JUNTOS, founded in 2002, is an organization for Mexican and Latino immigrants that "combines literacy education, leadership development and community organizing to help immigrants develop the necessary tools to advance economically, integrate into the social fabric of the city, and become active participants in civic life."[72] JUNTOS offers ESL classes; brings together the Latino community to organize on issues pertaining to education, security, and worker rights; and has a video project so that Mexican immigrants can document their experiences living in Philadelphia. The Mexican Cultural Center works closely with the Mexican Consulate to "serve as a networking hub for those interested in Mexican culture" in eastern Pennsylvania, southern New Jersey, and Delaware. In addition to organizing an annual Mexican Independence Day Festival at Penn's Landing in Philadelphia, it sponsors and advertises Mexican concerts, exhibits, and plays.[73]

In addition to JUNTOS and the Mexican Cultural Center, there are informal networks within the Mexican community. The social networking site www.mexicanosenphiladelphia.com, managed by Edgar Ramirez, diffuses information on Mexican and Latino cultural events, advertises Mexican businesses and restaurants, and lists different resources for the Mexican community, all in Spanish. Events advertised on the Web site are also disseminated through a listserv.[74] Annunciation Church at Tenth and Dickinson Streets and St. Thomas Aquinas Church at Eighteenth and Morris Streets are frequented by the Mexican population. These churches hold and advertise events and forums for the Mexican community and also have knitting groups, family counseling, ESL programs, and tutoring for elementary school children.[75]

These formal and informal networks show that there are community-building efforts occurring among the Mexican population in South Philadelphia. However, much of this community building is related to showcasing Mexican culture and not related to the direct provision of services. Considering that the migration of Mexican immigrants to Philadelphia is so recent, this is unsurprising. It takes both time and funding to establish institutions that have the depth and breadth that CONCILIO and CONGRESO have. Amanda Bergson-Shilcock of the Welcoming Center for New Pennsylvanians acknowledged in our interview that this problem is not specific to the Mexican population. Recent immigrants who establish community organizations routinely struggle with low budgets, few paid staff, and an unfamiliarity with the U.S. nonprofit landscape.[76]

Bergson-Shilcock thinks that over time this will change for Mexican immigrants in Philadelphia, as it has for Mexican immigrants in other locations, such as California. As second generation Mexicans receive U.S. educations and decide to start their own community organizations, there will be a "new generation of leadership" in Philadelphia.[77] The organizations and churches mentioned here are making people aware of the Mexican population in Philadelphia, are providing Mexicans with avenues of advocacy and educational services, and their efforts may ultimately lead to the establishment of larger institutions in south Philadelphia that provide healthcare services. The existence of clinics that serve Spanish-speaking immigrants in South Philadelphia, like Puentes de Salud and Latina Community Health Services, implies that healthcare services are an important need for the Mexican population and need to be included in such institutions.

Conclusions

In each of the three areas of health care—primary care, emergency care, and chronic care—there are shortages of services and barriers that prevent Mexican immigrants in Philadelphia from fully accessing the existing healthcare services and programs available to them. Inaccurate demographic data on the Mexican population in Philadelphia, past national legislation hindering immigrants' access to public welfare benefits, and early level of development in community-building efforts, have all worked in tandem to create, exacerbate, and sometimes even justify such a shortage of services.

In addition to the above factors, a phenomenon known as the "Hispanic Paradox" makes the lack of healthcare resources especially problematic for Mexican immigrant children. In this context, the term "Hispanic Paradox" refers to the health status of different generations of Hispanic immigrants and the fact that the health of Hispanic immigrants declines the longer they have been in the United States. Multiple health studies have found that "for virtually every indicator, second generation youth have poorer physical health outcomes."[78] In future studies of healthcare access within the Mexican immigrant population, it will be important to fully explore the consequences of the interplay between the Hispanic Paradox and the lack of access to healthcare services on the pediatric population and on future generations.

Efforts will need to come both from within and outside of the Mexican community in Philadelphia in order to continue to bring attention to and to improve Mexicans' healthcare situation. As the Mexican population continues to grow, the children of recent Mexican immigrants—the second generation—

could work together to establish new resources for the community and to improve healthcare infrastructure in particular. However, this process is a long-term one. Without more immediate action, such increases in community-building efforts will be infinitely more challenging. Lack of healthcare services for the burgeoning and largely undocumented Mexican immigrant population not only results in worse health outcomes for recent immigrants, but for their children as well, the second generation that will be essential in transforming Philadelphia's Mexican community in future years

With Barack Obama's presidential administration making changes to healthcare reform and the 2010 U.S. Census fast approaching, there is a real opportunity for nationwide change in the healthcare landscape for Mexican immigrants. There is also a real opportunity for Philadelphia to make health care a human right in practice, not just in ideology, for all men, women, and children.

Notes

1. U.S. Census Bureau, 2000 U.S. Census. Available at http://www.census.gov.

2. Welcoming Center for New Pennsylvanians, "PA & Immigration: Immigrant Communities: Pan-America." Available at http://www.welcomingcenter.org/immigrationPA/panamerica.php#mexico (accessed 24 Dec. 2008).

3. Maria R. Warda, "Mexican Americans' Perceptions of Culturally Competent Care," *Western Journal of Nursing Research* 22, no. 8 (2000): 203–224.

4. United Nations, *Universal Declaration of Human Rights,* art. XXV (1948).

5. Four separate interviews were conducted with leading immigrant advocates and healthcare providers in the fall of 2008 over a period of one to two hours at the sites of the Pennsylvania Health Law Project (Leonardo Cuello, 24 Oct.), the Children's Hospital of Philadelphia (Dr. Susmita Pati, 7 Nov.), the Health Federation of Philadelphia (Natalie Levkovich, 3 Dec.), and the Welcoming Center for New Pennsylvanians (Amanda Bergson-Shilcock, 5 Dec.).

6. Historical Society of Pennsylvania, "Early Enclaves." Available at http://www.hsp.org/default.aspx?id=361 (accessed 24 Dec. 2008).

7. David M. Cutler, Felicia Knaul, Rafael Lozano, Oscar Méndez, and Beatriz Zurita, "Financial Crisis, Health Outcomes, and Ageing: Mexico in the 1980s and 1990s," *Journal of Public Economics* 84 (2002): 279–303.

8. David Card and Ethan G. Lewis, "The Diffusion of Mexican Immigrants during the 1990s: Explanations and Impacts," in *Mexican Immigration to the United States,* ed. George J. Borjas (Chicago: University of Chicago Press, 2007).

9. Historical Society of Pennsylvania, "Latino Philadelphia." Available at http://www.hsp.org/default.aspx?id=103 (accessed 24 Dec. 2008).

10. Amanda Bergson-Shilcock, Director of Intake and Operations for the Welcoming Center for New Pennsylvanians. Personal interview, 5 Dec. 2008.

11. Ibid.

12. Peter Bloom, e-mail message to the author, 1 Nov. 2008.

13. Ibid.

14. World Health Organization, "Declaration of Alma-Ata." Policy statement from the International Conference on Primary Health Care, Kazakhstan, 12 Sept. 1978.

15. Ibid.

16. Leonardo Cuello, Pennsylvania Health Law Project. Personal interview, 24 Oct. 2008.

17. Amanda Bergson-Shilcock, interview.

18. Leonardo Cuello, "Health Care for Immigrants: A Manual for Advocates," Pennsylvania Health Law Project. Dec. 2008. Available at http://www.phlp.org/Website/ Immigrants/Immigrant%20Health%20Care%20Manual%20For%20Advocates.pdf.

19. "Section 330" (Public Health Service Act of 1946) is still used to describe these regulations, but in the U.S. Code it has been renumbered as Title 42, Chapter 6A, section 254b, last updated 8 Jan. 2008. The text of Section 330 is available at http://bphc.hrsa.gov/ about/legislation/section330.htm.

20. U.S. Department of Health and Human Services, Health Resources and Services Administration, "Benefits to the Health Center." Available at http://bphc.hrsa.gov/about/ benefits.htm (accessed 6 Nov. 2009).

21. Natalie Levkovich, Health Federation of Philadelphia." Personal interview, 3 Dec. 2008.

22. City of Philadelphia, Department of Public Health, "Health Care Centers." Available at http://www.phila.gov/Health/Commissioner/History/HistoryHealthCarePart6.html (accessed 22 Dec. 2008).

23. Greater Philadelphia Health Action, "Southeast Health Center" (advertisement). Available at http://www.gphainc.org/upload/healthcare_locations/6.pdf (accessed 23 Dec. 2008).

24. City of Philadelphia, "Patient Information on HCC-2 Services and Procedures" (brochure). Obtained by author in Feb. 2009.

25. Ibid.

26. Natalie Levkovich, interview.

27. Mayor Michael A. Nutter of Philadelphia, Executive Order No. 9-08, "Access to City Programs and Activities for Individuals with Limited English Proficiency," 9 June 2008.

28. Nelson A. Diaz, "Immigrant Access to City Services." Memorandum to All City Commissioners and Department Heads, 10 Oct. 2003. Available at the Pennsylvania Health Law Project Web site: http://www.phlp.org/Website/Immigrants/City%20Soloicitor%20 Oct%202003.pdf (accessed Dec. 2008).

29. Ibid.

30. Susan Pingree, "Patient Residency Policy." Memorandum to Health Center Directors, Clinical Directors, Health Care Coordinators, and Clerical Supervisors, 15 Mar. 2004. Available at the Pennsylvania Health Law Project Web site: http://www.phlp.org/Website/ Immigrants/Health%20Center%20Patient%20Residency%20Policy%203152004.pdf.

31. Leonardo Cuello, interview.

32. Ibid.

33. "Puentes de Salud—Mission and History." Available at http://www.puentesdesalud .org (accessed 18 Dec. 2008).

34. "Emergency Medical Treatment and Labor Act," U.S. Code 42 (1986) § 1395dd et seq., as explained on the Centers for Medicare and Medicaid Services Web site. Available at http://www.cms.hhs.gov/emtala/.

35. See 55 Pa Code 150.11, or see interpretation, "Healthcare for Immigrants," from the Pennsylvania Health Law Project. Available at http://www.phlp.org/Website/Immigrants/ Immigrant%20Health%20Care%20Manual%20For%20Advocates.pdf (accessed Dec. 2008).

36. Leonardo Cuello, "Healthcare for Immigrants."

37. Ibid.

38. See note 35.

39. Leonardo Cuello, interview.

40. Leonardo Cuello, "Healthcare for Immigrants."

41. Leonardo Cuello, interview.

42. Ibid.

43. Ibid.

44. C. A. DuBard and M. W. Massing, "Trends in Emergency Medicaid Expenditures for Recent and Undocumented Immigrants," *JAMA* 297 (2007): 1085–1092.

45. Leonardo Cuello, interview.

46. Leonardo Cuello, "Healthcare for Immigrants."

47. Leonardo Cuello, interview.

48. Ibid.

49. "Chronic Care in America." The Institute for Health and Aging, University of California San Francisco, report for the Robert Wood Johnson Foundation, 1996.

50. Leonardo Cuello, interview.

51. Figures from the Pan American Health Organization (2003) and from the World Health Organization (2003), reported in Nelda Mier, Alvaro A. Medina, and Marcia G. Ory, "Mexican Americans with Type 2 Diabetes: Perspectives on Definitions, Motivators, and Programs of Physical Activity," *Preventing Chronic Disease* [CDC serial online], April 2007. Available at http://www.cdc.gov/pcd/issues/2007/apr/06_0085.htm.

52. Verónica F. Gutiérrez, Steven P. Wallace, and Xóchitl Castañeda, *Health Policy Fact Sheet—Demographic Profile of Mexicans in the United States.* Health Initiative of the Americas. University of California Berkeley, School of Public Health, Oct. 2004.

53. National Center for Health Statistics, "Leading Causes of Death for Hispanic/Latina Females Compared with Females of Other Ethnic Groups, 2001," in *Minority Populations and Health: An Introduction to Health Disparities in the United States,* ed. Thomas A. LaVeist (San Francisco: Jossey-Bass, 2005).

54. Pamela Constable, "Adopting America's Bad Habits: Latinos' Poor Diets, Lack of Exercise Propels Social Agencies into Action," *Washington Post,* 5 Aug. 2008.

55. Gopal K. Singh and Barry A. Miller, "Health, Life Expectancy, and Mortality Patterns among Immigrant Populations in the United States," *Canadian Journal of Public Health* 95, no. 3 (2004): I14–I21.

56. Leonardo Cuello, "Healthcare for Immigrants."

57. Amanda Bergson-Shilcock, interview.

58. U.S. Census Bureau, 2006 American Community Survey; U.S. Census Bureau, 2000 U.S. Census. Both available at http://www.census.gov.

59. Natalie Levkovich, interview.

60. Audrey Singer, Michael Katz, Domenic Vilitello, and David Park, "Immigration to Philadelphia: Regional Change and Response" (press conference), 13 Nov. 2008.

61. National Immigration Law Center, "Immigrants & Public Benefits: Immigrant Children's Health Improvement Act (ICHIA)." Available at http://www.nilc.org/immspbs/cdev/ICHIA/ichia003.htm#sign (accessed 9 Feb. 2009).

62. Personal Responsibility and Work Opportunity Reconciliation Act of 1996, H.R. 3734, Public Law 104-193.

63. Qualified immigrant statuses include U.S. citizen (by birth or naturalization), legal permanent resident ("green card"), asylees/refugees, some Cuban/Haitian entrants, persons

paroled into United States for one year or more, VAWA-petitioning battered women and children, persons granted withholding of deportation or removal, immediate relative of U.S. citizen with filed I-130 petition, immediate relative with approved I-130 petition, and PRUCOLs (Persons Residing Under Color of Law), according to literature from the Pennsylvania Health Law Project Web site. Available at http://www.phlp.org/Website/Immigrants/Immigrant%20Health%20Care%20Manual%20For%20Advocates.pdf.

64. Personal Responsibility and Work Opportunity Reconciliation Act of 1996, H.R. 3734, Public Law 104-193.

65. Singer, Audrey, Michael Katz, Domenic Vilitello, and David Park, "Immigration to Philadelphia: Regional Change and Response" (press conference). Free Library of Philadelphia, Philadelphia, 13 Nov. 2008.

66. Julia C. Prentice, Anne Pebley, and Narayan Sastry, "Immigration Status and Health Coverage: Who Gains? Who Loses?" *American Journal of Public Health* 95 (2005): 1.

67. Alexander N. Ortega, Hai Fang, Victor H. Perez, et al. "Health Care Access, Use of Services, and Experiences among Undocumented Mexicans and Other Latinos," *Archives of Internal Medicine* 167, no. 21 (2007): 2354–2360; Arijit Nandi, Sandro Galea, Gerald Lopez, Vijay Nandi, Stacey Strongarone, and Danielle C. Ompad, "Access to and Use of Health Services among Undocumented Mexican Immigrants in a U.S. Urban Area," *American Journal of Public Health* 98, no. 11 (2008): 2011–2020.

68. Claudia L. Schur, Marc L. Berk, Cynthia D. Good, and Eric N. Gardner, *California's Undocumented Latino Immigrants: A Report on Access to Health Care Services.* Report prepared for Rep. Henry J. Kaiser Family Foundation by The Project HOPE Center for Health Affairs, May 1999.

69. Nandi, Galea, Lopez, et al., "Access to and Use of Health Services."

70. See Web site of Congreso de Latinos Unidos: http://www.congreso.net/home.php. Also see Web site of Council of Spanish Speaking Organizations (CONCILIO): http://elconcilio.net/. (Both sites accessed 24 Dec. 2008.)

71. Amanda Bergson-Shilcock, interview.

72. See Web site of JUNTOS/Casa de los Soles: http://www.vamosjuntos.org (accessed 27 Mar. 2009).

73. See Web site of Mexican Cultural Center: http://www.mexicanculturalcenter.org/Who_we_are.html (accessed 6 Apr. 2009).

74. See the site's mission statement: http://www.mexicanosenphiladelphia.com/mision.html (accessed 6 Apr. 2009).

75. Valeska Garay, e-mail message to the author, 3 Apr. 2009.

76. Amanda Bergson-Shilcock, interview.

77. Ibid.

78. Ruben Rumbaut, "Assimilation and Its Discontents: Between Rhetoric and Reality," *International Migration Review* 31, no. 4 (Winter 1997): 937. See also Tamara Dubowitz, Stephanie A. Smith-Warner, Dolores Acevedo-Garcia, et al., "Nativity and Duration of Time in the United States: Differences in Fruit and Vegetable Intake among Low-Income Postpartum Women," *American Journal of Public Health* 97, no. 10 (2007): 1787–1790; and Steven D. Barger and Linda C. Gallo, "Ability of Ethnic Self-Identification to Partition Modifiable Health Risk among U.S. Residents of Mexican Ancestry," *American Journal of Public Health* 98, no. 11 (2008): 1971–1978.

PART III

Identity Formation in a Transnational Context

Immigrants who came to the United States in the post-1965 period, particularly from Global South nations, have largely developed transnational identities, that is, they have maintained critical ties to their home nations while also developing strong relationships with populations and communities in their host society. With respect to one's nation of origin, these transnational ties often involve the sending of remittances, visiting home, frequent communication, and building family residences. Transnational linkages can also refer to the support of family businesses or establishing enterprises in one's "home" country. For those who are precluded from visiting home because of lack of resources or their status as refugees or asylum seekers who escaped dangerous situations in their homelands, transnational identities can still be apparent through their attempts to "imagine/remember" home. They join other immigrants in the practice and transmission of their culture to the second generation in their host society. The transnational equation is complete with the bonds that one creates with groups on this side of the Atlantic.

While some European immigrants from the First and Second Great Waves did maintain relationships with home, they were less apt to develop the strong linkages with their nations of origin that we see among today's newcomers from the Global South. What factors explain these distinct experiences? The transnational identities that are developed among today's immigrants are related to conditions in their homelands, such as economic crises wrought by contemporary globalization, their small numbers, and their encounters with racism in the United States. Thus, they have maintained their direct ties to home as well as attempted to keep their cultures alive in the United States. Such actions have strengthened their sense of ethnic identity and their self-esteem, while easing their adjustment in this country. The new transnational identities developed in this process differ from the ways in which they defined themselves while residing in their nations of birth (Osirim, Chapter 10).

The new transnational identities adopted by Haitians, Africans, South Asians, and Cambodians described in this volume are complex and multifaceted. As black populations, Haitian and African immigrants are frequently considered to be African Americans in their interactions with the broader society here. As Lundy and Osirim indicate (Chapters 9 and 10), these groups clearly have their own national identities and communities with which they identify. As the number of Haitian migrants has increased in the United States, they have increasingly tried to hold onto their Haitian identities, and in fact, they have exhibited transnational identities that for Lundy emphasize "unity," as opposed to the focus on "blood," noted in earlier studies. Lundy (Chapter 9) demonstrates the complicated nature of transnational identities for Haitians which, on the one hand, valorizes their glorious past as the first black independent nation in the New World, and on the other, reminds them of the conflicts they have encountered with the instability of the state and the class/color hierarchy in Haiti. The consequences of these negative historical and to some extent contemporary realities in Haiti lead to difficulties in forging a unified community in the United States.

In Chapter 10, Osirim argues that due to their experiences with racism in the United States, Africans (as well as the Haitians in Lundy's chapter) develop Pan-African identities that unite blacks across national groups. Although tensions have been noted in relations between Africans and African Americans in the United States and in Philadelphia, African immigrants have also forged linkages with African Americans and Afro-Caribbeans, which enhance their social mobility and contributions to urban renewal in the City of Brotherly Love. In fact, The Coalition of African Communities (AFRICOM) and the Mayor's Commission on African and Caribbean Immigrant Affairs, in which both Haitian and African organizations as members work in tandem with African American elected officials, are Pan-African organizations that serve as models for providing services to immigrants as well as revitalizing the city. Such relationships are especially possible in a city where blacks constitute about 44 percent of the population.

Both Chakravarthy and Nair's and Skilton-Sylvester and Chea-Young's studies (Chapters 11 and 12) illustrate transnational identities among South and Southeast Asians that unite these groups with their homelands through cultural practices in the United States. For both Malayalee Indians and Cambodians, Hinduism and Buddhism, as well as the teaching of the Khmer and Malayalee languages respectively and the creation of associations such as the Nair Society, are attempts to maintain their cultures and (re)create "home" in the Philadelphia area. Identity formation in their new host society, however, is complicated by other factors for each of these groups.

Adaptation to life in the United States has resulted in some changes in gender roles among Malayalee nurses and their husbands in Greater Philadelphia. While their commitment to a more traditional gender ideology has not changed, life in Philadelphia has meant that Malayalee nurses, who have higher incomes than their spouses, have assumed a breadwinning role. As a result of these more demanding careers, housework and childcare were increasingly shared between women and men in these families. At the same time, however, these South Asian men have been able to regain some of the status lost in the labor market and the household through their leadership of The Nair Society.

Unlike the other populations examined in this volume, the Cambodians have actually experienced "invisibility" and are characterized as the "other Asians" in Philadelphia (Skilton-Sylvester and Chea-Young, Chapter 12). According to these authors, their invisible status is the result of several factors including the power of the model minority myth, residential patterns in three non-contiguous sections of the city, and participation in informal jobs and services. Unlike the African and South Asian populations in this volume (Chapters 10 and 11), Cambodian Americans had low levels of educational attainment and high rates of poverty that were comparable to African Americans, and thus, they negated the Asian model minority stereotype. Some Cambodians, like some Haitians and Africans in this volume, also lived in close proximity to African Americans in West Philadelphia. In fact, the identities of these three populations were shaped to some extent by the significant presence of African Americans in the city. In the case of the Cambodians, this meant further invisibility for the second generation who attended schools that were predominantly African American.

With a greater international presence in Philadelphia in the contemporary period, however, we are slowly moving away from the black-white racial binary. In this process, we are becoming a more multicultural city fostering global citizenship for the twenty-first century.

9

Philadelphia's Haitian Community

Transnationalism and Unity in the
Formation of Identity

GARVEY F. LUNDY

On a cold fall Sunday evening, after a church service conducted in
Haitian Creole, about fifty Haitians gathered in the annex of a
Catholic Church in West Philadelphia waiting to hear a renowned
Haitian poet—now living in New York City—discuss the beauty of the Creole language and the glories of Haitian culture. The audience consisted
mostly of Haitian immigrant families and their children. The children were
running around speaking English with a dab of Creole; the parents, in contrast, were trying to control their children, speaking mostly in Creole with
a dab of English. It was a typical Haitian scene.

The speaker, to my surprise, did not read poetry, nor did he give a lecture
on the literary tradition of Haiti. Instead, he spoke about what Haitians need
to do in order to glorify and uplift their country. According to the speaker,
Haitians need to return to their indigenous culture: the Creole language, the
Vodou tradition, and the African rhythms that they brought with them to
the island of Hispaniola. The speaker also went through a litany of abuses
that Haiti has suffered under foreign domination and multinational exploitation, all of which prevented Haiti from achieving its full potential. He
concluded that Haitians must be the masters of their own country, and
despite centuries of abuse and pillage, he believes that Haiti is still full of
natural and human resources, and it is up to Haitians themselves to exploit
these resources in order to uplift the nation and bring it on par with other
leading nations of the world. In the end, one can infer that the speaker was

seeking to overcome, and perhaps conquer, the hegemonic construction of race, class, language, and nationhood that has plagued Haiti and Haitians.

Earlier that summer, on July 30, Haitians gathered in front of the African American Museum to celebrate Haitian Unity Day. Created to parallel the annual African American Unity Day the city celebrates, Haitian Unity Day has distinctly profound resonance for Haitians. In the Haitian flag, there is a white squared portion in the center that includes the country's arms and the famous phrase "*L'union fait la force,*" meaning that through unity they find strength. For Haitians at home and abroad, unity has profoundly shaped their consciousness and collective identity.

Working within the theoretical parameters of transnationalism, this chapter will address the theme of unity for Haitians and how unity shapes their collective identity in Philadelphia. More precisely, this chapter has three interrelated objectives in its examination of transnationalism and unity among Haitians in Philadelphia. The first is to place the Haitian community in its proper historical and demographic context. Because Philadelphia's Haitian community is understudied and less well known relative to the communities in New York City and Miami, this exercise will help introduce the reader to Haitians in Philadelphia and counter notions of the newness of this community. Indeed, the Haitian presence in Philadelphia dates back to the eighteenth century.

The second objective is to examine Haitians within the theoretical framework of transnationalism. To that end transnationalist theory is reviewed. In addition, because of the central role Haitian immigrants have played in the development of transnational theory, their contribution will be reviewed to shed light on the nature of transnationalism among Haitians in Philadelphia.

Finally, transnationalism is used to explore the theme of unity among Haitians. Unity (or lack of it) is a recurring theme among Haitians in Philadelphia. The hegemonic root of this term is examined, and its transnational application in Philadelphia is then explored. Unity is asserted to be a key element in Haitian identity, and it serves as a means (1) to connect others in the diaspora, (2) to engage in political discourse and activity back home, and (3) to shape the nature of local community organizations and politics.

In meeting these objectives, I hope to overcome some of the pitfalls of transnational research outlined by Cordero-Guzmán, Smith, and Grosfoguel (2001). In particular, they claim that research on transnationalism has failed to acknowledge the active role of the state in creating transnational public life. In addition, researchers have not properly contextualized in history the newness of transnationalism and the manner in which it currently occurs. Finally, researchers have failed to acknowledge the manifestation of transnational activities that are occurring at different levels of social reality.

The work of Glick Schiller and Fouron (2001) on Haitian transnationalism and the common discourse of "blood" among Haitians will serve as theoretical and intellectual points of departure to address the issue of unity. Using a snow-ball election procedure, seventy interviews were conducted between 2004 and 2006. Subjects included community leaders, professionals, recent immigrants, and long-standing residents of Philadelphia. All the subjects were first genera-tion Haitians. In addition to the interviews, I actively participated in Haitian political and social events in Philadelphia.

The Historical Legacy of Haitians in Philadelphia

In discussions of new immigrants in Philadelphia, one often hears of Haitians as the *new* immigrant group in Philadelphia (Gregory 2006). This assertion, however, is inaccurate for the Haitian presence in Philadelphia is not new, but rather has a long history that goes as far back as the eighteenth century. Perhaps the confusion lies in that this early Haitian presence existed prior to the forma-tion of the Haitian state in 1804. That is, prior to 1804, the western third of the island of Hispaniola was still a French colony and was known as Saint Domingue. That was to change with the Haitian Revolution.

With the onset of the Haitian revolution in 1791, and the subsequent upheaval it created, thousands of refugees found their way to port cities in the United States—of which Philadelphia was one. Of the 3,000 refugees from Saint Domingue who arrived between 1791 and 1794 in Philadelphia, about 30 per-cent were of African descent, still bound by slavery (see Table 9.1). Their coming to Philadelphia, a free city in a free state, was a particularly thorny issue from a legal and social standpoint. Although white Saint Domingans were able to rebuild their lives in Philadelphia with some measure of prosperity and develop a francophone social and cultural community, the situation was dramatically different for the blacks and the *gens de couleur*—as the mixed race population was known. These refugees or émigrés were more isolated and had fewer resources than their white counterparts. Although the blacks and *gens de couleur* leaving Saint Domingue were different from their host communities in terms of religion and language, it was their skin color that primarily determined their

TABLE 9.1   SAINT DOMINGUE REFUGEES' ARRIVAL IN PHILADELPHIA, 1791–1794

Year	Number of ships	White passengers	Gens de couleur	Enslaved Africans	Total passengers
1790	6	2			2
1791	13	93		31	124
1792	74	449	1	149	599
1793	158	1,659	29	629	2,317
1794	13	33	2	7	42
Total	262	2,236	32	816	3,084

Source: Nash (1998, 50).

fate. Moreover, white Philadelphians did not make the subtle distinction of skin color found in the West Indies, thus relegating *gens de couleur* to the inferior status of black (Branson and Patrick 2001).

A major obstacle for black Saint Domingans upon entering Philadelphia was the steadfast determination of French colonists to hold on to their human property despite the anti-slavery uprising in Saint Domingue and the 1794 decree that abolished slavery in the French colonies, and despite Pennsylvania laws that gradually abolished slavery. Perhaps more disturbing was the attempt by arriving French colonists to circumvent Pennsylvania laws requiring manumission. Sadly, however, Pennsylvania's abolition laws did not result in freedom at all for the majority of black refugees, but rather in a different type of servitude. Although legally released from slavery after six months from when an owner established residence, the law also allowed slaveholders to immediately sign their former enslaved blacks to lengthy periods of indenture. In this manner, French colonists could retain the labor of their human property until they were twenty-eight years old or, if they were older than age twenty-one, for seven years. Given how young most black refugees were, life as an indentured person meant many years of service.

In general, black refugees were denied the relief supplied by the French government, U.S. government, and private donors that was made available to white émigrés to compensate them for the loss of property and the opulent life they left behind. But for a few exceptions, poverty describes the life of many of these black immigrants coming to Philadelphia. These newly arriving blacks, like their fellow African Americans, worked as servants in white households. Although in hardship, these black emigrants were known to avoid the poorhouse as an alternative. The desire to remain invisible, the prison-like character of the poorhouse, and the stipulation of needing a recommendation for admittance all worked against black émigrés from seeking refuge in the poorhouse. As a consequence of these conditions, the black and *gens de couleur* who came to Philadelphia at the end of the eighteenth century "melted" away into the general black population.

Twentieth-Century Haitian Migration

After the eighteenth century, Haitian migration to the U.S. ceased, as Haitians were preoccupied with securing the new republic from external threats and rebuilding the nation after thirteen years of war. Haitian migration did not resume again until the twentieth century. Ira Reid, in 1937, provided one of the earliest documentations of twentieth century Haitian migrants when he recorded the presence of 500 Haitians in New York City (Reid 1970: 113). In general, postcolonial Haitian migration is divided into two periods: the first during the American occupation from 1915 to 1934, and the second associated

TABLE 9.2   IMMIGRATION TO THE U.S. BY REGION AND COUNTRY OF LAST RESIDENCE
FOR THE CARIBBEAN, 1960–2005 (%)

	1960–1969	1970–1979	1980–1989	1990–1999	2000	2001	2002	2003	2004	2005
Cuba	47.3	36.2	16.8	15.8	21.2	26.8	29.2	12.9	18.7	22.6
Dominican Republic	19.5	19.6	28.0	35.8	20.6	21.9	23.8	38.7	32.6	29.9
Haiti	6.8	7.8	15.4	17.7	26.1	23.3	20.4	17.7	16.7	14.8
Jamaica	14.6	18.4	24.5	17.6	18.5	15.6	26.1	19.3	16.5	19.4
Other Caribbean	11.8	18.0	15.3	13.1	13.5	12.4	11.1	11.4	11.4	13.2

Note: Percentages are based on the yearly total numbers of Caribbean immigrants.

Source: Department of Homeland Security (DHS). 2005. *Yearbook of Immigration Statistics: 2005.* Available at http://www.dhs.gov/files/statistics/publications/LPR05.shtm (accessed October 16, 2005).

with the rise and the subsequent brutality of the Duvalier dictatorships, beginning in 1957.

The first period, during the U.S. occupation, is considered minor, given that the bulk of the emigration was not destined for the United States, but rather Cuba and the Dominican Republic. During this period, many Haitians were forced to leave their land by U.S. agribusiness companies and made to work under slavelike conditions in the sugar fields of Cuba and the Dominican Republic (Perusek 1984).[1]

Later in 1957, with François Duvalier in power, Haitian intellectuals, politicians, and military officers opposed to his regime fled for the United States. These were members of the Haitian middle class and they saw their departure as temporary, as they anticipated the quick collapse of the Duvalier regime, which did not materialize until almost thirty years later. As François Duvalier held his power and expanded his reign of terror, U.S. residency became more permanent, and the desire to leave Haiti increased. In addition to the oppression Haitians faced at home, the 1965 Hart-Cellar Act liberalizing immigration also facilitated an increase in Haitian migration. Like their eighteenth century brethren, Haitians who came during the early half of the twentieth century tended to melt into the general African American population. However, as migration increased in response to the brutality of the Duvalier regime and liberalization of U.S. immigration policies, Haitians—as well as other Caribbean migrants—began to assume a more public identity apart from African Americans (Kasinitz 1992; Vickerman 1999).

With respect to Caribbean migration in general, Haiti has become among the leading sending countries to the United States (see Table 9.2). This migration flow reached its peak in 2000 when Haiti led all Caribbean nations in sending migrants to the United States. Since then, the numbers have gradually declined, with Cuba and the Dominican Republic—Haiti's island neighbors—assuming the lead. Traditionally, Haitian immigrants have been located in four states: New York, New Jersey, Massachusetts, and Florida. The populations of Haitians in these four states constitute 87 percent of the total Haitian population in the United States. Indeed, the literature on Haitian migration and their communities has often focused on Haitians in these four locations (e.g., Fontaine 1983; Laguerre 1984; Stepick 1998).

Philadelphia's Current Haitian Population

According to the 2000 U.S. Census, the current population of people with Haitian ancestry in Philadelphia is slightly over 4,000. Table 9.3 presents a demographic profile of the Haitian population in Philadelphia and the Haitian population in the United States. Aside from some slight variations, the two groups are fairly similar. Differences, however, are to be noted. Relative to the general Haitian population, Haitians in Philadelphia are less likely to be married and more likely to be widowed or divorced. In terms of nativity and education, Philadelphia has slightly fewer foreign-born Haitians and has a smaller population of Haitians with less than a high school degree. These two factors are associated. Given the well-established link between education and income, the greater educational attainment of Haitians in Philadelphia is perhaps the driving force behind their lower poverty level and higher employment rate relative to the general Haitian population. Finally, in terms of the occupational category, a large proportion of Haitians in Philadelphia find themselves employed in the production and transportation sector of the economy, which are low-skilled, labor intensive jobs.

Unlike the traditional Haitian centers of New York, Boston, and Miami, the growth of Philadelphia's Haitian community is not linked to direct arrivals from Haiti. Instead, Philadelphia is the second, or sometimes third, destination for Haitians after spending several years in more traditional Haitian communities. Based on interviews, the most common reason for Haitians migrating to Philadelphia is that New York (Brooklyn in particular) is too expensive, too large, and too dangerous to live in. Through a process of trickle or chain-like migration, Haitians visit a family member or a friend in Philadelphia and are impressed by the reasonable price of living and decide to relocate. Over the years Philadelphia has gained the reputation of being the sixth borough among trendy New Yorkers because of the high flow of New Yorkers leaving for the City of Brotherly Love (Pressler 2005). Apparently Philadelphia's reputation has extended to New York City's immigrant population. Indeed, as one interviewee suggests, the incentive to leave New York for more affordable housing and better living conditions sometimes takes on a transnational dimension as official members of the Haitian government become involved in the process:

**TABLE 9.3   DEMOGRAPHIC CHARACTERISTICS OF INDIVIDUALS
CLAIMING HAITI AS PRIMARY ANCESTRY FOR THE UNITED STATES
AND PHILADELPHIA COUNTY, 2000**

	United States	Philadelphia
Gender		
Male	48.2	48.3
Female	51.8	51.7
Age		
Median age (years)	30	29
Under 5 years	7.8	5.4
18 years and over	68.8	72.0
65 years and over	5.1	4.0
Marital status[a]		
Never married	39.3	40.5
Married	49.9	46.3
Widowed or divorced	10.8	13.2
Nativity and citizenship		
U.S. born	34.0	37.2
Foreign born	66.0	62.1
Naturalized U.S. citizen	42.5	43.5
Not U.S. citizen	57.5	56.2
Education[b]		
Less than a high school degree	36.2	31.8
High school graduate	22.9	24.4
Some college and associate degree	25.6	27.4
Bachelor degree	10.3	10.2
Graduate or professional degree	5.1	6.2
Occupational status[c]		
Management and professional	21.9	20.1
Service	33.7	31.8
Sales and office	21.3	19.2
Farming, fishing and forestry	0.8	0.2
Construction, extraction, and maintenance	5.9	7.4
Production and transportation	16.4	20.5
Economic status		
Employed (in labor force)	47.5	49.2
Median household income	$35,459	$34,481
Median family income	$36,503	$34,591
Per capita income	$13,210	$12,284
Families below poverty level	4.6	3.8
Individuals below poverty level	20.0	15.7
Total population	548,199	4,221

Note: Except for population numbers and incomes, values are percentages.

[a] Percentages are based on individuals 15 and older, for a population of 407,834 in United States and 3,240 in Philadelphia.

[b] Percentages are based on individuals 25 and older, for a population of 311,417 in United States and 2,348 in Philadelphia.

[c] Percentages are based on individuals 16 and older, for a population of 231,516 in United States and 1,752 in Philadelphia.

Source: 2000 U.S. Census. Available at http://www.census.gov.

> I was in New York, Brooklyn ... East New York [a section of Brooklyn]. ... I was thinking of leaving East New York for somewhere else ... something better probably in Brooklyn ... somewhere in Queens or Florida as I was thinking about at that time ... But money wise, it was a big problem. I heard on Haitian radio ... Wilson Desir, he was the Haitian consul, he said, "you people you're going to Queens, you're going to other areas in Brooklyn to purchase expensive homes, Florida is very cheap, so is Philadelphia. I would advise you to go to Philadelphia. If you go to Philadelphia, for at least $5,000 you can own your own house.[2]

In addition to this nondirect manner of arrival, a smaller group, which took a more direct route, was in place in the early 1970s and as far back as the 1960s. This cohort consisted primarily of professionals fleeing the oppressive regimes of François Duvalier ("Papa Doc") and his son Jean-Claude Duvalier ("Baby Doc") during the first and second waves of Haitian migration as outlined by Catanese (1999). Another important cohort, who came during the 1990s, were refugees fleeing Haiti following the 1991 coup d'état of President Jean-Bertrand Aristide. They came to Philadelphia as part of a resettlement program coordinated by the Nationalities Service Center of Philadelphia, various churches, and the Haitian Community Center.

Philadelphia is divided into twelve planning sections, or districts, in which there are sixty-three different neighborhoods (see Figure 9.1). Haitians can be found in almost every corner of Philadelphia. The Haitian community, however, is concentrated primarily in three districts: (1) the Olney–Oak Lane section, which is bordered by Ivy Hill Road to the northwest and Cheltenham Avenue to the northeast and includes the vicinity of Crittenden street, East Wister Street, and Cayuga Street; (2) the Near Northeast, which borders the Olney–Oak Lane section and is situated between Shackamaxon and the Bucks County line, generally northeast of Roosevelt Boulevard; and (3) West Philadelphia, located west of Schuylkill Avenue and north of Baltimore Avenue. Haitians are also known to reside in the nearby suburb of Upper Darby, which is out of the city limits bordering West Philadelphia, and is about six miles away from City Hall (see Figure 9.2).

The Olney–Oak Lane district contains nearly half of the Haitian population in Philadelphia (47.0 percent). The majority of Haitians in that district are to be found in the neighborhoods of Olney and Logan/Fern Rock. The Olney neighborhood, in particular, is perhaps the most recognized neighborhood for Haitians. Olney is in fact one of the most ethnically diverse neighborhoods in Philadelphia, attracting new immigrants at a level greater than other neighborhoods in the city (Goode 1998). In the city of Philadelphia, the black and white racial proportion is almost even, with blacks and whites each comprising about 45 percent of the population. The rest of the population is about 8 percent Hispanic and 5 percent Asian. In the neighborhood of Olney, however, we observe a more even distribution of groups, as the proportion of Asians, Hispanics, and "other groups" increase (17.9 percent, 21 percent, and 11.6 percent, respectively), accompanied by a decrease in the white population (21.13 percent), and no perceptible difference in the black population (44.6 percent).

The Near Northeast section of Philadelphia borders the Olney section and it contains the second largest concentration of Haitians at 16.7 percent. The division between the Olney neighborhood and the Near Northeast is almost

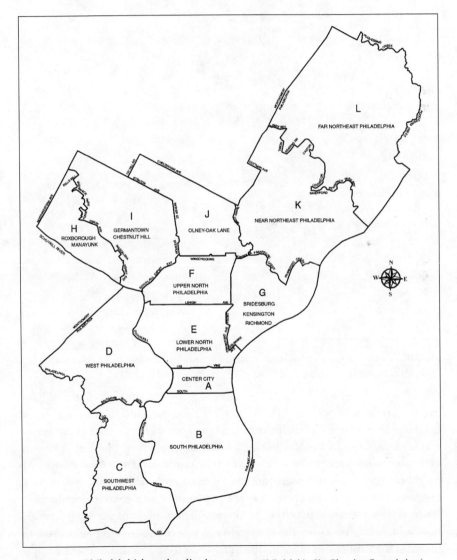

FIGURE 9.1 Philadelphia's twelve districts. (*Source:* Philadelphia City Planning Commission.)

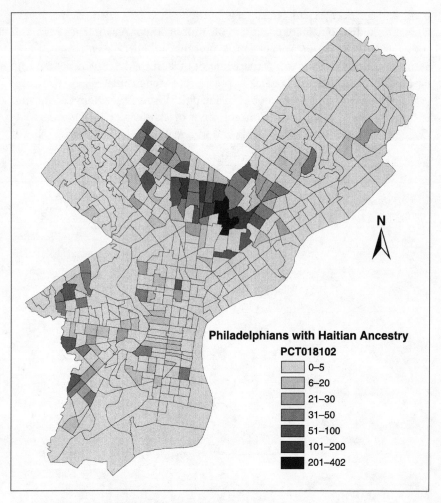

FIGURE 9.2 Philadelphia's population of Haitian ancestry. (*Source:* Cartographic Modeling Lab, University of Pennsylvania. January 2007.)

imperceptible until one begins to walk closer to Roosevelt Boulevard—a major corridor connecting Philadelphia to northern New Jersey—and head north, further away from Olney. Northeast Philadelphia (both Near and Far) is known as the working class, white section of Philadelphia, and the Near Northeast neighborhood of Lawncrest-Summerdale is a border neighborhood that divides blacks and whites. Over 60 percent of the population in Lawncrest-Summerdale is white, which is in sharp contrast to the overall percentage of the white population in Philadelphia. Given the pattern of racial segregation, it is not unusual to find that the majority of blacks living in Lawncrest-Summerdale (about 20 percent) reside in the blocks that immediately border the neighborhood of Olney.

West Philadelphia is the third section where there is a concentration of Haitians. Of the three primary districts with Haitians, West Philadelphia contains the smallest community with only 11.1 percent. West Philadelphia is situated west of the Schuylkill River and encompasses about fourteen square miles and twenty-five neighborhoods. Seventy-five percent of its population is black, and it has one of the highest crime rates in the city. West Philadelphia also borders Center City, the economic, cultural, and political center of Philadelphia. In addition, West Philadelphia is the home of the University of Pennsylvania, an Ivy League institution with an intimidating presence that exudes considerable capital in Philadelphia.

Transnationalism

As the Haitian identity emerges and becomes more public, the transnational nature of this identity becomes more apparent. Members of Philadelphia's Haitian community, like other groups such as African immigrants (see Osirim, Chapter 10 of this volume), are increasingly involved with City Hall politics, block associations, and school board issues, as well as seeking elective office. Coexisting with these local endeavors is the attempt by Haitians to maintain their ties to Haiti. In many instances, these local political actors have been involved in protesting U.S. government policies in Haiti, and they have been the voices of Haiti when local media outlets seek opinions during moments of political crisis back home. In essence, Haitians are living across borders, and this border crossing has shaped the identity of Haitian Americans in Philadelphia. Fundamentally, Haitian identity in America is a transnational identity.

Indeed, one can argue that transnationalism has become the preeminent theoretical framework to analyze and understand contemporary migration patterns and settlements (e.g., Massey et al. 1987; Basch, Glick Schiller, and Szanton Blanc 1994; Cordero-Guzmán, Smith, and Grosfoguel 2001). It allows researchers to incorporate the rapidly changing technological, political, and economic forces of society that currently impact the nature of migration. Transnationalism places contemporary immigrant communities in the globalized context of information technology where space and time have been significantly compressed; where there is a breakdown of the nation-state as the organizing structure for political, social, and economic life; and where the formidable and ubiquitous power of global capitalism greatly affects people's life choices.

According to anthropologist Linda Basch and her colleagues (Basch, Glick Schiller, and Szanton Blanc 1994: 7), transnationalism is defined as the processes by which immigrants forge and sustain multi-stranded social relations that link together their societies of origin and settlement. Contemporary migrants are thus seen as maintaining ties across borders, such that formerly concrete lines separating home and host society have become blurred, creating a single *arena of social action.* Unlike immigrant groups of the past, where the nation-state was characterized by its members sharing a common culture within internationally recognized boundaries, the nation-state for the current population of immigrants includes citizens who are physically dispersed within the boundaries of other states. And here lies the crux of transnationalism. These dispersed citizens remain socially, politically, culturally, and most often economically loyal to the nation-state of their ancestors (Basch, Glick Schiller, and Szanton Blanc 1994).

Researchers have vigorously engaged the intellectual merit of transnationalism and its utility to explain the contemporary nature of migration and transmigrants. Cordero-Guzmán, Smith, and Grosfoguel (2001), for example, find major problems with the current formulation of transnationalism. They argue that transnationalism has overemphasized global capitalism at the expense of the nation-state; many investigators have failed to place their research in a historical context; and investigators engaged in transnational research have often failed to consider transnationalism that occurs at a "different level of social reality from that engaged so fully with the nation-state" (Cordero-Guzmán, Smith, and Grosfoguel 2001: 19). That is, the transnationalism that occurs with transmigrants is burdened by the legacy of colonialism or contemporary global centers (i.e., *metropoles*).

Despite these shortcomings, Nancy Foner (2001) has convincingly argued for the merit of transnationalism as a social scientific construct by demonstrating the unique nature of contemporary immigrants relative to those of the past. She further suggests that transnational ties will persist among the second generation, and even perhaps the third generation, with the continued flow of migrants of all ages who enrich and replenish the immigrant stock and their children, ensuring a link to the ancestral land and the extension of dual citizenship to the second generation. As it stands, transnationalism has withstood the criticism and displayed an impressive degree of resilience (see Portes, Guarnizo, and Landolt 1999), while successfully being applied to various facets of the immigration process (see Vertovec 1999).

Transnationalism and the Haitian Community

Haitian immigrants are central characters in establishing transnationalism as an important sociological and anthropological concept. Their ubiquitous presence as subjects has propelled Haitian immigrants to the forefront of transnational research. Explored has been the Haitians' sense of nationhood (Glick Schiller and Fouron 1999, 2001), Haitian identity (Fouron and Glick Schiller 1997), and Haitian political transnationalism (Itzigsohn 2000). Indeed, in one of the first widely recognized works to outline a transnational perspective, Basch, Glick Schiller, and Szanton Blanc (1994) used the experience of Haitian immigrants in New York to explore dimensions of transnationalism and to examine the Haitian construction of identity. In the process, they historicize the global, capitalistic context that led to migration and the eventual formation of cross border ties. Indeed, it is in their research on Haitian immigrants that Glick Schiller and her colleagues (Glick Schiller and Fouron 1999: 344; 2001: n. 1; Fouron and Glick Schiller 2001) introduce the seminal concept *transnational social field*. Borrowing from the works of British social anthropology and Pierre Bourdieu, *transnational social field* refers to an unbounded terrain of interlocking egocentric networks. It is a network that entails more than the traditional sociological use of networks that suggest chains of social relationships associated with a particular actor. In particular, the term facilitates the investigation of larger—and thus multiple—social, economic, and political processes in which immigrant groups are embedded. Moreover, the concept facilitates an investigation of the *processes* by which immigrants actively participate in social organizations of two (or more) nation-states. The Haitian immigrant community in New York City becomes the social laboratory in which these concepts are investigated and explored.

The investigation of Philadelphia's Haitian community, like the aforementioned study of New York City's Haitian community, is examined within the concept of a transnational social field. The contemporary Haitian community in Philadelphia is embedded within a historic, social, economic, and regional matrix that is unique to Philadelphia. The forces that attracted Haitians to Philadelphia at the end of the eighteenth century and the forces that currently attract and affect them contribute to a unique social process of transnationalism that is germane to Philadelphia.[3]

Glick Schiller and Fouron (2001) have more recently addressed the issue of long distance nationalism among Haitians. Using the personal experiences of the second author, Georges Fouron, as the central narrative and a frequent point of departure to explore the experiences of others, they demonstrate how Haitians, although living abroad, still hold tightly to a nostalgic image of Haiti. These Haitians somehow simultaneously live in two countries, participating in personal and political events in both the United States and Haiti. For Glick Schiller and Fouron, it is in the context of long distance nationalism that Haitians can claim allegiance to Haiti and actively participate in her political formation while still residing outside her borders. As they put it, "Long distance nationalism is a claim to membership in a political community that stretches beyond the territorial borders of a homeland" (2001: 4).

The common discourse that Glick Schiller and Fouron uncovered in their research that identified this notion of long-distance nationalism is a discourse of a common "blood." When their subjects were asked to define what it meant to be Haitian, 82 percent of their respondents spoke of descent, and half began the exposition by speaking of "Haitian blood" (2001: 108).

In my own research, the common discourse that I uncovered was "unity." Similar to the findings of Glick Schiller and Fouron, unity is the discursive vehicle that creates long-distance nationalism within the Haitian community in Philadelphia. Unity—the lack of it or the need for it—became the refrain for Haitians as they described their state in Philadelphia or abroad. In a paradoxical manner, this sometimes-perceived absence of unity and the frequent reference to the epic manifestation of it during the Haitian Revolution connect Haitians to each other and to their struggles back home. Thus unity, like blood, becomes the substance that unifies and creates tension among this transnational community. What are the roots of this discourse?

Unity: Its Social Historical Roots

Whether couched in terms of blood or the historical legacy of their ancestors, unity is a theme that preoccupies the Haitian consciousness and is an important element of Haitian identity. The root of this particular line of discourse can be found in the long history of Haiti and the hegemonic construction of color, class, and nation that have plagued it since its inception as a nation-state (Basch, Glick Schiller, and Szanton Blanc 1994: 150; Nicholls 1996; Trouillot 1990).[4] Wherever Haitians find themselves in the diaspora, they carry with them the historical legacy of their country. News about political events back home is often at the center of discussions in barbershops, salons, restaurants, auto repair shops, or the living room of a friend or family member—wherever Haitians congregate. In these discussions and heated debates, the refrain calling for unity often emerges as a topic. To appreciate this call for unity by community leaders and among ordinary Haitians, one must properly appreciate that the history of Haiti is one in which a single act of sustained *unity* resulted in the most thorough case of revolutionary change anywhere in the history of the modern world, while paradoxically intense factional fighting and deep divisions have often plagued the island nation and created 200 years of instability with thirty-two coups d'état. Indeed, so pervasive is this theme of unity, or the perceived lack of it, that an entrepreneurial group of Haitians is marketing t-shirts that cater to this call (see http://www.sakapfetstore.com).

These divisions, however, are not of the Haitians' own making. In French colonial Saint Domingue, white supremacy effectively kept the population of Africans enslaved, and the French system of color stratification bestowed status, and oftentimes freedom, to members of the colony based on their pigmentation. Simply put, individuals who were the product of mixed race ancestry, *gens de couleur* or *mûlatres,* were more likely to acquire freedom and the status that came with it. The black Africans occupied the lowest position in the class structure of Saint Domingue. Since its birth in 1804, Haiti has found itself struggling with the divisive forces originating from these French hegemonic practices. The *gens de couleur* later became the political and economic power brokers in Haitian society. More commonly referred to in Haitian Creole as "*milat*," members of this group, as well as a few important black families, established a hegemonic legacy where French culture and the French language became the marker of one's humanity. They looked to Europe, and especially France, as their cultural reference. Their children were sent to be educated in Europe or elite institutions in North America, while the indigenous culture of Haiti, the practice of Vodou, and its language (Creole) were looked down upon.[5] In his much-debated book, Nicholls has argued that much of Haiti's political history in the nineteenth century is a conflict between mulattoes and blacks, such that the two groups would prefer to invite foreign intervention in Haiti's affairs rather than allow their rivals to gain power (1996: 8).[6]

The split within the nation came to an apex in 1915 when the U.S. Marines invaded the island nation and proceeded to occupy it for the next nineteen years. The invasion and the occupation had the effect of creating further divisions within Haitian society. The U.S. occupational forces had a preference for light-skinned Haitians and, as such, assigned them to major administrative posts and installed three light-skinned presidents.

Perhaps the most brutal legacy of the nineteen-year U.S. occupation was the creation of a Haitian army against the people (Farmer 2004; Trouillot 1990: 106; Schmidt 1971). The U.S. occupation established a military school that became the training ground for a series of Haitian presidents skilled in the art of crowd control through intimidation and threat from the army (Trouillot 1990: 106). Indeed, during and after the U.S. occupation, it could be said that Haiti was unable to provide any viable avenues for corrective civil discourse as the peasantry found itself marginalized and partisan struggles intensified in the absence of any viable political institutions that would allow a platform for political debate (Trouillot 1990: 86). The polarization created by French and U.S. self-interest in Haiti was masterfully exploited by the Duvalier governments of 1957–1986 (François Duvalier and Jean-Claude Duvalier).

More recently, even as Haitians have been able to dislodge the almost thirty-year stranglehold of the Duvalierist government, discord continues in the debate that surrounds Aristide and his two nonconsecutive terms as president, both of which were cut short in a coup d'état. During the Aristide period, Haitians were divided on a number of issues, from Aristide's favorable position toward Vodou, to his warm relationship with Cuba's Fidel Castro and his openly hostile rhetoric towards the small powerful elite that controls Haitian affairs.

François Pierre-Louis (2006) provides some insight into the nature of the debate surrounding Haiti, Duvalier, and Aristide in New York City, as members of the political right and left were divided as to the best approach to remove the Duvalier regime and in the debate surrounding Aristide's radicalism. The right or conservatives believed they could work with the U.S. government to expose the brutality and civil rights violation of Duvalier and remove him from power. The New York City–based paper *Haïti Observateur* perhaps best symbolizes this position. The left or progressives, in contrast, saw the United States as instrumental in human rights violations by Duvalier and as key to his sustained power.

The fall of Jean-Claude Duvalier brought together various political factions in Haiti and abroad. The opposition to the twenty-nine-year Duvalier regime and the prospect of starting anew brought many Haitians together in an effort to promote democratic change in Haiti. The ascendancy of Jean-Bertrand Aristide held promise for many Haitians. Indeed his presidency is considered by many to be the first sustained involvement by the Haitian masses in the Haitian political process since the Haitian Revolution. In September 1991, eight months into his presidency, Aristide was overthrown by a military coup d'état. The subsequent U.S.-led embargo and the dire economic conditions that followed created a wave of refugees heading for Florida.

This event also brought Haitians together to advocate for the fair treatment of these refugees by the U.S. government. Moreover, it was during this period of President Aristide's tenure as a president in exile that the Haitian effort, abroad and at home, to come together and overcome long-held antagonism was at its peak. Aristide significantly contributed to a unifying discourse and promoted a positive Haitian identity. After protracted negotiations, Aristide was forcefully returned to power to serve out the remaining days of his office. Because the Haitian constitution bars presidents from holding two consecutive terms, Aristide sought and gained reelection five years later in 2001. With only a year remaining in his second term as president, Aristide was once again the victim of a coup d'état in 2004.

Again, as in the past, foreign forces were instrumental in sharpening divisions within the country. By many accounts the coup d'état was orchestrated by U.S. forces, with the implicit backing of France, and this time Canada (Bogdanich and Nordberg 2006). In Aristide's second term as president he sought to redress the historical divisions and injustices that have held Haiti hostage. Aristide assumed a very open and at times confrontational discourse of economic justice for the poor and full political participation of the masses. He initiated a campaign of reparation and restitution for slavery under French rule and for the unjust "debt" repayment forced upon Haiti for French recognition that was started in 1825. He openly embraced Vodou and made it an officially recognized religion of the state. These and other political stances by Aristide resulted in a bitter anti-Aristide campaign by the elite that was supported by the United States and other Western agencies. In the end, Aristide's tenure served to fester some long-held divisions among Haitians as they struggled to build a nation of common interest.

Unity in Philadelphia's Haitian Community

For Glick Schiller and Fouron, the common discourse that ties Haitians together and establishes a transnational link is the discourse of "blood" ties. Haitians identify themselves and others to their ancestral home with reference to the idea that all Haitians share the same "blood." As they put it, "Members of this network used an ideology of blood to explain the continuing connection between Haitians living abroad and those in Haiti" (2001: 353).[7] Glick Schiller and Fouron allude only briefly to division as another theme or discourse within this transnational Haitian identity. They write, "while historical mythology and rituals of nationhood have been shared by all classes in Haiti and have linked them to a pride in nation, these nation-state building processes have not necessarily linked Haitians to one another" (2001: 348).

In my investigation of Haitians in Philadelphia, this division and the desire to overcome it has become a recurring theme among Haitians when describing themselves and the Haitian community. In the same way the Haitians will valorize their ancestral heroes for establishing the first black republic in the Western Hemisphere, they will discuss the partisanship that divides their country and, likewise, divides the Haitian community in Philadelphia.

As we have seen, this division lies in the hegemonic construction of color, class, and nation as established by France and exacerbated by the United States. Indeed, Haitians are not unique in engaging in this type of discourse. Guarnizo, Sánchez, and Roach (1999), for example, describe the Colombian community in New York City and Los Angeles as one mired in mistrust and fragmented solidarity. Itzigsohn (2000: 1146), as another example, alludes to the high level of political partisanship among Dominican immigrants in his research. The call for unity, or a discourse espousing various themes of unity, is not uncommon among dominated or oppressed groups. Tommie Shelby (2005) demonstrates this quite thoroughly in his exploration of the philosophical and historical dimensions of black solidarity among African Americans. The discussion of unity, however, among Haitians, a historically-oppressed immigrant group that has fought against colonial domination and chattel slavery—and has won—and has subsequently fought for international recognition and respect, takes a different tone in the postmodern era. Barbershop discussions and street corner debates about the state (condition) of Haiti and the need for unity reveal much more about the group in a transnational context of U.S. immigrant communities, where linkages between the country left behind and the new country have not been completely severed.

In my attempt to understand the root of this discourse, it occurred to me that unity serves as a transnational identity that may have similar functions as "blood." That is, like blood, unity is (1) a common reference point to create a Haitian identity; (2) it echoes the historical legacy of oppression and domination by outside forces that Haiti has suffered; and (3) more importantly, it is an attempt to correct those hegemonic forces that Haiti has suffered under for the past 200 years. Indeed, unity—like blood—is connected to the historical legacy of Haiti and may be seen as part of the collective identity of Haitians living in Haiti and abroad. As one Haitian man told me:

When you enter a large institution, you see pictures of founders and contributors who helped build that institution, *yo tout mete tèt ansanm* [they all put their heads together] . . . then the job is done. . . . Everything is built with unity. Haitians, however, we lack this unity. We have a saying that is very powerful: "*L'union fait la force*" [through unity we find strength]. . . . In all nations of the world, there were two countries that were powerful in uniting together: the United States and Haiti. . . . When you go into our history books, you will see a story of people who came together to overcome, just like the United States.

He further says:

Consider Dessalines and Christophe, when they came together they were able to defeat the French. These white French used rumors and misinformation to divide these leaders. They went over to Dessalines to spread rumors about Christophe, and they went over to Christophe to spread rumors about Dessalines. They went over to Pétion to do the same thing. Now these leaders are working against each other, against the greater good of the nation. When these guys began to see what was going on, Dessalines went over to Christophe and Pétion and he pleaded, "we must come together for the liberation of the nation . . . *annou mete tèt nou ansanm* [let us put our heads together]." . . . If it were not for unity, Haiti would never have gotten her independence.

This discourse on unity also links Haitians to other immigrant groups in the Philadelphia area, as community leaders are prone to make comparisons. Indeed, the most common comparison is made with the Korean community. In the Olney section of Philadelphia Korean-owned shops are a visible presence, and their overall economic power in Philadelphia is palpable. Haitian community leaders see Koreans as a model to follow and are quick to note this. Consider the following excerpts:

That is one of the reasons we have success with youth and the clergy is because we are doing: having people come in the community; having workshops; having doctors come in have free health clinics. . . . That's what we are doing . . . if we can do it more and more, we can be like the Koreans, but then again the Koreans have a different background. Your background has a lot to do with what you become.

My first experience in ethnic relations was with the Koreans. . . . They were so well organized and obedient to their internal structure. They followed those who came to the United States before them. They did not try to re-invent the wheel. They had institutionalized various methods for dealing with the U.S. and its institutions, thereby those who came after them could learn.

When you see Koreans, they help each other; Haitian people don't help each other. I'm not saying the whole community—Some Haitians people do help. In general, Haitian people don't help other Haitian people ... we got to be together.

These and other statements suggest that Haitian identity is not only based on unity but, to a minor extent, also on the contrast of Haitian life with that of other groups, for example, Koreans.

Despite Duvalier's attempt to create divisions between Haitians abroad and Haitians at home, there has been a concerted effort to overcome those gaps. The Haitian discourse on lack of unity, in describing the Haitian community, is also an attempt to correct the division and live up to the expectations of the founding fathers of the first black republic. Haiti's construction of unity is tied to its experience of hegemony by a foreign power, but it is also forward looking in its attempt to bring Haitians together. A pastor at a very popular church put it this way:

Some people put it as a political thing ... they try to refer it to whatever ... some regime before.... Me, personally, I don't say that. I don't put it as a regime, I don't put it as a political thing, that's why I say it goes back to our grandfathers ... our education, as a slave ... since we don't have nothing, what we have, we try to keep it for ourselves.... There is a proverb in Creole, in Haiti ... *depi nan Guinan, neg tap trayi neg* [since the times of Africa, men betrayed men] ... they refer to the slave days ... back then to the slave time ... we were traitors to each other. We cannot put on the political ... if it was the political, change it.

This discourse of unity, however, is not confined to the realm of history; it extends to community activity and many members of the Haitian community believe it has real consequences and implications for community strength and organization. In their own words, they believe Haitians are still living out the legacy of division created by the French and the United States. Although the context is different and the lines with which these divisions are created have shifted somewhat in Philadelphia, they still haunt community organization:

Sometimes we try to do things here in Philadelphia but it's difficult because people don't want to come together. This person does not like this person, or the fear that this organization has a particular political orientation I disagree with. You know, the Haitian community could do better for itself, here in Philadelphia, if only we learn to overcome these petty divisions.

The unity discourse is used as a reminder of the past that is possible again today, as well as the goal that must be achieved if Haitians are to make community progress in the city of Philadelphia. Comparisons are often made between the conditions of Haitians at home and Haitians in Philadelphia. For many Haitians in Philadelphia, the link is clear. Consider the following exchange between a prominent member of Philadelphia's Haitian community and me:

QUESTION: You say Haiti is at a crossroad . . . politics in Haiti. Do you see politics in Haiti affecting unity and cooperation among Haitians in Philadelphia?

ANSWER: It's very simple. Myself, for example, or other guys who think like me, who act like me, who speak like me, it's difficult, if not impossible, to join a group of people whom we know are against the change in Haiti. So, if they are against any change in Haiti, how could they possibly be for any change in the [Haitian] community? They may be pursing personal interest. But if you are against changes in Haiti, why would you be interested in changes [in Philadelphia] . . . because you're really talking about the same changes . . . you're talking about same changes . . . you know.

The current Haitian community in Philadelphia is still small compared to New York, Miami-Dade, and Boston. It is still at a nascent stage, not yet fully extending its political muscle and its full economic weight, as is the case for Haitians in these other locations. Others have documented the divisional lines that exist in these other locations to be a clear consequence of color and class stratification that grew out of Haiti's hegemonic experience under colonial France and the U.S. occupation. Of the early Haitian community in New York, Basch, Glick Schiller, and Szanton Blanc write, "Haitians of bourgeois backgrounds avoided any form of public organization because they did not wish to be associated publicly with Haitians of lower social strata. Lines of class, delineated by categories of class, shaped the initial Haitian settlement" (1994: 189). Likewise Laguerre writes about New York's Haitian community, "Queens provides a haven for light-skinned immigrants who used to belong to the old Haitian bourgeoisie. Many former Pétionville residents may be found here" (1984: 55, n. 5).

To the credit of the Haitian community in Philadelphia and through the progress Haitians have made in combating the hegemonic legacy of revolutionary Saint Domingue, the acute color division does not seem to be prominent in Philadelphia.[8] Nevertheless, there is a status hierarchy based on manner of entry into the United States—which is inevitably tied to class differences back in Haiti. In particular, those who entered through refugee status occupy lower status, versus those who entered by means of a U.S.-issued visa. Comparing Philadelphia's Haitian community with other prominent Haitian communities, one Haitian community leader who provides immigration services described the Haitian community as fractured, where many Haitians are fighting for territorial control, which at times prevents unity for a common goal. Based on his observation, that is not the case for Boston, where he had previously worked under the same capacity—providing immigration services to the Haitian community. In discussing the instrument Haitians use to demarcate status, he says:

> Haitians are status conscious here in Philadelphia. The way you enter the country makes a difference on how you are perceived. Take the example of Miami: Many Haitians look down on Little Haiti in Miami. The people who make up Little Haiti are recent immigrants from the lower sectors of Haitian society. A large number of them came to Miami illegally by boat [*Kantor*]. In Little Haiti, they have more or less transplanted the lower class Haitian culture to the streets of Miami. As a consequence, middle and upper class Haitians are embarrassed by their behavior and they look down on them.

Another interviewee I spoke to had this to say about Little Haiti in Miami, which reveals the class differences that are still felt and expressed through rural vs. urban residence in Haiti:

> I don't like Little Haiti. The people there do not carry themselves well. I don't know Little Haiti, but from what I hear. . . . The people of Little Haiti are not from the towns of Haiti, not just Port-au-Prince, or other cities that are well developed back home, like Au-Cap [Cap Haitian], Jacmel. These people are coming from far away, they take a boat and arrive in Florida. . . . I hear that they walk barefooted. It's *wo-wo* all the way. . . . They don't carry themselves well. . . . I am making an effort for myself. . . . I did not bring myself up to this level to be carried back down.

Other than the manner of entry, class distinctions are often made based on level of education. One often hears the phrase *Yo pa gen edikasyon* or *yo pa edike*.[9] As one interviewee stated in describing the most recent Haitian immigrants coming to Philadelphia:

> I've been in the United States since the 1970s . . . it seems they are these different brands of Haitians coming to the United States, [different from] those of us that were already educated in Haiti. We came into the system and after two or three months we were ready to go. We did that for a good period of time. Nowadays, like I said to you, I volunteer my time at the

school district, the ESL students, especially the Haitian students, they are not the same caliber of students like us [during my time].

To describe the whole of the Haitian community in Philadelphia as completely fractured, however, would be a mistake. Indeed, coordination among various sectors of the Haitian community does occur with some measure of regularity. These two somewhat contradictory facets of the community are not unusual. As many observers have asserted (e.g., Leyburn 1980), Haiti is a society divided along many lines (e.g., masses and elites, rural and urban, *mûlatre* and black, French and Creole, Christian and Vodou), but these divisions exist alongside contact that allows economic and other exchanges.[10] The social "penetration" that exists among the different sectors of Haitian society carries over to the United States and Philadelphia, in particular. The penetration that occurs in the United States is perhaps greater than the penetration that occurs in Haiti. The important difference being that in the U.S. context, Haitians are able to escape more effectively the historical and cultural legacies of class, social, language, and religious differences that are imbedded in Haitian culture. Being relegated to the second-class status of "black" in the United States, without regard to the subtle distinctions that are inherent in Haitian society, has its benefits. These contradictory elements of the Haitian community—unity and division—create openings for new possibilities in the formation of Haitian identity in this transnational and postindustrial society.

Conclusion

Since the time of the Haitian Revolution, Haitians have always had a presence in Philadelphia—the City of Brotherly Love. This presence contributed to the anti-slavery discourse of the period and forced the city and the nation at large to confront the immorality of human bondage. Through time, after Philadelphia had lost its title as the nation's capital, Haitian migration to the city dwindled, and the distinctive identity of these émigrés faded away as they became part of the larger African American community.

Philadelphia, however, never lost its connection to Haiti, and Haitians are again migrating to this historic city. The current global economy and the growth of the northeastern megalopolis that extends from Boston to Washington, D.C., has benefited Philadelphia and made it a respite from the more costly cities along the eastern seaboard. Within this context, transnationalism has become an indispensable theoretical instrument to describe and understand the shaping of the Haitian community. This chapter has shown how the lives and experiences of Haitian immigrants have broadened the development of transnational theory, and, furthermore, how the specific experiences of Haitians in Philadelphia has widened our understanding of transnationalism.

The exploration of unity and its transnational implications among Haitians in Philadelphia has provided insight into a key component of Haitian identity. The centrality of unity as a recurring theme exemplifies the transnational and historic connection Haitians have to each other. But unlike blood—the concept introduced by Glick Schiller and Fouron (2001)—which emphasizes unfettered relationships among Haitians in the diaspora—the term unity includes the fractious nature of Haitian politics and class relations, as well as the effort to overcome these divisions. Unity, thus, is a vehicle for all Haitians to connect to a glorious history where unity resulted in an unprecedented victory that overturned the oppressive system of slavery and created the first black republic in the Western Hemisphere. Unity is also the vehicle used to connect to events back home as Haitians engage in heated political discourse and become increasingly involved in the outcomes of events in Haiti. Finally, unity is the vehicle used to describe and engage the Haitian community in Philadelphia. In an unspoken manner, Haitians imply that unity has successfully liberated their people from French domination. Therefore, unity can once again resolve factional differences that currently exist in the Philadelphia community.

Notes

1. In 1937, in the Dominican Republic, President Trujillo orchestrated the massacre of some 30,000 Haitians in an attempt to rid his country of their presence.

2. Wilson Desir was Council General for Haiti in New York.

3. The work of Pierre-Louis Jr. (2006) on Haitian hometown associations in New York City serves as an interesting comparison to Haitians in Philadelphia. In my research, I have not encountered any hometown associations in Philadelphia. Philadelphia's Haitian community is a product of New York City and other much larger communities along the East Coast. As such, their ties to their hometown often occur through organizations and compatriots in New York City, rather than institutions in Philadelphia.

4. Portes, Guarnizo, and Landolt (1999: 220) have argued that the most efficient way to learn about transnationalism and its institutional underpinnings is to understand the history of individuals.

5. Basch, Glick Schiller, and Szanton Blanc (1994: 152) argue that this sector of the Haitian population was in a sense always transnational because of its economic and cultural links to Haiti and Europe.

6. See Dupuy's (1989: 81) critique of Nicholls's argument for the assassination of Dessalines.

7. They find the "blood" theme pervasive among first-generation Haitians, while those born in the United States are less likely to speak of "blood" ties and more likely to speak of heroic ancestors and strong family ties (Glick Schiller and Fouron 1999: 356).

8. Nina Glick Schiller provides a lengthy and informative historical outline on the identity changes of the Haitian community in New York, from its early days where language (Creole vs. French), class, and color differences were major obstacles to forming a public Haitian identity (included in Basch, Glick Schiller, and Szanton Blanc 1994: 184–210).

9. Depending on the context, when Haitians refer to someone as not being educated [*yo pa gen ediksyon*] it can refer to a lack of manners or it can refer to a lack of formal education. In some cases it can refer to both. In context of the current quote, it refers to both.

10. Trouillot (1990: 81) writes, "Though Haiti is split in two, it does not consist of two societies. On the contrary: the very mechanisms that have produced the split keep the two parts in an unequal but complementary relationship."

References

Basch, Linda, Nina Glick Schiller, and Cristina Szanton Blanc. 1994. *Nations Unbound: Transnational Projects, Postcolonial Predicaments, and Deterritorialized Nation-States.* Langhorne, PA: Gordon and Breach.

Bogdanich, Walt, and Jenny Nordberg. 2006. "Democracy Undone: Mixed U.S. Signals Helped Tilt Haiti toward Chaos." *New York Times,* January 30.

Branson, Susan, and Leslie Patrick. 2001. "Étrangers dans un Pays Étrange: Saint-Domingan Refugees of Color in Philadelphia." In *The Impact of the Haitian Revolution in the Atlantic World,* ed. D. P. Geggus. Columbia: University of South Carolina.

Catanese, Anthony. 1999. *Haitians: Migration and Diaspora.* Boulder, CO: Westview Press.

Cordero-Guzmán, Héctor R., Robert C. Smith, and Ramon Grosfoguel. 2001. *Migration, Transnationalization, and Race in a Changing New York.* Philadelphia: Temple University Press.

Dupuy, Alex. 1989. *Haiti in the World Economy: Class, Race, and Underdevelopment since 1700.* Boulder, CO: Westview Press.

Farmer, Paul. 2004. "Who Removed Aristide?" *London Review of Books,* April 13.

Foner, Nancy. 2001. "Transnationalism Then and Now: New York Immigrants Today and at the Turn of the Twentieth Century." In *Migration, Transnationalization, and Race in a Changing New York,* ed. Héctor R. Cordero-Guzmán, Robert C. Smith, and Ramon Grosfoguel, 35–57. Philadelphia: Temple University Press.

Fouron, Georges E., and Nina Glick Schiller. 1997. "Haitian Identities at the Juncture between Diaspora and Homeland." In *Caribbean Circuits,* ed. Patricia Pessar, 127–159. Staten Island, NY: Center for Migration Studies.

———. 2001. "The Generation of Identity: Redefining the Second Generation within a Transnational Social Field." In *Migration, Transnationalization, and Race in a Changing New York,* ed. Héctor R. Cordero-Guzmán, Robert C. Smith, and Ramon Grosfoguel, 58–86. Philadelphia: Temple University Press.

Glick Schiller, Nina, and Georges E. Fouron. 1999. "Terrains of Blood and Nation: Haitian Transnational Social Fields." *Ethnic and Racial Studies* 22 (2): 340–366.

———. 2001. *Georges Woke Up Laughing: Long-Distance Nationalism and the Search for Home.* Durham, NC: Duke University Press.

Goode, Judith. 1998. "The Contingent Construction of Local Identities: Koreans and Puerto Ricans in Philadelphia." *Identities* 5:33–64.

Gregory, Kia. 2006. "American Try: A Haitian Transplant Struggles to Make Life Easier for his Fellow Immigrants." *Philadelphia Weekly,* January 4.

Guarnizo, Luis Eduardo, Arturo Ignacio Sánchez, and Elizabeth M. Roach. 1999. "Mistrust, Fragmented Solidarity, and Transnational Migration: Colombians in New York City and Los Angeles." *Ethnic and Racial Studies* 22 (2): 367–396.

Itzigsohn, José. 2000. "Immigration and the Boundaries of Citizenship: The Institutions of Immigrant's Political Transnationalism." *International Migration Review* 34 (4): 1126–1153.

Kasinitz, Philip. 1992. *Caribbean New York: Black Immigrants and the Politics of Race.* New York: Cornell University Press.

Laguerre, Michel S. 1984. *American Odyssey: Haitians in New York City.* Ithaca, NY: Cornell University Press.

Leyburn, James Graham. 1980. *The Haitian People.* Westport, CT: Greenwood Press.

Massey, Douglas, Rafael Alarcón, Jorge Durand, and Humberto González. 1987. *Return to Aztlan: The Social Process of International Migration from Western Mexico.* Berkeley: University of California Press.

Nash, Gary B. 1998. "Reverberations of Haiti in the American North: Black Saint Dominguans in Philadelphia." *Pennsylvania History* 65:44–73.

Nicholls, David. 1996. *From Dessalines to Duvalier: Race, Colour and National Independence in Haiti.* New Brunswick, NJ: Rutgers University Press.

Perusek, G. 1984. "Haitian Emigration in the Early Twentieth Century." *International Migration Review* 18 (1): 4–18.

Pierre-Louis, François, Jr. 2006. *Haitians in New York City: Transnationalism and Hometown Associations.* Gainesville: University Press of Florida.

Portes, Alejandro, Jaime Guarnizo, and Patricia Landolt. 1999. "Introduction: Pitfalls and Promise of an Emergent Research Field." *Ethnic and Racial Studies* 22 (2): 217–237.

Pressler, Jessica. 2005. "Philadelphia Story: The Next Borough." *New York Times,* August 14.

Reid, Ira De A. 1970 [1939]. *The Negro Immigrant: His Background, Characteristics and Social Adjustment, 1899–1937.* New York: AMS Press.

Schmidt, Hans. 1971. *The U.S. Occupation of Haiti, 1915–1934.* New Brunswick, NJ: Rutgers University Press.

Shelby, Tommie. 2005. *We Who Are Dark: The Philosophical Foundations of Black Solidarity.* Cambridge, MA: Harvard University Press.

Stepick, Alex. 1998. *Pride against Prejudice: Haitian in the United States.* Boston: Allyn and Bacon.

Trouillot, Michel-Rolph. 1990. *Haiti, State against Nation: The Origins and Legacy of Duvalierism.* New York: Monthly Review Press.

Vertovec, Steven. 1999. "Conceiving and Researching Transnationalism." *Ethnic and Racial Studies* 22 (2): 447–462.

Vickerman, Milton. 1999. *Crosscurrents: West Indian Immigrants and Race.* Oxford: Oxford University Press.

10

The New African Diaspora

Transnationalism and Transformation in Philadelphia

Mary Johnson Osirim

> *Neighborhood revitalization is a big part of what I am trying to do with my real estate business. You see a lot of this going on in Old City, but I don't have the capital to do anything there. But here, I feel like I can be more effective. I have helped boost the economy here. On this block, by next year, nothing will be abandoned.*
>
> —Interview with Mr. Jion, June 2006

Over the past twenty-five years, the United States has been witnessing the growth of a new African Diaspora with an increase in immigration from Africa and the Caribbean. Although the Greater Philadelphia area has been an understudied site in the general literature on immigration, it is becoming an increasingly important location for Africans, ranking among the top ten metropolitan areas with respect to the percentage of the African-born in the population. The above quotation from an African entrepreneur in Philadelphia begins to indicate the significant presence and commitment of African immigrants to business ownership and community development, particularly in a historically African American section of the city, West Philadelphia.

This chapter will explore a small segment of the New African Diaspora that resides in the Greater Philadelphia area—a segment that is characterized by many as successful—African business owners and leaders of community organizations. Drawing on in-depth interviews with twenty entrepreneurs and leaders of African organizations, this exploratory study will examine how their business acumen and leadership are contributing to the revitalization of the city, but most especially to West Philadelphia. This work will also situate their experiences within the context of the literature on migration studies, interrogate how these migrants define themselves, and delineate their views on race and race relations in the United States. In this study, African immigrants developed transnational and new Pan-African identities, which led to their successful efforts in urban renewal. Further, their efforts in fostering the revitalization of the city strengthened these identities. African immigrants were able to achieve this level of success due in large part to the significant black population in the city—the latter constitutes 44.7 percent of the urban residents.

The African Presence in the United States and in Philadelphia

How did Africans come to play an important role in the revitalization of West Philadelphia? In order to answer this question, we must first examine changes in U.S. immigration policies. Changes in immigration legislation beginning with the Hart-Cellar Immigration Act of 1965, the Immigration Reform and Control Act of 1986, and the Immigration Reform Act of 1990, which included the establishment of the Diversity Lottery,[1] among other laws, have made it possible for immigrants to enter the United States from Africa, as well as from other regions in the Global South. In addition to the changes in immigration law, the United States became an increasingly attractive option for Africans seeking to leave the continent due to the prospects for enhanced socioeconomic mobility and the position of the United States as a technological leader (and superpower) in the past few decades. From the late 1980s to the present, political and socioeconomic conditions on the African continent have also served as major "push" factors for increased migration to the United States. Included among these factors are: the current phase of globalization (and the related consequences of economic crisis and adjustment), political instability and corruption, wars, civil unrest, and natural disasters. As a result, some Africans have migrated to the United States in an effort to further their educations, to escape poverty, and to seek asylum. Most have legally entered the United States under provisions in immigration law for family reunification, to meet the demand for highly trained specialists, or in the status of refugees, asylum seekers, or students. Since the terrorist attacks on September 11, 2001, however, it has become increasingly difficult for Africans to visit or settle in the United States.[2]

The largest number of African-born immigrants in the United States come from West Africa, constituting about 36 percent of this population in 2000, followed by East Africans with 24 percent and North Africa with 22 percent of the African-born population (http://www.migrationinformation.org). Among the most significant sending countries in Africa are Nigeria, Ghana, Ethiopia, Sierra Leone, Egypt, South Africa, Kenya, and Liberia. By the end of the 1990's, Nigerians were the largest population of migrants from the continent constituting about 17 percent of all African immigrants, followed by Ethiopians at about 13 percent (Arthur 2000).

African-born populations are somewhat scattered throughout the United States, with the greatest concentrations found near large cities and in the northeast. According to the 2000 U.S. Census (U.S. Census Bureau 2000), over 2 percent of all African-born individuals in the United States reside in Philadelphia—about 20,392 persons. (Slightly over 11 percent of the population of the city is foreign-born.) They constitute about 6–7 percent of the foreign-born in Philadelphia (Welcoming Center for New Pennsylvanians 2006; http://www.migrationinformation.org). Migrants from most African nations reside in the Delaware Valley with the largest numbers coming from Liberia, followed by such nations as Nigeria, Ethiopia, and Ghana (Swigart 2001; Welcoming Center for New Pennsylvanians 2006). This region has also been an important site for resettlement of refugees from Sierra Leone, Ethiopia, and Sudan (Swigart 2001).

An African presence can be found in several areas of the city. West Philadelphia has become the most important commercial district for African-owned businesses, as noted in my study, with several enterprises dotting the Baltimore Avenue corridor. Several other communities are now home to Africans—a small Kenyan population lives in Norristown; the Sudanese tend to concentrate in West or Northeast Philadelphia; while Sierra Leoneans, Liberians, and Ethiopians tend to live in Southwest Philadelphia (Welcoming Center for New Pennsylvanians 2004). The region is home to at least three African mosques and eleven churches, several of which are located in West Philadelphia. The city has also been an important locale for African community organizations and annual events, such as the Odunde Festival. The Coalition of African Communities (AFRICOM) is a model association in the city and nationwide. It facilitates African immigrants' access to many vital city services.

Much of the success that Africans have realized in their immigration and business experiences has stemmed from their high levels of educational attainment in their nations of origin and their strong commitment to education over the life-course. African immigrants, like their South Asian counterparts (see Chakravarthy and Nair, Chapter 11 of this volume) are among the most highly educated migrant populations in the United States, with at least half of their population holding college degrees (Yetman 1999; Arthur 2000; Swigart 2001). Most of the immigrants in this study compose what has been called the African "brain drain"—populations that are also referred to as "model minorities" (Dodoo 1997). The business owners and leaders of community organizations in this study are no exception to this pattern—eight of these respondents earned bachelor's degrees before migrating to the United States. How can we begin to understand their experiences in and their attitudes about the United States? What paradigms are most useful in making sense of their lives?

Migration Studies: What Theories Shed Light on the New African Diaspora?

Within the sociological tradition, the current phase of globalization character-ized by the substantial movements of capital, populations, and ideas suggests that a new body of theory is needed, beyond the assimilation and conflict per-spectives of the past, to account for the experiences of populations of color who have recently migrated to the United States or elsewhere.[3] Migration Studies far surpasses the earlier field of race and ethnic relations and provides greater breadth and specificity in understanding the experiences of migrants around the world. This new field enables us to accord agency to the global movements of populations involved in multiple sites and stages in the process of immigra-tion. It also provides us with the tools to comprehend how the current phase of globalization presents new "push" and "pull" factors for migrants linked to eco-nomic crisis and political instability in their home countries. The current phase of globalization facilitates transportation and the spread of technology in such a way as to make information about, communication with, and travel to foreign shores easier and to some extent more affordable. Of course, this stage of capital-ist development in the North has demands for migrant labor that are both simi-lar to and different from the earlier periods.[4]

It is precisely in the field of Migration Studies where we can begin to under-stand the experiences of New African Diaspora immigrants. African immigrants to the United States, as well as those migrating elsewhere, are perhaps best under-stood through the concept of transnationalism. According to Lundy (Chapter 9 of this volume) transnationalism has arguably become the most important con-struct in understanding contemporary immigration. Transnationals maintain "identities that extend across national borders and involve participation in both their home countries and new societies of settlement" (Swigart 2001: 3). These immigrants engage in "transnational practices" which involve:

> multistranded social relations along family, economic and political lines, that link together migrants' societies of origin and settlement. In this way, migrants are said to build transnational social fields that cross geo-graphic, cultural and political borders. (Basch 2001 as cited in Foner 2001: 9)

These multi-stranded social relations involve African immigrants sending remit-tances back to relatives in their home countries, which are often the critical means of support for many poor and low-income families, and indeed, are major con-tributors to the economies of these nations.[5] These transnational ties, however, are also maintained by migrants' abilities to frequently visit home, to call, to correspond by regular mail or email, and by sponsoring relatives from abroad (Arthur 2000). While earlier European immigrants to the United States were also likely to maintain ties to their homelands, I argue that the ties of contemporary immigrants of color are far stronger, likely to be very current and of longer duration, than the ties of old. This is partly due to the changes in technology and economic development (or the lack thereof) linked to globalization and to the issue of "race" and exclusion in the United States, which often leads immigrants of color to maintain close ties to home and to their national identities. As Vickerman has observed, "transnationalism, by orienting immigrants back to their homelands, strengthens ethnicity and slows the process of assimilation" (2001: 220).

Portes (1996) also discusses the increased importance of transnational communities in the United States, especially in relation to immigrant entrepreneurship. In their travels back and forth between their home and host nations, transnationals carry both their cultural and political attitudes in both directions. In the case of African immigrants, they share information, develop contacts, and establish trust on both sides of the Atlantic, which contributes to the development of their businesses and other ventures in their host societies. As Stoller (2002) observes for many Francophone African traders, they have maintained strong ties to their communities of origin, which has facilitated their access to West African crafts and other goods to sell in the United States.

This leads us to the question of how Africans are treated by and respond to the "host" society? What ties do Africans develop on this side of the Atlantic? Here, I suggest a return to the concept of assimilation, although in a more complex, distinctive form than found in the earlier studies. Portes and Rumbaut's concept, "segmented assimilation" is useful here, defined as a situation "where outcomes vary across immigrant minorities and where rapid integration and acceptance into the American mainstream represent just one possible alternative" (2001: 45). Although this term was developed with reference to the immigrant second generation, it also holds relevance in the study of first-generation African immigrants, since it maintains that assimilation is not a uniform process that all groups experience equally and is not a desirable process from the perspective of all migrants, especially those who see their stay as temporary. The idea of a temporary stay describes the experiences of some of the participants in my study, who hope to return home upon retirement. Portes and Rumbaut's (2001) work takes a comprehensive approach to examining the processes of incorporation of new groups into the United States, finding that assimilation is one possible outcome among others, including remaining part of an immigrant enclave or, as also noted by Ogbu (1978), becoming part of a minority oppositional culture (also see Portes and Zhou 1993).

Moreover, in this theory and in other contemporary empirical works, race plays a critical role in the processes of incorporation as well as in socioeconomic mobility for immigrants in the United States. In this regard, are first generation African immigrants likely to be viewed by mainstream society as African Americans or as Africans? How might their association with African Americans or Caribbean immigrants in major cities affect how they are treated by European Americans and, in turn, lead to upward or downward mobility? Do Africans experience "favored treatment" in gaining access to resources in the United States, as many scholars have observed for first generation Caribbean immigrants, or are they likely to be viewed as African Americans, in keeping with the treatment of second-generation Caribbean immigrants, and experience downward mobility (Apraku 1991; Portes and Zhou 1993; Waters 1999)? Research by sociologists and others has revealed that African immigrants do not experience the returns to education that are realized by Caribbean immigrants, namely they earn lower salaries than one would expect given their educational attainment (Dodoo 1997). While this chapter will not answer all of these questions, it will explore African immigrants' notions of identity and their experience with race relations. Transnationalism and to some extent, segmented assimilation, appear to be the best starting points for such analyses.

African Entrepreneurs and Civic Leaders in Philadelphia: Who Are They?

In the summers of 2006 and 2007, along with research assistants from Bryn Mawr College, I began the study of African business and civic leaders in the Greater Philadelphia area. We conducted in-depth interviews with twenty African immigrants using the snowball sampling method and lists of businesses and organizations from the study *Extended Lives: The African Immigrant Experience in Philadelphia* (Swigart 2001) and from *Immigrant Philadelphia: From Cobblestone Streets to Korean Soap-Operas* (Welcoming Center for New Pennsylvanians 2004).[6] This small sample is part of a much larger study of African immigrants in Philadelphia and Boston. The interview measures consisted of about 150 fixed-choice and open-ended questions on such issues as: the personal backgrounds of the participants and their connections to home; their educational, occupational, and family histories; their reasons for coming to the United States, their self-definitions; the operation of their businesses; and their leadership of civic groups and their ethnic celebrations. Interviews lasted approximately 1.5–2.5 hours and were conducted in the home or office of the respondents. This chapter will focus on some of their personal background characteristics, relationships and identities, connections to home, and some of the activities associated with their businesses and associations. Pseudonyms will be used to protect the identities of each participant in the sample.

Of the twenty interviews conducted with individuals, seven of the participants were women and thirteen were men. Eleven respondents were entrepreneurs, while thirteen were leaders of African community organizations. Unlike the West African traders in Stoller's studies (2001, 2002) who had little connection to the communities in New York City, the participants in my study were very involved in community associations in Philadelphia.[7] In addition to being members of several local, national, and international organizations, six of the thirteen respondents were founding members or members of the Executive Council of AFRICOM. The ages of the twenty participants ranged from thirty-four to sixty-one, with a mean age of fifty-two for the women and forty-seven for the men. The interviewees have been in the United States for a period ranging from eight to thirty-six years, with most immigrants being in the United States for about twenty years.

My sample resembles the local and national statistics on the countries of origin for African immigrants. Nine of the participants in my study are Nigerian, three are Liberian, two are Eritrean, and one each are from the following countries: Ethiopia, Cote d'Ivoire, Guinea, Sierra Leone, Sudan, and Uganda. Thus, Anglophone West Africa and the Horn, which are the homelands of many émigrés to the United States were also the regions of origin for individuals in this study. Nine of the interviewees came directly from their country of origin, while the remainder came from other nations, including three who identified themselves as refugees/ asylum seekers. Those who did not enter from their homeland came from Cote d'Ivoire, Brazil, India, Oman, Britain, Italy, and Canada.

As was the case in Arthur's (2000) and Swigart's (2001) studies, the majority of participants in my study were highly educated and committed to further educational attainment. Eight of these interviewees had received bachelor's degrees before coming to the United States; sixteen participants completed their first degree or earned higher degrees, or both, in the United States. Some earned master's degrees in business administration and public administration while others earned doctorates in such fields as education and engineering. With respect to annual earnings, six of the entrepreneurs in this study earned over $85,000/year, with the remaining four stating incomes in the range of $40,000–$70,000. Of the remaining immigrants leading organizations, a broader range of incomes was noted—from $10,000 to over $85,000. Most of these participants earned in the $45,000–over $85,000 range; only one participant, a minister, stated that he earned a salary at the bottom of the scale ($10,000–$15,000). Included among those who led civic associations were two professors (one combined this position with work as a diplomat), a social worker, a minister, a business manager, and an administrator in a government agency. Therefore, for the most part, in considering their occupational, income, and educational attainment, these immigrants could be considered middle–upper middle class.

Thirteen of the respondents in this study were married, two were divorced, and five were single. Fifteen of them have children, and in six of these cases, their children were primarily adults. Women in this study had three children on average compared to two for the men (the latter were slightly younger in age).

Transnational Ties: Connections to Home, Relationships in the Philadelphia Area

African immigrants (like their Haitian counterparts as noted by Lundy in Chapter 9) embodied many of the characteristics of transnationalism discussed in the more recent theoretical and empirical literature mentioned above. They had strong connections to home as illustrated by sending remittances to relatives in their countries of origin and by their visits home. While frequent phone calls and electronic and "snail" mail are also important barometers of connections to home, this study did not explore these ties. On this side of the Atlantic, these immigrants also developed important relationships with co-ethnics, other Africans, African Americans and Afro-Caribbeans/West Indians at their workplaces and in their organizations, which signified strong linkages to Philadelphia, a city with a very large black population.[8] In the United States, Africans were often regarded as African Americans by the mainstream population. Such experiences point to the role of race and racism in their lives and the salience of segmented assimilation theory (Apraku 1991; Portes and Zhou 1993; Bryce-Laporte 1993; Portes and Rumbaut 2001). In describing themselves, several of these immigrants discussed the multi-faceted nature of their current identities—as residents of the United States with outstretched arms to their countries of origin across the Atlantic. As this study will show, not all immigrants had equally strong ties with their nations of origin and their adopted homes. Further, while some longed to return home for retirement, others were committed to staying in the United States. Moreover, most of these immigrants were now conscious of the racial quagmire that they had stepped into in the United States and not only noted conflicts in relationships between blacks and whites, but some also observed tensions between Africans and African Americans.

The majority of participants in this study (eighteen of twenty interviewees) send money to relatives in their homelands either on a regular basis or as requested. For many respondents during their early years in the United States, this meant sending several hundred dollars every two to three months to their family members abroad, largely to parents and siblings to educate children in the family, especially siblings, nieces, and nephews. Money was also sent to meet the medical needs of their relatives and to supplement their family's income. Eight of the participants send amounts ranging from $3000 to over $6000 per year. In addition to depositing money in accounts abroad, immigrants frequently send remittances via Western Union and through relatives and friends who are traveling to their home countries.

The vast majority (seventeen) of the immigrants in this study had visited home since they left. Half (eight) of these respondents go home on a regular basis, ranging from every year to every three years. Those respondents whose nations have been embroiled in civil wars and ethnic conflicts, such as Sudan and Liberia, have generally not visited their countries.

Although these participants did demonstrate close ties to home, fewer than half of them (eight) stated that they plan to return home permanently. Respondents in the latter category were looking forward to retiring in their home countries, although even they expressed some ambivalence about this. They first wanted to make sure that all of their children received higher education in the United States and that they had been able to earn enough money to return home for a comfortable retirement. Five of the interviewees stated that they had no intention of returning to their home nations permanently, while six respondents were much more unsure about future plans. Those who were negative about the prospects of returning home were from nations where political turmoil through wars, state instability, and natural disasters had taken a harsh toll: Eritrea, Ethiopia, and Sudan. Those who were most unsure about this issue stated that in part, it depended on what happened with their children. Moreover, most African nations have been beset with various forms of political and economic crises in recent decades, which led many of them to come to the United States in the first place. Thus, the unpredictability of political stability and an adequate quality of life make such plans about the future very difficult, if not futile.

In addition to their close relationships with their children and other relatives in the United States, these African immigrants have developed ties with other populations in the Philadelphia area, as well as in the United States more generally. Only four respondents mentioned having many friends that were European American; the majority of respondents had developed close ties with other Africans, African Americans, and West Indians. First, for these respondents, working and living in a city with a large African American population and specifically owning businesses and leading organizations based in West Philadelphia, one of the very established African American communities in the city, explains the close connections to black populations there and to the success that they experienced. Given the location of their establishments and, in some cases, the nature of the goods and services that they provide, African entrepreneurs in this study have a significantly black clientele. Second, many of these respondents are leaders of AFRICOM and members of the Mayor's Commission on African and Caribbean Immigrants' Affairs, both groups serving the needs of immigrants from Africa and the Caribbean. Third, the history of race relations and the persistence of racism in this nation makes it more likely that at some point in the psyches of European Americans, Africans will be taken for or linked to African Americans, and thus, most Africans will be less likely to form close bonds primarily with whites.

Participants in this study generally saw Philadelphia as a good location for African immigrants. Eight of these interviewees settled in Philadelphia directly upon their arrival in the United States. The twelve others in this study moved here after living in such southern locations as Raleigh and Atlanta, the northeast, the New York/New Jersey area, and such cities as Detroit, Sioux Falls, and Omaha in the midwest. Several factors influence the decision to come to Philadelphia for many immigrants and these individuals in particular: the nature, quality, and number of educational institutions in this region, especially in the fields of engineering, medicine, and technology; employment prospects in these and other professional fields; lower housing prices than in many other cities (similar to what Lundy reports in Chapter 9 for Haitian immigrants), and the presence of relatives and friends in the city or in nearby areas. Mr. Mon comments on the attractiveness of Philadelphia as an immigrant destination:

I came here first because it was where my friends were, but it was a comfortable place to be in terms of my transition and getting settled in as an immigrant. Pennsylvania is easier to get situated as an immigrant than compared to other U.S. cities like New York. It was easy to assimilate here. There is a big Liberian community here in Philadelphia and a large African community in general. So there were some cultures already here that I was familiar with in terms of things like food or language. Those elements make it much easier to assimilate. The last reason is education. I knew about Temple because a lot of people graduated from there and moved back home. I knew it was affordable and run as a government institution. That's something that immigrants look for. It was easily accessible. (Interview with Mr. Mon, July 2006)

While all respondents remarked that they had relationships with African Americans and West Indians, and many of these had close friendships with members of these populations; six immigrants stated that the sole group with whom they had the most friendships was Africans. Only one respondent noted that she did not have close friendships with Africans in the United States—her close African friends lived on the continent.

Over half of the respondents in this study (eleven) commented that they had no real idea about race relations in the United States before coming here. Others were aware that there had been a civil rights movement to address racial issues. A few interviewees mentioned some of the prominent leaders of this period, such as Dr. Martin Luther King, Jr., and Malcolm X and politicians with more positive attitudes towards blacks, such as Jimmy Carter.

Once these immigrants settled in the United States, they noticed that tensions between blacks and whites persisted. For several, racism was clearly alive and well and was revealed in specific interactions that some of them had with

European Americans and more broadly in dealing with U.S. institutions. As noted by a member of the AFRICOM Executive Council:

> It was my husband's birthday. I had made reservations for dinner at a local restaurant. Then, a white couple came and stood behind us. The maitre' d went and helped the white couple. I decided the establishment did not need my money and I said this. I didn't play the race card, but it is there. (Interview with Ms. Nei, July 2006)

In discussing race relations, a Nigerian businessman commented:

> I never experienced any of it back home. Well, believe me if a white guy comes to Nigeria, the natives will take him in as one of their own! Coming here it's the opposite. I remember my first time on the subway here. I was looking forward and my eyes met with another guy. It looked like he was furious at me, just because we made eye contact. . . . You learn to know your place. . . . Now, I'll give a friendly hello but that's it. If I acted the way I would have acted back home, people would see that as a threat or a weakness. (Interview with Mr. Jion, June 2006)

For Ms. Nei, the institutional racism in a suburban school district led her to start an organization to protect the rights of her children and those of other blacks:

> My daughter was in the 99th percentile. North Penn had a two year accelerated math program in middle school. My daughter came home and cried when she told me what was happening in school. [The teachers] had to screen the children. The teacher said that since my daughter wanted to become a medical doctor, she did not need to be tested further. She was then told that she draws so well and she does not need this. I went to look at my daughter's folder with 99th percentile scores. Why was she not screened? The Principal said that he did not want to set my daughter up to fail. . . . Due to a racial incident in the North Penn School District, I organized "Concerned Parents for Equity in Education," from 1989–1996. Parents had many issues as black parents living in the suburbs. Our children were the only black children in their classes. . . . Many children were assigned to special education classes. Parents would ask me to go with them to their children's classes and to their parents' meetings. (Interview with Ms. Nei, July 2006)

These examples of race relations between African immigrants and European Americans closely resemble the experiences of many African Americans. Such experiences do create bonds between Africans and African Americans and further illustrate how Africans come to be viewed as African Americans by mainstream society.

On the other hand, as noted by previous researchers such as Arthur (2000), some respondents in this study also noted tensions in relations with African Americans, even though most participants enjoyed close relationships with African Americans and some even identified as "African American" (although most of these individuals probably meant that they are "Africans in America"):

> Since I came to this country, I have a better understanding of what African Americans and Native Americans have gone through and deal with currently. I have also noticed negative race relations between African Americans and Africans and West Indians in some pockets of Philadelphia. (Interview with Mr. Astu, July 2006)

> Yeah, I found out that there is a lot of tension between blacks and whites, but also between African Americans and immigrants. It's this notion that Africans come and take jobs away from African Americans and on the other side, Africans think African Americans are not as hardworking. I think the relationship between blacks and whites is a bit more, sure. But just because you don't see the tension between African Americans and Africans as much, that doesn't mean it's not there. (Interview with Mr. Tige, July 2006)

> It was a new thing for me to see the relationship between Africans and African Americans. You notice this all the time in the school system. . . . There is a tension that exists. A lot of African Americans can't understand how we excel so quickly economically. To them, we are living good. But to us, we are not living good. Many of us had better lives before we came to America. They feel we are taking their businesses and their jobs away from them. Feel like we are messing with their government. (Interview with Mr. Jah, June 2006)

The formation of such attitudes among Africans has many roots, including the images and stories presented in the media, the school system, and from other socializing agents, such as parents and peers. Okome (2005) observes how in some cases, Africans make conscious decisions to distance themselves from African Americans:

> [There is a] conscious decision of black immigrants to distance themselves from the "undeserving underclass" [meaning African Americans] without consciously apprehending that they are necessarily part of the

under-class. It takes events like the Amadou Diallo shooting by the New York City Police to send the clarion call to most African immigrants that they are part of the discreditable, undeserving underclass.

It is likely to be the case that if the Africans in this study did not locate their businesses and organizations in the African American community within a city whose population is nearly half black, and thus did not have as much contact as they currently do with African Americans, such negative attitudes on both sides would be even more prevalent.

In this study, African immigrants' experiences with racism were not limited to their interactions with European Americans and African Americans, but were also noted in their dealings with other populations of color, especially those who dominated certain segments of the small business sector and the institutions that serve them. Entrepreneurs further experienced racism from their customers, particularly when they were engaged in such "niche" businesses as black hair products. Customers often held onto perceptions of "who the owner of a particular type of business should be" which led them to conclude that those who controlled the niche sold the better products (in terms of quality, price, or both). In her comments below, while Ms. Esor views Korean Americans as the source of many of her problems as a businesswoman, she also expresses a desire to distinguish herself and her business from African Americans:

> In everything you do in life, there are problems. Overcoming them is what is important. This business is not supposed to be a black business. There are more Asian businesses [in this field]. Many blacks come here and ask to speak to the owner. This used to be a problem. Because of this, we lose some customers to the Koreans. They think you [we] go to the Koreans, buy from them, and then raise the price. They think the Koreans are going to be cheaper. They come to this store and also think that I am not the owner. Even when we go to trade shows. . . . When the Koreans come, they come with money. The Koreans have their own banks, blacks have difficulty getting loans. Often you cannot compete with the Korean-owned businesses. If you are not strong on this, they will buy you out. Many black businesses have closed. . . . You can't go to the bank and get money and the Koreans have their own institutions. If I go to a bank, when you check the application line for black, they do not want to differentiate you from African Americans. (Interview with Ms. Esor, July 2007)

Although all of their negative encounters are not revealed here, on the whole, African immigrants in this research had more experiences with racism from European Americans than from other groups.

In addition to their relationships with populations in their home countries and on this side of the Atlantic, African immigrants' transnational ties also revealed themselves in their self-descriptions. When asked how they would describe themselves today, participants in this study gave responses that illustrate the multi-layered notions of who they are. Half of the participants defined themselves in national terms—e.g., Liberian, Ethiopian, Nigerian. A few respondents immediately stated that they were "Africans," while some others discussed their identities as hyphenated Americans—e.g., Ghanaian-American, Nigerian-American. Six of the participants in this study described themselves as African American, but as stated above, this was more likely to mean for most of them, "Africans in America."

In their self-descriptions and discussions about race, these immigrants frequently stated that they are regarded as African American or black by the larger society, a similar finding to that discovered in earlier sociological studies for Africans and other groups of color (Portes and Zhou 1993; Bryce-Laporte 1993; Waters 1999; Arthur 2000). They also noted that they had to check-off "African American/black" frequently on official documents, such as employment forms, since no category existed for "Africans." One could detect some displeasure from these respondents in finding themselves in or having to place oneself in the category of African American/black. The uncomfortable nature of categorizing oneself as "black" did not come from denial on the part of these respondents that they are black, but rather, from what this means in the United States, especially when European Americans "lump" all black groups, regardless of ethnicity, into one category. While they have formed bonds with other Africans, African Americans, and West Indians, these African immigrants were conscious of ethnic/cultural differences, even though they largely put these aside in descriptions of themselves in the United States. As they noted:

In Africa, I had no idea that I was Black. In Eritrea, there are different ethnicities. In Eritrea, I would have been Tigrinya and Orthodox Christian. (Interview with Mr. Astu, July 2006)

In most cases, being black and being from Africa, you are labeled as a black person. Sometimes I get the same treatment as African Americans and I'm African. In terms of statistics, I get pushed into the African American category because there is no category for Africans. Because of that, we don't get to be defined as who we really are. . . . I still consider myself African, in that light. But my American heritage does share part of African American history in terms of the slave trade. But I still consider myself African. (Interview with Mr. Mon, July 2006)

[Describe yourself.] That's often a tough one for most Africans. When you have to fill out employment forms, there is only one section: African

American. I am an American citizen, so I am African American, but I describe myself as African.... [In Africa] I would have called myself Nigerian. It's funny. I always correct my cousin, who lives with me, when he says, "we do this or we do that back in Africa." But there are over forty countries and hundreds of cultures in Africa. "Be specific!" I tell him. (Interview with Mr. Yire, July 2006)

These statements from immigrants in Philadelphia reveal a strong commitment to their African identities, while at the same time many also reveal a connection to the United States. The experience of these African immigrants living in the United States in relatively small numbers has created a Pan-African community here and, for many, a Pan-African identity. As Bryce-Laporte notes for Caribbean immigrants, much of this Pan-African identity stems from the way that black immigrants "find themselves branded and thus bond along racial, regional, or pan-ethnic lines" (1993: 40). Under these circumstances, these immigrants are more likely to identify as Africans or as African Americans/blacks rather than as, for example, Yoruba, Efik, Igbo, Ashanti, or Mande. Living and working alongside other Africans, African Americans, and to some extent West Indians, also forges new identities and strengthens their sense of transnationalism.

Finally, these immigrants were asked, "Where has life been better—in your country of origin or in the United States?" Participants were quite split on this matter and, in fact, about half had mixed responses. Only one stated adamantly that life was better at home (in Africa). Nine respondents stated that life had been better in the United States. Both the positive and mixed statements were generally made in the context of political and economic stability, better infrastructure and institutions in the United States, with a longing for home for some, as noted by these Liberians:

In some areas, it has been better in America and in some areas it has been better back home. I don't know. Well, health care and facilities are much better in the United States. But in areas involving stress-related activities, I would say America is by far a more stressful place. I feel underutilized, like I'm wasting my time here. The Center and the Ministry give me hope, but I'm homesick. (Interview with Mr. Jah, June 2006)

Both places are special. I was very involved in politics back home, civic responsibilities and political processes. In terms of education, it has been better here in the U.S. because I've been able to go beyond what I had before. Economics, it has definitely been better here. But in terms of my journalism career, not much has happened/changed. (Interview with Mr. Mon, July 2006)

In an earlier study of African immigrants, Apraku (1991) reported similar findings. He noted that even though many African immigrants encounter racism, are lumped together with African Americans, and disapprove of the way the latter are treated, they stay in the United States largely for monetary reasons.

African immigrants in this study have revealed that they are indeed transnationals with strong ties on both sides of the Atlantic. Through their remittances, frequent visits home, relationships with other Africans, and their sense of identity, they are connected to the continent, but they also have ties to the United States, Philadelphia and the black community here, which also (re)creates a sense of home.

African Businesses in Philadelphia: Toward Revitalizing the Urban Landscape

Although this is a very small sample, most of the participants have been engaged to some extent—either as business owners[9] or as leaders in African community organizations (or both)—in the revitalization of West Philadelphia. Admittedly, they are a small part of this equation—long-time African American residents and other populations in the city, along with the University of Pennsylvania as a large landowner in the area, have been significantly involved in this endeavor for the past few decades. African immigrants, particularly in the last fifteen years, have also been important actors in this process. While much data was gathered on African-owned businesses, this section will only explore a few key issues regarding these activities. I will examine the businesses and practices of ten entrepreneurs: their resources at start-up, the goods/services that they provide, their contributions to human capital development, and some of the successes and problems they have encountered, as well as explore their contributions to urban renewal. Few figures will be provided on the financial viability of these firms, since several entrepreneurs were reluctant to provide data on the profitability of their enterprises.

One of the very interesting findings about African immigrant entrepreneurship in this study is that it does not consist of businesses focused solely on meeting the needs of the African population. While my sample does include a grocery store, restaurants, a cultural center, and a future nightclub designed to meet the needs of African customers, this sample also includes firms that provide business services, particularly in accounting and advertising, an insurance company, real estate offices, an architectural firm, and a parking lot. In addition, two of the eight entrepreneurs in this study,[10] both from Nigeria, have diversified their business holdings to include various unrelated establishments and, as such, they will be featured somewhat more prominently here.[11]

Of the eleven firms for which the years of establishment were available, the mean and median age of the enterprises was twelve years. The age of firms ranged from two to twenty-four years.[12] The median amount of start-up-capital for these firms was $20,000 with an average of $29,222.[13] Capital at the start of these businesses ranged from $5,000 to $110,000. These firms have about six workers on average and are classified here as small.[14] To understand the development, growth, and overall prospects of success for small firms, knowledge of the available resources accessible to entrepreneurs is important. In this study, most of these businesspersons obtained the money to establish their enterprises from their personal savings or from gifts and loans from relatives and friends. Three of the entrepreneurs did obtain money from other sources. The two Nigerians who owned multiple businesses were able to secure bank loans for the cultural center and the nightclub after they had used their personal savings to open their earlier businesses (a grocery store and a parking lot, respectively). A third entrepreneur, a Ugandan, obtained money from business brokers at a very high rate of interest to start his bar and restaurant. Most of these businesspersons, like micro- and small-scale entrepreneurs around the world, noted that they had problems securing adequate finance, problems that continued to plague them years after the establishment of their enterprises.[15]

These immigrants commented that they began the types of businesses that they did for several reasons: (1) they had developed expertise in an area based on their education or previous work experience and wanted to "establish something of their own" (e.g., business services such as advertising and accounting); (2) there were few barriers to entry in the activity they began, namely real estate; and (3) they perceived a need for services that would address the needs of their community (e.g., the night club would serve as a social center).

[I entered this business] because of the realization that at that time there was a need for entertainment that I wanted to get involved in. A lot of foreigners, myself included, had no place to go to listen to African music and meet other Africans. (Interview with Mr. Leo, June 2006)

Well, the Petro Parking Company I was working for was big and I was paid well, but once you reach the position I was in, I knew I couldn't go any higher. I am ambitious and wanted to go out on my own. . . . For this club, I know the easiest way to arouse attention is to find places where people can socialize. This is a place where Africans can come and celebrate their culture. (Interview with Mr. Jion, June 2006)

I felt a need for the food market. In the early 1990s, the Chinese and Koreans were selling our food. Most of the food they do not use (nor) eat. They did not know how to present them, how to keep them. Decided to open a food market so our people can have a choice. I decided to compete with them. (Interview with Mr. Maj, June 2006)

My sister and I entered the business together. My husband was looking for a job for the two of us. There was an Indian restaurant located on Baltimore Avenue and the owner was seeking a cook and a waitress. The owner of the restaurant offered me the opportunity to run the restaurant if I could pay the rent because the owner could no longer afford the rent. A friend of my sponsor . . . helped me start the business. She provided assistance with negotiating the rent and completing the paperwork. (Interview with Ms. Aram, July 2007)

While immigrant businesses are often characterized by their use of family labor, this was not the case in most of the firms studied here. Only two businesses employed family members as workers—one restaurant/bar owned by a Ugandan immigrant employed the entrepreneur's nephew in addition to nineteen U.S.-born workers, while the grocery store employed one regular worker but also relied on labor from the Nigerian business owner's wife and brother. Although micro- and small-scale businesses do not employ many workers, they collectively account for most workers in nation-states around the globe (Mead 1999). They are also important sources for human capital development, which assists the businesses in which they work and other firms that they or their employees may develop, as well as overall community and national development. Enterprises in this study employed six workers on average and had a median of four workers. At one end of the spectrum, there were two businesses that did not employ any workers—one real estate firm and one advertising business. In the case of the latter, however, the entrepreneur hired subcontractors from Temple University and trained them to conduct some of the survey research. In this regard, he was very conscious of his position as a Nigerian entrepreneur and a graduate student and tried to provide opportunities for other African students:[16]

To begin the company, I hired a bunch of people [subcontractors]. I sought out African students at Temple University to hand out surveys on the street. . . . I use my alma mater, Temple. I talk to African clubs on the campus and there is always someone willing to help. The survey project was set-up as an internship for the students. (Interview with Mr. Yire, July 2006)

These enterprises also provided jobs for other Africans, both co-ethnics and African immigrants from different nations than the owners, such as a Ugandan bar/restaurant owner who used to employ a few Ethiopian immigrants. Over the years, these entrepreneurs trained workers who went on to start other businesses of their own, some in the same field, while others started firms in unrelated areas. These workers have left to start an insurance company (left employment in an insurance company to begin his own), a gas station, convenience stores, bars/restaurants (left a restaurant to start his own), a taxi business, and a carpentry shop, as well as other ventures. Undoubtedly, the training and experience these employees received working in these immigrants' firms helped them in their quest to become entrepreneurs. Thus, in creating various employment and internship opportunities, these entrepreneurs have contributed to human capital development in both West Philadelphia and the broader region.

These businesspersons provide services to African clients as well as other residents of West Philadelphia and the region. As stated above, West Philadelphia is home to a very established African American community, but it is also the residence of many students in University City (from both Drexel University and the University of Pennsylvania), some faculty from the universities, and other populations of color. Entrepreneurs in this study mainly discussed having customers who are African, African American, and Afro-Caribbean, but some such as Mr. Jion in real estate and Mr. Sak in insurance stated that they have also had European American customers in the former case and Hispanic and Vietnamese customers in the latter. Even African-focused businesses have had appeal to those outside of the African community, particularly those from various groups in the African Diaspora:

> Africans buy goods from the market, African Americans and other people in the neighborhood. . . . We looked around and added some other goods. We now added Western Union, keys, calling cards, African wares. In the beginning, it was mainly groceries, but now, sell a range of goods. These goods have changed who the customers are somewhat. The Western Union was a draw. In the beginning, the Western Union brought more immigrants but as time wore on, it brought folks from the neighborhood. (Interview with Mr. Maj, June 2006)

Nine of the ten businesspersons studied stated that they have achieved success in their firms and that although they have experienced many challenges, overall they have experienced more successes. The respondents made these claims based on the fact that they are still in business and have remained in business since they first opened, that they have provided employment, have purchased buildings, have supported their families, and in some cases, have been able to support nonprofit activities in their "home" and "host" countries. While many of the entrepreneurs did not provide information on the growth and profitability of their establishments, the few who did have experienced growth for the most part, such as an increase in profits in insurance from $20,000 at the end of the first year to $250,000 today and an increase in assets in a real estate firm that began with $13,000 and is now worth over one million dollars. Significant growth in assets and profits can also be noted in the parking lot, the other real estate business, the accounting firm, the market, and the cultural center. Mr. Maj, the owner of the latter two establishments, talked about the redevelopment of West Philadelphia as a major reason for the growth in his assets:

> Growth in assets is mainly accounted for by the redevelopment and incentives in University City. In the last fifteen years, the University of Pennsylvania has given money to faculty to buy properties in this neighborhood. Between here and the university, 25 percent of all properties are owned by the university system. Property values in University City have increased but there are a combination of factors responsible for this—the university system was the key drive re: keeping certain folks in the city. So now, from the Clinton and Street eras, we also see a real change. Several new properties were built where projects used to exist. This was a very strong drive in determining re-development in the area and has led to increased property values. (Interview with Mr. Maj, June 2006)

While it is true that the University of Pennsylvania has spearheaded a good deal of redevelopment in West Philadelphia, it is also the case that these African entrepreneurs are contributing to this endeavor through purchasing abandoned buildings, establishing businesses, developing human capital, and in turn, contributing to the local economy. They are also creating stronger bonds among the African community. As noted by Mr. Jion and Mr. Leo, who are committed to enhancing development:

> Neighborhood revitalization is a big part of what I am trying to do with my real estate business. You see a lot of this going on in Olde City, but I don't have the capital to do anything there. But here, I feel like I can be more effective. I have helped boost the economy here. On this block, by next year, nothing will be abandoned. (Interview with Mr. Jion, June 2006)

> I pay taxes, everything I buy has taxes on them, so I contribute to the economy. Also the people I hire contribute to the economy because they buy other goods in the community with that payment. But I think an important thing to talk about is the fact that my businesses bring Africans together. I think two weeks ago, a gentleman approached me and said he was new in town and wondered if he could call a cab. He was South African. We started talking and he told me my club is talked about back home. And he's not the only one—a man from Paris told me the

same thing. This is a place where you can come to Philly and not know anyone, but before long, you meet people who make your stay more meaningful. (Interview with Mr. Leo July 2006)

While these firms are mainly experiencing financial success, they are not without their problems. In addition to the problems of finance stated above, others such as Mr. Jion also believe that their status as immigrants makes them more vulnerable to problems regarding government regulations, such as zoning:

A lot of African businesses experience the same thing. When you're not familiar with the protocol, punishment should be a slap on the wrist, not capital punishment. I am running into all of these roadblocks with the zoning regulations. They say, I should have gotten zoning information before I started. But before, where I come from, you do it differently. You can start a business where and when you want. I didn't know all of the zoning details when I started renovating this building. Give me a chance, don't kick me to the curb just because I have never done this before. (Interview with Mr. Jion, June 2006)

Mr. Leo also remarked that he has encountered difficulties in his business as an immigrant:

I wouldn't call them problems, but I sell alcohol and you're dealing with people who drink and don't know how to handle themselves. It's only a minor problem. Initially, when I started, this neighborhood was bad. Young people used to stand on the corner and say things to me like, "You foreigner! Go home!" that sort of thing. (Interview with Mr. Leo, June 2006)

African Community Organizations: Striving for Solutions and Success

Today, problems encountered with one's immigration status and business development are being addressed in three notable organizations based in Philadelphia—The Coalition of African Communities–Philadelphia (AFRICOM), the Mayor's Commission on African and Caribbean Immigrants' Affairs, and the African and Caribbean Business Council. These groups are important vehicles in facilitating settlement in the area, accessing resources such as health care and education, and assisting in enterprise development. Moreover, these associations also help forge strong relationships with other Black Diaspora populations, such as Afro-Caribbeans/West Indians and African Americans. As such, they make major contributions to building a strong Pan-African community that contributes to success among African immigrants.

AFRICOM, which was established in 2001, states its mission as:

> to empower the African refugee and immigrant communities by: a) facilitating family access to health and social services, with special focus on women, children and the youth; b) promoting economic development; c) facilitating resolution of inter and intra-group conflicts; d) advocating on issues of concern to African communities; and e) educating the media and broader public on African cultures and experiences. (http://africom-philly.blogspot.com and interview with Ms. Nei, July 2006)

In its efforts to make health care available to all Africans, AFRICOM encouraged the Philadelphia Health Department to hire a French-speaking health worker to do outreach in the Francophone African immigrant community. The group also assists immigrants and refugees with immigration issues and refers individuals to appropriate legal counsel. Educational initiatives are also very important to AFRICOM, as noted by Mr. Mon, one of the founding members:

> We also work with the School District of Philadelphia to assist in improving the cultural awareness, to increase security using cultural dynamics and also maybe helping to reform the school curriculum to ensure it is culturally sensitive. AFRICOM is also in the process of establishing a charter school. (Interview with Mr. Mon, July 2006)

Among the special events sponsored by AFRICOM is an Annual Health Fair, which includes on-site HIV testing, and social events, such as "Echoes of Africa" to promote knowledge about the diversity of African cultures to the broader Philadelphia community.

While membership in AFRICOM is open to individuals, the organization mainly consists of representatives from African and Caribbean organizations in the Philadelphia area. AFRICOM has an elected executive council and a board of directors. Meetings are held every month in West Philadelphia. Six respondents in this study have been involved as founding members, as members of the Executive Council, or as both. Today, one respondent is the current president and another is a board member.

Linked to AFRICOM and sharing a similar mission is the Mayor's Commission on African and Caribbean Immigrants' Affairs. Under the leadership of City Council Majority Leader Jannie Blackwell, this group, established in 2005, takes as its mission: "to encourage the development and implementation of policies and practices intended to improve conditions affecting the cultural, social, economic, educational, health and general well-being of the African and Caribbean immigrants, refugees, and asylees residing in Philadelphia" (http://ework .phila.gov/philagov/news/prelease.asp?id=150). AFRICOM sends representatives to the Mayor's Commission and has worked with the Commission on several issues, including discrimination and violence experienced by African children in Philadelphia schools (interview with Ms. Nei, July 2006). This Commission has been focal in promoting the development of the West Philadelphia commercial district/Empowerment Zone that clearly benefits African business owners, including those in this study. A trade commission has also been established which seeks to promote trade relations with Caribbean and African nations. Moreover, the Mayor's Commission provides further opportunities for Africans to develop working relationships with African Americans.

To specifically address business and community needs, the African and Caribbean Business Council was formed in 2006 as an outgrowth of the Mayor's Commission. This group, which is in its formative stage, serves as a conduit for exchange of information among African and Caribbean entrepreneurs. It plans to offer job training and create directories of African and Caribbean businesses in the area. At the time of my interview with Mr. Nywu, the interim chair, the organization had about thirty members and plans to offer different levels of membership in the group including to students in business schools, professionals, enterprises, and associate members who do not have to be African or Caribbean but could be African American, Latino, or another ethnicity. This group also seeks to establish partnerships with companies involved in African countries, such as Hershey's Cocoa and Western Union. Their current office is the African Cultural Center owned by Mr. Maj (interview with Mr. Nywu, June 2006). Respondents in this study have been very involved in the establishment of this group, and they look forward to the assistance it might provide to the African business community in the future:

> Recently, I joined the African/Caribbean Business Council. My situation is typical. I wanted to avoid the limelight, get things started all by myself. But I ran into all of these complications with the zoning. Had I had a group to back me up and support me, things may have been different. . . . Once it (Council) is in place, it will assist not only me, but other people in the same boat as me. (Interview with Mr. Jion, June 2006)

In establishing and participating in these organizations, African immigrants in this study have made valuable contacts, which not only enrich their businesses, work, and personal lives, but also create strong bonds with others in their community. Members of AFRICOM, indeed many participants in this study, have strong working relationships with the Mayor's Office, the City Council, and the Commission, which also fosters strong linkages with members of the African

American and Caribbean communities. In the process of establishing strong ties to the Philadelphia area, African immigrants are also playing a key role in urban renewal and strengthening and re-energizing civil society, especially in West Philadelphia. As noted by Jannie Blackwell during the establishment of the Mayor's Commission on African and Caribbean Immigrants' Affairs: "We appreciate the investment that so many of our African and Caribbean immigrants have made toward the revitalization of Philadelphia, especially in recognition of the hardships that they have endured" (http://ework.phila.gov/philagov/news/prelease.asp?id=150).

Conclusion

Africans migrating to the Greater Philadelphia area over the past two and a half decades are indeed transnationals with strong bonds to their homelands and close ties to African Diasporic communities in Philadelphia. For many, the forces of globalization have led them to leave their countries of origin to seek a better life away from economic and political crises, civil wars, and natural disasters. While they remain connected to "home" through the sending of remittances and frequent visits, they have also established themselves as engaged residents of West Philadelphia. Although several participants in this study have encountered racism in the United States and other problems as immigrants, they have managed to maintain successful enterprises and to begin vibrant civic organizations in Philadelphia. Through these actions, they have demonstrated that they are important actors in the revitalization of West Philadelphia and in the formation of a dynamic, Pan-African community.

Notes

1. The Hart-Cellar Act opened the United States to immigrants from the Global South. The Immigration Reform and Control Act required employers to certify their employees' immigration status. It also granted amnesty to those who were out of status and who could prove they had been living in the United States for at least two consecutive years before January 1982. The Diversity Program of the Immigration Act of 1990 was instituted to increase the admission of immigrants from nations that have been underrepresented in the United States.

2. Since the attacks on the World Trade Center and the Pentagon on September 11, 2001, the U.S. State Department has increased the requirements to obtain visas for foreigners to enter the United States, especially for those coming from the Global South.

3. I do believe that conflict theories, such as internal colonialism and middlemen minorities, are still important in understanding the vestiges of colonization that persist for several groups in the United States including African Americans, Native Americans, Chicanos, Puerto Ricans, and Chinese Americans (see Blauner 1972; Bonacich 1980).

4. Therefore, the United States still has great needs for cheap agricultural labor while at the same time having demands for highly skilled professionals.

5. In some cases, remittances from relatives in the Global North have been found to exceed the GDP in some nations in the Global South, such as Bolivia. About a decade ago in Ghana, remittances were found to be a major contributor to the Ghanaian economy.

6. Very special thanks are extended to Mike Fratangelo, Tia Burroughs, and Nia Turner for working with me as research assistants on this project. Two of these interviewers are African American women and the other was a European American male.

7. Differences in community participation noted in Stoller's and my studies can also be explained by the class differences in our samples. My sample consisted largely of members of the middle and upper-middle classes, while Stoller's participants were largely low-income traders in the microenterprise sector of the economy.

8. According to the 2000 U.S. Census, the African American population of Philadelphia was 655,824 or 43.2 percent of the total population of the city. As of 2005, African Americans constitute 44.7 percent of the city's population. U.S. Census Bureau (2000, 2005).

9. Of the ten entrepreneurs considered in this section, only one is a woman. There is more than one businesswomen in the overall study, but only one has a business in West Philadelphia. On the whole, however, men are more highly represented in this occupation than women given the significant structural blockage that women still experience here and around the globe in becoming entrepreneurs. Access to capital, although not the only challenge, remains a major problem for women. See Osirim 1992, 2001; Carter and Cannon 1992; Berger 1995; and Bolles 2007.

10. There are more than ten African entrepreneurs in this study. However, some of these businesspersons are not included in this section of the paper because their enterprises are not located in West Philadelphia but at other sites in Greater Philadelphia.

11. Compared to several other sub-Saharan African nations, Nigeria has a long history of creative, dynamic entrepreneurship. See Harris 1970; Kilby 1965, 1971; and Schatz 1977, among many other works.

12. Some entrepreneurs in this study own more than one business. At the time of his interview, one businessman, who owns a parking lot and a real-estate firm, planned to open a nightclub.

13. Only nine entrepreneurs supplied figures for the amount of establishment capital.

14. There is a great deal of literature that categorizes size of firm by financial data, such as the amount of sales or the number of employees. In my studies of entrepreneurship in microenterprises in sub-Saharan Africa, I have chosen to use number of employees as the more significant indicator of size. See Osirim 1998.

15. Although several studies on the development of entrepreneurship in sub-Saharan Africa, as well as in the Global South more generally, state that the need for finance is overestimated by business owners, it is the case nevertheless, that a good deal of discrimination in obtaining bank loans based on class, gender, ethnicity and race prevails in many nations, including our own. See Schatz 1977 and Osirim 1992, 2008.

16. Of course, it is also the case that hiring students as interns lowered his business expenses.

References

Apraku, Kofi. 1991. *African Emigres in the United States: A Missing Link in Africa's Social and Economic Development.* New York: Praeger.

———. 1996. *Outside Looking In: An African Perspective on American Pluralistic Society.* Westport, CT: Praeger.

Arthur, John. 2000. *Invisible Sojourners: African Immigrant Diaspora in the United States.* Westport, CT: Praeger.

Basch, Linda. 2001. "Transnational Social Relations and the Politics of National Identity: An Eastern Caribbean Case Study." In *Islands in the City: West Indian Migration to New York,* ed. Nancy Foner. Berkeley: University of California Press.

Berger, Marguerite. 1995. "Key Issues on Women's Access to and Use of Credit in the Micro- and Small-Scale Sector." In *Women in Micro- and Small-Scale Enterprise Development,* ed. Louise Dignard and Jose Havet. Boulder: Westview Press.

Blauner, Robert. 1972. *Racial Oppression in America.* New York: Harper and Row.

Bolles, A. Lynn. 2007. "Of Land and Sea: Women Entrepreneurs in Negril, Jamaica." In *Women's Labor in the Global Economy: Speaking in Multiple Voices,* ed. Sharon Harley. New Brunswick, NJ: Rutgers University Press.

Bonacich, Edna. 1980. "Class Approaches to Ethnicity and Race." *Insurgent Sociologist* 10 (2): 9–23.

Bryce-Laporte, Roy S. 1993. "Voluntary Immigration and Continuing Encounters between Blacks: Post-Quincentenary Challenge." *Annals of the American Academy of Political and Social Science* 530 (1): 28–41.

Carter, Sara, and Tom Cannon. 1992. *Women as Entrepreneurs.* London: Academic Press.

City of Philadelphia. 2005. "Mayor Street Announces Commission on African and Immigrant Affairs." Available at http://ework.phila.gov/philagov/news/prelease.asp?id =150.

Coalition of African Communities (AFRICOM) Web site: http://africom-philly.blogspot.com.

Dodoo, Francis Nii-Amoo. 1997. "Assimilation Differences among Africans in America." *Social Forces* 76 (2): 527–546.

Foner, Nancy. 2001. *New Immigrants in New York.* New York: Columbia University Press.

Harris, John. 1970. "Nigerian Entrepreneurship in Industry." In *Growth and Development of the Nigerian Economy,* ed. Carl Eicher and Carl Liedholm. East Lansing: Michigan State University Press.

Kilby, Peter. 1965. *African Enterprises: The Nigerian Bread Industry.* Palo Alto, CA: Stanford University Institute Studies.

———. 1971. *Entrepreneurship and Economic Development.* New York: Free Press.

Mead, Donald. 1999. "MSE's Tackle Both Poverty and Growth." In *Enterprise in Africa: Between Poverty and Growth,* ed. Kenneth King and Simon McGrath. London: Intermediate Technology Publications.

Ogbu, John. 1978. *Minority Education and Caste.* New York: Academic Press.

Okome, Mojúbàolú Olúfúnké. 2005. "Antinomies of Globalization: Causes & Consequences of African Immigration to the USA." In *Globalization and Its Discontents,* ed. Olufemi Vaughan, M. Birch, and C. Smalls. Ibadan, Nigeria: Sefer Academic Press. The article is also available at http://www.africamigration.com/archive_01/m_okome_globalization _02.htm.

Osirim, Mary J. 1992. "Gender and Entrepreneurship: Issues of Capital and Technology in Nigerian Small Firms." In *Privatization and Investment in Sub-Saharan Africa,* ed. Rexford Ahene and Bernard Katz. New York: Praeger.

———. 1998. "Negotiating Identities during Adjustment Programs: Women and Microenterprise Development in Urban Zimbabwe." In *African Entrepreneurship: Theory and Reality,* ed. Anita Spring and Barbara McDade. Gainesville: University Press of Florida.

————. 2001. "Making Good on Commitments to Grassroots Women: NGOs and Empowerment for Women in Contemporary Zimbabwe." *Women's Studies International Forum* 24 (2): 167–180.

————. 2008. "African Women in the New Diaspora: Transnationalism and the (Re)Creation of Home." *African and Asian Studies* 7 (4): 367–394.

Portes, Alejandro. 1996. "Global Villagers: The Rise of Transnational Communities." *American Prospect* 7 (25): 74–77.

Portes, Alejandro, and Ruben Rumbaut. 2001. *Legacies: The Story of the Immigrant Second Generation*. Berkeley: University of California Press.

Portes, Alejandro, and Min Zhou. 1993. "The New Second Generation: Segmented Assimilation and Its Variants." *Annals of the American Academy of Political and Social Science* 530 (1): 74–96.

Schatz, Sayre. 1977. *Nigerian Capitalism*. Berkeley: University of Califorrnia Press.

Stoller, Paul. 2001. "West Africans: Trading Places in New York." In *New Immigrants in New York*, ed. Nancy Foner. New York: Columbia University Press.

————. 2002. *Money Has No Smell: The Africanization of New York City*. Chicago: University of Chicago Press.

Swigart, Leigh. 2001. *Extended Lives: The African Immigrant Experience in Philadelphia*. Philadelphia: Balch Institute of Ethnic Studies.

U.S. Census Bureau. 2000. United States Census 2000. Available at http://www.census.gov/main/www/cen2000.html.

————. 2005. American Community Survey. Available at http://www.census.gov/acs/www/.

Vickerman, Milton. 2001. "Jamaicans: Balancing Race and Ethnicity." In *New Immigrants in New York*, ed. Nancy Foner. New York: Columbia University Press.

Waters, Mary. 1999. *Black Identities: West Indian Immigrant Dreams and American Realities*. New York: Russell Sage Foundation.

Welcoming Center for New Pennsylvanians. 2004. *Immigrant Philadelphia: From Cobblestone Streets to Korean Soap-Operas*. Philadelphia: Welcoming Center for New Pennsylvanians in collaboration with the Historical Society of Pennsylvania.

————. 2006. *Immigrants Resource Manual: What Every Immigrant Needs to Know*. Philadelphia: Welcoming Center for New Pennsylvanians in collaboration with the Historical Society of Pennsylvania.

Yetman, Norman, ed. 1999. *Majority and Minority: The Dynamics of Race and Ethnicity in American Life*. Boston: Allyn and Bacon.

11

From Kerala to Philadelphia

The Experiences of Malayalee,
Hindu Nurses in Philadelphia

RASIKA CHAKRAVARTHY AND AJAY NAIR

B etween 1972 and 1976, three South Indian women came to the United
States in search of economic opportunity and a gateway for the
immigration of their families. The following is a look into the lives
of Malayalee nurses in America, as well as the complexities surrounding
ethnic identity and adaptation in Indian immigrant populations.

The portrait of Indian Americans in much of the scholarly literature and
in the mass media fails to acknowledge the diversity of the community and
the unique experiences and challenges of subgroups within Indian America.
The ethnic label "Indian American" encompasses all of the various regional
subgroups in India, but more often than not, the term is more closely associated with people of North Indian[1] background. In this case study, the
researchers focus on the unique immigrant experience of South Indian Keralite Hindus in the Nair community of Philadelphia.

Coming from a primarily patriarchal Indian society in which traditional
gender roles place the husband as the primary breadwinner of the family
and in which females are socialized to be dutiful wives, mothers, and homemakers (Choudhry 2001), the women of this study are unique in that most
are the primary earners of the family and have opened the gateway to America for their husbands and future children.[2] By investigating the interactive
roles of gender and religion in the Indian household, with a particular focus
on the relevance and impact of community organizations, we hope to shed
light on the complexities surrounding ethnic identity and acculturation of
Indian women in the United States.

Demographic Background:
Philadelphia and the United States

The earliest accounts of Indians in Philadelphia are of those who were brought to the colonies as indentured servants or slaves. The Pennsylvania Abolition Society has a record of a James Dunn from Calcutta who was indentured as an eight-year-old boy (Prasad 1999). An "East Indian from Scotland" named Anthony Adams was indentured to Thomas Mullen of Philadelphia from 1745 to 1751. In 1788, an eighteen-year-old Joseph Green from Calcutta became an apprentice to William Richardson of Middletown, Bucks County, Pennsylvania. A Philadelphia merchant named James Boland had possession of a fifteen-year-old East Indian slave named John Bally (Muhkerjee and Wycliffe 2006).

Today, a little over 3 percent of the 2,319,222 Indian Americans in the United States reside in Pennsylvania (U.S. Census 2005). Approximately 75,000 Indian Americans live in Pennsylvania, which reflects a 31 percent growth rate between 2000 and 2005. Philadelphia is unique in its economic diversity as well as its central access to the South Asian communities of New York, New Jersey, and the District of Columbia, which together have the greatest number of South Asians in the United States (Sinha 1996). In fact, Milbourne, a town that borders Philadelphia, has a 40 percent Indian population, whereas Indians constitute only 0.6 percent of the U.S. population (U.S. Census 2000).

Nurses from Kerala, many of whom were sponsored for jobs in Philadelphia, were among the first to settle in the area (Melwani 2005). All of the participants in this study have at some point lived near or in Milbourne, and they continue to maintain strong connections to this community. Despite the fact that more than 300,000 of the 2.3 million Indian Americans have roots in Kerala (information available at http://www.fokanaonline.com/), very little research has focused on this segment of the Indian American community.

Asian Indian Immigration

Immigration from South Asia to the United States occurred in two contrasting phases of Asian migration to the United States. In the early stages, between 1903 and 1908, about 6,000 Punjabis immigrated to Canada and nearly 3,000 crossed into the United States (Leonard 1997). These immigrants were largely men from Punjab who worked on farms. Subsequently the immigration laws of 1917 and 1924 were changed to ban most immigration from Asia. In the next phase, the Immigration and Naturalization Act of 1965 gave preferential treatment to skilled labor. Hence the two sets of immigrants were dissimilar: the earlier immigrants were men, primarily from the state of Punjab in India, and from rural backgrounds, while the later ones were families, from all over India, Pakistan, Bangladesh, Sri Lanka, and Nepal, and from urban, educated backgrounds.

The surge in South Asian immigration to the United States post-1965 was due not only to the change in U.S. immigration policies, but also due to capitalist market forces, differences in wages in various parts of the world, unstable governments in South Asian countries, and family reunification in the United States. South Asian countries did not disallow emigration, as it alleviated their unemployment problems and foreign currency imbalances (Leonard 1997: 68). In addition, the 1970s saw an influx of healthcare professionals and the status change from students to permanent residents for Indian students who had completed their graduate studies (Leonard 1997: 81). As many of these Indian Americans are practicing professionals, such as scientists, engineers, or medical personnel, they are found in greater concentration near metropolitan areas, primarily in the states of New York, California, New Jersey, Texas, Pennsylvania, Michigan, Illinois, and Ohio (Leonard 1997: 70). Revisions in immigration law in 1976 led to a decrease in professional Indian immigrants, which has contributed to the lower educational level of the recent immigrant population (Sheth 1995: 177).

In the five-year periods between 1955 and 1980, the largest Keralite immigration took place in the years 1971–1975, representing 38 percent of the Malayalee immigrant population up to that point, with the year 1975 boasting 11 percent of the Malayalee population, the largest immigration in one year. The decade of 1970–1980 saw an overwhelming 74 percent of the immigration up to that point. Forty percent of Malayalees were in the healthcare field, either as doctors, nurses, or technicians, and 45 percent had bachelor's, master's, or doctoral degrees. One survey showed 85 percent of Keralite immigrants to be Christians, 14 percent to be Hindus, and the remaining to be Muslim or other denominations (Andrews 1983: 103).

Ethnicity, Religion, and Cultural Organizations

Ethnic identity in the United States is defined by the identification of immigrants with their group's race, nationality, language, food, clothing, or any other values or symbols that will render the group unique. There are several sources of Indian ethnicity: religion, language and history, values such as nonviolence and educational and professional excellence (Sheth 1995: 183–184), tradition, position in life, and individual experiences (Joseph 1992: 15). Indians are able to maintain their identity by consuming culturally marked goods, attendance at public festivals, and religious worship, among other things (Lessinger 1995: 27).

Religion is crucial to ethnic construction because it serves as a medium for the transmission of culture and supplies a framework for the formation of communities (Kurien 1999: 649). The importance of religion in the United States permits immigrants to reinforce their identity as well as gain acceptance in the host community (Leonard 1997: 108). As one scholar purports, "In the United

States, religion is the social category with clearest meaning and acceptance in the host society, so the emphasis on religious affiliation and identity is one of the strategies that allows the immigrant to maintain self-identity while simultaneously acquiring community acceptance" (Williams 1988: 11–12). Religion is a significant part of immigrant life as it provides the anchor to a memory of the past and helps the transmission of tradition wherein both personal and group identities can be preserved (Williams 1992: 229).

Looking at the religious development of Asian immigrants in the United States (Leonard 1997: 107–108), one finds that in the early years the immigrants acted on their own, either practicing religion in private or abandoning it. It is during the 1970s that a "national" stage emerged wherein the immigrant population grew in numbers and sought its own identity. These immigrants grouped themselves according to nationality and prompted the growth of mosques, temples, and churches. Then came the "ecumenical" stage, when temples and mosques became more international and people of various national origins attended them. The "ethnic" stage followed, with Hindus and others dividing and subdividing into smaller and smaller groups. As the number of Indian immigrants increased, so did the importance of religion to this group (Leonard 1997: 107–108), as it helped them preserve their identity and cohesiveness. Indeed, Indians are more religious in the United States than they were back home (Williams 1988: 11).

Since 1965, organizations have become another important vehicle for fulfilling the various cultural needs of the South Asian community (Sheth 1995: 185). Religious institutions provide immigrants a physical and social space to freely practice their customs and traditions and pass these on to the next generation (Ebaugh and Chafetz 2000: 396). Regional organizations help bring together people who share a common language, cuisine, religion, dress, and so forth (Williams 1988: 48) and also serve to accommodate similar professional and educational backgrounds. In fact, when there is a large number of Indians in one area that share a particular regional background, it is fairly common for immigrants to form caste-specific organizations, similar to the Nairs of Philadelphia (Kurien 1998: 45–46). Pan-Indian organizations, on the other hand, aim to address the more general political and economic needs of Indians as a minority group. Whereas prior to the 1970s Indian immigrant organizations could mainly be found on college campuses, many more have since sprouted in urban and suburban areas. In fact, there was a proliferation of Indian immigrant organizations in Philadelphia and South Jersey in the 1970s (Sheth 1995: 186–187).

In 1983, the first Kerala Convention was held in New York City, which led to the founding of the Federation of Kerala Associations in North America (FOKANA). In the same year, the Council of Indian Organizations (CIO) was founded in Philadelphia. There are twenty-five organizations represented by

CIO, a group that works to build community among people of Asian Indian origin. At least four of the groups represented by CIO are Malayalee organizations that represent the interests of Indian immigrants from Kerala. In the Philadelphia region there are two Malayalee organizations that focus specifically on the Nair community: the Nair Society of Delaware Valley (NSD) and the Nair Service Society of Pennsylvania (NSS). Three other pan-Kerala organizations exist in Philadelphia: Kerala Art and Literary Association of Philadelphia (KALA), the Malayalee Association of Greater Philadelphia (MAP), and PAMPA, a non-profit organization for charitable, educational, and civic activities. The existence of multiple umbrella organizations in Philadelphia speaks to the diversity of the community.

Background on Kerala Nurses in the United States

Comprising only about 1.3 percent of the country's land, Kerala is a small, isolated, but extremely distinctive part of India. While Malayalam is the official language of Kerala, English is widely spoken and understood. Along with Hindus, thriving communities of Christians, Muslims, and Jews coexist in Kerala. Compared to the rest of India, Kerala has a higher proportion of Christians in the population, 22 percent as compared to 2.6 percent nationally (Thomas and Thomas 1984: 62).

The Keralite Hindus are not homogeneous but are divided into several castes, such as the Brahmins, Nairs, and Ezhavas. In the olden days, Nairs were warriors and took part in the constant wars between native states (Thomas and Thomas 1984: 63–64). The Nairs were always an honored class, and historically have maintained a close relationship with the Brahmins. Even though they constitute less than 20 percent of the populace in Kerala, the Nairs have become an extremely organized and powerful group in Kerala (Thomas and Thomas 1984: 63–64).

Nursing has been in practice in India since the Vedic times, but it only began to be recognized as a profession in the late eighteenth century (Raghavachari 1990: 30). To give an example of the tremendous need for nurses in India, the Bhore Report (Report of the Health Survey and Development Committee 1946) compared the proportion of medical personnel to population in India and the United Kingdom (Wilkinson 1965: 93). In India the ratios were: one doctor to 6,300; one nurse to 43,000; one health visitor to 400,000; and one midwife to 60,000 people. The Report observed that though "doctors should be increased fourfold, a corresponding increase in nurses and health visitors should be a hundred times" (Wilkinson 1965: 93–94).

Though India was in dire need of nurses, the main obstacle to enrollment was the strong prejudice that such work was somehow degrading, as it involved contact with sick people and unfamiliar men (Wilkinson 1965: 31). Initially, the nurses were from the Christian or Anglo-Indian communities, which were less restrictive in their views of women in this profession. With India's independence came emancipation for women in other communities, and nursing became a popular career choice as it required little training or investment (Raghavachari 1990: 31). With time, training became more organized and a nursing service was established to handle the supervision and training of other nurses (Wilkinson 1965: 31).

Due to the shortage of nurses in the United States in the 1960s, nurses today constitute one of the largest immigrant groups to the United States from India (Bloom 2004). The demand for nurses can be attributed to several factors, including the expansion of Medicare and Medicaid and greater medical insurance coverage provided by employers to workers, which increased the need for health care professionals. There was also a decline in U.S.-born nurses, as many women took up other attractive careers, and many quit the profession due to poor working conditions or sex-based discrimination (George 2005: 50). To meet this demand, the U.S. government had to lift restrictive immigration quotas several times to allow for more foreign recruitment of nurses, the majority of whom were from the Philippines, India, and Korea (George 1998: 269). Before 1965, most foreign nurses could enter the United States only as exchange visitors but the Immigration and Nationality Act Amendments of 1965 gave them an occupational status (Choy 2003: 168). Keralite nurses were prime candidates for emigration to the United States; many nurses born in Kerala traveled all over India to obtain their professional degrees, and then emigrated all over the world. In addition, Kerala has the highest literacy rates in India and very progressive educational programs that have brought very competitive émigrés to the United States and Europe (Bloom 2004: 26).

Methodology

This research employed qualitative methods in gathering and analyzing data. The data is contextualized through narrative and categorized around emergent themes. Data was collected through personal interviews and participant observation using nonprobability and purposive sampling; that is, selecting participants on the basis of their availability and obtaining the best data possible. In this case study, in-depth interviews were conducted with the husbands and wives of three Malayalee, Nair couples who reside in the greater Philadelphia area. The interviews were conducted in the participants' homes, which allowed the researcher to engage in limited participant observation of these couples.

In his study of Kerala immigrant couples in Chicago, Ramola Joseph found that husbands and wives had very different perceptions about attitudes and behavior, and that there were considerable discrepancies between husbands' and wives' responses, which yielded insights into family dynamics and patterns of authority and influence (1992: 22–23). A study conducted by Blumberg and

Coleman (1989) found similar discrepancies between what husbands and wives report when both are interviewed. Because in this study any such discrepancies might point to larger phenomena, it was important to the researchers to be able to compare the responses of husband and wife and to allow each person to be able to answer questions as freely and comfortably as possible. Thus, the researchers asked to interview husband and wife separately. In all three cases, the researchers observed some degree of hesitation, puzzlement, or both, from the husband upon the request, and indifference from the wife, if she was even present at the time. Though in all cases husband and wife were interviewed separately, they were not necessarily out of earshot of one another.

Each interview entailed a set list of questions that consisted of a combination of life history and experiential questions, which were primarily open-ended. If the subjects mentioned something of particular significance or interest, the researchers asked follow-up questions on the topic and in this way hoped to learn as much as possible from each individual. However, as can be expected, some subjects were more talkative than others. All of the interviews were tape recorded and subsequently transcribed for further analysis. The researchers also attempted to simultaneously engage in participant observation of both the subject and the surrounding activities in the household.

One of the researchers is a Nair community member. The researchers' subject criteria was for the couples to have originated from Kerala, to be part of the post-1965 wave of immigration to the United States, to be active and established members of the Nair Society of Delaware Valley, and for the wife to be a nurse who immigrated to the United States before her husband. The six participants in this study ranged from age 55 to 63, with the women ranging from 59 to 62 years old. All participants arrived in the United States between 1972 and 1977, and all wives came to the United States at least one year before their husbands. All couples immigrated directly to the United States from India, though for one couple Australia was also an option. No participant's real name will be used in the course of this paper; we will instead refer to "Radha," "Lela," and "Uma" and their respective husbands "Murali," "Arun," and "Raghu."

The Maintenance and Modification of Identity

Coming to America

Being in a new country with little or no family or social support was a source of hardship for each couple, and especially for the wives, who immigrated first. As Radha described, "When I came it was very hard, because nobody was there to help us ... one of my friends sponsored me, that's why I came—I struggled a lot." Although Uma stayed with relatives when she first arrived in the United States, she struggled with having very little freedom. She was also the only participant who expressed distinct displeasure about coming to America; it seems she had very little say in the decision and did not want to leave home, but her husband was adamant about it.

All of the nurse wives followed similar paths of being educated in India and working there, then coming to the United States and completing whatever education was necessary before passing the State Boards, during which time they worked as "nurse technicians" and after which they worked as registered nurses. After finishing her nursing education in India, Radha worked five years as a staff nurse in Bombay before coming to the United States and working at the University of Pennsylvania in Philadelphia. Leaving Kerala in order to work may have been a valuable intermediary step before taking an even bigger step toward independence by coming to America.

While the wives all had the same level of education, that of the husbands varied; one had a high school level education, one had a Master's in Economics from India, and then completed his certificate in accountancy here, and one had a high school education from India, and went to respiratory school while here. Upon coming to America, the husbands worked various jobs before getting some sort of certification to be able to get slightly more advanced jobs here. For example, Murali worked in a string of technical jobs and only afterwards went to school for becoming an ultrasound technician. He then worked at the Children's Hospital of Philadelphia for five years and subsequently at another hospital for ten years before retiring for health reasons.

While reasons for going into nursing varied, "helping people" was a compelling factor for all three women. In addition, Lela said that she saw the girls who became nurses all come back wearing nice new clothes, which made it seem like a "good profession." Uma expressed that she did not particularly want to be a nurse, but her family did not have enough money to send her to school to become a teacher; she would also be making more money as a nurse and would be able to send that money to her family. All three women started out working irregular shifts, such as night shifts, but have since graduated to regular, forty hours a week, day shifts. During the night shift period, husband and wife would juggle care of the kids, and often had to rely on a babysitter for supplementary care.

Life was not easy upon arriving to the United States. Radha's first job was in Northeast Philadelphia, quite a distance from her home, where she worked until getting a job at the University of Pennsylvania. She described having to wake up at 4:00 A.M. in order to catch the train to work, and then walking a great distance to her destination. In addition to taking an extra course in psychiatry, one of the burdens of becoming a nurse in America was the difficulty of passing the State Boards. None of the three women were able to pass on their first attempt. Uma attributed this partly to the nature of the exam: "[In India] we used to read and write and all that stuff. Here it's almost all multiple choice questions and that's the first time we ever saw that." As she described, "Mentally you are a little down; you are a nurse, but you cannot perform as a nurse."

There was a general trend in relocation patterns once the couples arrived in Philadelphia. After living in the Fortieth Street area in an apartment, each couple moved to Upper Darby, particularly the Milbourne area. In addition to larger residences with more room for the children, the couples were drawn to Upper Darby because it offered more safety than the city. All participants seemed to value a quiet neighborhood close to public transportation. After many years in Upper Darby, Raghu and Uma moved recently to Broomall, a wealthier but neighboring town, which traces their additional upward economic progress.

The Gender Evolution

The modification of gender relations and constructs during immigration and settlement are central to Hindu American ethnicity (Kurien 1999: 648). In the Indian milieu, women have for centuries played supportive, passive, and even submissive roles, living under the protection or dominance of fathers, brothers, and sons. Women were given respect and responsibility, but not power and authority. In the post-independence era, a sea change took place. Women slowly started competing with men for education, employment, and even professional choices. They were no longer merely traditional homemakers and caretakers of traditions and cultures placing paramount importance on the family, but were fulfilling their own passions and dreams and vying with men for educational and professional achievements.

With the women eroding the stronghold of men in the workplace, there is some change in views on gender roles, but women are still a long way from achieving parity with men. One would think that in the case of the Keralite nurses in particular, there would be a redefinition of gender roles, as these women are the primary breadwinners in the United States. In addition, except in the case of Keralite nurses, few women, even those well educated, venture to move to the United States on their own (Lessinger 1995: 110), and typically an Indian woman's immigration status in the United States depends on her husband's sponsorship (Bhattacharjee 1992: 14). It is interesting, then, that traditional gender roles continue to pervade the Keralite immigrant household.

While Keralites seem to be transitioning toward more democratic husband and wife relations, equality is not yet within reach, as wives still end up doing most or all of the household work (Thomas and Thomas 1984: 126). Though role reversal is not a common occurrence among Keralites, role sharing is becoming more acceptable (Thomas and Thomas 1984: 127). As more and more women work outside the home, they are able to persuade the husbands to help out a bit with the housework, particularly as they do not have domestic workers to help out as they did in India (Kurien 1999: 659). In addition, research in the

United States and in the Global South shows that women experience greater self-esteem, respect from others in the family, and assertiveness when they begin earning higher wages. The rise in earnings or earnings potential gives them self-confidence and the sense of control and the ability to have greater bargaining power in family situations (Blumberg and Coleman 1989: 239). Unfortunately, however, various factors can hinder a woman's ability to get a dollar's worth of economic power from every dollar that she brings to the household (Blumberg and Coleman 1989: 234).

Ironically, breadwinner wives and dependent husbands end up adopting more traditional gender roles for the sake of marital stability. These couples may return to traditional housework arrangements to reclaim gender accountability for their own sake, for the sake of partners, or for the outside world (Brines 1994: 665). Housework is the hallmark of women's work, though with the change in employment patterns for women and change in attitudes toward the sexual division of labor, more husbands are participating in domestic chores than in 1965 (Brines 1994: 652). But if a man is severely threatened by his wife's higher financial earnings, he cannot afford to be seen doing "women's work at home" (Brines 1994: 665).

Indian men have a wide range of answers when presented with questions on women's employment. Some men encourage and guide their wives, take pride in their success, and even pitch in with household chores and child rearing. Other men reluctantly allow their wives to work; they are happy with the money their wives can make but are threatened by the possible loss of male control. These husbands are quick to deride any modern or feminist ideas the wives may espouse (Lessinger 1995: 112). While in India gender roles are considered complementary, in the West they are considered dichotomous and oppositional; a woman cannot be strong or dynamic without the man appearing weak or passive (Dasgupta and Dasgupta 1996: 386). Interestingly, Rayaprol found gaps between women's ideology and their practice; it is often strategically convenient for them to pursue egalitarian practices, but externally they advocate a transitional ideology, in which it is accepted that men can have more power (1997: 132). This would enable women to empower themselves while at the same time giving men the satisfaction of having some control.

Even though Radha, Lela, and Uma had worked in India, their husbands did not take part in the household work, due to the availability of household servants and the presence of relatives from the extended family system. Also, nursing in India did not pay the women enough to overtake the men as primary breadwinners. Hence with the move to the United States, the women experienced upward mobility in status, while the reverse was true for the men (George 1998: 271), thus affecting gender roles here.

Around the house, Radha, Lela, and Uma dominate the household activities, though all of the men help out to varying degrees. While Murali claimed to be involved in the cooking, cleaning, washing, and shopping for the household, it was clear that Radha did the majority of the housework. She complained that when she is at home, she does not have a chance to sit down, because she does all the cooking, cleaning, and laundry. In fact, while Murali relaxed in the adjoining room watching Malayalee television during Radha's interview, as soon as her interview was over she departed to wash the dishes and the laundry. She did concede, however, that her husband helps her with the cooking and shopping and was the primary caregiver of their daughter during her childhood and adolescence.

When asked if anything had changed in each household since moving to the United States, both wives and their husbands admitted that since working women could not do everything, the husband helped out more around the house here, though in India the woman would take care of the children and the house all on her own. However, this was simply a factor of time and not a change in ideology on the part of the men; women simply did not have the time to work full-time and take care of all the household activities, so help was a necessity. Lela agreed that here the wife and husband share the household chores more: "If I am doing housework, he's taking care of the kids and taking care of other things." However, when Lela was asked what she thought would happen if women had enough time to both work and take care of all the housework, she responded matter-of-factly that in such a case, the woman would probably end up doing everything herself. So while we see a new sharing of household labor between husband and wife, a quasi-reversal in terms of traditional gender roles, it seems to be more a function of woman's available time than a change in ideology by men. Interestingly, for all three couples, childcare seemed to be juggled equally between husband and wife.

When each nurse was asked whether there was some sort of expectation about a woman's role in the Indian household, the answer was overwhelmingly that of "housewife." Radha's response was, "Yea, I mean housewife. We always do the housework. We listen to the husband. We don't work, watch the children, make dinner. The values of the family you respect, the men of the house, and listen to everything of the man." When asked whether this was the expectation, or the practice, she replied that it was the practice: "That's how you learn it in your culture and you try to practice it as much as you can." Lela added, "You know, in India most times they think, you know, it is not equal. They think the ladies are only sitting in the kitchen and making [food] and taking care of the kids." When Lela was asked how people in India would perceive it if a man did the cooking and cleaning and she said, "They think that is below the dignity of the men."

While Murali did not acknowledge an expectation in the Indian household about men's and women's roles, he struggled with the changes in his household that took place after coming here. He claimed that women were getting more progressive, and were increasingly involved in the money matters, which created tension in his and many others' households. According to Murali, when the women "jump ahead of the man, it creates a problem"; decision making is a boundary that once crossed creates discord in the household. He explained that women were taking more charge in the household and attributed this partly to their making more money, but also to their mixing with American female coworkers, who would describe how they took care of their own money in their households. As Murali described, "When they come home, it's 'You don't do that, that's my money, I get paycheck, I do that.' . . . All the cultural things gone."

Religion, Community, and the "Invisible Circle"

When individuals were asked how they maintain their cultural identity in the United States, religiosity was the resounding theme. Almost every participant admitted to being more religious now than when they were in India, noting that the Nair Society has been an integral part of this change. Contrary to the general fear that upon moving here, immigrants will gradually abandon their cultural identities and practices, Indians here seem to have become "more community-oriented, more religious and more 'Indianized' over time" (Kurien 1998: 45). Religion becomes an integral part of everyday life and is primarily practiced within the home, though temples provide a central location to celebrate special occasions. For immigrants, places of worship serve also as social and cultural centers where people can meet and converse with fellow immigrants while maintaining contact with traditional culture (Lessinger 1995: 47).

When asked how she maintains her cultural identity in the United States, Radha described her religious routines: "I keep up in a good way so far . . . every morning we get up, take shower and go to the puja room, pray ten minutes and then whenever we get the time to go [to] the temple; there is a Delaware *Narasimha* temple so we go there. And every month we have *bhajan,* you know we meet the people and especially in this house we pray double, morning and evening." Both Murali and Arun were eager to show the researcher their home altars and in Arun's home religious *bhajans* were playing from the kitchen throughout the interviews. In fact, while interviewing Arun, a *Swami* from the Chinmaya Mission called and Arun insisted on introducing the researcher to the Swami over the phone. Lela explicitly stated that religion was the main factor that ties her and her husband to their cultural identity in the United States.

It would be impossible to ignore the importance of religion in Murali's life; the first half hour of the interview was an almost evangelical description of Hinduism's origins and philosophical tenets. He also gave the researcher a "religious tour" of the house after the interview, showing their prayer room and home altar, where Radha was praying at the time, and where they pray at sunset and sunrise daily. He proudly showed the researcher numerous images of deities, the favorite being Krishna, as well as the large Indian flag in his foyer. Murali practices Hinduism by reading many lyrics and books, which give him "peace of mind," and by having many religious images around the house, which symbolize the invisible presence of God. Raghu observed that because in India religiosity is part of a systematic routine, "you don't even think about religion at all." It was only upon coming to America that he began questioning and trying to understand his faith.

Indeed, Kurien found that many Indian immigrants are more aware of their religious identity in the United States than in India, as they are forced to analyze and explain its meaning to themselves and their children (1999: 653). Especially significant is the multitude of home altars in America. Images of gods and goddesses can be found in almost all Hindu households—in a kitchen cabinet, a coat closet, a corner in the family room, and so forth, demonstrating the presence of domestic worship (Eck 2000: 223). It is not uncommon to call a few friends or acquaintances for religious gatherings, special prayers, or study groups (Williams 1988: 46). The practice of Hinduism at home is by far the most fundamental and influential tool for passing the torch of religious beliefs and customs to the next generation of Indian immigrants (Williams 1988: 43). As language is another component in reinforcing religious and ethnic identity, the native language is maintained in the households (Jacob and Thaku 2000: 237). Indeed, all of the couples the researchers met with spoke Malayalam primarily in the home, and almost all agreed that it was important that their children also be fluent in Malayalam.

In the Nair community, maintaining one's cultural identity is heavily intertwined with community organizations. The couples the researchers spoke with were all members of at least two organizations, the Nair Society, which includes families of this particular Hindu caste, and a broader Malayalee organization, which sponsors general activities for Keralite Indians. However, all members were more involved with the Nair Society than the Malayalee organization. Most agreed that this stemmed from the religious and homogeneous nature of the Nair Society—Malayalee organization events were more inclusive, and more cultural and social, rather than religious. Raghu observed that, "When you reach a certain age, you like to stay with your own religion." As Lela put it, the Nair Society is "our own community. The other one is, you know, so many other people too. . . . This is just like a family."

The role of the extended family in providing an anchor for the immigrant group cannot be overstated. The "private space" for the Indian community is unique in that it consists of the domestic sphere of one's own family as well as the extended family of Indians (Bhattacharjee 1992: 15). Almost everyone interviewed preferred an extended family to a nuclear one, and one of the couples,

Raghu and Uma, actually did live with their son, his wife, and their young child. During the interview itself the researcher witnessed both grandparents interacting with and taking care of the grandchild.

In the case of the Nairs, both husbands and wives agreed that Nair men were more active in their organizations, in terms of leadership, than Nair women. However, the researchers could not uncover any sort of gendered basis; women were encouraged to take leadership in the Nair Society, and there have been female presidents, but their busy work schedules and additional household duties prevent them from doing so. According to Uma, women "have other things to do—to take care of the family and the house, cooking, cleaning and all that stuff," in addition to a full day at work. So perhaps while Nair men do not actively hinder women's participation in the organizations, the insufficient transfer of gendered responsibility in the household is an impediment to their increased involvement. Moreover, while the husbands seemed rather proud of their leadership positions and involvement in the Nair Society, none of the women expressed even remote discontent about their lack of involvement in the organization.

Though responses varied as to what is the exact purpose of the Nair Society, the most prevalent theme was that it is a social and cultural organization that allows the Nairs to pass on their culture to their children. Various activities such as picnics and religious celebrations (such as *Onam*) help the children identify themselves as Nairs. In Raghu's words, it is about "teaching the kids religion, how to do the prayers, how to respect the elders." Murali's commentary was particularly insightful: "We are making a little boundary between us, making a circle around us. There's an invisible circle around every group." Rayaprol observed similar phenomena in her study of South Indian immigrants in Pittsburgh; most participants made a conscious and deliberate effort to mark "boundaries" of ethnicity, so that their Indian and Hindu identities were emphasized upon interaction with the broader American environment (1997: 74). It is in this need to build community that we begin to discover the essence of the Indian immigrant experience.

Conclusion

Assimilation and acculturation occur when different cultures encounter each other and different components from these cultures are fused together to form a new cultural milieu (Joseph 1992: 30). However, immigrants often carry with them culturally imagined roles and values that muddy the process of acculturation. Many immigrants prefer to preserve their ethnic individuality rather than assimilate (Rayaprol 1997: 61), as culture serves as a lifeline from the native land that immigrants can hold onto while trying to establish the basis of their identity in a new place (Espiritu 2001: 415). One way immigrants cope with the new environment is by remaining allied to the values and beliefs of their homeland.

Another way is to try to integrate the aspects of both cultures that are most conducive to developing that identity (Rayaprol 1997: 61). Indeed, many immigrants from India try to preserve their culture even while merging with mainstream American life (Bhattacharjee 1992: 6). Whatever strategy they choose, immigrants are above all concerned with "cultural reproduction," or the process by which their knowledge, beliefs, values, and behavioral norms are transmitted to the next generation (Rayaprol 1997: 61).

The Nair community of Philadelphia is unique in that contrary to traditional patterns of Indian immigration, it is mostly women who opened the gateway to America for their husbands and children through nursing, and women are the primary breadwinners of the household. Despite various hardships and initial obstacles, all of the couples in this study fulfilled their professional and economic goals and demonstrated upward economic progress. Surprisingly, Nair couples in the United States seem to have maintained a traditional ideology about the domestic division of labor, though time constraints and the demands of the nursing profession have necessitated increased involvement by the husbands in household chores in the United States than was customary in India. In addition, Nair couples in Philadelphia have maintained their cultural identity primarily through increased religiosity, language, transnational ties, and active participation in community organizations. The Nair Society in particular serves as a vehicle for the transmission of religious and cultural practices to the next generation of Nairs in the United States.

Notes

1. In this paper, we regard Maharashtra as the dividing line between North and South India.

2. It is important to note that Nair communities in Kerala are unique in their cultural traditions. Although it is not commonly practiced today, Nair communities in the state of Kerala had a unique matrilineal system of inheritance called Marumakkathayam.

References

Andrews, K. P. 1983. *Keralites in America.* Glen Oaks, NY: Literary Market Review.

Bhattacharjee, Anannya. 1992. "The Habit of Ex-Nomination: Nation, Woman, and the Indian Immigrant Bourgeoisie." *Public Culture* 5:19–44.

Bloom, Barbara DiCicco. 2004. "The Racial and Gendered Experiences of Immigrant Nurses from Kerala, India." *Journal of Transcultural Nursing* 15:26–33.

Blumberg, R. L., and M. T. Coleman. 1989. "A Theoretical Look at the Gender Balance of Power in the American Couple." *Journal of Family Issues* 10 (2): 225–250.

Brines, Julie. 1994. "Economic Dependency, Gender, and the Division of Labor at Home." *American Journal of Sociology* 100 (3): 652–688.

Choudhry, U. K. 2001. "Uprooting and Resettlement Experiences of South Asian Immigrant Women." *Western Journal of Nursing Research* 23:376–393.

Choy, Catherine Ceniza. 2003. *Empire of Care: Nursing and Immigration in Filipino American History.* Durham, NC: Duke University Press.

Dasgupta, Sayantani, and Shamita Das Dasgupta. 1996. "Women in Exile: Gender Relations in the Asian Indian Community in the United States." In *Contours of the Heart: South Asians Map North America,* ed. Sunaina Maira and Rajini Srikanth. New York: Asian American Writers' Workshop.

Ebaugh, Helen Rose, and Janet Saltzman Chafetz, eds. 2000. *Religion and the New Immigrants: Continuities and Adaptations in Immigrant Congregations.* Walnut Creek, CA: AltaMira Press.

Eck, Diana L. 2000. "Negotiating Hindu Identities in America." In *The South Asian Religious Diaspora in Britain, Canada, and the United States,* ed. Harold Coward, John R. Hinnells, and Raymond Brady Williams. Albany: State University of New York Press.

Espiritu, Yen Le. 2001. "'We Don't Sleep Around Like White Girls Do': Family, Culture, and Gender in Filipina American Lives." *Signs* 26 (2): 415–440.

George, Sheba. 1998. "Caroling with the Keralites: The Negotiation of Gendered Space in an Indian Immigrant Church." In *Gatherings in Diaspora: Religious Communities and the New Immigration,* ed. R. Stephen Warner and Judith G. Wittner. Philadelphia: Temple University Press.

———. 2005. *When Women Come First: Gender and Class in Transnational Migration.* Berkeley: University of California Press.

Jacob, Simon, and Pallavi Thaku. 2000. "Jyothi Hindu Temple: One Religion, Many Practices." In *Religion and the New Immigrants: Continuities and Adaptations in Immigrant Congregations,* ed. Helen Rose Ebaugh and Janet Saltzman Chafetz. Walnut Creek, CA: AltaMira Press.

Joseph, Ramola B. 1992. *Perceived Change of Immigrants in the United States: A Study of Kerala (Asian Indian) Immigrant Couples in Greater Chicago.* PhD diss., Loyola University of Chicago.

Kurien, Prema. 1998. "Becoming Americans by Becoming Hindu: Indian Americans Take Their Place at the Multicultural Table." In *Gatherings in Diaspora: Religious Communities and the New Immigration,* ed. R. Stephen Warner and Judith G. Wittner. Philadelphia: Temple University Press.

———. 1999. "Gendered Ethnicity: Creating a Hindu Indian Identity in the United States." *American Behavioral Scientist* 42 (4): 648–670.

Leonard, Karen Isaksen. 1997. *The South Asian Americans.* Westport, CT: Greenwood Press.

Lessinger, Johanna. 1995. *From the Ganges to the Hudson: Indian Immigrants in New York City.* Boston: Allyn and Bacon.

Melwani, Lavina. 2005. "Indian Majority." *Little India.* Available at http://www.littleindia.com/news/123/ARTICLE/1315/2005-10-15.html (accessed January 8, 2007).

———. 2007. "Generation Next." *Little India.* Available at http://www.littleindia.com/news/142/ARTICLE/1702/2007-03-02.html (accessed March 21, 2007).

Muhkerjee, Tapan, and J. J. Wycliffe. 2006. "The History of the Early Arrivals of Asian Indians to America." Available at http://www.iafpe.org/php/showNewsDetails.php?linkid=5&newsid=5.

Prasad, Leela. 1999. *Live Like the Banyan Tree: Images of the Indian American Experience: An Exhibition at The Balch Institute for Ethnic Studies.* Philadelphia: Historical Society of Pennsylvania.

Raghavachari, Ranjana. 1990. *Conflicts and Adjustments: Indian Nurses in an Urban Milieu.* Delhi: Academic Foundation.

————. 1997. *Negotiating Identities: Women in the Indian Diaspora.* Delhi: Oxford University Press.

Sheth, Manju. 1995. "Asian Indian Americans." In *Asian Americans: Contemporary Trends and Issues,* ed. Pyong Gap Min. Thousand Oaks, CA: Sage Publications.

Sinha, Vaswati R. 1996. "South Asians in Philadelphia, 1996: Reflections on an Oral History." Available at http://ww2.lafayette.edu/~sinhav/madone.html (accessed January 8, 2007).

Thomas, Annamma, and T. M. Thomas. 1984. *Kerala Immigrants in America: A Sociological Study of the St. Thomas Christians.* Cochin, India: Simons Printers and Publishers.

Wilkinson, Alice. 1965. *A Brief History of Nursing in India and Pakistan.* Madras: Trained Nurses' Association of India.

Williams, Raymond Brady. 1988. *Religions of Immigrants from India and Pakistan.* Cambridge: Cambridge University Press.

————. 1992. "Sacred Threads of Several Textures." In *A Sacred Thread: Modern Transmission of Hindu Traditions in India and Abroad,* ed. Raymond Brady Williams, 228–257. Chambersburg, PA: Anima.

12

The Other Asians in the Other Philadelphia

Understanding Cambodian Experiences in Neighborhoods, Classrooms, and Workplaces

ELLEN SKILTON-SYLVESTER AND KEO CHEA-YOUNG

I mages of Philadelphia typically include glistening skyscrapers or restored colonial architecture, discussions of the robustness of center city's business district or the drafting of the U.S. Constitution. Similarly, Asian Americans are typically discussed in relation to educational and economic success on the one hand or in terms of traditional values that have provided the foundation for achieving in a new land. Ong has suggested that immigrant and refugee discourses that have at times focused on long-standing cultural traditions or the strife that groups have encountered before arriving in the United States have been replaced by discourses that focus on any newcomer's chances of becoming "individually responsible subjects of a neoliberal market society" (2003: 89). Both in terms of the challenging economic realities faced by many Cambodians in the United States and in terms of the limited economic value of the Khmer language in the global marketplace (Heller 1999; Lo Bianco 1999; Tse 2001), it is easy to see how the global economy has made some aspects of Philadelphia more visible than others and some Asian Americans more hidden than others. In Global Philadelphia, when it is defined in terms of the marketplace, Cambodians and the neighborhoods in which they live are often obscured from view.

There is an implicit assumption in the United States that Asian Americans are over-achievers in both educational and economic spheres. The "model minority" myth is powerful and has had a big impact on why the challenges that Cambodians have faced in Philadelphia (and elsewhere) have been so invisible (Ancheta 2000; Lee 1994; Ong 2003; Reyes 2007; Takaki 1989; Tuan 1999). As Ong suggests:

> Newspapers have pointed to the increasing number of wealthy and skilled immigrants from Taiwan, China, India, and South Korea who constitute an upwardly mobile or upper class fraction of Asian Americans. The media also cover those "other Asians"—Cambodians, Laotians, and Mien—not so much identified with their high-tech expertise as with their "high fertility rates." (2003: 2)

Similarly, Reyes (2007) has documented the experiences of 1.5-generation and second-generation Southeast Asian youth—including several Cambodians—in Philadelphia and has shown the ways that this concept of "the Other Asians" has traction as they attempt to explain their place within a Pan-Asian identity. As one of her Cambodian informants explains:

> I feel like post-Vietnam wave of immigrant, that we really don't have the Asian American identity that's been identified [as] the American experience. . . . We should be able to identify ourselves and categorize ourselves into the "Other Asian". . . . For the Other Asian, my kind came here for liberation, to liberate, to be free as opposed to come here to see America as a prospect. We came here because it was bad in our country, and it's better here for us. So our reason to be here is to start a whole new life, but not start a whole new life and put ourselves as part of the American pie. . . . We're here because we're running away from what happened. (Reyes 2007: 1)

While some have talked of Asian Americans as forever foreigners or honorary whites (Tuan 1999), Reyes makes the case that within broader U.S. and local Philadelphia racial discourses, this category of "Other Asian" is synonymous with the label of "problem minority" and categorizes them alongside African Americans living in poverty.

In addition to the ways that Cambodians in Philadelphia and in the United States may not fit the stereotype of successful Asian Americans, many have also experienced not just the trauma and upheaval of the Pol Pot regime, but also what Long (1993) calls the "liminality" of the refugee camp, where they were not allowed to make decisions for themselves, and the realities of living in poverty in the United States. The national data on poverty and educational attainment illustrate why the model minority myth remains pervasive when Asian American groups are all lumped together and why Cambodians are largely invisible in discussions of the Asian American experience. Whereas Neidzwiecki and Duong (2004) cite 1999 statistics that show that 12.4 percent of Americans,

12.6 percent of Asian Americans and 24.7 percent of African Americans live below the federal poverty line, 29.3 percent of Cambodian Americans live in poverty. National educational statistics paint a similar picture. For 1999, whereas 80.4 percent of Americans, 80.6 percent of Asian Americans and 71.3 percent of African Americans have a high school diploma, just 47.1 percent of Cambodian Americans do. In terms of higher education, 24.4 percent of Americans, 14.2 percent of African Americans, and 42.7 percent of Asian Americans have received at least a Bachelor's degree, whereas just 9.1 percent of Cambodian Americans have. These national statistics mirror the data on Cambodians in Philadelphia. As Fifield (2004) suggests, they are the fourth largest foreign language population receiving public assistance in the city, at least a third live below the federal poverty level, and they have a graduation rate from high school of just 47 percent.

As the city with the fourth largest population of Cambodians in the United States, Philadelphia is a city that should feel the presence of the Khmer people in its midst. Even though the *Philadelphia Inquirer* describes Cambodians as the second most concentrated immigrant group in the city and the largest Asian group in the School District of Philadelphia, the leader of the Cambodian Association of Greater Philadelphia says: "I think we are unknown to most Philadelphians . . . unless you live next to a Cambodian, you're not going to know them. . . . I guess the squeaky wheel gets the grease. . . . Our wheel is wobbling and about to fall off, but it doesn't make the squeaking noise" (Fifield 2004). This quotation illustrates the ways that Cambodians in Philadelphia are often invisible and, at the same time, in need of support.

In this chapter, we are arguing that the only way to understand the experience of Philadelphia Cambodians is to counter their categorization as an invisible "problem minority" by making visible the incredible heterogeneity and cultural and linguistic richness of Khmer people in the city and their participation in neighborhoods, classrooms, and workplaces. We are arguing that the roots of this invisibility have three key elements:

1. The geographic distribution across three distinct and largely poor neighborhoods in Philadelphia leaves them without a critical, organized, and visible mass in the city.
2. Social, economic, and cultural orientations towards private, local, and informal networks (e.g., Cambodian Buddhist temples, structures for distributing knowledge/services, work) leave their economic and cultural contributions unrecognized and invisible to those outside of the community.
3. The power of the model minority myth often obscures the needs that do exist (e.g., in educational contexts) and makes their legitimate need for social support somewhat invisible.

In the sections that follow, we will first highlight our distinct roles as researchers and authors and outline the data sources, frame the arrival of Cambodians to Philadelphia in historical terms, and illustrate and analyze each of these three roots of Khmer invisibility in Philadelphia. Our goal is to make visible both the critical issues being faced in the city, but also the strength, resilience, and variety of experiences of these newcomers to Philadelphia. We are especially interested in the ways that the particular experiences of Cambodians in the city are connected to the wider theme of investigating the roles of Philadelphia institutions and communities in this volume as a whole.

Researcher Roles and Data Sources

We are writing as co-authors with two very different vantage points, but a common passion for understanding Cambodian communities in the city, particularly in relation to education. Skilton-Sylvester has been involved in various Cambodian communities in Philadelphia since 1990 when she first tutored a small group of Cambodian women in South Philadelphia. For the following fifteen years, she has been both a teacher and researcher in various educational and community contexts. She has worked as a researcher for the Education Law Center, investigating the implications of a class-action suit filed on behalf of Asian students in the School District of Philadelphia in 1985 by collecting interview and observational data from all schools with significant Asian student populations. At the National Center on Adult Literacy, Skilton-Sylvester interviewed and assessed more than one hundred adult ESL learners (Skilton-Sylvester and Carlo 1998). Her activities as a tutor and researcher continued in a three-year ethnographic study of identity, literacy, and policy in the classrooms and homes of Cambodian women and girls in South, West, and North Philadelphia, and in ongoing contacts and extended life-history interviews with the young girls that were a part of her ethnographic study as they have become adults, joined the labor market, and moved to other neighborhoods in and around the city.

As someone who arrived in Philadelphia when she was five years old, having been born in a refugee camp on the Thai-Cambodian border, and having attended Philadelphia public schools for all of her elementary and secondary education, Chea-Young contributes to this chapter an insider knowledge of Khmer communities in the city. In particular, her experiences growing up and currently living in Logan have added substantial depth to the ways that this chapter addresses Khmer experiences in the city. As someone who has defied the statistics on educational attainment for Cambodians by getting both a Bachelor's and Master's degree and pursuing a Doctorate at a local Ivy League university, she has a unique insider/outsider perspective. As she wrote in a recent graduate course:

I have always felt out of place. I rebelled against the usual pattern of Cambodian rearing by finishing high school, not getting pregnant young, not "marrying" at 14 and earning college degrees. But, I grew up differently. I never had to persuade my grand/parents that reading, studying and going to church were not lazy activities. They didn't believe that "true" work was physical labor. So, as one of a handful of Cambodian Americans in the academy, it is lonely.

Chea-Young's deep personal knowledge and experience of growing up Khmer in Philadelphia, her recent interviews with several additional Cambodian informants, her own autobiographical writing, and her interviews with her mother are also key data sources in our attempts to make visible the heterogeneity and resilience of these Philadelphia residents whose families have come so far and went through so much to be here.

The Arrival of Cambodians in Philadelphia

A majority of the Cambodians in Philadelphia were part of what Long (1993) describes as the Second Wave (1978–1982). This wave is sandwiched between an earlier wave (1975–1977) and a later wave (1983–1986) of Southeast Asian refugees. The data she presents from refugee camps in Thailand shows that the number of Cambodian arrivals peaked in 1979 and 1980, reaching nearly 150,000 in a single year. In describing this period of flight, Long states,

In December 1978, Vietnam invaded Cambodia, which was followed by China's invasion of Vietnam. Since the Khmer Rouge had massacred several million of their own people, the Vietnamese justified their invasion of Cambodia on the grounds that they were liberating the country. The Vietnamese were therefore astonished when they were subsequently universally condemned. The Vietnamese precipitated the Second Wave of Khmer refugees. Escaping fighting between the Khmer Rouge and the advancing Vietnamese, approximately 100,000 Khmer fled into Thailand. . . . Crossing mine fields for three days, the Khmer had little food or water. Several thousand died. Others remained stranded in the border zone for months. . . . The outside world did not really know what was happening in Cambodia. . . . The refugees themselves said that they fled both Khmer Rouge and Vietnamese forces and few wanted to return until they knew the conflict had ended. (1993: 41–44)

This description of flight, death, and confusion about the dangers of the Khmer Rouge and the Vietnamese troops and long periods of waiting in refugee camps is a part of many of the stories Cambodians in Philadelphia have told us. Many talk of working and starving in work camps, and watching members of their families be tortured and killed (Chan 2003, 2004; Ong 2003; Ledgerwood, Ebihara, and Mortland 1994; Skilton-Sylvester 1997; Smith-Hefner 1990, 1993; Ung 2001). The following story was told by Cambodian women in South Philadelphia:

> I got hurt. I got sick on the border Thailand and Cambodia and fever, cold too much, chills and diarrhea and thin. I got sick. No fat. The same as die, but big hand, feet. The knife cut the arm. Sometimes they have the water. The people died. No sugar, salt, rice. They died. No home. In 1979, sleep outside; sleep on the ground. The people fighting. Vietnam and Cambodia fighting. The people run into Thailand border. No clothes, no home, no food ... two or three clothes. The Americans go to the Thailand camp, Sakeo. Take the people in border to the Sakeo camp. My sister died on the border. No medicine and she sick. One day, two days, she died. To run away the mountain, river, town to Thailand. Swim the river. I am scared of soldiers fighting Vietnam. One month, I am walking from Cambodia to Thailand. I sleep a little. At Sakeo, they have fish and food. No thin anymore.

In an article on the immigration patterns of the Indochinese in the United States, Thuy describes the second wave of Indochinese arrivals to the United States in this way:

> These refugees have come to the U.S. in poor health, with much lower educational and socioeconomic backgrounds, and with fewer marketable skills than their predecessors. They also seem to have less capability in the English language and little or no exposure to Western culture and urban living. A substantial number have been semiilliterate or illiterate. (1983: 107)

Although initially, flight from Cambodia was the impetus for settling in Philadelphia, more recent arrivals have typically come from other U.S. cities.

The Current Population of Cambodians in Philadelphia

The 2000 U.S. Census puts the Philadelphia Cambodian population at 6,570 people (*Philadelphia Inquirer*, December 4, 2004) with a concentration in neighborhoods in three main sections of the city: Olney/Logan (North), West Philadelphia, and South Philadelphia (see Figure 12.1). The Cambodian Association

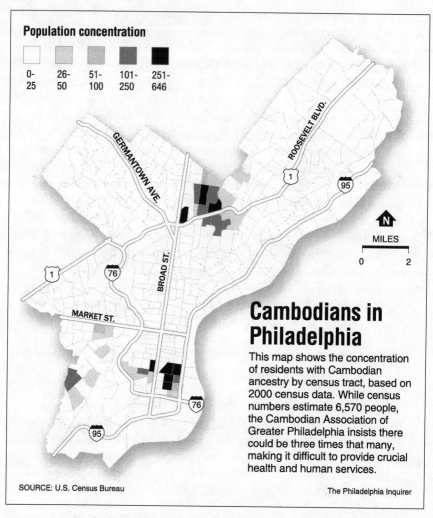

FIGURE 12.1 Cambodians in Philadelphia. (*Philadelphia Inquirer,* December 4, 2004. Used with permission of the *Philadelphia Inquirer.* Copyright © 2009. All rights reserved.)

says Philadelphia's Cambodian population is three times the census figure (nearly 20,000); this higher estimate is confirmed by the director of the Southeast Asian Mutual Aid Assistance Coalition, who suggests that the size of the Cambodian population in the city "grew in the late 1990s as a result of secondary migration from California and the New England states and was estimated at the turn of the twentieth century to be somewhere between 15,000 and 20,000" (Chan 2003: 173). According to Fifield (2004), there are four Cambodian Buddhist temples in the city, with many being frequented by older Cambodians.

How Geographic Distribution Contributes to Invisibility

One of the most striking aspects of Cambodian resettlement in the Philadelphia region has to do with how dispersed the population is in the city. Key Khmer clusters in the city include West, North (Olney/Logan), and South Philadelphia. Other newer areas of settlement are even more diffuse and appear to be extensions growing in the direction of Northeast Philadelphia and the outskirts of Philadelphia, their population manifesting distinct indicators of upward socioeconomic mobility, such as skilled white-collar workers, business ownership, greater income earning levels, and home ownership. In this chapter, we focus primarily on the three most concentrated groups of Cambodians in Philadelphia. Each neighborhood has its own flavor and its own reasons for obscuring Cambodians from the view of the rest of the city. In describing each neighborhood below, we provide specifics about the particular kinds of invisibility found in that neighborhood, as well as short vignettes (particularly in educational contexts) that illustrate the implications of that invisibility in the classrooms of residents of those neighborhoods.

Informal Cambodian Networks and Formal U.S. Educational Contexts as Sites for Invisibility

In the data and analysis that follow, we use examples of the role of both informal Cambodian "institutions" and formal educational institutions to illustrate the ways that support comes primarily through informal networks, and negotiations of the community's public identity comes primarily through more formal institutions. In each case, and for different reasons, their interactions with local institutions contribute to their invisibility. In the case of informal Khmer networks, it is because the networks themselves are not visible to the public, and in the case of formal institutions like schools, it is because the stereotypes that are often constructed in schools render the lived realities of Philadelphia Cambodians more invisible. In this way, schools are not being analyzed primarily in relation to their educational function, but more in relation to their socializing and public identity-formation functions.

West Philadelphia

Although West Philadelphia was the original settlement site for many Cambodians arriving in Philadelphia in the 1980s, in the past decade, this neighborhood has seen a significant reduction in its Cambodian population. Some now suggest (interviews, June 2007) that there are probably only four to six Khmer families living in this region. The statistics on enrollment at the local elementary school tell the story in quite dramatic ways. During the 1992–1993 school year, the school's population was 25.5 percent Asian (primarily Khmer) and 73.2 percent African American. By the 1999–2000 academic year, this same elementary school was 7.6 percent Asian, and in the 2006–2007 academic year, that number had dropped to 5.4 percent. The school and the neighborhood have remained predominantly African American, but there has been a significant shift over the past fifteen years from a cluster of Cambodian families and businesses that saw themselves and their children as part of a local Cambodian community to a very small number of families. The biggest causes of this shift (with families migrating south and west) are the gentrification of this neighborhood that borders a large university. As housing costs have risen, Cambodians have moved to find more affordable apartments.

Even at the height of the Cambodian population in West Philadelphia, the neighborhood had a majority of African American residents. In many ways, it was as if the Cambodians had moved into what remained an African American neighborhood. Although other immigrant groups (especially Africans—see Osirim, Chapter 10) have now settled in this community, there has been little or no contact across these groups as a result of language and cultural barriers. A striking example of the invisibility some Cambodian residents have felt in this neighborhood comes from two Khmer sisters who grew up in West Philadelphia while they were in high school.

When we think about the levels of belonging that the Cambodians in West Philadelphia felt in school, we immediately think of two questions—one posed by a high school senior in 1995 and the other posed by a teacher to her sister when she was a high school senior in 2002. The first question came after Skilton-Sylvester was reading Maxine Hong Kingston's *The Woman Warrior* with the older sister during her senior year. At one point in the discussion, after comparing the protagonist's experiences with school in a new language to her own, she looked up from the text and asked, "*Is she the only Asian writer?*" Skilton-Sylvester heard this question with a sense of shock, even though she knew that in the three years she had visited that student's school, she had not come across any mention of Asians or Asian Americans in the curriculum. Seven years later, as she ate dinner with this student's younger sister, the sister recounted a story that started with another unforgettable question from a teacher at her largely African-American, West Philadelphia high school. The teacher told the class that they were going to write an essay and that they needed to answer the following question: "How does it feel to be black?" As the only Asian student in the class, her response is perhaps not surprising. She, a seventeen-year-old Cambodian American student, shrugged and wrote about what it feels like to be black. The level of invisibility of Asian American experiences in the curriculum illustrated in the first question is unsettling, the level of invisibility in the second question, and perhaps even more the acceptance of that invisibility in her response, is shocking. Although the first level of invisibility was felt in schools across the city, the second question is strongly connected to the experiences of being Cambodian in West Philadelphia.

Another kind of invisibility can be seen in the experiences of Cambodian adults in West Philadelphia. The vast majority of women in this part of town (and in the city as a whole) had had very little schooling (less than three years for most) in Cambodia. Many women did not attend adult education programs, but those that did encountered a teacher who tapped into their lived experiences as mothers, wives, and West Philadelphia residents. The program, housed in a Southeast Asian community organization, had adults with a mixture of languages and ethnic backgrounds, but the majority were Khmer. Some of the invisibility of their classroom work came from the fact that it was seen as a part of their work at home while children were at school, and as such, was invisible in some of the same ways that women's housework is often not seen in the public sphere. Another form of invisibility came from the assumptions—not just from the outside community but also from within the organization—that these women were not interested in workplace goals.

For one of the women, future work goals (along with wanting a better life for her children) were a big part of her investment in coming to class. She believed that her limited English proficiency was the key thing keeping her from a job. During the fieldwork period, she did not work outside of the home. Interestingly, it took a teacher who was committed to understanding the goals and needs of her students to find this out; one of the Cambodian administrators of the program for the organization that hosted the class (who had much more education than the local residents) had told the teacher that students were not interested in workplace issues. As the teacher explains in talking about her students' ability to talk about their goals:

> I was amazed at how specific students were able to be. And also how many of them articulated employment-related goals, because I had been told that students weren't really interested in working, that there was no reason for them to work because they were on welfare. . . . When I was . . . collecting materials, I almost didn't even consider any employment-related stuff. I thought, 'Well, I might as well just get some just in case,' and I realized that on the basis of this information, not from the students, but from another source, I was sort of censoring what I might bring into the classroom, which is pretty easy to do, I think.

In this way, these adult students' identities as "welfare recipients" had made the administrators of the program miss the ways in which being a worker was a desire of many in the program.

In West Philadelphia, invisibility came as a result of being in the minority in a relatively homogeneous African American neighborhood, being female, poor and on welfare, and as a result of the limitations of the curriculum, as well as from the role of stereotypes both inside and outside of the Cambodian community.

North Philadelphia: Olney/Logan

Neighborhood designations such as Logan and Olney are not exact, but both are residential neighborhoods located in the northern section of Philadelphia. Although these two neighborhoods are in very close proximity and are often lumped together when people look at where there are concentrations of Cambodians in the city, they are not considered one community. In fact, they are divided along gang lines with Logan being more Blood and considered less affluent and less well-kept and with Olney being more connected to the Crips and considered more clean, more diverse in terms of multiple immigrant groups, and more middle class. These divisions might not be visible to the outsider, but are a part of how these neighborhoods are seen from within (Chea-Young, personal experience).

With Korean-American and Hispanic businesses flourishing in the southern part of the Olney neighborhood, mostly on Fifth Street, Olney appears to be the more ethnically and socioeconomically diverse neighborhood of the two (and one of the most diverse neighborhoods in Philadelphia). Cambodians are dispersed across blocks of neighborhoods in Olney, living in houses where they are only one small element in multiethnic neighborhoods. However, as the site of the largest Cambodian organization in the city, Olney includes a concentrated set of both formal (ESL and Khmer classes, translation services) and informal (advice from Khmer elders, socializing with other Cambodians) services.

The more educated and ethnolinguistically diverse nature of Cambodian residents of Olney can be seen in looking at the experiences of two women who attended a local adult education program (Skilton-Sylvester 2002). The kinds of invisibility they experienced had to do with erroneous assumptions made by the education program that students would prefer to come to class at night because they were working during the day. On the contrary, this was not the case for these women because of the safety issues they faced in walking home after dark, the workplace demands of one of the women at her family's restaurant, and the ways that the curriculum did not address the lived experiences of these students (e.g., by making assumptions that all of the women had children and by materials that portrayed a white, middle-class lifestyle).

There is a concentrated group of Cambodians living in nearby Logan, an old inner-city neighborhood that betrays signs of deterioration caused by urban flight: boarded-up houses, more than twenty-one acres of vacant lots (located primarily in the southern part of the Logan neighborhood), and lack of any rental housing stock, a gauge of little developer interest (Philadelphia City Planning Commission 2002). Vacant lots and a lack of commercial areas may be painful and constant reminders of the personal and communal deprivations of these residents (aside from a block of Southeast Asian–owned stores). Once predominantly a Jewish community, some of the neighborhoods in Logan are among the most economically, physically, and academically depressed areas of the city. The steady out-migration of whites and the significant influx of African Americans in the 1950s and Southeast Asian immigrants in the 1980s has not only changed the complexion, but has contributed to the erosion of the middle class and lower middle class. Racially mixed communities in Logan are those where Cambodians, despite the presence of growing numbers, still do not constitute an absolute majority relative to the local population; yet a strong Cambodian flavor is palpable due to the clustering effect. They are communities within larger communities, sharing and competing with other populations for the territory, resources, and services of the community.

Although Cambodians are not in the majority in this predominantly black and Asian neighborhood, it is much more common to be an immigrant newcomer than in West Philadelphia. Chea-Young's experiences growing up in her family and in the Logan neighborhood provide a portrait of relative invisibility, but also significant at-home and in-school learning. They also show the geographic mobility that she had in her schooling experiences, starting in Logan, being bused to a mostly white middle school in another neighborhood, and later attending a public, ethnically mixed magnet high school in Logan. The connections that Chea-Young felt with her father and grandfather in relation to Khmer literacy and the ways that her mother's schooling experiences were connected to her learning at home contrast dramatically with the disconnections she felt in Philadelphia schools. As she writes:

> School was indeed a political place; I had assumptions about being less capable than my white peers, that I was inferior somehow. . . . Experiences of institutionalized racism in schools, of finding two Philadelphians—one privileged and the other vibrant but virtually abandoned—maintained in part by a substandard public education system and policy decisions at every level, sparked questions and opened gates of inquiry that shape me to this day. . . . Against the backdrop of the mostly White school, I became acutely aware of my "yellow" Asian-ness, like having other children (Black and White) chanting "Ching Chong" in my face as a form of greeting, molestations on school buses that bus attendants would wave off; I was literally "invisible." . . . I realized early on that my appearance, culture and stories, gifts that parents/grandparents shared and passed on, were sometimes great barriers at school. Throughout my

schooling years, I experienced an extraordinary misreading of the world—that being "normal" and "okay" meant being White.

In spite of the challenges of living and going to school in Logan, the significant gang activity that surrounded their home, and the complexity of going to monolingual schools as a Khmer-speaking student, the heterogeneity of Logan that made it so that she represented one of several ethnolinguistic/racial groups, her father's beliefs and actions that she could go to a better public school, her early Khmer literacy and her parents' belief in the power of education have influenced her trajectory, but it is a story of succeeding in spite of the supports and services available in her Philadelphia neighborhood rather than because of them.

South Philadelphia

South Philadelphia is a densely populated neighborhood and home to the highest concentration of Cambodians and Cambodian-owned businesses in the city. Almost half of all Cambodian newcomers to the city settle around Seventh Street in South Philadelphia, the majority of families on thirty blocks (P. Hong, personal communication). Although popularly known as an "Italian" neighborhood, South Philadelphia is home to a growing and thriving community that is redefining blocks and neighborhoods with their culture and language. Residential areas in South Philadelphia are typically heterogeneous in population, and are typified by one-way streets, small row homes, and tight parking spots. Termed "South" by Cambodians across the city, this area is vibrant, visually and physically crowded, and what some would call "booming." The neighborhoods or corners are more "Cambodian friendly," with eclectic small businesses such as mom-and-pop shops, laundromats, video stores, barber shops, distinctive Cambodian restaurants, eateries, coffee shops, and neighborhood services owned and run by Cambodians (N. Ros, interview, May 31, 2007). Two streets in particular, Fifth Street and Seventh Street, are commuter streets specializing in service businesses (R. Sorn, interview, May 29, 2007).

While many Cambodians have congregated in healthy and noticeable numbers in South Philadelphia and maintained a strong shared cultural tradition (at least among the elderly Cambodians), they have only been able to share that culture or make a small visible imprint on the urban scene around them: through the three Cambodian Buddhist temples, or wats, and small businesses with store signs in distinct Khmer letters. If more organized and recognized as a legitimate marketplace similar to that of the thriving Ninth Street Italian Market, this area could have real potential to improve Philadelphia by providing employment and income, and integrating into the urban market framework (P. Hong, personal communication, June 14, 2007). While Cambodian residents may have some nodding acquaintance with the wider South Philadelphia neighborhood, it is with other Cambodians clustered on and around their surrounding streets that they share an intimate life. Concentrated houses or apartment buildings and businesses indicate how Cambodians have structured a sense of place and community in South Philadelphia.

In the South Philadelphia neighborhood, Cambodians do have a critical mass with a significant number of people and businesses. However, the community as a whole remains somewhat invisible to the rest of Philadelphia. It is a relatively insular community in many ways. As one Cambodian leader who has lived in South Philadelphia explained:

> In South Philly, if you want to rent movies you want entertainment, you can go rent Cambodian movies, you want live entertainment, you can go to a Cambodian party and see a live Cambodian singer. . . . It doesn't matter what the need is, you can go to other Cambodians and Cambodian [stores], even with like money, it's sad to say and it's probably not the most effective way to save money, but there's the Cambodian bank. . . . [In South Philly], you can get all your food, you can get all your clothes . . . there really isn't like a critical pressing need for Cambodians to go outside of the community to get what they need. (N. Ros, interview, May 31, 2007)

Similarly, Skilton-Sylvester remembers that when tutoring a group of women in a home in this neighborhood, the Philadelphia Folklore Project was doing a photo exhibit on Cambodians living in South Philadelphia. She took her adult students to the show—literally less than ten blocks away—and none of them had ever traveled that far outside of the few blocks where other Cambodians lived since their arrival in the city. One of the potential contributions to this insularity is that adults are not in a position to need to learn English for daily social interaction *because* there is such a vibrant local economy, as well as the most active of the Cambodian temples for spiritual and cultural connections. Twenty years after arrival in the United States, many still have difficulty conversing in English even though many of their children and grandchildren have long since abandoned fluency in Khmer.

Informal Social and Economic Networks as a Source of Invisibility

In interviews with several Cambodian leaders, one thing that became increasingly clear is that traditional U.S-based institutions are not utilized by Cambodians in the ways that they are by many other immigrant groups. Even now, there remain a large number of Cambodian immigrants who are reluctant to use formal structures such as financial institutions or to access formal econo-mies, feeling these offerings do not meet their needs or present other entry bar-riers. The director of the Cambodian Association said that she understands the reluctance, as many Cambodians have been victimized by a corrupt government in their homeland and have not been able to express themselves at problematic social settings such as health service environments in the United States. Typi-cally, issues of access and trust are compounded by a poor flow of information between Cambodian immigrant communities and institutions, an extreme lan-guage barrier, and the paperwork responsibilities usually attached to more for-malized institutions and networks. The main challenging communicative encounters, especially in terms of accessing a service, take place in health and educational settings, as well as in stores outside their community.

For some Cambodians, their first introduction to a "permanent institution" may have been the Khmer Rouge, a guerilla army that emptied Cambodia's cities and executed an estimated 1.3 million Khmer people, the majority of whom were military officers, professionals, educated people, even those wearing glasses. Local Khmer leaders have described the Khmer Rouge as a "permanent," not to mention debilitating, institution that was well established and above all, "untrust-worthy." As aptly observed by Navy:

> [The Khmer Rouge] called themselves [an] institution, and that's how it was drilled into [Cambodians] and so, then, like, even now, [you] can't trust the current government, you can't trust like police officers in Cam-bodia. [Based on this history], it might [not be] worth trusting [institu-tions or formalized networks]. (Interview, June 2007)

Thus, accessing institutions or services in this country not only requires a level of familiarity and knowledge of the English language, it involves a level of trust in people. But, remarkably noticeable is the high level of trust that Cambodian immigrants give to identifiable Cambodian or Southeast Asian community offi-cials, many of whom have helped Cambodians in the area of real estate, finances, and health. Although the majority of Cambodian immigrants have legal status here in the United States, fear and a general distrust of officials and institutions keeps particularly older Cambodians from seeking out mainstream social ser-vices. Many elderly Cambodian immigrants in particular are wary of interacting with city workers, including the police, emergency medical providers, doctors, lawyers, and other public officials. Instead, they rely primarily on other social networks within the Cambodian community for support, whether that support be financial or psychological.

A recent interview with Cambodian leaders at the Cambodian Association suggested that Cambodians are not accessing essential services. Their experience shows that many Cambodian immigrants will not access essential social services if doing so could result in sharing of information related to local welfare agencies. Still many others may not be accessing these services because of their general unfamiliarity with and distrust of formal institutions, which stems from their experience as farmers in Cambodia and subsequently as war refugees. One informant explained how Cambodians' lack of familiarity with schooling has resulted in their inability to either obtain or access the necessary resources and capital for their children:

> Here in the United States, [we] work with [former] farmers and fishermen where there's no education background at all. I think if they had [some schooling] they [would be] better equipped to deal with [their] children here going to school. At least they [would] have a concept of school. So, your children coming back, ah there's supposed to be something in their notebook, [they are] supposed to learn or you know there's homework and things like that . . . my dad, he [went] to school . . . they introduced the French language [to him and] at least he [knew] what to look for such as the As, the Bs, and things like that. (Interview, June 2007)

This example shows the ways that previous experiences with formal institutions in Cambodia—whether they be schools or the government—have profoundly influenced interactions with formal institutions in the United States.

In addition to participation in more informal networks of support than formal ones, Cambodians in Philadelphia are regularly involved in underground, informal jobs. There is a twenty-year history of Cambodian men and women, as well as children, working in "invisible" or underground industries including the garment industry, assembly factory lines (including paper, envelope, and cough drops), the metal-packing industry, vegetable and fruit farms, and other factories. Farm labor, however, is the most common occupation of Cambodian immigrant men, women, even children. In factories, they often work in shifts, day and night, and typically spend sixty to ninety hours per week in front of their machines. Such employment is often characterized by poor working conditions, both in terms of compensation and the existence and enforcement of basic labor standards. Although Cambodians involved in underground economic activities are on public assistance or own informal businesses, many have to multiply their working hours in order to survive financially.

This is the situation for thousands of Cambodians, young and old, from all three Cambodian clusters in Philadelphia. Both women and men build their lives in these worlds. Informal economic activity is not a panacea and does not always foster economic success, but for many Cambodian families it is the difference between extreme poverty and economic self-sufficiency; for others, it is a pathway to business ownership. Not only does it provide income-earning opportunities for Cambodians, it absorbs surplus labor and helps maintain a low cost of living in the city by providing cheaper sources of food and services.

Much of what accounts for "informal" employment situations consists of invisible features of an economy's landscape, like home-based garment assembly and manufacturing factories. Other informal employment situations are more familiar even to the most casual observers: street vendors, for example. The more visible industries or agencies have Cambodians concentrated at the bottom of wage categories such as positions in social work, for example. It would be hard to imagine these industries or agencies in Philadelphia's peripheries functioning without immigrants; although this role is central to the economy, it is also largely invisible. Similarly, as the Executive Director of the Cambodian Association of Greater Philadelphia explains, much of the networking done in relation to work is largely outside of the officially funded program framework:

> Oh it's like with everything else in the community word of mouth so I mean you know none of this stuff is like ever advertised anywhere but you know you talk to other people and who are already working and see you know who else needs more jobs and then or who else needs more workers and then you know the "crew leaders" will know other crew leaders and so forth. (C. Suy, interview, June 3, 2007)

Once again, this illustrates the role of familiarity and trust in the development of informal, invisible networks through which participation is orchestrated. Although Cambodians work incredibly hard within these informal economies, the image of them relying on welfare is not contested in part because this hard work happens outside of the view of mainstream Philadelphians. As a 1.5-generation young woman discussed her work picking fruit:

> I guess the general feeling was I can't believe I worked so hard and it really, really opened my eye to what my parents really went through to I mean like thinking about how hard I worked, and how much money I made at the end of the day it was kind of bad for me and to really finally comprehend that that was what my family did every day like for practically all of my life with no kind of like raises or anything like that so I mean people are still earning you know five dollars an hour and so and at the same job that they've been at for you know twenty years and so it's a hard reality check I guess.

The irony is that although this "under the table" work is part of what keeps Philadelphia going, it means that Cambodians in these jobs are frozen out of the networks they need access to in order to advance. As in many immigrant communities, the hard work of parents, often in dead-end jobs, is framed in terms of supporting the younger generation to have more choices. The girls involved in Skilton-Sylvester's ethnographic study would often talk about how when they grew up, they wanted to have an "inside" job, in an office, not outside in the blueberry fields where they and the adults in their families worked. Although this was not available to the first generation, each of these three sisters did end up with "inside" work—one as a teacher's aide, one as an administrative assistant, and one as a small business owner. Each of them now participates in the formal economy, but, with the exception of the business owner, still at the lowest rungs of the employment structure. The expanded opportunities for 1.5-generation and second-generation children are inextricably linked to schooling. Although there were many good teachers that this generation encountered, the system as a whole has not adequately met the needs of these students.

Classroom Invisibility in Relation to the Model Minority Myth

The invisibility profiled above in relation to particular neighborhoods and the prevalence of informal and private economic and social networks is largely connected to the dispersed nature of the community and the realities of living in poverty. Classroom-based invisibility is connected in part to the ways that Cambodians in Philadelphia do not fit the stereotype of the Asian American model minority and in part due to the fact that they largely attend schools that are struggling for resources in low income neighborhoods in the city.

The role of the model minority myth may appear to be largely an academic debate, but key policy decisions in the school district were made based on these erroneous assumptions. For example, all of the children in Skilton-Sylvester's (1997) ethnographic study were pulled out for English instruction during their math class—based on the assumption that "Asians are good at math." The class action lawsuit filed in 1985 had two Cambodian students as the original plantiffs. Each of them had been placed in special education without adequate testing or communication with parents. The lawyers working on the case had previously attempted to get the district to address their concerns that Cambodian students were struggling in school, but this was so contrary to the district's sense of how Asian students do in school that only a lawsuit, Y.S. v. School District of Philadelphia, was able to bring about new services (such as bilingual counselors, counseling assistants, and tutors) for Khmer and other language minority students in the city.

The concentration of Cambodians in the urban core puts them in close contact with native-born minorities, serving to cement the identification of these "new immigrants" as racially different from the majority, and "exposes second-generation to the adversarial culture developed by marginalized native youths" (Portes and Zhou 1993). Moreover, the residence of families in these enclaves also puts them in schools dominated by other low-income students, both from their own group and from the native-born minority poor. Cambodian children, thus, typically attend "schools with a demoralized educational climate" (Hirschman 2001) compounded by a public education that fosters the neglect of these students' complex identities, experiences, and educational needs.

Our data show that school discrimination may take shape in several forms: violent harassment by other students, unaccommodating curricula, or being misunderstood or stereotyped by school personnel. Often, the most traumatic new reality for immigrant students is the behavior of their peers, who ignore, reject, and sometimes taunt them. According to a focus group led by Rorng Sorn in 1999 at the Cambodian Association of Greater Philadelphia, there were reports by high school adolescents of being singled out or isolated, stereotyped, or harassed. Incidents as reported by these focus groups and other individuals range from racial slurs and fights to subtle comments that singled them out as different (Rorng, personal communication). These adolescents also reported being pushed or "picked on" because of their race, size, stature, language difficulties, accent, or foreign dress, and being deliberately teased, laughed at, and "jumped." At the extreme, kinds of sexual harassment, such as verbal abuse, sexist remarks about a young woman's clothing, and unnecessary touching have been known to occur among Cambodian female students (Chea-Young, personal experience).

Although there is a substantial literature on established ethnic groups, this body of work is generally silent about the particular needs and problems of immigrant children, especially Cambodian children in the inner cities. There is a frustrating lack of data about the experiences of immigrant children in general (Olsen, 1998). While many studies have described the pervasive nature of the differential educational achievements across all ethnic groups (Erickson 1987; Ogbu 1978), studies focusing on these factors have unfortunately ignored the complexity of the process in which immigrants, and particularly refugees, also endure hardships and drastic social and cultural changes, rendering these experiences virtually invisible to educators and to the public at large.

Through our years of teaching experiences with Cambodian students, we find that a number of educators still come to the classroom with a priori assumptions about the profound foreignness of their Asian American students. It is that sense of profound cultural difference that underlies the model minority stereotype as well. Often, as Rizvi and Lingard (2006) note, the educational system and educational policy come from one's perceived notions of how the "Other" lives. As one of the now-adult informants in Skilton-Sylvester's study explained of her high school experience:

Before me, there were a lot of Cambodians that went to my school and there was a lot of gangs going on and there was a lot of kids dropping out and becoming pregnant and everything and I guess a lot of teachers thought they know Cambodian people or Asian people. . . . I have this counselor that was working at my school . . . and I can tell he's like "you guys come to this country and aren't even happy to come to this country, you guys don't even try to learn, you know." And he'd look at everybody as just one category which really upset me a lot. . . . So one day my boy-friend dropped me off at school and he's like "Are you gonna drop out and just have kids?" which I thought was really rude. . . . He was a white man and I was like, you know, "you're saying this to me because I'm Asian, because I can feel it like if I was a black girl you wouldn't be saying this to me because it would be looked at as prejudice, as color, but for an Asian girl it wouldn't really look at it like color or prejudice or any-thing," so I was upset.

In addition to the stereotyping that leads to feeling invisible in schools, the absence of Asian and Cambodian contributions to Philadelphia and the United States in the curriculum is striking. If one skims through a school textbook, a bulletin, or the history shelf at a local library, the likelihood of finding informa-tion about Cambodians—or Southeast Asians for that matter—is relatively slim. Visit a school ESL classroom, and the likelihood of finding it physically isolated from the mainstream, or scheduled so that participants' schooling is interrupted, is very high.

Conclusion

In analyzing the data for this chapter, we have seen many ways that invisibility permeates Cambodian experiences in Philadelphia and have illustrated the ways that this invisibility is shaped by the neighborhoods and institutions of the city. As the unit of analysis has shifted from individual experiences to contexts and institutions that shape and are shaped by Cambodians in the city, one may be tempted to believe at the end of this chapter that it is possible to generalize about Cambodians in Philadelphia. We urge the reader to resist this temptation. In spite of the tremendous obstacles Cambodians have faced and do face, we have seen portraits of resilience and strength in families and individuals as they live as Cambodians in the United States. Each time we are tempted to conclude that we have "figured out" the Khmer experience in the city, we encounter someone who defies that generalization. Even so, one of Ong's Cambodian informants makes a statement that rings true for many Cambodians in the city: "To be American is not an easy thing" (2003: 219). In our analysis of neighborhoods and institutions, we have found a geographically dispersed community and a significant disconnect between the formal networks available in the city and the informal Khmer neighborhood networks utilized by many Philadelphia Cambodians. Addressing the significant needs *and* tapping into the cultural richness of this community will require work, not just from newcomers, but from mainstream institutions and thoughtful Philadelphians—Cambodians and non-Cambodians alike.

Note

1. The 1.5 generation includes those born in Cambodia who came to the United States as youngsters and have grown up mainly in the United States.

References

Ancheta, A. 2000. *Race, Rights and the Asian American Experience.* New Brunswick, NJ: Rutgers University Press.

Chan, S., ed. 2003. *Not Just Victims: Conversations with Cambodian Community Leaders in the United States.* Urbana: University of Illinois Press.

———. 2004. *Survivors: Cambodian Refugees in the United States.* Urbana: University of Illinois Press.

Erickson, F. 1987. "Transformation and School Success: The Politics of Culture and Educational Achievement." *Anthropology and Education Quarterly* 18 (4): 335–356.

Fifield, A. 2004. "A Cruel Past Lingers: Cambodians in Philadelphia Are Still Haunted, Years Later and a World Away." *Philadelphia Inquirer,* December 4.

Heller, M. 1999. *Linguistic Minorities and Modernity: A Sociolinguistic Ethnography.* New York: Longman.

Hirschman, C. 2001. "The Educational Enrollment of Immigrant Youth: A Test of the Segmented-Assimilation Hypothesis." *Demography* 38:317–336.

Ledgerwood, J., M. M. Ebihara, and C. A. Mortland. 1994. "Introduction." In *Cambodian Culture since 1975: Homeland and Exile,* ed. M. M. Ebihara, C. A. Mortland, and J. Ledgerwood, 1–26. Ithaca, NY: Cornell University Press.

Lee, S. J. 1994. "Behind the Model Minority Stereotype: Voices of High- and Low-Achieving Asian American Students." *Anthropology and Education Quarterly* 25:413–429.

Lo Bianco, J. 1999. "The Language of Policy: What Sort of Policy Making Is the Officialization of English in the United States?" In *Sociopolitical Perspectives on Language Policy and Planning in the USA,* ed. T. Huebner and K. Davis, 38–65. Philadelphia: John Benjamins.

Long, L. 1993. *Ban Vinai: The Refugee Camp.* New York: Columbia University Press.

Niedzweicki, M., and T. C. Duong. 2004. *Southeast Asian American Statistical Profile.* Washington, DC: Southeast Asian Resource Action Center (SEARAC).

Ogbu, J. U. 1978. *Minority Education and Caste: The American System in Cross-Cultural Perspective.* New York: Academic Press.

Olsen, L. 1998. *Made in America: Immigrant Students in Our Public Schools.* New York: The New Press.

Ong, A. 2003. *Buddha Is Hiding: Refugees, Citizenship, the New America.* Vol. 5. Berkeley: University of California Press.

Philadelphia City Planning Commission. 2002. "Logan: Redevelopment Area Plan." Available at http://www.philaplanning.org/plans/areaplans/loganrap.pdf (accessed June 2, 2007).

Portes, A., and M. Zhou. 1993. "The New Second Generation: Segmented Assimilation and Its Variants." *Annals of the American Academy of Political and Social Sciences* 530:74–96.

Reyes, A. 2007. *Language, Identity and Stereotype among Southeast Asian American Youth: The Other Asian.* Mahwah, NJ: Lawrence Erlbaum Associates.

Rizvi, F., and B. Lingard. 2006. "Globalization and the Changing Nature of the OECD's Educational Work." In *Education, Globalization & Social Change*, ed. H. Lauder, P. Brown, J. Dillabough, and A. Halsey, 247–260. Oxford: Oxford University Press.

Skilton-Sylvester, E. 1997. *Inside, Outside and In-Between: Identities, Literacies, and Educational Policies in the Lives of Cambodian Women and Girls in Philadelphia.* Unpublished doctoral dissertation, University of Pennsylvania.

———. 2002. "Should I Stay or Should I Go? Investigating Cambodian Women's Participation and Investment in Adult ESL Programs." *Adult Education Quarterly* 53 (1): 9–26.

Skilton-Sylvester, E., and M. Carlo. 1998. "'I Want to Learn English': Examining the Goals and Motivations of Adult ESL Learners in Three Philadelphia Learning Sites." Report No. TR9808. Philadelphia: University of Pennsylvania, National Center on Adult Literacy.

Smith-Hefner, N. J. 1990. "Language and Identity in the Education of Boston-Area Khmer." *Anthropology and Education Quarterly* 21:250–268.

———. 1993. "Education, Gender and Generational Conflict among Khmer Refugees." *Anthropology and Education Quarterly* 24 (2): 135–158.

Takaki, R. 1989. *Strangers from a Different Shore: A History of Asian Americans.* New York: Penguin.

Thuy, V. 1983. "The Indochinese in America: Who Are They and How Are They Doing?" In *The Education of Asian and Pacific Americans: Historical Perspectives and Prescriptions for the Future*, ed. D. T. Nakanishi and M. Hirano-Nakanishi, 103–122. Phoenix, AZ: Oryx Press.

Tse, L. 2001. "Resisting and Reversing Language Shift: Heritage-Language Resilience among U.S. Native Biliterates." *Harvard Educational Review* 71 (4): 676–709.

Tuan, M. 1999. *Forever Foreigners or Honorary Whites? The Asian Ethnic Experience Today.* New Brunswick, NJ: Rutgers University Press.

Ung, L. 2001. *First They Killed My Father: A Daughter of Cambodia Remembers.* New York: Harper Perennial.

Contributors

Jennifer Atlas graduated magna cum laude from Haverford College in 2009 with a bachelor of arts in community and population health and in Latin American and Iberian studies. She has worked extensively on improving cultural competence in health care and healthcare access for Spanish-speaking immigrants through the National Institutes of Health Clinical Center, Michigan's Mott Children's Health Center, and the Philadelphia nonprofits Puentes de Salud, Philadelphia Legal Assistance, Congreso de Latinos Unidos, and the National Nursing Centers Consortium. Atlas has a particular research interest in pediatric health access issues.

Rasika Chakravarthy graduated from the University of Pennsylvania in 2006 with degrees in economics, psychology, and South Asia studies, and with distinction in South Asia studies. She is currently pursuing a law degree at Georgetown University Law Center in Washington, DC.

Keo Chea-Young, a 1.5-generation Khmer American, is a Gates Millennium scholar and a doctoral candidate in reading/writing/literacy at the University of Pennsylvania Graduate School of Education. She holds a master's degree in language and literacy and a reading specialist certification from the Harvard Graduate School of Education. She consults for two literacy organizations in Philadelphia, instructs part-time at Arcadia University, and is currently preparing her dissertation on the literacy practices of inner-city Khmer American high school adolescents. Chea-Young also serves as a member of the doctoral student editorial board for the *Journal of Southeast Asian American Education and Advancement*.

Noel J. J. Farley taught at Bryn Mawr College, where he was the Harvey Wexler professor in economics. He retired in 2002 and now has the title of research professor at the college. Irish research has been his life's work, especially the era of the Irish Tiger. Since his retirement, he has been working on nineteenth-century Irish economic history as well as many of the activities of the Irish Americans. In addition to what he has published with Philip Kilbride, he is currently working on a project entitled "Irish Immigrants: Deposits and Immigrants' Remittances in Kenrick's Bishops Bank, 1848–1880."

Philip L. Kilbride is professor of anthropology at Bryn Mawr College. His research specialties include childhood and family in Africa, about which he has published *Street Children in Kenya: Voices of Children in Search of a Childhood* with Collette Suda and Enos Njeru (2001) and *Changing Family Life in East Africa: Women and Children at Risk* with Janet Kilbride (1990). He was recently a Fulbright teaching fellow in the Czech Republic where he published on childhood and taught a course entitled "The Irish American" at Pardubice University. With Noel Farley, he has written on the Irish diaspora, most recently *Faith, Morality and Being Irish: A Caring Tradition in Africa* (2007).

Garvey F. Lundy received a Ph.D. in sociology from Pennsylvania State University and currently teaches sociology at the Blue Bell campus of Montgomery County Community College in Pennsylvania. Prior to that, he was an adjunct professor of sociology at the University of Pennsylvania and an Andrew Mellon postdoctoral fellow at the Population Studies Center, also at the University of Pennsylvania. Lundy was born in Haiti and has lived in the United States for several years. His research interests are the sociology of education, race and ethnic relations, and Haitian migration. He is coauthor of *The Source of the River: The Social Origins of Freshmen at America's Selective Colleges and Universities* (2003) and has published a number of articles on migration and on oppositional culture theory. He has also contributed several entries in the *Encyclopedia of Black Studies* (2005) and the *Encyclopedia of African Religion* (2009).

Ajay Nair is the associate vice provost at the University of Pennsylvania. He serves as Penn's chief student affairs officer for offices and services charged with integrating academic, residential, co-curricular, developmental, and recreational activities. He was previously associate dean of student affairs at Columbia University and held positions at Penn State University and the University of Virginia, where he served in a variety of capacities as faculty member, student affairs administrator, and academic administrator. Nair's research interests include quality assurance in educational systems, service learning and civic engagement, and second-generation Asian American identity. His current book project, *Desi Rap: Hip-Hop in South Asian America* (2008), focuses on the complexities of second-generation South Asian American identity. Nair holds B.S. and Ph.D. degrees in education from Penn State. He was born and raised in Philadelphia.

Mary Johnson Osirim is professor and chair of the department of sociology and faculty diversity liaison at Bryn Mawr College. Her teaching and research interests have focused on gender and development, race and ethnic relations, immigration, the family, and economic sociology in Sub-Saharan Africa, the English-speaking Caribbean, and the United States. During the past twenty years, she has conducted fieldwork on women, entrepreneurship, and the roles of the state and nongovernmental organizations in the microenterprise sectors of Nigeria and Zimbabwe, in which Bryn Mawr students participated as research assistants. She has many publications in these areas in such journals as *International Sociology, Gender and Society,* and *Women's Studies International Forum,* a coedited special issue of *African and Asian Studies,* and a recently published book in this field, *Enterprising Women in Urban Zimbabwe: Gender, Microbusiness and Globalization.* Currently, her research is focused on transnationalism and community development among African immigrants in the northeastern United States.

Rakhmiel Peltz is the founding director of Judaic studies and professor of sociolinguistics at Drexel University. He received a Ph.D. in molecular and cellular biology (University of Pennsylvania) and a Ph.D. in Yiddish studies and linguistics (Columbia University), and has published extensively in both fields. Before coming to Drexel, he was on the faculty of Boston University and was a professor and director of the Yiddish studies program at Columbia from 1990 to 1998. He is the author of *From Immigrant to Ethnic Culture: American Yiddish in South Philadelphia* (1998), the first book on spoken Yiddish in the United States. More recently, he was coeditor of *Language Loyalty, Continuity and Change* (2006) and served as project director and producer of the film *Toby's Sunshine: The Life and Art of Holocaust Survivor Toby Knobel Fluek* (2008). He is currently editing a volume of Uriel Weinreich's scholarly writings on Yiddish: *The Language and Culture of Jews in Eastern Europe.*

Birte Pfleger is associate professor of history at California State University, Los Angeles. A specialist in early American history, Pfleger focuses on immigration and ethnicity. She is the author of *Ethnicity Matters: A History of the German Society of Pennsylvania* (2006). She is currently working on a book that explores eighteenth-century German language print culture in Pennsylvania to understand how German-speakers dealt with racial, ethnic, and religious diversity and how they constructed ideas about citizenship and gender roles. In addition, she is writing an article that analyzes the meaning of ethnicity, language, and citizenship during and after the American revolution for German-born revolutionary war veterans. Born in Germany, Pfleger studied in the United States and earned a Ph.D. in history at the University of California, Irvine, in 2003.

Joan Saverino is the director of education and outreach at the Historical Society of Pennsylvania, where she initiated and directs PhilaPlace (www.philaplace.org), an interactive Web site and collaborative neighborhood history and culture project. She is a specialist on Italian American immigration and ethnicity and has taught courses in immigration and ethnicity, gender and culture, folklore, and material culture at the University of Pennsylvania. She is currently working on a manuscript of a multisited study that investigates the embodied social relations of Calabrian and immigrant women to West Virginia. Saverino has a Ph.D. from the University of Pennsylvania, and her work on Italian Americans has appeared in both popular and academic publications, including the books *Sunday Dinners and Basement Kitchens: Rethinking Italian-American Folk Cultures* and *Embroidered Lines and Cut Threads: Women's Domestic Needlework from the Italian Diaspora* (both 2010, forthcoming).

Ellen Skilton-Sylvester is a professor of education at Arcadia University. Her work with Cambodians in Philadelphia began in 1990 when she tutored Cambodian women in South Philadelphia, continued in her work with the Education Law Center looking at the impact of local educational policies on Cambodian students in the School District of Philadelphia, and concluded with a multiyear ethnographic study of literacy, policy, and identity among Cambodian women and girls in the city. In 1997, she received an Outstanding Dissertation Award from the Council on Anthropology and Education of the American Anthropological Association. She has published articles about Cambodian experiences in Philadelphia in several academic journals as well as in the book *School's Out: Bridging Out-of-School Literacies with Classroom Practice* (2001). As an educational anthropologist, her scholarship emphasizes biliteracy, immigrant education, and citizenship education in a global context.

Lena Sze is a doctoral candidate in American studies at New York University. Her research interests include race, citizenship, and identity in relation to cultural policy, urbanism, immigration, and Asian American studies. Drawing on prior arts and cultural work in Philadelphia, she edited *Chinatown Live(s): Oral Histories from Philadelphia's Chinatown* (2004).

Ayumi Takenaka is an associate professor of sociology at Bryn Mawr College. She has worked in the fields of immigration and immigrant communities across countries. Her current research includes the re-migration of immigrants from the United Kingdom to the United States and from Japan to the United States. Recently, she has published the articles "Salir Adelante: The Relationship between Geographical and Social Mobility in the Peruvian Context" (with Karen Pren) in *Latin American Perspectives* and "How Diasporic Ties Emerge: Pan-American Nikkei Communities and the Japanese State" in *Ethnic and Racial Studies*.

Victor Vazquez-Hernandez is an associate professor of history at Miami Dade College—Wolfson Campus, where he teaches survey courses in American, Latin American, and world history. His publications include *The Puerto Rican Diaspora: Historical Perspectives* (Temple University Press, 2005), coedited with Dr. Carmen T. Whalen; "Development of Pan-Latino Philadelphia, 1892–1945" in *Pennsylvania Magazine of History and Biography*; and "Formation of Spanish-Speaking Enclaves in Philadelphia, 1920–1936" in *Legacies Magazine* (Historical Society of Pennsylvania). He is currently conducting research on Puerto Ricans in Florida. Vazquez-Hernandez is also the president of the National Congress for Puerto Rican Rights (NCPRR), a civil and human rights organization.

Index